The Police and the Community: Studies

GLENCOE PRESS CRIMINAL JUSTICE SERIES

Bloomquist: **Marijuana: The Second Trip**

Brandstatter/Hyman: **Fundamentals of Law Enforcement**

Brandstatter/Radelet: **Police and Community Relations**

Eldefonso: **Readings in Criminal Justice**

Gourley: **Effective Municipal Police Organization**

Koga/Nelson: **The Koga Method: Police Weaponless Control and Defense Techniques**

Koga/Nelson: **The Koga Method: Police Baton Techniques**

LeGrande: **The Basic Processes of Criminal Justice**

McArthur: **Police Patrol Pointers**

Melnicoe/Mennig: **Elements of Police Supervision**

Nelson: **Preliminary Investigation and Police Reporting: A Complete Guide to Police Written Communication**

Radelet: **The Police and the Community**

Radelet: **The Police and the Community: Studies**

Roberts/Bristow: **An Introduction to Modern Police Firearms**

Williams: **Narcotics and Drug Dependence**

General Editor:

G. DOUGLAS GOURLEY

Inspector (Ret.), LA Police Department
Chairman, Department of Criminal Justice
California State University at Los Angeles
Los Angeles, California

The Police and the Community: Studies

Louis A. Radelet

Director, National Center on Police
and Community Relations
Michigan State University

Hoyt Coe Reed

Coordinator, Research Library
National Center for Police and Community Relations

GLENCOE PRESS
A division of Benziger Bruce & Glencoe, Inc.
Beverly Hills

77635

GLENCOE PRESS
A division of Benziger Bruce & Glencoe, Inc.
8701 Wilshire Boulevard
Beverly Hills, California 90211
Collier-Macmillan Canada, Ltd., Toronto, Ontario

Library of Congress Catalog Card Number: 72-11489

3 4 5 6 7 8 9 BWe 80 79 78 77 76

Contents

Introduction   *vii*

Part One.   The Scope of the Field   **1**

Study 1.   An Early Police Training Program in Human Relations   *3*
Study 2.   The Lohman Texts on Police Work with
            Minority Groups   *10*
Study 3.   Perceptions of the Police Role   *14*
Study 4.   Attitudes of Victims of Crime   *19*
Study 5.   Professionalization of the Police   *22*
Study 6.   Perceptions of Police and Community Relations   *25*
Study 7.   Role Attributes   *33*
Study 8.   Police Discretion   *38*

Part Two.   Psychological Considerations   **43**

Study 1.   The Structure of the Community   *45*
Study 2.   Systemic Model of Police Morale: A Personality and
            Social Structure Analysis   *49*
Study 3.   Profile of the Police Subculture   *56*
Study 4.   Points on Perception   *69*
Study 5.   Points on Prejudice   *80*
Study 6.   Points on Rumor   *92*

Part Three.   Sociological Considerations   **99**

Study 1.   The Negro Population of the United States   *101*
Study 2.   Countercultural Conflict: The Police and Insular
            Culture Groups   *109*

77635 v

Study 3.   The Police and Black Teen-age Culture   *119*
Study 4.   Mexican-Americans and the Administration of
           Justice in the Southwest   *127*
Study 5.   The Black Panther Phenomenon   *133*
Study 6.   A Model for Handling Citizen Complaints   *145*

Part Four.   Special Considerations   151

Study 1.   Juvenile Justice: System or Nonsystem?   *153*
Study 2.   Misdemeanant Probation   *185*
Study 3.   The Free Press—Fair Trial Issue   *195*
Study 4.   Blue Power   *212*
Study 5.   Assessment of Attica . . . A Symposium
           (December 4, 1971)   *224*

Part Five.   Programs   255

Study 1.   The National Institutes on Police and
           Community Relations   *257*
Study 2.   Michigan Institute on Community Relations and
           the Administration of Justice   *260*
Study 3.   The Flint, Michigan, Police-School Liaison Program *269*
Study 4.   Sensitivity Training in Police-Community Relations *275*
Study 5.   Conflict Management and Crisis Intervention—
           Oakland, California   *281*
Study 6.   Police Role and Organization for the 1970s   *288*
Study 7.   The Saint Louis PCR Program   *293*
Study 8.   Community Service Programs   *300*
Study 9.   Ride-Along Programs   *308*
Study 10. Project PACE: San Francisco   *312*
Study 11. Crisis Intervention: Dayton   *319*
Study 12. Prosecutors, Courts, and Community Relations   *326*
Study 13. The POST Leadership Training Program: California   *333*
Study 14. The North Philadelphia Program   *339*
Study 15. Job Description: Police and Community
           Relations Coordinator   *345*
Study 16. Police-Community Relations in Britain   *348*

Works Cited   *355*

Bibliography   *359*

Index   *Name*   *381*

        Subject   *385*

Introduction

In an area of research and activity as new, vast, and changing as the one of relationships between the police and their communities, the student is faced—all at once—with the necessity of getting an overview of the history, theory, practices, and responses of police and community people to one another. Many of these people have already had a wide variety of experiences in their efforts to redefine their respective roles and realistically apply programs that will improve their relationships.

Almost with a sense of panic, the student as well as the administrator feels he must move from total ignorance to total mastery of the subject if he is to avoid disaster. But such misgivings are the mark of the innovator. In this or any other dynamic field of endeavor, the more he learns the more aware he becomes of alternative ways of achieving goals. Even so, there will for an indefinite period of time be a dire feeling in the pit of the stomach of the would-be practitioner that makes him ask himself, "Have I learned all that I could?" or, "Am I doing all that I should?" And as programs continue to snag as they develop, there will always be misgivings about whether he had done the right things.

The value of *Police and the Community: Studies* then becomes clear. The *Studies* expands and enlarges upon various aspects of police and community relations as set down in the text, *Police and the Community;* and it does so through some of the experiences of those who have already worked in the field.

Addressed to college students, policemen and women, sociologists, and all others interested in learning how societal relationships affect law and order within their communities, it will complement any number of basic textbooks. The *Studies* volume does not rely on the text alone, although the reader will, of course, gain immeasurably by including *Police and the Community* in his study. The special value of *Studies* is that it stands out as a volume independent of a particular basic text.

To encourage and guide further study, and to aid review, an extensive bibliography has been included, consisting primarily of works written since 1967. This list does not include the titles in Works Cited, which contains all texts references in the studies.

In addition, questions have been added to the first few studies in the hope that they will suggest what to look for in these and in the later studies for which the student can formulate his own questions.

A final word: the great difference in length of the various studies should not be taken as a criterion of their relative importance. Some programs simply take longer to describe than others. All of them are important in developing attitudes and procedures.

Part One

The Scope
of the Field

To understand how the idea of "police-community relations" has developed, the student should have some knowledge of the history of the police in Europe—particularly in Britain—which is the base from which American police philosophy and procedures have evolved. This background is given in Part I of the basic textbook *The Police and the Community* (Louis A. Radelet), in which the concept of police-community relations is described as a product of the role of the police in today's society.

But the various views of why and how police relationships with the community are to be organized are often conflicting. The resulting confusion is further complicated by current efforts to professionalize the police and by divergent views on the discretionary use of police power.

The Studies presented here in Part I provide illustrative materials to deepen the reader's understanding of the scope of the field and to familiarize both student and administrator with current thinking in these areas. Valuable background information is given in Studies 1 and 2, which describe early training programs in human relations that antedate what came to be known as *police-community relations*. Studies 3 and 4 suggest the differences between how the police see police-community relations in the light of their understanding of their role, and how some elements of the community—such as victims of crime—see the relationship. Studies 5 through 8 examine some of the factors that complicate the process of achieving consensus on what police and community relations might become.

1

STUDY 1

An Early Police Training Program in Human Relations

Since the 1940s, the National Conference of Christians and
Jews (NCCJ) has conducted summer workshops in human
relations on many college campuses for leaders in community
activities including government officials, teachers, civic and
religious leaders, policemen, and others. As his project for
one of these workshops (1947), the then Patrolman Irvin D.
Lawler of the Detroit Police Department prepared "A Training
Program in Human Relations for Cadet and In-Service Police
Officers." It is condensed here for critical study of its per-
tinence to today's circumstances.

Lawler's Introduction stated that the program was designed to
give police officers a better view of the work they must perform as
representatives of a law enforcement agency, to give them an understanding of the people with whom they worked, and to do so by
involving them in the conduct of the course. He cautioned that much
time must pass before the effects of the course would be felt, especially
by the older officers. He also advised that all segments of the community
should be made aware of the program if it were to be effective.

The purposes of human relations training, in his view, included
enabling officers to anticipate tensions between racial and ethnic groups
and helping them to understand and curb their prejudices so that they
might discount rumors and act on the merits of individual people,
rather than on the basis of their group stereotypes.

What police officers need to know if they are to be effective in
handling people includes the areas of residence in the community of
all racial and ethnic groups as well as their origins and expectations

Used by special permission of Irvin D. Lawler, Detroit Police Department (Ret.),
with the explanation: "This material was written by an experienced police officer
for the training and use of all policemen, for a better understanding of their duties
and the people with whom they come in contact in the performance of their official
duties as law enforcement officers."

based on their cultural backgrounds, and the areas of residential contact between these groups as possible points of friction. The way police deal with citizens affects their reputation and thus their relations with the public, and the way police handle disturbances influences tension levels.

Objectives of the Course

1. *Information and Ideas:* (a) the structural (ecological) pattern of the city; (b) how the city is changing and how changes affect people; (c) important minority groups and their particular concerns; (d) what prejudice is, its sources and its effects on police conduct and the people with whom they deal, and (e) how people feel toward the police, based on group identifications.

2. *Attitudes and Sensitivity:* (a) minority groups want much the same things that policemen want, and strive for them in the same ways; (b) police must feel responsible for making and maintaining a good reputation with all groups in the city.

3. *Skills:* Officers must learn how to work with and understand the needs of people and what people expect of them. They must learn to judge people as individuals rather than as members of stereotyped groups. They must learn to accept criticism and benefit from it.

Outline of Course

Four subjects, covered in six periods, eight hours total, as follows:

First Period (2 hours)
A. *Orientation* (1 hour): (a) Purpose of human relations training for the police. (b) What a police officer needs to know about the people he serves. (c) What police should hope to gain from such training.

B. *Structural pattern of the city and population distribution* (1 hour):

1. Distribute a mimeoed map of areas of city. Have students fill in their copies to show: (a) where each lives (mark with X); (b) mark "Y" place where you were raised, or parents' home; (c) mark "B" location of big businesses; (d) mark "H" economically above average areas; (e) mark "L" below average areas; mark "A" economically average areas; mark "S" slum areas.

2. Instructor sketches blackboard outline of city and indicates on it: (a) students' ideas of cultural changes in neighborhoods in which they were raised, and (b) assists students in marking map with symbols for areas missed.

3. Have students fill in on their maps communities of Jews, Poles, Italians, Spanish, etc., as appropriate for the city.

4. Assist students in transferring this data to blackboard map. Ask students for origins of groups shown on map and discuss cultural patterns of each group.

Second Period (1 hour)
Changes in the city-population growth and movement:

1. Discuss changes that have occurred in the past 50 (or 25 or 10) years as different racial and ethnic groups arrived, as to: (a) why industry came to city; (b) why certain people came; (c) where they settled; (d) how industry expanded and where; (e) what happened to older residents as changes occurred, and (f) how groups moved up social ladder as newer groups came.

2. Make a case study of a particular neighborhood as to such changes.

3. Compare map of city today with X years ago.

Third Period (1 hour)
Cultural patterns of minority groups:
A. *How minority groups behave and why:*

1. Customs, traditions and characteristics: (a) first and second generation Americans more likely to stick to old customs; (b) third generation likely to forget old-country habits.

2. Most minority group members feel they are held down by: (a) segregation in recreation, eating places, entertainment; (b) poor housing, slums—can't move into better areas; (c) employment limited by type of jobs, with promotion difficult; (d) prejudiced remarks directed at minorities, etc.

3. Pressure and prejudice cause certain behavior patterns: (a) segregated by race, nationality, religion; (b) the desire of minority individuals to continue family and cultural ways; (c) conflicting with others who want to change and adapt; (d) minority individuals reciprocate prejudices against them; and (e) older Americans suspicious of minority ways and customs.

B. *How minority groups find social activity:*

1. Crowded living conditions cause them to seek pleasure outside their homes at: (a) public beaches and parks; (b) amusement places; (c) theatres, public, and private exhibitions.

2. Segregation and nature of their employment cause them to: (a) spend their money (if employed) in bars, dives, etc., in their own communities instead of spending it on homes or home improvements, and (b) organize their own social, neighborhood, and church groups.

Fourth Period (1 hour)
Cultural patterns of minority groups (continued):
C. *How minority groups get what they want:*

1. Recognition as citizens of the community: (a) personal merit; (b) court decisions; (c) pressure groups; (d) minority group newspapers; (e) appeal to Congressmen through organized groups; (f) joining groups in sympathy with them.

2. Better housing: most are seeking an opportunity to move to a better neighborhood.

3. Employment and unions: many businesses and most unions have public relations departments.

4. Education: opportunities much greater today than ever before.

5. Political influence: attempt to get members of their groups elected to various offices.

Fifth Period (1 hour)

1. *Status of entire police department is affected:* (a) by manner in which minority group persons are treated by officers; (b) by attitudes of police; (c) by complaints against members of the department, whether valid or not; (d) by newspaper articles, including the minority press; (e) by their personal reputations as police officers.

2. Police generally deal with individuals or small groups, seldom with entire minority groups, therefore: (a) must treat people as individuals, not stereotype them as members of groups; (b) groups are seldom responsible for behavior of their individual members; (c) crime may be higher in a given area, but it is the conditions of the community rather than any group characteristics that create these situations.

3. The police department is itself a minority group, in some sense.

4. People whom the police generally come in contact with: (a) are often but not always law violators, and (b) only have contacts with the members of their own segregated group.

5. Police may act from two different attitudes in contacts with minority groups: (a) the human approach, treating persons as individuals, or (b) the stereotype approach, viewing all members of a group as the same.

6. Police officers can come to understand minority groups, including what group members expect of police officers while on assignment: (a) by getting acquainted through personal contacts; (b) studying neighborhood organizations; (c) reading about such groups; (d) studying the social agencies having frequent contacts with these groups.

7. The approach of police officers, as representatives of city government, may mean: (a) the difference between peaceful settlement of a dispute or conflict, and (b) the gain or loss of respect of citizens for their government.

8. Know when and how to act as a police officer, according to departmental procedures: (a) in police conduct, (b) in civil cases.

9. Discretion is one of the best tools of a good officer: (a) in the way in which he conducts himself; (b) the way in which he is able to handle people; (c) his interpretation of the law and his duties as an officer.

Sixth Period (2 hours)
First hour:
A. *How prejudiced remarks affect minority groups:*

1. Prejudice toward groups is made evident: (a) by officers in remarks either to or about them; (b) by methods used by police; (c) by daily contacts of officers on their beats; (d) by rumors passed by members of a group who want to "get even" for previous arrests; (e) by remarks made by persons of another group.

2. Prejudice directed at other group members by members of a minority group: (a) in retaliation for remarks directed at them; (b) create stereotypes within their own groups from hearing rumors; (c) may be based on media stories of "brutality."

3. Prejudice of persons within their own groups: (a) class hatreds may develop between different economic levels within a group; (b) differences of opinion within a group regarding what is regarded as prejudice and what is not.

Second hour:
B. *Minority groups and prejudice:*

1. All people have prejudices in one way or another: (a) may result from lack of understanding, hearsay evidence, or other prejudgments; (b) people are not born with prejudice; heredity has nothing to do with it; (c) many persons acquire prejudices in childhood from parental remarks, or not being allowed to play with other minority groups' children; (d) many people react to prejudice with prejudice.

2. Police officers also have prejudices: (a) regarding certain members of the department who they feel are "out to get them"; (b) regarding the kind of police work they want to do and where they want to work; (c) regarding minority groups. Yet departmental policy requires: (a) impartiality to all people; (b) using the same discretion and fairness with all, with ap-

propriate firmness as needed; (c) remembering that some people in any group are prone to do certain things; (d) and refusing to be swayed by attitudes of other members of the department.

3. Attitude of minority people may be resentment for being made scapegoat, which they show: (a) by attitudes toward other groups; (b) trying to prove they are no different from anyone else; or (c) "throwing in the towel," by turning to crime, feeling they have no chance anyway.

Means of Presentation for First Unit

(A similar technique for each segment of the course.)

1. Review what was done at last session without explaining what was said.

2. Ask what points were brought out.

3. Ask if there are other points to be added.

4. List any remarks (from 2 and 3) as they are given.

5. Have class discuss why minority groups behave as they do.

6. Ask for observations on minority group members' behavior.

7. List on board all points made.

8. Discuss these points, asking, "What do you base this on? Have you seen it or just heard about it?"

9. Ask which seem accurate, which seem based on rumor, hearsay.

10. Ask, "Why do you think people behave this way?" Select one case for study and have class discuss it.

11. At this point, a suitable film might be shown.

12. Ask "why" again and analyze the picture.

Following the syllabus outline above, Lawler appends supplements as student aids:

1. "How Minority Groups Affect the Structural Pattern of the City" —a study of the history of the city in terms of changing patterns of residential areas and industrialization.

2. "Riots and Social Disorders"—including a study of the Detroit race riot of 1943: its causes, mishandling, and damages, as well as the tendency of all groups to blame others for the situation.

3. "Official Attitude of Police Toward Race Relations"—which states:

A. Both the individual officer and the department want to operate from a strong position of stated policies; charges of discrimination and brutality (true or not) are damaging to effective enforcement, as is lack of public confidence.

B. To attain their objectives, officers should: (a) be prepared to suppress a riot; (b) exert all efforts to prevent riots; because (c) conditions are always worse after riots.

C. A professional approach to riot prevention is essential: (a) in keeping with professional status of the police; (b) including maintenance of a neutral position, since all citizens are equal before the law; (c) avoidance of use of epithets ("nigger," "kike," "wop," etc.) as self-defeating; (d) with professional conduct based on training in psychology of prejudice, sociology of cultures, attitudes, etc., plus training providing an understanding of economic forces that affect human behavior.

Questions for Discussion

1. Why is a knowledge of the cultural backgrounds of racial and ethnic groups important to a police officer? What is the difference between *racial* and *ethnic*?

2. How can the ways in which police handle disturbances affect tension levels? Can you cite examples from the recent news?

3. Does the program, as outlined above, give police a better understanding of the human relations aspects of their work?

4. Why is it suggested that older officers may take longer to benefit from a human relations training course?

5. Can prejudices be modified or curbed? If not, what then?

6. Why is it important for the police to know where ethnic and racial groups live in the city, and how and why these patterns are changing?

7. Can you give contrasting examples of minority groups' behavior and account for it in terms of their cultural backgrounds?

8. Why do some groups become socially assimilated more easily than others?

9. What does "The Means of Presentation" attempt to do in this program?

10. Do you feel that the Supplements at the end of the Training Program would be helpful? Would "outside readings" be better?

11. Would this be an acceptable training curriculum for the police under today's circumstances, recalling that it was devised in 1947?

STUDY 2

The Lohman Texts on Police Work with Minority Groups

During the 1940s, Dr. Joseph D. Lohman was both Pro-
fessorial Lecturer in Sociology at the University of Chicago,
and Chairman of the Division of Corrections of the State of
Illinois.* At that time, he developed for classes in The
Chicago Park District Police Training School mimeographed
materials and census tract maps of the city to demonstrate
the imperative necessity for police officers to understand
the nature and causes of intergroup tensions in big cities,
that is, the ecological factors at work among the people
whom they were to serve.

These materials were the basis of Lohman's book,
The Police and Minority Groups. In 1950, the Division of
Police, Louisville, Kentucky, produced *Principles of Police
Work With Minority Groups* with the assistance of Dr. Loh-
man, who served as a consultant for the program and per-
mitted the extensive use of passages from his earlier work.
Similar courses were prepared by him for other cities.

Since these Lohman texts became the basis for subsequent training materials in police-community relations,
their combined contents are described here for the guidance of students in the field.

The science of ecology is the study of the relationships of plants and
animals to their environment. Sociologists have found it useful to borrow
the concept for analyzing the relationships of people with each other
and with their physical environments. An important purpose of the Lohman courses was to apprise police officers of the nature and consequences of these two types of relationships—group with group, and group

---

*Dr. Lohman later served as Sheriff of Cook County, as State Treasurer of
Illinois and, finally, as Dean of the School of Criminology, University of California at Berkeley. He died in 1968. The material is used here with the permission of The Chicago Park District.

with habitat; in brief, to provide a basic understanding of human ecology.

For example, Lohman showed that where two or more minority groups live side by side and compete for scarce jobs, housing, and community services, each group tends to blame the other for the existing shortages and to relieve their frustrations in such hostile activities as name-calling, developing prejudices from false notions of superiority, and even physical violence. Moreover, the actual environment of slum living consequent to poverty and overcrowding has, in itself, a debilitating and demoralizing effect that feeds the frictions between groups.

For the police to try to handle incidents in such areas without studying the ecological factors of human behavior is self-defeating. Their job becomes infinitely more difficult. Therefore, the Lohman courses of study began by analyzing a series of census tract maps that showed for each area of the city such factors as

Density of population, by persons per square mile

Native white population, by percent of total

Rental areas, by typical rent paid

Juvenile delinquency, by number of cases

Infant mortality rates, by number per tract

Educational status, by number of years of schooling

Incidence of serious crimes, by number

Number of suicides occurring

Black population, by percent of inhabitants

Various nationality groups, by percent of population

Age of dwelling units, by percent built before 1899

Dwelling units, by percent needing major repairs

Average insanity rate, age 15 and over

Nationality and racial migrations

The subjects of the maps for a given city would, of course, vary with local demography. When such maps were printed on transparent plastics, they could be overlaid to show where living conditions were most desperate, and therefore where social frictions and tensions were most likely to develop. Such evidence was realistic since it was based on composite indices of personal and social disorganization.

With the understanding of their clientele that resulted from such courses of study, a police department could realistically deploy its manpower and other resources. But the Lohman courses did not rest there. It is one thing to know *where* incidents may occur; it is quite another to predict their *nature*. Therefore, the courses included so-called *conferences* that analyzed the qualitative factors influencing the behavior of people in cities. These covered a variety of subjects.

Conference I stressed the need to understand the ethnic groups in our cities in terms of their origins, traditions and expectations when they find themselves living across the street from each other. For example, the tensions that arise when the children acquire the behavioral patterns of their peers in public schools and become alienated from their parents' cultural ways, and even from their parents themselves. The results may be that the parents lose control, and the children, needing affection and guidance, join street gangs to seek peer acceptance.

Conferences II and III considered the origins and characteristics of races as we find them in our cities, and offered proofs that there is no superior race: that all men are, biologically, born with the same potentials. They may be handicapped by the effects of their cultural environment; but that is all the more reason for the professional policeman to work with them understandingly and to try to discover their potential responses when they are treated as equals.

Conference IV described the social situations in which tensions are likely to develop into incidents requiring police attention. First, from frustrations, in searching for jobs and finding employment limited by prejudice. Second, from conflict, in searching for decent housing where there is racial segregation. Third, from resentments and discrimination, in seeking recreational and personal services and finding restricted admittance and condescending attitudes. Data were supplied to show how ideas of racial superiority militate against minorities in all their efforts to achieve equality.

Conference V discussed the proper role of police officers in dealing with tension situations, and treated the situations of day-to-day contacts, controlling mobs, using adequate versus inadequate or excessive force, and handling rumors. Cases were cited for each type of situation to illustrate both right and wrong procedures.

Conference VI considered the effects of law and administrative controls upon human relations. The discussion included a consideration of possible conflicts between federal, state, and local laws; and of possible conflicts between these laws and local customs. To which situation should the police be responsive? To clarify the position of the police in such situations, the mobilization of community resources was shown to be imperative. To this end, methods of establishing a plan of action were suggested and illustrated.

Appendixes on police procedures were included in the Lohman texts for the convenience of students: for example, a list of the appropriate state laws on race relations and city ordinances that bear on the police function. Lists of films, pamphlets, and books on related subjects were also included to use for further study.

Questions for Discussion

1. Which of these two approaches seems preferable:
   a. Would it really help to know all about the people you have to deal with in your work? or,
   b. Would it be easier to do your job as experience dictates?

2. Which of the materials in the Lohman courses seems most helpful to the man on the beat?

3. Which do you think are irrelevant to police work? Why?

4. What other kinds of data would you use census tracts to show?

5. Until recently, police in major cities had relatively little trouble with Oriental juveniles. Why?

6. Do you think that Lohman-type courses did the job? What would you have added? What would you have omitted?

7. For example, would you have included a section on the use of mace and other nonlethal methods in handling mobs or demonstrations?

STUDY 3

Perceptions of the Police Role

In *The Police and the Community* by Louis A. Radelet, especially in Chapter III, various concepts of the police role have been discussed from the viewpoints of the police and of the communities they serve, as seen by several writers, largely in a theoretical way. A number of surveys have been conducted to elicit, through questionnaires, the attitudes of individual officers and community people on a more concrete basis.

One such survey was done by Nelson A. Watson and James W. Sterling and published by the International Association of Chiefs of Police in 1969 under the title *Police and Their Opinions.* It analyzes the responses of 4,844 officers and community people to 79 questions designed to reveal their feelings about aspects of the police-community relationship. From the responses selected here, can you form a profile of the average officer's ideas about his role, the community, selective enforcement, and his understanding of "professionalism"?

Note to Students: Except where otherwise indicated, the figures show the percentages of *officers* who *agree* with the statements (and, where stated, *civilians*).

Percent

PERCEPTION OF CRIMINALS:

Q. 22—Criminal ways are acquired through experience; they are not inherited 90.6

Q. 56—An experienced officer "can tell a criminal by his looks" 25

Q. 32—A person of "beatnik" or "mod" appearance needs to be watched .... (majority disagreed)

Percent

PUBLIC RELATIONS:

Q. 23—Many people look on a policeman as an impersonal cog
in a government machine 82
Q. 26—Public support for the police seems to be growing 50
Q. 29—Police are not receiving support from the political power
structure in our cities 73

CIVIL DISOBEDIENCE:

Q. 25—A person has a right to deliberately disobey a law which
he believes is immoral or unjust 10
Q. 52—Persons who deliberately violate the law should be arrested 90

COMPLAINTS:

Q. 35—The public has a right to pass judgment on the way
police do their job 64
Q. 44—Police need not be concerned about public scrutiny 69
Q. 51—There is nothing wrong with the *idea* of civilian review
boards 48
Liberal Civilians (LC)*...... 94

COURT DECISIONS:

Q. 28—Court decisions on interrogating suspects will result in
fewer solutions to criminal cases 76
LC...... 11
Q. 37—It is absolutely essential for police to learn how to do
their work in compliance with court decisions 91
LC...... 97
Q. 41—Experience shows police that there is a big difference
between whether a man is guilty and whether the court
says he is 79
Q. 42—Police are often responsible for defendants being found
"not guilty" 70

POLICE ETHICS:

Q. 46—Persons who give officers free meals, etc., expect something in return 76
Q. 55—Under no conditions is it right or proper for a policeman to accept gifts for his services 73

---

*The definition and sampling of "Liberal Civilians" were acknowledged by the
researchers in this study to be inadequate. Therefore, the results reflected here,
while indicating interesting contrasts, may not be entirely trustworthy.

Percent

SOCIAL QUESTIONS:
Q. 24—Good police work requires that officers concern themselves with the *consequences* of crime, not with its *causes*   14
                                            LC......   15
Q. 36—The trouble with psychology and sociology is that they
are not related to everyday realities of police life   40
                                            LC......   .09
Q. 43—In hiring, assigning and promoting officers, race should
not be a consideration   87
                                            LC......   88

POLICE-COMMUNITY RELATIONS UNIT:
Q. 65—A PCR Unit is needed to open communications with the
community   69
                                            LC......   97

VALUE OF EDUCATION:
Q. 31—Police service requires more college trained men   77
                                            LC......   97
Q. 49—The best officers generally *have* more education   38
                                            LC......   79
Q. 50—Certain college courses should be required for initial
employment   63
                                            LC......   85

HARD LINE APPROACH TO POLICE WORK:
Q. 33—In certain areas of the city, physical combat skills and
aggressiveness will be more useful than book learning
and a courteous manner   46
Q. 54—Some ideals of politeness and decency taught in police
schools are unworkable on the beat   57
Q. 58—Preservation of the peace legitimatizes "move along"
even when no law is being violated   71
Q. 72—Police should permit violators to "tell their side" before
making an arrest   53

RELATIONS TO AUTHORITY:
Q. 30—The good policeman unquestionably obeys his superior
officer   50
Q. 34—The best officer knows when to depart from rules   67
Q. 57—As long as a law is on the books, it should be enforced   59

ORIENTATION TO POLICE WORK:
Q. 63—Officer chose police work after being in other occupations .... white officers   46
                               black officers   52
                               women officers   54

Percent

Q. 69—Found police work different from what they expected . .   65

Q. 74—Have not seriously considered leaving police work   78
(Note: College trained officers showed the greatest
inclination to seek other jobs.)

NEGRO vs. WHITE OFFICER RESPONSES:

Q. 60—The best means of reducing crime is to get tough
whites   79
Negroes.   58

MALE vs. FEMALE RESPONSES:
(Note: For the most part there were no real differences in responses by sex.)

Q. 53—An officer should consider a juvenile's socio-economic
status and home situation in deciding what to do with
him . . . . .women.   85
men   64

ANALYSIS OF PROBLEMS FACING POLICE:

Q. 79—What is the most important problem confronting our
profession?
A. group conflict and civil disorder   15
B. limitations on wire tapping 03
C. citizen review boards   3
D. leniency of courts in sentencing 25.5
E. corruption   2
F. developing effective methods for conforming to court
decisions re: interrogation and search 14.5
G. need for more dedicated officers at all levels   38

Q. 76—Which problem is most pressing in your *department*?
A. lack of manpower; inability to recruit   47
B. inadequate equipment and facilities   7
C. reliance on old-fashioned methods and procedures. .   4
D. lack of modern technological advances   3
E. inadequate training   6
F. lack of understanding/support of citizens   14
G. lack of clear-cut policies   5
H. political interference in department operations   12

Q. 78—What is the most important problem you face *on the
job*?
A. too much paper work   27
B. not enough freedom; too many rules   12
C. boredom   2
D. many officers don't know what they're doing   13
E. physical danger/brutality against the police   6

Percent

F. ineffective supervision 13
G. not enough chance for advancement 22

Q. 77—What is the most important problem that you *as an individual face*?

A. irregular hours and ill-timed vacations 8
B. inability to relax at home; can't leave the job behind (mainly administrators answered) 15
C. not enough pay 57
D. little respect shown by others for my profession ... 16
E. gradual drifting away from non-police friends 3
F. marital difficulties connected with my work 3

ANALYSIS OF RESPONSES BY YEARS OF EXPERIENCE:

Page 89: "As experience increases, the proportion of officers who believe public support for the police is growing increases, as does their belief that police have nothing to hide from public scrutiny."

Questions for Discussion

1. What do you think about the officer's perception of criminals?
2. Do the police feel they're supported by the public?
3. Are they conservative in their views about protestors?
4. Do the responses indicate that civilian review boards have a chance of being instituted?
5. Are police and civilians far apart in their ideas on courts?
6. Police and civilians seem close on causes of crime. Why?
7. How realistic are the figures on racial discrimination in employment?
8. Does the degree of approval of a PCR Unit imply that police-community relations would be the concern of all personnel?
9. Are the views on higher education for police consistent?
10. Is there general agreement on the "hard line" approach?
11. Do the respondents approve of "selective enforcement"?
12. Do the figures show police *are* a para-military organization?
13. Discuss the role of men vs. women in handling juveniles.
14. Is the statement quoted from page 89 of Watson and Sterling convincing?
15. Do the responses to questions on Problems Facing the Police suggest a universal police problem? Are any of the problems peculiar to the police as a profession?
16. Judging from all responses, how "professional" do you feel these police officers were?

STUDY 4

Attitudes of Victims of Crime

This section of *Field Surveys I, Report on a Pilot Study in the District of Columbia on Victimization and Attitudes Toward Law Enforcement* (page 145) contains some surprises about minority group attitudes on the functions and methods of the police. Written by Albert Biderman and his associates at the Bureau of Social Science Research, Inc., the survey is part of the President's Commission on Law Enforcement and Administration of Justice, 1967.

Note to Students: Remember that this was a study of the attitudes of persons in the District of Columbia who had been victimized by crime.

Negro respondents, particularly the men, believed that they received less than equitable treatment from the police. They had somewhat less respect and regard for the police—how much less depending in part on their own experiences. The single most outstanding finding concerning attitudes toward the police was not so much the difference between groups, but rather the generally high regard for the police among all groups, including Negro men. In spite of perceptions of differential treatment, over half the Negro men thought that there are "just a few policemen who are responsible for the bad publicity the force sometimes gets." Eighty percent of the Negro men said that policemen "deserve a lot more respect and thanks than they get."

When it is remembered that it was the Negroes who expressed the most worry about being the victims of crime, and that there was a general reliance on the police to prevent and control crime, it is not so surprising to find this potential for good will toward the police, even among Negro men who are not well educated and who live in the poorer areas of the city. Random samples of the public would disagree with the highly selective impressions the police and community leaders have of various aspects of police performance. The pictures about what "the Negro thinks of the police" that are derived from offenders, from com-

19

plainants, from special clienteles such as merchants, and from activists of various sorts, are all at variance with what this study indicates as majority opinion.

Examination of the Issues

1. We hear much contention about "over-policing" of minority areas. What are the implications of the study report on this subject?

2. Discuss the passage in terms of *selective enforcement*.

3. Compare the ideas in the above with the following findings from *Field Surveys II* by Philip Ennis, National Opinion Research Center, University of Chicago, 1967, a Report of a study done for the President's Commission on Law Enforcement and Administration of Justice; U.S. Government Printing Office, Washington, D.C. (page 52 ff.). This study of *Attitudes Toward the Police, Law Enforcement, and Individual Security* drew the following conclusions from a national sample of 14,000 adults who had been victims of crime.

   a. For all issues, at all income levels, and for both sexes, blacks are far more critical of the police than whites.

   b. Among whites of both sexes, the higher the respondent's income, the more favorable his view of the police.

   c. Among blacks, attitudes toward the police change in a complex and not always understandable way with differences in income. There is a recurrent tendency for blacks of *higher* incomes to be harsher on the police than those with lower incomes. Blacks in the $6,000–$9,999 category sometimes show stronger antipathy to the police than those in the highest bracket; but in the matter of the police showing respect to blacks, Negroes in the highest income group are sharply more critical than the rest.

   d. Differences in opinion are relatively minor between sexes; but perhaps a tendency exists for black women to be more critical than the men on occasion.

   e. The widest divergence between whites and Negroes, not surprisingly, occurs on the question of police showing respect to the citizenry. About two-thirds of the white—males and females, regardless of income—say their police are "very good" about being courteous, but only about one-third of the blacks have this view. Finally, about 15 percent of blacks are explicitly negative compared with about 3 percent of the whites.

A separate question in this study was: "Should the police devote their energies toward preventing crime, or should they concentrate on catching criminals?" In reflecting the results, the report states: "The full meaning of these responses is not fully clear . . . It is obvious and important, however, to note that there is no consensus as to which view is right."

In an effort to determine what the respondents felt was the main function of the police, not all possible functions were explored. Instead, the concentration was on two critical issues, both with strong moral and political overtones. The first pertained to organized gambling. This area was selected because it represents a sensitive boundary point between the necessity of public authority to maintain "law and order" and the right of individuals to exercise their private preferences. The second issue concerned the role of the police in allowing demonstrations for civil and political matters. This is another boundary between public order and individual expression.

On the gambling issue, not surprisingly, about three-fourths of the respondents wanted to stop gambling, the respectable moral position. The remaining one-fourth showed some tolerance.

The respondents were more evenly divided regarding the control of demonstrations; only the smallest minority favored full freedom. But Negroes were overwhelmingly more favorable toward demonstrations than whites.

Questions for Discussion

1. How do you account for the relationship between the incomes of white people and their view of police?

2. How would you explain the data about the incomes of black people and their attitudes toward the police?

3. Bearing in mind that the respondents had been victims of crime, do you feel that they were competent to judge whether the police should "prevent crime" or "catch criminals"?

4. Are the responses about gambling and civil demonstrations plausible indications of what the respondents might feel about other possible functions of the police (handling juveniles, street arrests, etc.)?

5. What over-all conclusions can be drawn from the data quoted from these two studies?

STUDY 5

Professionalization of the Police

The following study is directly quoted from a speech with
the same title, made at Michigan State University to the
Thirteenth Annual National Institute on Police and Community Relations, May 1967, by Professor Albert J. Reiss,
Jr., then chairman of the Department of Sociology, University of Michigan.

The passage is quoted here to stimulate discussion of the
effects of police professionalization on the improvement of
police and community relationships.

Americans are losing their respect for law and order. They have lost the
code of the Good Samaritan, and they do not support their local police.
But these themes are far from new ... It is clear that waves of crime
and public protest have made for changes in police organization, strategy
and tactics. While local police departments have undergone organizational changes as a consequence of police scandals and waves of reform,
major changes in policing across the country generally have followed
public definition of crime or policing as a national problem of political,
legal or moral scope ...

In some studies we have done of actual contacts between police
officers and citizens [*Studies in Crime and Law Enforcement in Major
Metropolitan Areas*] ... we examined 14,697 encounters ... (and) two
paradoxes are suggested by our findings ... The dominant mode of behavior of police toward citizens is to treat them in a "businesslike,"
"routinized," or impersonal fashion. Such conduct is often termed
"bureaucratic" or "civil" and attributed to officials in civil service systems. At the same time we find that the dominant mode of behavior of
citizens toward officers is to respond in a "civil" fashion ...

Herein lies the paradox, however. *The citizen who treats the
officer with civility often regards civility in the officer as a sign of dis-*

Reprinted by permission of the author.

respect—and the the officer who meets civility in the citizen often perceives it as a sign of disrespect. The paradox arises because of differences in their expectations of one another . . . the citizen wants the officer to behave with more than civility; he wants to be treated as a "person" . . . and the officers want the citizen to behave with more than civility rather than to show deference toward their authority . . . The problem of differences in expectations arises in part because the police continue to operate within a "traditional bureaucracy," while the citizen increasingly operates in civil-rights-oriented democracy where "human relations" is at the center. Clearly these problems lie in the structure . . . of organizations.

The second paradox arises from the differential treatment officers give citizens according to their race, and the responses citizens make to such treatment. When the officer departs from the model of civil treatment of citizens in a *positive* fashion by good humored or jovial treatment, he is more likely to do so toward white than Negro citizens: 21 percent of white citizens were treated this way as contrasted with 12 percent of Negroes . . . When the officer departs from the model of civil treatment in a *negative* fashion, with hostile, authoritarian or belittling behavior, he is more likely to do so toward white than Negro citizens. Roughly twice as many whites as Negro citizens were treated with aggressive behavior by the police. Furthermore, the police act more harshly toward antagonistic white than they do toward antagonistic Negro citizens. The differences in treatment of whites and Negroes are largely accounted for by the fact that the police are more likely to treat Negro citizens with civility (80 percent of Negroes vs. 66 percent of whites).

This suggests that when the police depart from the model of "civil treatment" of citizens, they are more likely to treat white than Negro citizens with both "traditional human relations" and "traditional punitive" perspectives . . . Despite the police academy and its human relations training, police line culture supports traditional ways of handling citizens, ways that the classroom has not overcome . . . police officers are more likely to respond to a white citizen's behavior in this traditional fashion since whites are expected to behave toward the officer in traditional ways.

Negroes present a somewhat different problem . . . given the strong pressures both within and without police systems to have officers behave positively toward the Negro citizen. The outcome is not a human relations approach (often presumed to be taught to police officers), but increased civility in conduct toward them . . . What is lacking is not only a "human relations" approach toward Negro citizens, but an approach to *both* white and Negro citizens that is based on the rights and dignity of individuals . . . as *persons* rather than as *clients* . . . That problem is at the center of *all* bureaucracies.

Questions for Discussion

1. In what ways does the bureaucratic behavior of police toward citizens have a detrimental effect upon police and community relations?

2. How does the paradox of racial differential treatment actually work out?

3. What professional approach does Reiss suggest is needed in the way the police treat clients?

Perceptions of Police and Community Relations

People perceive "police and community relations" in a variety of ways, largely due to their own occupations and experiences. The following quotations illustrate the point.

James Q. Wilson*

> This opinion has been taken from an article in the March 1969 issue of *The Atlantic,* entitled "What Makes a Better Policeman?"

Criticisms of the police arise out of radically different perceptions of the police function. Some people see the police as the chief means of ending or reducing crime in the streets. Others see them as an agency by which white society confines and suppresses black ghettos. Still others view them as an organization caught on the grinding edge of a class conflict. . . . One reason for this confusion [lies] in the fact that police perform a variety of functions . . . various departments emphasize crime prevention, or law enforcement, or the maintenance of order, or political power.

William H. Parker

> The widely respected late chief of the Los Angeles Police Department addressed the first National Institute on Police and Community Relations at Michigan State University in 1955. The quotation is from the Institute *Proceedings*.

My initial premise is that community problems are not an unrealistic and relatively unimportant concern, but a vital issue—a question of human weakness and society's failure to control that weakness. . . . My

---

77635

second premise is that social order is the first concern of those interested
in improving community relations. It provides a peaceful arena in which
inequities can ultimately be solved. Community order works another
advantage. . . . Man is a creature of habit, not of hate. Order, even
though enforced . . . creates among the peoples of the community
habitual patterns of conduct. . . . Our laws are far from perfect, but
they are sufficient for the maintenance of human intercourse without
violent conflict. . . .

The community relations detail is, first, a public information
agency; secondly, it keeps the police staff informed about minority
problems and activities. Third, it reports police activities which are
discriminatory and, lastly, it acts as a listening post for rumors and
activities which might prelude violent conflict, and flashes word to
citizen groups organized to combat just such emergencies.

Police field deployment is not a social agency activity. In deploy-
ing to suppress crime, we are not interested in *why* a certain group tends
toward crime; we are interested in maintaining order.

Jerome H. Skolnick

> In "Police and the Urban Ghetto" from Research Contributions
> of the American Bar Foundation, 1968 (No. 3, p. 10 ff.),
> Jerome Skolnick looks at police roles under William H. Parker.

The late Chief Parker infused into police work a new kind of professionalism based on a para-military model. The goals were efficiency,
integrity and widespread law enforcement . . . in practice . . . accompanied by a failure to recognize the human dimension in police work . . .
and the legal values of a free society . . . (But) legality alone is not
sufficient to bridge the ever-widening gulf between police and minority
groups. Emphasis upon legality will help cut down on unreasonable
police interrogations, detentions and friskings. . . . In addition, we must
work out ways to change the perception of the police role. (Police are,
in fact, performing social agency activities, whether they like it or not.)
Nor is it irrelevant for police to understand *why* a certain group tends
toward crime. The police are legal officials enjoying considerable discretion, and they can use this discretion in constructive rather than
destructive ways.

Linda McVeigh Matthews

> Also in the March 1969 issue of *The Atlantic* magazine, Linda
> McVeigh Matthews describes in the article "Chief Reddin: New
> Style at the Top," Thomas Reddin's police-community relations
> program after he succeeded Parker.

His assistants are out breaking bread with the people and selling
community relations. . . . the top administrators keep whirlwind sched-

ules . . . to reach as many people as possible and gain their trust. . . .
Reddin has two distinct constituencies—the WASPish middle class, and
the other, including 30 percent of the Latin and Negro population in the
ghettos who, copwise, feel threatened by the police themselves, of whom
Reddin says, "Our men were faceless badges behind the windshields
of patrol cars, and the only time they ever talked to Negroes was when
they were making an arrest." Reddin established community relations
councils, but they petered out (despite some implementation of their
recommendations). What most poor black and Latin people were waiting for was a sign that attitudes and actions of the lowly patrolman had
changed.

The patrolmen's behavior was one of the things that Reddin could
not control . . . Many resented the innocuous concessions that had come
out of the community councils. He tried to convince them that the
community relations program was not just window dressing but would
make their job easier. But patrolmen are tough customers. Community
relations strikes them as softness—antithetical to their self-image. . . .
No one has yet found an adequate reward for the man who displays
positive attitudes except to promote him—right out of the patrol division.

If patrolmen are one aspect Reddin *cannot* reform, there is one
aspect he *will not* reform, though doing so might be the one demonstration of sincerity that would win over minority groups. This is the old
bugbear: internal disciplinary procedures. . . . Reddin's tragedy is that,
like other top police administrators, he is held accountable for matters
over which he has no control.

James Baldwin

> In the book *Nobody Knows My Name* (pp. 65 ff.), James Bald-
> win provides a dramatic statement of the perception of the
> policeman in the ghetto.

The only way to police a ghetto is to be oppressive. None of the
Police Commissioner's men, even with the best will in the world, have
any way of understanding the lives led by the people they swagger about
in twos and threes controlling. Their very presence is an insult, and it
would be, even if they spent their entire day feeding gumdrops to
children. They represent the force of the white world, and that world's
criminal profit and ease, to keep the black man corralled up here, in his
place. The badge, the gun in the holster, and the swinging club make
vivid what will happen should his rebellion become overt. . . .

It is hard, on the other hand, to blame the policeman—blank,
good-natured, thoughtless, and insuperably innocent—for being such a
perfect representative of the people he serves. He, too, believes in good
intentions and is astounded and offended when they are not taken for
the deed. . . . He is facing, daily and nightly, people who would gladly

see him dead, and he knows it. . . . There are few things under heaven more unnerving than the silent, accumulating contempt and hatred of a people. He moves through Harlem, therefore, like an occupying soldier in a bitterly hostile country; which is precisely what and where he is, and is the reason he walks in twos and threes.

Ed Cray

> Director of publications for the American Civil Liberties Union of Southern California and author of *The Enemy in the Streets,* writes in "The Politics of Blue Power," in *The Nation.*

As never before in the 126-year history of organized police forces in the United States, law enforcement has figured in the daily prints. Yet for all the hue and cry and the accompanying polarization of public opinion, the major issue has barely surfaced. Who is to control the nation's police forces: the police themselves, or the community? . . .

In the face of threats, real or imaginary, the police have openly girded themselves with a new-found armor—political influence, supported by public fear of rising crime rates and ghetto rebellion. . . .

The political power of the police nationally is considerable. In both Cleveland and Los Angeles, police have gone directly to the ballot for pay raises or retirement benefits refused by the city fathers. In Los Angeles, too, the third successive bond issue for more police facilities was approved, while voters were turning down school bond measures.

Law enforcement is testing its political muscle, emboldened by the easily sensed mood of a public demanding domestic tranquility at any price. The police claim they can provide instant peace of mind—the slogan is "law and order" and until the campaign collapses in futility, they will muster ever greater support. And with that support, the police will push even harder for complete control of law enforcement.

> The Skolnick paper referred to earlier continues (p. 12 ff., *passim.*):

The San Francisco Police Department, until five years ago, devoted most of its energy to apprehending criminals. In May, 1962, Police Chief Thomas Cahill, at the recommendation of such civic groups as the National Association for the Advancement of Colored People and the National Conference of Christians and Jews, established a community relations bureau . . . to create a better understanding and closer relationship between the police department and the community, and to promote greater public cooperation with the police department.

Implicit in the creation of this unit was a recognition that changing social needs required a more expansive concept of police work. . . . The PCR idea gave organizational meaning to the notion that police prevent crime, not only by the threat of deterrence but also by a sympathetic understanding of the problems of people residing in high-crime areas. Crime was not, in this view, simply an act of perverted will but . . . arose out of frustrations and degradations felt by disadvantaged people; thus the police would help reduce crime by reducing despair— by acting as a social service agency to ameliorate some of the difficulties encountered by minority group persons.

The history of the San Francisco PCR unit reflects a struggle between two opposing interpretations of the role of the policeman and his relationship to the community. . . . Each faction developed a secure power base whose function was to undermine the validity of the position of the other side. . . . The chief of police [had] to mediate between [them]. When he supported the PCR Unit . . . it was able to function successfully. When with time his enthusiasm for the Unit waned, the influence of the Unit diminished until it could no longer function as it once had. . . .

The Unit was established in May 1962 with Lieutenant Dante Andreotti as commanding officer. . . . In the beginning [he] was given considerable support. He was flown to Michigan to study at the Community Relations Institute there, was the object of supportive newspaper publicity, and received public praise by the Chief of Police. . . . By January 1964, the success of the PCR Unit . . . was so great that four members of the unit were invited to work out of the Office of Economic Opportunity in four poverty pockets. In the Spring of 1967, there were two men in the Hunters Point OEO office, one in Chinatown, two in Central City, etc. . . .

As the duties and responsibilities of the men in the PCR Unit increased, so did the hostility of the rest of the police force . . . A gripe against the Unit stemmed from the fact that its men worked in plain clothes, even though they were not of detective rank. The hostility that minority group communities felt toward police was so great that for a uniformed officer to enter a new community was out of the question. On the other hand, the police outside the Unit were unwilling to accept the idea that their uniforms elicited as much hostility as they did. They saw the unwillingness of the PCR men to wear uniforms as either disrespect for their fellow policemen, or a special attempt to show that they were "better" than other members of the force, or part of some sinister Communist plot to disparage the uniform.

The PCR Unit suffered from the stigma . . . of deviation from standard police practices. The role of the PCR man was often described as "social work" by other police. Many members of the force [said] "social worker = socialist = communist." . . . social work activities undercut the basic conception of the police role. Police like to see themselves as strong, aggressive, masculine hunters protecting the weak. . . . "I'm a cop, that's all I want to be and that's all I'm going to be." . . .

Probably the greatest barrier to . . . acceptance of the PCR Unit was the informal complaint procedure the unit developed . . . for complaints against the police . . . and other units of the city government. . . . The unit became the informal "ombudsman" of San Francisco. . . .

As hostility within the Police Department grew, there were increasing pressures upon Cahill to disband the Unit. . . . In December 1966 a committee of the Grand Jury of San Francisco recommended that the Central PCR Unit be broken up and its men assigned to do the same work in uniform under district captains. . . . Chief Cahill promised that this would not take place . . . [But] he announced a new plan: Each district captain was to select two men from his station to work in close connection with the Central Unit, to carry the work of the unit to the local stations. Significantly, however, these men were to be responsible to their captains, and not to Lieutenant Andreotti. The significance of this procedure was clear: if the captain was unsympathetic to minorities and to the concept of community relations, he would prevail over Andreotti. . . .

As Cahill took this position, his personal relations with Andreotti deteriorated . . . [and] . . . Andreotti was finally eased out of the department, was given a farewell party attended by the mayor and was vigorously praised when he left for a job in the Justice Department. . . .

There is a real question as to what we can learn from San Francisco's attempt to introduce a PCR Unit. First, it seems to me that we can distinguish three types of police-community relations approaches that have been tried in this country:

1. The public relations approach, exemplified by Chief Parker [which] emphasizes relations with press and contacts with "responsible" citizens, including minority group leaders. It does not seek police contact on a person-to-person basis with the grass roots of minority populations. In my opinion, this approach must fail.

2. The second approach is exemplified by Andreotti and his Unit. It gives help to minority people in a social work approach. It was successful insofar as it improved relations between the PCR Unit and minority groups; it did not succeed in bringing around the remainder of the police department.

3. The third approach is the "variation" suggested by Chief Cahill. The problem with this has to do with the special training of men and the complicated area of rank and responsibility . . . It is too easy for this approach to regress to the public relations concept. Even a well-intentioned precinct captain may have to succumb to pressures generated by the men under him.

I know no easy answers, but I would suggest the following. First, for each major police department, there should be a centralized PCR unit, headed by a man like Andreotti. . . . It is important that the men in his unit can count on him to get them out of conflicts . . . with other high ranking officers. Second, it would be a good idea to rotate general duty police through the PCR unit while at the same time maintaining a strong continuing cadre in the central PCR unit. The PCR unit would thus serve as a training agency for men to be fed into other units. The difficulty with this approach is that there are relatively few police who are really interested in PCR work, so that there is a risk that men assigned to the unit against their will would emerge even less sympathetic to minority group peoples. Nobody really knows the answer to this problem. It may be necessary to experiment by establishing different types of PCR work over a period of two or three years to learn what would be the most favorable structure for a PCR unit.

Thurgood Marshall

> Thurgood Marshall, now Associate Justice of the U.S. Supreme Court, then Director-Counsel, NAACP Legal and Educational Fund, New York, addressing the sixth National Institute on Police and Community Relations, May 1960, spoke on "Racial Factors in Law Enforcement." Mr. Marshall stated his position on police and minority groups:

Some years ago, I was staying at the home of a Negro who lived in a block predominantly settled by Negroes and one adjoining a white community. Sitting on the porch of that home, I noticed a policeman coming through the white block, patting the white children on the head, saying nice things to them with an obvious exhibition of good feelings on both sides. The same policeman, when he reached the Negro block, yelled at the Negro children, told them to get out of his way, and brushed by them, with antagonism exhibited on both sides. . . .

Human beings must be treated as human beings and the policeman must convince himself that, under the law, this government requires non-discrimination in terms of race and religion. He must convince himself that this is the law of the land and that he cannot overrule or disregard it. He must realize that when he is on duty, his every action must be on that basis. He cannot make a practice of calling one man "Mr." and another man "boy." He must recognize that a Negro in the eyes of the law is innocent until he is proved guilty, the same as anyone else. He must realize that he has no more right, unlawfully and without provocation, on the pretense of defending himself, to beat a defenseless Negro, any more than to take his billy to the leading white citizen of the city. . . . In other words, it is my thesis that the police official in the United States has a tremendous responsibility, on the one hand, to recognize the quality of the man without regard to race, and on the other, to do his part to destroy the image that the policeman is the oppressor of the civil rights of minority groups.

Questions for Discussion

1. Is there an inconsistency between Parker's two premises?

2. Did Parker see his police-community relations unit as having primarily a *service* or an *intelligence* function?

3. What does Skolnick think was lacking in Parker's police-community relations program?

4. What basic changes did Reddin make in the Los Angeles approach to police and community relations? Were they adequate to assure success?

5. Is there a relationship between "the aspect Reddin cannot reform" and "the aspect he will not reform"?

6. Baldwin, a successful black novelist, sees both cause and effect in blacks-police and police-blacks attitudes. Do you see any hope for improving police-community relations in this deadlock?

7. Is it the proper function of police, or of a police association, to lobby for the kinds of gains that Cray mentions?

8. Concerning Skolnick's description of PCR efforts in San Francisco:
   a. What made Cahill decide to introduce a PCR program?
   b. Why did most of his men resist it?
   c. To what pressures did he finally capitulate when he reorganized the program?
   d. What function of the program was apparently most offensive to many of the men in his department?

9. Can you suggest other possible patterns for organizing a PCR program than the three Skolnick proposes?

10. Could an officer accept Marshall's comments on the role of a policeman and still maintain his freedom to exercise his discretionary judgments on duty?

STUDY 7

Role Attributes

James W. Sterling, Project Director of the Management
and Research Division, International Association of Chiefs
of Police, has authored a report of a longitudinal research
project entitled, *Changes in Role Concepts of Police Officers.*
The phase from which this study is extracted investigates
"Changes in Role Concepts of Police Officers During Recruit
Training." The research was done in the police departments
of Baltimore, Cincinnati, Columbus, and Indianapolis.

Sterling, in the *Preface,* says:

> With regard to learning within the context of this research, it seems
> appropriate to recall the adage that not all which is taught is learned,
> and not all that is learned is actually taught. Some of the ideas pre-
> sented in police recruit schools are simply unlearned. Others are
> conditionally learned, while still other ideas are learned and rejected
> as having no value. On the other hand, much is learned beyond that
> which is contained within the formal curriculum. Within the school,
> the incidental comments of instructors and other recruits may pro-
> duce unintended learning. Outside the school, the actions, expressions,
> and words of friends and the general public may teach the recruit
> lessons of great significance. This expanded view of learning an occu-
> pational role is taken within this report.

Sterling continues:

> The role of the police patrolman is a complex one. Not only in
> terms of the variety of demands placed on the individual enacting the
> role during his on-duty hours, but it is also complicated by the intense
> and pervasive character of the vocational role which impinges on his
> non-duty hours. As a consequence of this, an inquiry into the social-

The material here is used with the permission of the International Association of
Chiefs of Police.

ization* process for the police initiate will reflect that complexity. The perspective of role theory has been adopted for this research because it offers a means by which the process of taking on the police role can be studied with greater clarity and deeper understanding than is possible with the usual common sense approaches or, for that matter, other theoretical approaches.

"One of the most important concepts within role theory," Sterling explains in discussing the role conflict instrument used as the basis for the study,

> ... is that of role conflict, the exposure to and awareness of conflicting role expectations. In this regard, one of the most frequently mentioned views of the police officer is that he is a man in the middle, caught in a chaos of conflicting expectations.
>
> He is truly the "man in the middle." He stands between the lawless and the law abiding and between the rioter and society. And no matter what course of action he takes, he is between Scylla and Charibdis for one side will always take him to task.**
>
> The intra-role conflict arises out of the differential expectations held by various reference groups about the role performance of the police ... How much of the behavior of a police officer is determined by the behavioral expectations of significant others? We don't know, but a consideration of the following examples ... will suggest that a large part of what we do is determined by the behavioral expectations held by other people.
>
> A former member of a state highway patrol recalled his feelings at the time he was assigned to work in a Negro area:
>
>> I found myself roughing up Negroes routinely in the back seat of the patrol car—not because I disliked Negroes, but because in the police group it was the thing to do. [Turner, *The Police Establishment,* p. 317]
>
> Not only are police officers perceptive of the expectations of other fellow officers but they are also sensitive to the expectations of the public. Consider the statement of an officer from a large city department:
>
>> If there was a real bad murder, you would get the feeling that the public wanted the killer and they didn't care how we caught him ... We also used to have the feeling that the public

---

Socialization is defined as a formal or informal learning process by which an individual becomes aware of and committed to behavioral norms that are seen as appropriate and right for specific role performances. Conversely, socialization includes the learning of expected behavioral responses to the performances of specific roles by other people.

**Thomas Reddin, *Law Enforcement in a Complex Society,* (General Telephone Company of California, undated pamphlet), p. 2.

wanted us to keep pushing around homosexuals and other per-
verts. [Burnham, "Police Violence," p. 34]

In the first instance, the police officer perceived of an expectation
held by some of his fellow officers that he should engage in behavior
which violates not only departmental rules and regulations but also the
very laws he should be enforcing. In the second instance, the officer was
expressing an awareness of an expectation on the part of the public to
engage in extralegal activities in the enforcement of the law. This is the
nature of the role conflict we are concerned with.

In his analysis of role attributes, Sterling considers (pp. 240, 241)
the changed evaluations of the recruits' ideas on characteristics they held
as most important to a police officer, at the beginning and at the completion of their formal recruit training:

Inter-City Comparison of Role Attributes Chosen by Police Recruits

Attribute	Balt.	Cin.	Col.	Ind.
Test 1, at the start of recruit training (T_1)				
Dedication	X	X	X	X
Alertness	X	X	X	X
Good training	X	X	X	X
Common sense	X	X	X	X
Job knowledge	X	X		X
Intelligence	X	X	X	
Honesty	X	X		
Appearance			X	X
Courage	X	X		
Respect for superiors				X
Patience			X	
Responsibility			X	
Reliability			X	
Test 2, on completion of recruit training (T_2)				
Alertness	X	X	X	X
Common sense	X	X	X	X
Well trained	X	X	X	X
Dedication	X	X	X	X
Job knowledge	X	X	X	X
Courtesy	X	X	X	X
Appearance	X		X	X
Honesty		X	X	X
Intelligence	X	X	X	
Responsibility	X	X		X
Initiative				X
Courage				

One's concept of what attributes are essential for the enactment of the police role is, at bottom, a reflection of what the role of the police is thought to be. Changes in conceptions of role attributes over time will take place to the degree that one's concept of the police role is altered. If a recruit at the start of training conceives of police work as consisting largely of physical tasks carried on in a hostile environment, then logically the attributes which are seen to be essential for work of this kind are physical strength and courage. After training, if the recruit now recognizes a legitimate role for the police in performing a variety of public service functions and sees that people can, in many instances, be manipulated more easily through verbal skills, then courtesy and knowledge come to be valued more highly.

The recruits sampled in the four cities were given a list of traits from which they were to choose those that they considered as attributes essential to the enactment of the police role.

The list of those qualities which were common to all four cities rose from four on T_1 (the test at the start of training) to six on T_2 (on the completion of training).

The attributes named on the first test included dedication, alertness, well trained, and common sense, in that order. On the second test, the order of preference became: alertness, common sense, well trained, and dedication, and to these all four cities added job knowledge and courtesy.

Probably the most striking change between the two sets of data relates to the attribute of courtesy. Courtesy was not included in the list of attributes chosen by the subjects at the start of their training. By the end of training, the recruits of all four cities chose this attribute. Thus ... whereas at the start of training the subjects did not conceive of police work as a role calling for the human relations skill of courtesy, by the end of training the subjects in all four cities had apparently experienced the role concept which was reflected in the choice of courtesy as an essential attribute.

Questions for Discussion

1. Does Sterling's *Preface* discredit the value of recruit training schools?

2. How is role theory helpful in contributing to an understanding of police function?

3. Explain *socialization* in your own words. Give some examples.

4. Why can't an officer "just go by the book" and avoid conflicts in role expectations?

5. Have *you* ever acted as you were "expected" to act rather than according to your own inclinations?

6. If you had been an instructor of these recruits, would you have conveyed the importance of courtesy? If so, how would you have done it?

7. Study all the attributes listed, noting their positions on the scale. Do you agree with the order of ratings? Can you account for them?

8. Do you think a patrolman of 10 years' experience would agree with the ratings?

Stop Crime, or Respect Civil Liberties?

Some persons feel strongly that crime among minority groups ought to be stamped out even at a high cost in the violation of civil liberties; others feel that civil liberties ought to be safeguarded even at a high cost of crime. [James Q. Wilson, "Police and their Problems"]

On which Sterling comments:

There is probably no conflict within the field of law enforcement which is more heatedly argued by both police and the public than that which is presented in this conflict situation ... Nearly 24 percent of the respondents perceive of the expectation held by patrolmen as being one of stopping crime even if it requires sacrificing certain civil liberties ... The opposite view was attributed to civil rights leaders (by the recruits).

Question for Discussion

What significance do you attach to the argument reflected in this quotation and commentary?

STUDY 8

Police Discretion

In his *Varieties of Police Behavior,* James Q. Wilson delin-
eates four types of situations in which police discretion
must be used, and illustrates each with cases.

The patrolman's decision whether and how to intervene in a situation
depends on his evaluation of the costs and benefits of various kinds of
action. Though the substantive criminal law seems to imply a mandate,
based on duty or morality, that the law be applied whenever and wherever its injunctions have been violated, in fact for most officers there
are considerations of utility that equal or exceed in importance those
of duty or morality, especially for the more common and less serious
laws. . . . His actual decision whether and how to intervene involves
such questions as these: Has anyone been hurt or deprived? Will anyone
be hurt or deprived if I do nothing? Will an arrest improve the situation
or only make matters worse? Is a complaint more likely if there is *no*
arrest, or if there *is* an arrest? What does the sergeant expect of me?
Am I getting near the end of my tour of duty? Will I have to go to court
on my day off? If I do appear in court, will the charge stand up or will
it be withdrawn or dismissed by the prosecutor? Will my partner think
an arrest shows I can handle things or that I can't handle things? What
will the guy do if I let him go? . . .
  To explain fully the uses of discretion many factors would have
to be considered. For simplicity, two major determinants (major in the
sense that they explain "enough" of the variation) suffice: whether the
situation is primarily one of *law enforcement,* or one of *order maintenance* and whether the police response is *police-invoked,* or *citizen-
invoked.* . . . Law enforcement involves a violation of a law in which
only guilt need be assessed; order maintenance, though it often entails

Reprinted by permission of the publishers from James Q. Wilson, *Varieties of
Police Behavior.* (Cambridge, Mass.: Harvard University Press, Copyright, 1968,
by the President and Fellows of Harvard College.)

a legal infraction, involves in addition a dispute in which the law must be interpreted, standards of right conduct determined, and blame assigned. A police-invoked response is one in which the officer acts on his own authority, rather than as the agent of a citizen who has made a specific verbal or sworn complaint (though citizens "in general" may have complained about "the situation"); a citizen-invoked response is one in which the officer acts on a particular complaint or warrant of the citizen. Although some situations cannot be neatly placed in any category, enough can . . . so that we can imagine four kinds of situations in which discretion is exercised, as illustrated by the following figure:

Four Kinds of Discretionary Situations

| | | Basis of police response | |
		Police-invoked action	Citizen-invoked action
Nature of situation	Law enforcement	I	II
	Order maintenance	III	IV

Each case offers a different degree of discretion for the patrolman, the department, or both.

Case I: Police-invoked Law Enforcement

In this situation, the police themselves initiate the action in the specific instance, though sometimes in response to a general public concern over the problem, and whatever action they take is on their own authority. If there is an arrest, the officer is the complaining witness. Many crimes handled in this way are "crimes without victims"—that is, no citizen has been deprived and thus no citizen has called the police. Such calls as the police may get are from "busybodies"—persons who dislike "what is going on" but who themselves are not participants. Enforcement of laws dealing with vice, gambling, and traffic offenses are of this character. The rate and form of police interventions in these situations can be strongly influenced by the policy of the administrator. He can apply a performance measure to his subordinates. . . . The performance is *goal-oriented* . . . based on whether the substantive law enforcement goal has been attained (e.g., closing down brothels). . . . With regard to traffic enforcement, however, the administrator's measure

will be how many traffic tickets the officers have written, not how safe
the streets are . . . in which case his performance measure will be *means-
oriented.*

Case II: Citizen-invoked Law Enforcement

Here a citizen is the victim of a crime and he or she complains to
the police. The vast majority of crimes with victims are those against
property—larceny, auto theft, and burglary—and the vast majority of
these are crimes of stealth for which the suspect is unknown. As a result,
only a small percentage are solved by an arrest. The patrolman in these
circumstances functions primarily as a report taker . . . except when
the suspect is still on the scene or has been caught by the victim or an
onlooker . . . for example, shoplifting. Here the patrolman must decide
whether to make an arrest, to tell the citizen that it is up to him to handle the matter by getting a complaint and taking the suspect to court
himself, or to encourage him to effect a citizen's arrest on the spot. . . .
In the case of juveniles [the patrolman] can decide, if not *whether* to
intervene (to arrest, take into temporary custody, warn and release,
etc.) The police administrator can influence the use of that discretion
significantly . . . by setting guidelines on how such cases will be handled.

Case III: Police-invoked Order Maintenance

In this instance, the police on their own authority and initiative
intervene in situations of actual or potential disorder. The most common
charges are drunkenness, disorderly conduct, or breach of the peace
. . . Because the police invoke the law, the administrator has some control over the patrolman's discretion. He can urge them to "keep things
quiet" but he cannot, as in traffic enforcement, judge each officer's "production" by how many arrests he makes . . . Nor can he insist, as he
might in cases of shoplifting, that an arrest is always the best way to
handle the situation . . .

Case IV: Citizen-invoked Order Maintenance

In this last case, a citizen calls for police assistance because of a
public or private disorder . . . In almost every department, such a citizen
call must be followed by a police response to avoid the charge of "doing
nothing." The way the patrolman handles these situations will depend
on his assessment of them and on the extent to which the participants
are inclined to be tractable, and victims prepared to sign a formal complaint. . . . Young college-educated patrolmen in a pleasant suburb may
handle these matters one way; older, working-class officers in a racially
mixed central-city may handle them in another.

In sum, in Cases I and IV the patrolman has great discretion, but in the former instance, it can be brought under departmental control, and in the latter it cannot. In Case II the patrolman has the least discretion, except when the suspects are juveniles, and then the discretion is substantial and can be affected by general departmental policies and organization. Case III is intermediate in both the degree of discretion and the possibility of departmental control.

Questions for Discussion

1. By what legal or moral right, or both, does an officer depart from "the book" in exercising discretion in handling incidents?

2. Implicit in "police-invoked law enforcement" (Case I) is the idea that the officer plays the roles of judge and jury as well as that of enforcer. Is this what the public expects of him?

3. In "citizen-invoked actions," is there more—or less—expectation on the part of the public that the officer will exercise discretion than is true in police-invoked actions? Give examples.

4. In situations of mass violations of the law (e.g., drug use, nudity, rock festivals), are the officers justified in merely containing such obvious infractions, without making arrests?

5. This passage reflects the heart of Wilson's book on *varieties* of police behavior. Do you feel his ideas are merely theoretical, or are they realistic and helpful?

Part Two

Psychological Considerations

As police work today moves toward a deeper understanding of the interrelationship of the police and the community they serve, it is important for the student to understand the psychological forces that mold police and community feelings about each other. For an overview of the basic psychological considerations in this context, the reader is referred to Part II of *The Police and the Community* (Radelet).

Some of the major problems arise from the difference between the way the police see themselves and the way various parts of the public see them. To help understand this difference, Studies 1 and 2 that follow examine the complex structure of the community and the numerous dynamic factors that affect police morale. Study 3 shows the nature of police subcultures that sometimes evolve as a result of the need of police to retreat from the conflicting expectations of the community.

To throw further light on the psychological factors that affect how we perceive, how we form our attitudes and beliefs, and how we develop our sense of values, Studies 4 and 5 develop points on prejudice and perception that the student may well find enlightening about his own attitudes as well as valuable in understanding police and community attitudes. Study 6, "Points on Rumor," discusses the various forms that rumor may take and suggests the devastating effects that unconfirmed reports can have on both the police and the community.

STUDY 1

The Structure of the Community

There are several possible ways of portraying the elements of community structure. None of them is fully satisfactory because any diagrammatic presentation is static, whereas the elements of a community are dynamic and, in their interplay on each other, are better visualized as a riptide: the waves on a shore break, rush up the beach, flow back, and shape the size and force of the waves to follow. Or the components of a community might be compared to the constantly changing color effects of a kaleidoscope, in which each of the colors may be thought of as representing individuals or groups of people in their ever-changing relationships. In short, the concept of the community should convey a sense of dynamic diversity.

Nevertheless, graphics are of some limited instructional value, and there is no shortage of them in efforts to suggest the nature of community structure. Carson H. McGuire's schematic diagram of a community, shown in Fig. 2–1, depicts four dimensions of community structure.

The first dimension (upper right in the figure) is *social status,* based on age of family, wealth, degree of influence or tradition. This classification follows the general pattern developed by W. Lloyd Warner, which goes further and divides the social hierarchy into class subdivisions for the upper, middle, and lower classes. In small communities, of course, these may not all be present.

A second element of community structure (lower right in the figure) is the community's *institutions.* These consist of the established, organized ways of behaving and include political, economic, religious, educational, and family organizational arrangements, as well as formal and informal groupings such as service clubs and friendship patterns.

A third element concerns *life styles* (upper left in the figure) of people—their degrees of conformity to accepted ways of behaving, as measured against community expectations. The range may be from the superordinate behavior of the socially most accepted citizens through such instances of social deviance as homosexuality and hippie culture.

45

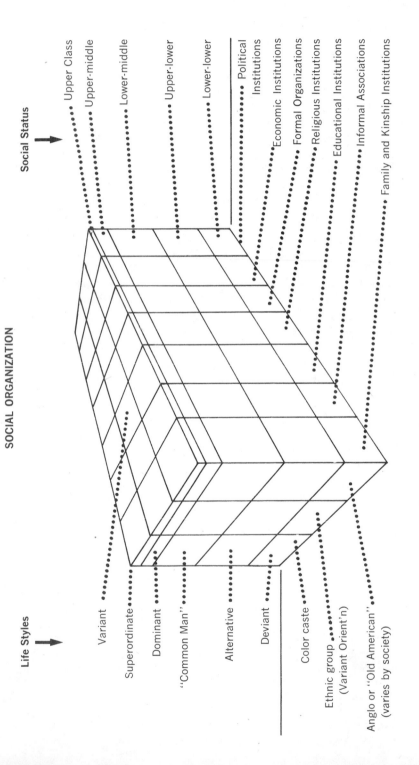

Figure 2–1.   Schematic diagram of a community

Variants may occur in any classification, however, as illustrated by two classic cases of upper-class personages, Oscar Wilde and Bertrand Russell.

A fourth method of categorizing groups (lower left in the figure) is based on the more or less *visible differences* between people. Color of skin is an example, but ethnic groupings by national origin marked by language differences or religious customs, or by the mere fact of being a "newcomer" are all possible.

But difficulties arise in any attempt to classify people. Individuals usually belong to several different groups and have varying degrees of allegiance to them. Moreover, people change. Through acculturation, newcomers—and even long-time inhabitants—adopt the ways of behaving of the more dominant groups and become examples of social mobility, moving up the social scale. Or established citizens may fall into a pattern of downward mobility: "Three generations from shirtsleeves to shirtsleeves." One author refers to the "climbers" and the "clingers."

Technology, too, may play a role by accelerating the upward mobility of the son of a laborer who, by reason, perhaps, of his college education (and perhaps his character), advances rapidly to a higher social status. The influence of technology on acculturation is complex. Television, for example, is a technological gadget, almost universally available. But the question arises: is television an integrative or disintegrative force in society?

In Fig. 2–2, on page 48, we see how a community can be visualized as a composite of several methods of classifying its inhabitants. The police are represented as the central subculture (the characteristics of which are described in Study 3). The overlapping circles can be conceived as representing any of the four classifications in the McGuire schema in Fig. 2–1, as well as other possible systems. Thus, circle 1 could represent "upper class," "Republican," "conformity," or "Spanish."

Whatever the classification, it is evident from the diagram in Fig. 2–2 that the police impinge on all groups, although not as equally and consistently as the drawing suggests. Likewise, each of the other groups (by whichever system) impinge on the police and on one another and are therefore clearly "a part of and not apart from" the totality of the community, as are the police.

Questions for Discussion

1. What is a riptide? Give examples (analogies) in the operations of community relations.

2. Compare Figures 2–1 and 2–2 as to their effectiveness in dramatizing the relationships of community forces. How is each superior to the other in its purpose?

3. Wherein is Warner's social status classification unreliable?

4. Compare the sociological and conversational meanings of the word "institution."

5. How do Oscar Wilde and Bertrand Russell illustrate the weaknesses of classification by life styles? Does this render the method useless?

6. Give examples of how nationality or religious customs might be visible differences that could disturb a community?

7. Do all groups in a community affect all the others? Equally? Give examples.

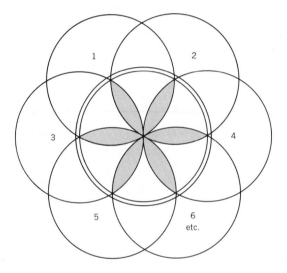

The central circle represents the police subculture. Each of the overlapping circles might represent a different method of classifying the groups in a community:

1. *social status:* upper, upper-middle, lower-middle, etc.
2. *institutions:* political, economic, religious, family
3. *life styles:* superordinate, dominant, conforming
4. *visibility differences:* color, religious customs
5. *business:* industry, manufacturing, marketing, services
6. *organizations:* labor, service, civic, fraternal, sports

Figure 2–2.   Classification of a community

Systemic Model of Police Morale:
A Personality and Social Structure Analysis

Theoretical views of the police and public adversary relationship are of minimal heuristic research value. None of the theorists clearly define terms or present a consistent theory based on environmental, organizational, and personality variables. The systemic model presented here attempts to rectify this deficiency with the interactional approach needed to understand the effects of police and citizen relationships on police morale. The model is based on an open systems approach that considers organizational interval development and environmental adaptation (Katz and Kahn, *The Social Psychology of Organizations*) and incorporates a role and self-identity theory in understanding the police organization (James Q. Wilson, *The Police and Their Problems*). It is intended to serve as a basis for investigating such crucial police and community relations issues as poor morale, police isolation, the respect syndrome of police, and so on. It should be noted that the model is a highly simplified theory of real-life situations and is presently in its early developmental stage. Its verification and modification is contingent on future research.

The theoretical model addresses itself to these questions:

1. How does the community contribute to the problem of poor police morale?

2. Is there a causal link between police isolation and alienation *and* community perceptions of police?

The model presented in this study was developed by Martin G. Miller while he was a member of the faculty of the (then) School of Police Administration and Public Safety, Michigan State University (1965–69), as assistant director of the National Center on Police and Community Relations. He is presently assistant professor of sociology, Iowa State University. The model and its accompanying explanation and bibliography were prepared by Professor Miller specifically for inclusion in this text. © 1973 by Martin G. Miller.

The model centers on the following terms and their definitions:

1. *Social system:* an ordered arrangement of social roles, patterned through allocative and integrative processes, and having boundaries relative to an environment.

2. *Personality system:* an ordered arrangement of self-identities, patterned through allocative and integrative processes, that is characteristic of a particular individual.

3. *Cultural values:* consensually validated standards for evaluating social acts that are characteristic of a particular social system. In other words, conceptions of desirable states of affairs (Robin Williams).

4. *Social role:* a set of expectations defining what is appropriate behavior in a particular position in a system of social relationships.

5. *Self-identity:* a set of need-dispositions or tendencies toward behavior expressed in the form of an image of self in a particular position in a system of social relationships.

6. *Norm:* a consensually validated behavioral prescription or proscription.

7. *Isomorphism:* a condition in which the content of a role expectation, a need-disposition, and a cultural value are identical.

8. *Congruence:* a condition in which the content of a role expectation, a need-disposition, or a cultural value are appropriate to the content of one or more of the others.

9. *Social structure:* form and distribution of, and relationships among, units within a social system.

10. *Degree of structural differentiation:* the number of units within a social system.

11. *Degree of structuring:* the extent to which the functioning of a social system is normatively regulated.

12. *Self-esteem maintenance system* (to be referred to as SMS): the hierarchical ordering of cultural values and social roles within a *personality* system. The ones on top are most important to self-esteem, the ones on the bottom least. It is a process of maintaining favorable images of self.

13. *Status assignment system* (to be referred to as SAS): the process of status ordering and giving within a *social* system. The hierarchical ordering of cultural values and social roles by the participants of a social system. The ones on top possess the most status (prestige) in the system, the ones on the bottom least. This reflects the central value system of the social system.

The key to understanding the effects of social structure on personality is the analysis of the structure of the social system's SAS and a
personality system's SMS. This calls for a determination of isomorphism
and congruency between the systems. What processes produce isomorphism and congruency or no isomorphism and congruency?

The theory is based on the following assumptions:

1. People try to maintain favorable self-identities.

2. Any kind of favorable image of self needs social support and con-
   firmation (as Cooley and Mead have stated).

3. We are part of many social systems, therefore many SASs feed
   into our SMSs.

4. In contemporary unstructured society, people are socialized within
   highly structurally differentiated social systems; thus, they possess
   many self-identities.

5. In contemporary unstructured society, high structural differentiation has led to people possessing a complexity of values and roles.

6. The degree to which there is isomorphism and congruency between
   our SASs and our SMSs is the degree to which we possess favorable
   self-identities.

A hypothesis of our theoretical model is that isomorphism and
congruence do not exist between the SMS of the *policeman* (personality
system)—particularly the low-ranked patrolman—and the SAS of the
police department (social system) and the SAS of the *community* (social system). Talcott Parsons defines a community as a social system
in which people share an area, and this shared area is the base of operations for their daily activities. The hypothesis stated above is supported
by Preiss and Ehrlich's finding (*An Examination of Role Theory*) that
in the state police organization studied, there was a low order of consensus on role areas of policemen among officers' audience groups.

Table 2–1 presents a hypothetical example of SMS and SAS hierarchical ordering that shows divergences between the systems with respect to the policeman's role and status. It is evident that little congruency or isomorphism exists between the SMS and the SASs. As a result,
there develops status discrepancy, i.e., "a lack of consistency between
property, occupation, education on the one hand and prestige on the
other" (J. C. Davis, *Human Nature in Politics*). Fig. 2–3 is a graphic
scheme of the interrelationships of these systems.

When the SMS is not identical to (isomorphic) the SASs, then the
subjects (in this case, police officers) suffer from:

1. *Alienation:* a rejection of the legitimacy of status assignment systems (*isolation* in Seeman's terms, "On the Meaning of Alienation")

and self-estrangement, an awareness of the discrepancy between one's ideal self and one's actual self image.

2. *Psychological stress:* (stress used in a broad sense of anxiety, inability to function normally, fright, etc.) A. Pepitone has written a most pertinent article, "Self, Social Environment, and Stress," relating to our concern for the reaction of stress to the unequal SMS and SASs. He states that the amount of stress experienced is

TABLE 2–1
Systemic Model of Police Morale: An Example

Self-esteem Maintenance System (SMS) of Patrolman

Hierarchies

	Cultural Values	Role Concepts: Community	Role Concepts: Police Department
High	Respect	Policeman	Patrolman
	Wealth	Doctor	Detective
	Power	Grocer	Juvenile Officer
Low	Honesty	Banker	PCR Officer

Status Assignment System (SAS) of Police Social System (Department)

Hierarchies

	Cultural Values	Role Concepts: Community	Role Concepts: Police Department
High	Respect	Policeman	Detective
	Power	Doctor	Juvenile Officer
	Honesty	Banker	PCR Officer
Low	Wealth	Grocer	Patrolman

Status Assignment System (SAS) of Community Social System

Hierarchies

	Cultural Values	Role Concepts: Community	Role Concepts: Police Department
High	Honesty	Doctor	PCR Officer
	Wealth	Banker	Juvenile Officer
	Power	Grocer	Detective
Low	Respect	Policeman	Patrolman

- - - - - = Important divergences in ordering that indicate lack of isomorphism between systems.

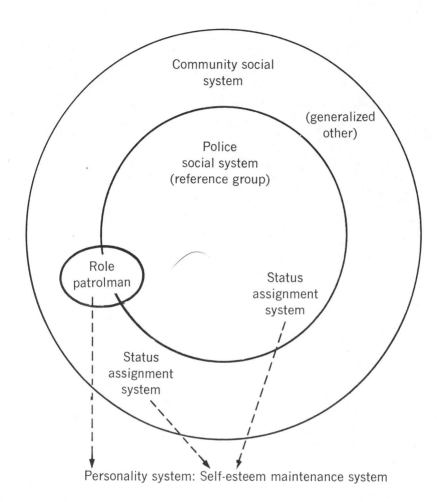

Figure 2–3.   Interrelationships of systems

dependent on losing status. Pepitone presents several laboratory experiments showing that stress reactions are correlated with threat of loss of personal esteem. If a person does not achieve status, he evaluates himself negatively. Such a person, in a situation where status is won or lost, defends himself from further loss at any cost. Another significant point is that organizations having a pattern of vertical structural differentiation shaped as a triangle, i.e., few positions on top, many on the bottom (as in the case of police departments), cause stress due to lack of mobility opportunity.

   The problems of alienation and psychological stress resulting from status discrepancy may be lessened to the extent that ways can be found to form isomorphism and congruency among the SMS of the policeman's personality system and the SASs of the police department and community social systems.

REFERENCES FOR FURTHER STUDY

I. PRO-ADVERSARY THEORISTS: PSYCHOANALYTIC/ PSYCHOLOGICAL PERSPECTIVE

Freud, Sigmund. *Civilization and Its Discontents (1930)*. Translated from the German and edited by J. Strachey. New York: W. W. Norton, 1961.

Pierce, Chester. "Psychiatric Aspects of Police-Community Relations." *Mental Hygiene,* 1962, 46: 107–115.

Stinchcombe, Arthur L. "The Control of Citizen's Resentment in Police Work." Unpublished manuscript, no date.

Toch, Hans. "Psychological Consequences of the Police Role." *Police,* 1965, 10: 22–25.

Westley, William A. "Violence and the Police." *American Journal of Sociology,* 1953, 39: 34–41.

Wirths, Claudine Gibson. "The Development of Attitudes Toward Law Enforcement." *Police,* 1958, 3: 50–52.

Supporting material:

Merton, Robert K. *Social Theory and Social Structure.* New York: The Free Press of Glencoe, 1957.

II. ANTI-ADVERSARY THEORISTS: SOCIOLOGICAL PERSPECTIVE

Banton, Michael. "Social Integration and Police." *The Police Chief,* 1963, 30: 8–20.

Gorer, Geoffrey. "Modification of National Character: The Role of the Police in England." *Journal of Social Issues,* 1955, 11: 11–24.

Supporting material:

Blau, Peter M. *Exchange and Power in Social Life.* New York: John Wiley and Sons, 1964.

Parsons, Talcott (ed. and tr. of Max Weber): *The Theory of Social and Economic Organization.* First American Edition. New York: Oxford University Press, 1947. (A translation of parts of Weber's *Wirtschaft und Gessellschaft.*)

III. RESEARCH

Clark, John P. "Isolation of the Police: A Comparison of the British and American Situations." *Journal of Criminal Law, Criminology, and Police Science,* 1965, 56: 307–319.

Preiss, Jack J. and Ehrlich, Howard J. *An Examination of Role Theory: The Case of the State Police.* Lincoln, Nebraska: University of Nebraska Press, 1966.

IV. THE SOCIAL PSYCHOLOGY OF THE POLICE

Becker, Howard S. *Outsiders: Studies in the Sociology of Deviance.* New York: The Free Press, 1963.

McNamara, John H. "Uncertainties in Police Work: The Relevance of Police Recruits' Background and Training." In David J. Bordua (ed.), *The Police: Six Sociological Essays.* New York: John Wiley and Sons, 1967.

Reiss, Albert J., Jr. "Professionalization of the Police." In A. F. Brandstatter and Louis A. Radelet (eds.), *Police and Community Relations: A Sourcebook.* Beverly Hills, California: The Glencoe Press, 1968.

Reiss, Albert J., Jr., and Bordua, David J. "Environment and Organization: A Perspective on the Police." In David J. Bordua (ed.), *The Police: Six Sociological Essays.* New York: John Wiley and Sons, 1967.

Skolnick, Jerome and Woodworth, J. Richard. "Bureaucracy, Information, and Social Control: A Study of a Morals Detail." In David J. Bordua (ed.), *The Police: Six Sociological Essays.* New York: John Wiley and Sons, 1967.

Werthman, Carl and Piliavin, Irving. "Gang Members and the Police." In David J. Bordua (ed.), *The Police: Six Sociological Essays.* New York: John Wiley and Sons, 1967.

Westley, William A. "Violence and the Police." *American Journal of Sociology,* 1953, 39: 34–41.

Wilson, James Q. "Police Morale, Reform, and Citizen Respect: The Chicago Case." In David J. Bordua (ed.), *The Police: Six Sociological Essays.* New York: John Wiley and Sons, 1967.

Wilson, James Q. "The Police and Their Problems: A Theory." *Public Policy,* (Harvard University), 1963, 12: 189–216.

Profile of the Police Subculture

When a group of people has meanings, values, and behavior patterns distinct from those of a larger group of which they are part, the group is said to constitute a subculture. Additional points about subcultures may be made:

1. The meanings, values, and behavior patterns may change.

2. Subcultures may contain organized *subgroups* which, though not large enough to constitute subcultures in themselves, are important enough to influence the character of the larger entity.

3. In addition to various subgroups, a subculture contains *classes of people* having their commonalities and differences.

4. The members of a subgroup have their *personal characteristics.*

5. The public holds certain *stereotypes* of members of a subculture: bankers (conservative), scientists (analytical), lawyers (deliberative). These may vary with individuals' experiences with them, as with the police (protector, "dumb cop," friend, enemy).

6. Members of an occupational subculture act differently when off their job and play many roles apart from, but reflecting and affecting their occupational role.

7. Subcultures have distinctive characteristics, such as "shoptalk," anecdotes, language, and "slanguage" which have meanings only to their members.

In the light of the above, let us look at the *police* subculture. *By the term police subculture we mean the body of collective understanding among policemen about matters related to their roles as officers.* (Victor G. Strecher, "When Subcultures Meet.") Expanding the seven points mentioned, we can profile the police occupational subculture as follows:

1. The meanings, values, and behavior patterns of the police as a whole, and of its individual members, do not remain constant. Many writers, for example, characterize the police as cynical. But Niederhoffer's analysis in Fig. 2–4 shows that an officer's degree of cynicism varies with length of time on the job.

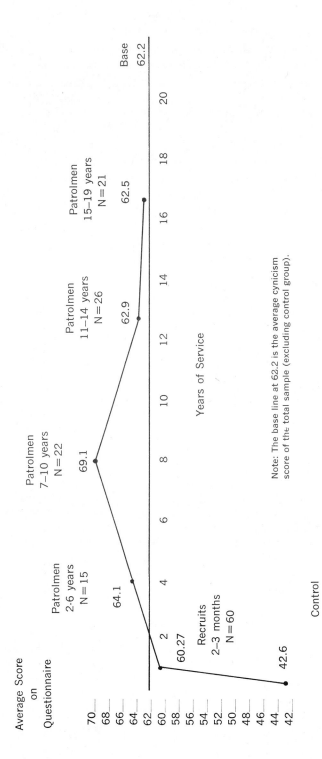

Figure 2–4. How cynicism among patrolmen varies with time
on the job in New York City (N=178)

The individual's cynicism increases up to the midpoint of his career, as the frustrations of his work increase. This is related to the fact that up to that point, he still has the option of resigning to seek what he might hope would be a more satisfying occupation. But at midpoint, the risk of loss of pension looms larger than his frustrations, and he begins to rationalize them as being tolerable in view of his now "downhill" road to retirement. With this caution—that characteristics of police personnel may vary—let us proceed to other aspects of the police subculture.

2. Subcultures may contain *subgroups* of more or less influence. In the large metropolitan force in New York City (41,000 employees), there are many such subgroups, with varying degrees of impact on the police organization. The largest and most powerful is the Patrolman's Benevolent Association (PBA), whose power was demonstrated by its successful crusade to eliminate the Civilian Review Board (1966). There are also ethnic and racial societies whose memberships presumably reflect the numbers of Irish, Negro, etc., employees of the total force. Table 2–2 (based on Niederhoffer, *Behind the Shield,* p. 135) shows the relative strength of these organizations among New York City police.

TABLE 2–2
Comparison of Membership of Selected Police Societies in the New York City Police Department

Association	Membership	Members	Percent
Emerald Society	Irish	8,500	42
Columbia Association	Italian	5,000	25
Shomrim Society	Jewish	2,270	11.2
Steuben Association	German	1,500	7.4
Guardians Association	Negro	1,320	6.5
Pulaski Association	Polish	1,100	5.4
St. Paul Society	Greek/Russian	300	1.5
Hispanic Society	Puerto Rican/ Spanish	250	1.
	Total	20,240	100.

Niederhoffer estimated there were approximately 11,000 Irish on the force. The significance of such subgroups in the police subculture lies in their potentials for divisiveness on the one hand and for morale building on the other.

3. *Classes of people* within the police subculture have commonalities and differences. In New York City, there are 5,000 civilian per-

sonnel employed in the police department whose orientations (salaries and pensions, for example) differ from those of the actual police. Other groupings may be based on sex, age, amount of education, social class origin, police family background, length of service, assignments (detective, traffic, juvenile, public relations, patrolmen), rank, service areas (ghetto, middle-class), etc., all classifications that constitute sufficiently large numbers of people in so large a department as to generate special interests, biases, and points of view. Moreover, there exist combinations of groupings (young-black-patrolman or Jewish-sergeant-detective). These both complicate and strengthen allegiances which, taken together, reinforce the concept of the police subculture. "I'm proud to be Irish; I'm proud to be a cop; I'm proud to be an Irish cop!" The impact of such varieties of groupings upon one another is suggested by the diagram in Fig. 2–5, in which the various overlapping circles indicate the unreality of conceiving of the police as a monolith of homogeniety.

4. As in other major occupational subcultures, policemen differ also in terms of their *personal characteristics*. The force includes introverts and extroverts, married and single, variations of mental and physical

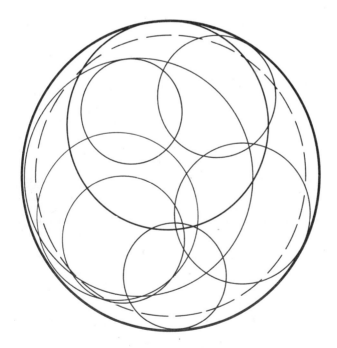

The broken circle represents the PBA. The overlapping circles of various sizes suggest subgroups with varying degrees of influence on the total police force.

Figure 2–5.   Diagram of a police subculture

health, parents and childless, etc., all of which are factors that contribute to police attitudes toward their jobs (cynical or challenged), effectiveness (healthy outlook or marking time), ambition (still striving or resigned to the way the "machine" works). Some find security (others don't) in the uniform, the pay and pension system, the early retirement prospect, or the paramilitary nature of the organization. Some have capitulated; others who have assignments they enjoy (the detective who gets his man; the juvenile officer who salvages a wayward youngster) are happily working at their jobs and attending night classes in college to qualify for promotion. Morale is both an institutional and a personal matter.

5. Little wonder, then, that various segments of the public and individual citizens see "the police" in various ways. In some instances, their views are based on personal contacts (pleasant or unpleasant), as a result of which they see all police as "the fuzz," "pigs," "flat-foots," or as "the guy that got my car back," "saved my daughter from attack," or "revived my baby when it turned blue."

But where the public attitude is generalized—based on rumor or on what civilians read or hear—they view the police on a scale ranging from total apathy, through phoning in evidence, to helping an officer make an arrest. The range is from a hostile adversary relationship to admiration and total cooperation. And the morale of individual policemen tends to be affected accordingly.

The esprit de corps of a department as a whole is further affected by the status ascribed to it by its public. But it is reflected differently for different groups within the department. Negro officers tend to respond differently than whites, for example. Even where the department has a satisfactory ascribed status, some or all Negro members may be scorned by their white colleagues as a necessary evil, employed to hold the ghetto in check, while ghetto citizens see them as Uncle Toms who have sold out to the "Establishment." They suffer the double marginality of being blacks and being cops. Similarly, the families of Jewish officers may look down on them (low prestige job) until they "make it to captain" or better. For such minority personnel, this personal "pariah" feeling is more pertinent than whatever prestige the department may enjoy.

6. So far we have discussed the police while acting as police, but it is important to note that their occupational traits carry over into their private lives in ways that may affect their job performance. Like other men, they play many roles: father, husband, club or church member, sportsman. Some consciously avoid "talking shop" at home to protect their families from fears. But carrying such burdens alone can affect job morale. "Cops are human, too." They are as varied as their backgrounds and personalities. There is no one "cop-type," any more than there is a typical doctor.

7. Any subculture has its characteristic "shoptalk" and jargon. In New York City, when a young officer gets unexpected preferred assignments, his buddies wonder who his "rabbi" is. The word means "teacher," but it has gained the connotation in that setting of one who can help a rookie to get ahead.

As in any subculture, the members exchange anecdotes, the language and substance of which are meaningful only to members of the occupation. They serve to brighten the day, convey information, and to build morale, because merely being able to understand them gives one a feeling of being part of the ingroup.

It is one thing to generalize about the police subculture, but it is more to the point to examine the actual statements of police officers themselves. The following quotations are from "Why I'm a Cop: Interviews from a Reporter's Notebook" by Patricia Lynden (*The Atlantic,* March 1969).

Background of officers interviewed

Veterans

A.N.:   Came out of the service in 1953. Worked in warehouse as laborer, like his father. Policeman ten years.

J.F.:   Thirty, white, Catholic, detective in D.A.'s office.

P.V.:   Thirty-eight, detective assigned to investigate organized crime.

Rookies

F.M.:   Irish-German background, Catholic, married to a Puerto Rican girl.

T.A.:   Jewish, middle class, Ivy League college, single.

S.M.:   Negro, Catholic, married to Negro girl of mixed racial background: her mother is white, Jewish, manager of a Stouffer's restaurant.

F.M.:   My father was a mechanic for a time; owned a bar while I was growing up. My uncle works for Transit Authority. As a child I always respected the police department. I thought it was a fine profession. Worked for Con Ed for six years. Private industry was a little callous ... You could have a number of years on the job there and then become disabled and you were through.

S.M.:   Mother raised me and my brother working as a domestic. Mother always told me: "If you want something, make sure you're qualified to get it. Don't ask for anything, and don't cry if you don't get it." Mother was strict.

F.M.:   My father gave me respect for authority. He was an old chief in the Navy.

T.A.:   Education was the most important thing in our family. I was raised to question values and establish my own. I think the highest value is education. I plan to make a career of the department. I'm going to make inspector. Before I came on the force, I wore my hair long and had a beard. I believed in absolute freedom and absolute responsibility. Most of my friends are behind bars now. They got caught doing everything from auto theft to rape and burglary. I went to Bayside High School, a middle-class neighborhood. These were middle-class and upper-class kids. They did it for kicks.

    My parents were very liberal people but they laid down certain laws: don't be brought home by the police. If I was, my father threatened to break my back.

S.M.:   When I was in high school I didn't smoke or drink or do anything. But some of the kids did. I think it's the family life when you make it out of a rough situation.

T.A.:   I think you have to put more blame on the individual, on his *moral* fortitude. If a guy has self-respect . . . he'll pull himself up. If not, he'll stay at the bottom of the barrel.

S.M.:   Yes, but you can't expect someone of 13 or 14 to have *mental* fortitude.

F.M.:   A girl who is a hooker today, you can't say it's because of the money. It's the individual herself. The family has a lot to do with it . . . the girl can say no. Her family ain't there now.

S.M.:   You have to have a background to make the right decisions. You have to have a basis of respect. It's love in a family . . . You can't keep your daughter cooped up.

T.A.:   Being a cop will change my attitude with my kids.

J.F.:   I was raised partly in Harlem, partly in Washington Heights. My father was a retired fire lieutenant. I went to high school and had a year at a mechanical institute to take architectural drafting . . . After the Marine Corps, I worked in a copper company. White collar job. I took the police test. I don't know why . . . My father was a quiet guy . . . My parents taught me to be honorable . . . I left home at 17 to play baseball professionally. After grammar school I was on my own as far as school work went. I had none of the Judaic impulse to succeed in school.

Attitudes on specific subjects

POLITICAL ATTITUDES

A.N.:   The majority of the men in the police department are conservative thinkers. I think it is obvious that they represent the system. They think like the establishment. A lot of this is for their own self-protection on the street. Cops are not broad enough to look at the over-all scope of the picture. It's hard enough for the average citizen, let alone for the cop who is always on the defensive. You're damned if you do and damned if you don't.

S.M.: I'm a liberal, but I'm not a social liberal.

F.M.: I'm a registered Democrat, but I'm a conservative. I voted for Buckley and Goldwater. Goldwater was crucified for a lot of things he said which actually came about, like the escalation of the war. He believes that America should stand on its own two feet and not depend on social security. Buckley was a truthful man.

T.A.: My mother is a Democrat, my father votes for the man— Dewey and Stevenson. I lean toward the conservative.

J.F.: I'm liberal and I'm a conservative. I'm not a liberal as far as politics go. I'm a conservative. I voted for Buckley instead of John Lindsay, and for Goldwater. I'm a liberal in my relations toward people.

JOB ATTITUDES

T.A.: We're overworked and underpaid and doing a sacrificial job ... We're out there rain or shine to protect society. Only 10 percent of our actual duty is in real crime fighting.

J.F.: I went first into a very quiet precinct, and I think because of that I have a different attitude than most cops. I like my work and I like people. Other cops approach people as the police- man to the community, which means automatic hostility. I approach people on a person to person basis ... As far as I am concerned everyone is an American ... I'm against verbal bru- tality but it exists anyway. I think you should start off being nice and respectful. If you have to, you can get harder. I believe in killing them with kindness if I can ... I don't like people to put their hands on me, so I don't put my hands on them.

P.V.: I think it's the greatest work a person can get into. There's something in it for everybody. It can give you the greatest satisfaction if you're a liberal or a conservative or a do-gooder, no matter what you are. I get a lot of personal satisfaction from it.

In the burglary squad we worked on criminals who would normally never be caught. It gives you a tremendous amount of satisfaction to know that when you catch a really good thief, and you catch him right, well, you really have something.

I'm a restless person. I like excitement. I feel that this is one thing all good policemen have . . . Why do people turn to crime? Because they make a good living at it, or because he's an addict trying to support a habit . . . When I arrest an addict I really feel for her, and more for her family . . . I would go to any length to help them if they wanted me to.

ATTITUDES TOWARD MINORITIES

A.N.: When I was first on the force I was sent up to Harlem, and I'd never been there in my life. I'd heard all sorts of things about how awful it is. I had to go get a guy out of a store who was causing a ruckus in there. I didn't want to arrest him, just get him out of there. He's high, and he calls me a white bastard. So there you are. If you touch him, you've got a potential riot on your hands . . . A Negro cop I knew came along, and I asked him to give me a hand . . . So you realize you're not effective in certain situations . . . Then, after a while, you think maybe you should have segregation. Let the Negro cops work Harlem . . . That's wrong, but I can see how it happens to a lot of the guys . . .

Look at all the stores in Harlem. Most of them are owned by whites, just like the Negroes say all the time. But what is stopping a Negro from owning a store? The Puerto Ricans open stores as soon as they arrive here. They're willing to accept the responsibility. You start to feel you don't want to hear crying stories anymore from Negroes, and you start to accept the cliché'd notions about them.

When whites quarrel with each other, they wind up in court, but nothing has happened. But when Negroes quarrel, they cut each other up and the courts look the other way when it's two Negroes. I saw a Negro woman once who had really gotten badly cut up, but she wouldn't press charges against the man because he was still her man. Cops look, after a while, at this as a whole way of life. Negroes are just different.

Cops see the filth and realize a lot of the filth they see is caused by the Negroes themselves . . . The cop doesn't want his kids to have any part of these people . . . But the old cop had a lot over the new one. He had a lot of street sense and a lot of heart. He had a lot of compassion. He grew up in the neighborhood. He knew the people and he knew their mores. The cop used to catch you playing hooky and he'd boot you in the rear and call your mother, and there were no records and no stigma . . . I think there's a total lack of communication now with the new system of moving cops around from precinct to precinct.

How many times do you hear of a cop breathing air into a Negro baby's mouth or helping firemen go into burning buildings?

S.M.: The problem today is "Give me, give me, I want." I don't think the cry of the black man today is that. He doesn't say

"Give me $100 and let me live in this shack." He says, "Just give me a chance and let me do something for this country." When I worked in a Brooklyn ghetto, I just looked around me and thought, "This is a damned shame."

[On the attitude of other cops toward Negroes]:

They don't have enough education. The police are in a position to understand the ghetto problems more than the middle-class people . . . But you can't explain the Negro problem in America in relation to the Irish and Italian immigrants coming over here. After all, they came voluntarily.

But the Negro has to cut out the attitude of "I want this, I deserve that." He'll have to say, "I have my degree. I can do this.". . . The poverty program is a big hoax. I don't think black pride will hurt people. I don't know why people get so upset about black power. I think black power means, "Learn, baby, learn so you can earn." Every Negro doesn't take the phrase to mean, "Let's loot, let's burn!"

J.F.:   Harlem *people* are not primitive. The *conditions* are primitive. This is as much because of self-apathy as because society has imposed it. The family structure is lacking there. Period. I'm speaking about the Negro community rather than the Spanish community.

The lack of family structure gives them little regard for each other . . . The Negro community has a genuine lack of morality as our society accepts it. The Spanish community is more aggressive . . . and that's how they've made the progress they have even though they're here for such a short time. I think self-help is the answer, but I think the Muslims are as bad as the Mafia.

ATTITUDES ABOUT SOCIAL LIFE

F.M.:   It requires readjustment of your social life. I was only married a year prior to coming on the job. I had weekends and holidays off, and a summer vacation. Now I don't . . . and I have odd hours and I have become distant with old friends.

T.A.:   I was a student for a few years but as soon as I donned the blue uniform, I was no longer me. I am socially limited now. I'm no longer me to old friends.

J.F.:   I don't socialize with cops. The job is so demanding, and it's really a way of life like normal jobs just aren't . . . If you're trying to relax, it's hard to be around other policemen without talking about the job. I don't think it's a good idea for cops to socialize with each other.

Our closest friends—he's a director of a boy's club on the lower East Side, a social worker, and his wife is a painter. She's on the other side of the political spectrum from me. We have some interesting arguments. Ben and I grew up together.

From their appearance, cop's wives are not exactly like

Barnard girls. Their manner and dress is not like that. They're really clean and neat. Cop's wives have to work harder and longer at being good wives than Joe Average's wife.

P.V.:   My wife knows very little about police work. I'd just as soon keep it that way. She won't worry as much. I put in five years with the burglary squad and it's rare that I would ever discuss a case with her. I may tell a funny incident that happened . . . but it's mostly things that you'd rather not talk about at home . . . The average policeman's wife has to be a very understanding person. He keeps bad hours. I think there are more divorces among police . . . You don't realize what a cold world this can be until you're a policeman. It's probably made me a stricter father with my own children . . . because you don't want your child to fall into it.

T.A.:   A typical person thinks the cop is the man who stands there to pick on you . . . I'm no longer me to my old friends. People have trouble seeing us as part of society, as ones who have given up some of our freedom to protect theirs.

J.F.:   People misunderstand what cops are all about; and their misunderstanding is getting bigger every day. Because of our unique position in society, an officer's presence is as a godlike figure or, to some people, the lowest on earth. But no matter what, the patrolman feels he has to be mechanical and not to reflect his emotions, and this is why people feel as they do toward him.

The uniforms are ridiculous and they have a lot to do with it. They can't possibly look good on you unless you are 21 and just out of the academy. Also, the lack of communication: cops act without face. When talking to an individual in the street, people feel they're talking to a robot.

Questions for Discussion

1. Do the individual members of a subculture have personal characteristics that reflect their identification with it?

2. In what ways may individuals and groups in a subculture show change in their "typical" traits?

3. Can one accurately state that a subculture is a microcosm of the larger society of which it is a part?

4. What are the strengths and weaknesses of the diagram of the police subculture in Fig. 2–5?

Regarding the quotations from "Why I'm a Cop":

5. How are the ethnic and racial backgrounds of the men reflected in their remarks?

6. In what ways do the officers differentiate between their own and "other cops' " views? Significance of this?

7. When discussing Negro characteristics, does A.N. really reflect his own or "other cops' " views? Examples?

8. How useful is the distinction S.M. makes between Irish and Italian immigrants' social adjustments and those of Negroes?

9. When S.M. interprets "black power," is he being realistic? (Are you being stereotypic in your answer?)

10. Is the description of police social life patterns consistent?

Exercise

Writers have attributed certain characteristics to subcultures in general and to the police subculture in particular. Similarly, various segments of the public have attached convenient labels to different occupational groups. Presumably, the writers' attributions are based on scholarly research. But the public's attributions are more often stereotypic—based on hearsay or personal experiences.

Furthermore, there is little consensus as to whether certain characteristics are "good" or "bad" qualities for an occupational incumbent to possess.

As a test of your own judgments, check the columns in the following chart and compare your opinions with those of others. Consensus does not necessarily mean the judgments are correct. As you make your decisions, ask yourself whether you are being stereotypic.

Does the chart itself induce or encourage stereotypic thinking?

CHARACTERISTICS OF A SUBCULTURE
Check the columns you believe are appropriate:

Trait	Is the trait:		Is the trait typical of:												
	Good	Bad	Police	Doctors	Lawyers	Teachers	Artists	Plumbers	Mayors	Husbands	Minorities	Judges	Military	Merchants	**Any** Occupation
alienated															
authoritarian															
bureaucratic															
clannish															
conformist															
conservative															
corrupt															
cynical															
defensive															
disciplined															
erotic															
expedient															
Fascist															
innovative															
insecure															
marginal															
masculine															
militaristic															
moralistic															
negative															
paternalistic															
politic															
pragmatic															
prejudiced															
professional															
racist															
regimented															
rigid															
secretive															
sensitive															

STUDY 4

Points on Perception

We actually *perceive* only a small fraction of the stimuli that our senses of sight, sound, smell, taste, and touch receive. Moreover, our five senses are far less sensitive than those of lower animals. A dog hears more, smells more. But if we did perceive each and every stimulus our senses send to our brains—if we were actually *conscious* of each of them—we would soon have a nervous breakdown.

In self-defense, and quite unconsciously, we therefore select what we wish to perceive, namely, those stimuli which seem relevant to our needs or our current interests. Not only do we wish to perceive, but we perceive these stimuli according to the perceptual history that has developed our prejudices—our prejudgments, which are the outgrowth of our experiences. For example, in Fig. 2–6, each of us will label the four postures of the stick figures according to our personal experiences with these particular postures.

When we compare the attitudes we have checked with those checked by other people, we find we do not agree: our experiences have been different. And we may even be unsure of which attitudes to check because we ourselves have had experiences that conflict with each other, leaving us with a sense of ambiguity or uncertainty.

This ambiguity becomes important in the testimony of two or more witnesses to a crime. Not only do the witnesses have different backgrounds and therefore different perceptive responses to the same stimuli at the scene of the crime, but the actual positions from which they view the scene may vary—even though they are standing next to each other when they become witnesses. Individual experiences are never identical.

A vivid illustration of this occurs when three people are shown the same photograph of a busy street scene. Depending on their interests of

This study leans heavily on a special issue on "Communications" of *The Kaiser Aluminum news,* Vol. 23, No. 3, Copyright, 1965, by the Kaiser Aluminum and Chemical Corporation, Oakland, Calif. We are also indebted to Donald M. Johnson, Professor of Psychology, Michigan State University, for his counsel in reviewing this material.

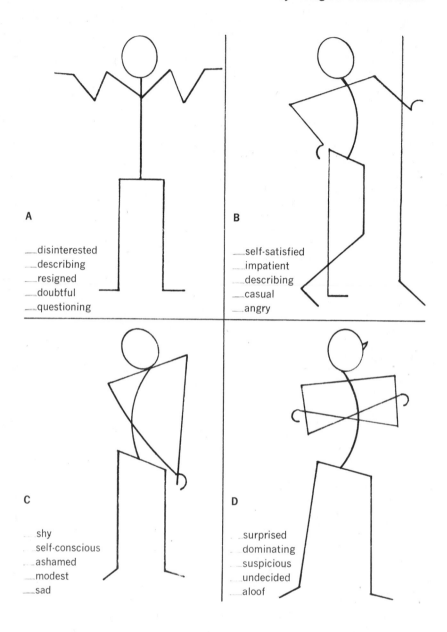

A

___disinterested
___describing
___resigned
___doubtful
___questioning

B

___self-satisfied
___impatient
___describing
___casual
___angry

C

___shy
___self-conscious
___ashamed
___modest
___sad

D

___surprised
___dominating
___suspicious
___undecided
___aloof

From materials developed by Leadership Resources, Inc.,
March 23, 1967.

Which of the characteristics would YOU check?

Figure 2–6.   Perception: What do you **see?** As the umpire said,
"They ain't nothing till I calls 'em." What is the **meaning** of
"meaning"?

the moment, (a) a young man "on the town" might see only a pretty girl in the picture, (b) a man wishing to cash a check might see only a bank sign, (c) while a person late for an appointment might see only the clock on the bank. Thus, motivation plays a role in perception.

Our point of view (even disregarding one's prejudice-building personal history—which, of course, is impossible) has a tremendous effect on what we perceive. Two people sitting opposite each other not only see each other, but see each other against entirely different backgrounds. Sitting in a garden behind a house, one sees the back of the house while his opposite number is seeing the back of the neighbor's house beyond the fence.

A six-foot-tall husband and his five-foot wife have entirely different perceptions of the ceiling heights, the closet shelves, and the views from the windows in their home.

In the parable of the six blind men examining an elephant, by John Godfrey Saxe, the men perceive, respectively, depending on their imaginations and what part of the animal their hands are touching: a wall (side of the elephant), a spear (tusk), a snake (trunk), a tree (knee), a fan (ear), and a rope (tail). And they are all correct—from their individual points of view. But what would a judge or jury make of their evidence in court?

Again, two people see an old sofa in a second-hand store. One (the average viewer) sees simply an old sofa; the other (an antique dealer) sees a potential fortune in the piece. Or take two boys looking in a store window. One (a casual observer) may see one or two items of interest; the other, a Boy Scout who is practicing for his observation merit badge, may mentally photograph the entire contents of the window.

But even without motivation as a factor in what we actually do perceive, the aggregate of what we *are* bears heavily on how we interpret stimuli. This is the basis of the Rohrschach test—the ink spots we called "ghosts" when we were children. When psychologists ask prospective parolees what they "see" in such images, the answers reveal the experiences of the subjects. "I see a man about to strangle his wife" as distinct from, "That guy is about to take that dame" (what *does* he mean?), as distinct from, "That's two trees on a windy night."

One's prejudicial background can make one an introvert or an extrovert: one habitually interprets the world from his own criteria; the other habitually reacts to external stimuli. The extrovert looks through the bars of the monkey's cage and wonders, perhaps, about life in there. The subjective introvert, empathizing with the ape, may wonder if the ape is asking himself what *that man* did to have to be put behind bars!

Our background gets in the way of our realistic perceptions when we attend a class reunion and are horrified at how our classmates of 20 years ago have changed. Our memory thus constitutes a kind of sixth sense influencing what we think we are thinking.

In the same way, we tend to categorize (stereotype) people on the basis of our "experience" with them. "All Jews are _____," "all Polacks are _____," "Greeks will _____ every time," "Negroes have _____," "All whites are _____," etc., ad nauseum. Such childhood "concepts," of course, prevent true perception and retard growth of character and maturation. And they get us into trouble!

Hans Toch, in "A Note on Police Experience," describes such a case:

> One late evening, Officer Geronimo Jones notices a young Negro casually standing against a wall smoking a cigarette, in an area in which car theft has been a problem. The officer's "experience" tells him that the person . . . is suspicious, and that investigation is in order. Officer Jones' "experience" also informs him that individuals . . . like that cannot be addressed as middle-class citizens (you can't say "sir" to them), and "experience" also dictates a firm but polite approach. Thus . . . the officer firmly and without preliminaries requests name and identification. The response to this request is an equally firm (the Negro also has had his "experience"), "I don't have to tell you nothin', and I'm not goin' to show you nothin' 'cause I didn't do nothin'!"

Toch points out that the inevitable antagonisms (resulting perhaps in a physical contest) allow no opportunity for any rational communication to take place, or for the men's "experiences" to be modified. "Neither has been able to take account of the other's viewpoint because each has been so sure of his own." The men simply have failed to perceive accurately or adequately. Thus there is no opportunity, or even inclination, for the officer to explain that car theft suspects are being checked, nor for the Negro citizen to explain (why should he *have* to?) that he was just taking the air in front of his own home. Stereotypic hostility perpetuates an intolerable status quo and is mutually reinforcing, each way. Thus, prospective employers reject job applications of mature, highly qualified people because of police records incurred in their youth. Their perception: once a so-and-so, always _____.

Not only our "experience" gets in our way, but words are often barriers to communication, too. This is so because words are symbols, with as many meanings as there are people to use them, on the one hand, and to hear or read them on the other. And this is not the academic matter of wondering whether an orange is called an orange because it is orange in color, or vice versa. It is a real problem of perception.

Common words cannot possibly have meanings in themselves—only people can provide meanings. The 500 English words most frequently used have 14,000 dictionary definitions. The number of definitions of the word *lead* requires several pages in a large dictionary. Check, too, on *run, cut, go, come, lie, tell, table, well, man, dog, aid, it* for other examples. Even in the sentence "I have a dog," the word-symbol "dog" conveys nothing definite. Man or beast? Male or female? Breed? Pet or pest?

Medium-sized words, too, have many meanings. One gropes in vain for universal meanings for such words as *country, patriotism, society, government, democracy, republic, brotherhood, people, delinquent, officer, insanity, white, Negro, Indian, mongol,* and *communism.*

Of course big words tend to be more explicit and definitive, for example, *hexagon,* but they can acquire new meanings, as in the case of *pentagon.* And then there are the fad words that change in meaning with the times, like *square, establishment, rock,* and *gay.*

Even in sentences, word-symbols startle our perceptions, as in the case of the tourist in the New England countryside who asked the sweet little old lady, "Do you think it's going to rain, Granny?" and got the terse, "Be a long dry spell if it don't" in reply. Or the farmer who joined a town square gathering, listening to a soapbox campaigner. "What's he talking about?" and was told, "He don't say."

Sometimes we perceive meanings that were never intended, as in the case of the milquetoast employee whose desk was in the path of the boss as he invariably passed on his way to his private office saying, "Good morning, Smith, 'morning Miss Jones, Miss Brown, Miss—" One morning the boss (still burning from a breakfast fight with his wife), missed "Smith" in his routine, and Smith worried himself into a tizzy of fear of being fired for some fancied dereliction. "The boss didn't say 'good morning'!"

In any language, there may be no words to say what we really want to say. The Japanese, for example, have no written word for "prejudice." They require three "characters" or symbols to convey the idea—those for "previous," "enter" and "dominant," which taken together in the context of "idea" convey more than our casually used single word.

To further complicate perception through symbols, there is the matter of such character traits as authoritarianism (the policeman in Toch's case above), or defensiveness (the Negro in that case). Hypersensitivity is illustrated by the exchanges in Fig. 2–7. George will doubtless not last long in his job if he doesn't answer with the possible responses in column 1, or if he doesn't mature from the chronic self-pity that shows through the responses in columns 2 and 3.

"What did he (or you) *mean* by *that?*" is often the panic cry of the defensive. But it is also the question we all should ask in any communicating. Meanings, of course, change with speakers, regions, occupations, context, time, tone of voice, accompanying gestures, the word stressed ("Can you come?" changes with the word one underscores), and so on. And no words at all can convey clear or wholly confusing impressions. A friendly (?) pat on the back; a smile (derisive, reassur-

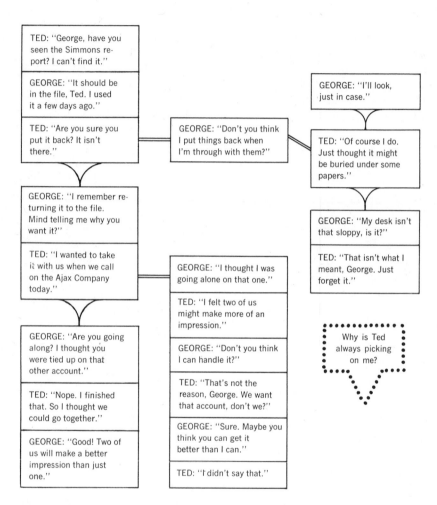

Figure 2–7.   Perception: What do you HEAR? What part do
your emotions play?

ing, affectionate?), or just a touch of the hand (warmth, or an intrusion on one's physical integrity?)—all have infinite *meanings,* complicated by the experience, prejudices, and relationships of those involved.

Perhaps the greatest communicator of all time was Jesus, whose use of the parable left his listener to develop meaning in accord with his own perceptive readiness.

What *is* the meaning of *meaning?* If instead of asking, "What does *that* mean?" we ask "What does *he* mean?," remembering that *he* is the product of all his experience, as are we ourselves, we can check our impulse to ill-considered reactions. Moreover, we sometimes don't even dare *say* what we *mean.* We only hope the listener will know what we mean because of where we are, because of the situation and even the mood of the moment. When the shy young man, sitting with his loved one in the moonlight looking out over the sea on a warm Spring night says, "Gee, this is great!" and the girl doesn't read that as, "God, how I love you"—well, he better get another girl. She may have a lot of things, but not accurate perception!

Another idea in the matter of communication is that ours is not a black and white world. We find it difficult to describe the multitude of "in-betweens," because our language doesn't provide adequate in-between words. Try, for example, to fill in the blank spaces below with words that indicate the degrees of possibility between these "either-or" perceptions:

good	_____	_____	_____	evil
pleasant	_____	_____	_____	unpleasant
sweet	_____	_____	_____	sour

There are *not* just two sides to every question.

When a trial lawyer demands a "yes" or "no" answer of a witness, he may be compounding the felony by requiring a reply as alien to truth as a conscious lie. "Did you, or did you not see him?" Perhaps the eyes of the witness had been looking but the consciousness was in shock of disbelief and thereby insulated from perception. The cliché, "When you've seen one, you've seen 'em all" is belied by the question, "Have you really *perceived* any?"

Of course in one's despair at ever mastering the arts of perception, one could simply fall back on pure fantasy. Or, since we do have to live in *this* world, we can use the following little catechism every time we read or hear something:

1. WHO said so? (Don't accept "they.")
2. WHAT did *he* say? (What someone says he *thinks* someone else said—forget it!)
3. What did he MEAN? (Check, ask questions.)
4. HOW does he *know?* (Was he there?)

Marshall McLuhan says that "the medium is the message." Whatever television, for example, chooses to broadcast is what the public gets. Television producers *say* they produce what the public wants. However, their perception of what is wanted is based in part on "the ratings," but more on what the producers and advertisers (with their dollar-oriented experiences) *think* the public wants. *They* are the medium, and meanings are in people—both "senders" and "receivers."

This is made clear in an analysis of communication by William R. Carmack of the University of Oklahoma, in a lecture delivered to the Police Community Relations Institute at Michigan State University in 1963. Man learns, he said, primarily through experience—mostly vicarious. The components of communication (compare with the preceding "catechism") are:

1. The source or sender—is he an authority?

2. The message—what does it actually say; in the light of what?

3. The channel or medium—what is its bias, motive, reliability, integrity?

4. The receiver—individual or group? What is *their* background?

Carmack spoke of an experiment in which the same taped message on military strategy was played to four classes in a college, each class being told the speaker was a different person: a student, a Russian visiting this country, the surgeon general of the United States, and General MacArthur. The class hearing the tape attributed to the last "authority" was the most impressed—the most influenced by the speech because of *their* perception of who was supposedly speaking.

But it is "the authority" that one should be most on guard against. For example, we tend to accept anything appearing in a standard encyclopedia as being sacrosanct. However, if one compares the article in *Britannica* on the American Revolution as it appeared in the last British edition with that in the first American edition, one would not know it was the same war. Here the "authority" was "the medium," in effect. Even more startling is the revelation that many college undergraduates have "earned their way through school" by ghost-writing articles for their professors who were contributors to the major encyclopedias.

Following are some examples of various techniques for checking on the mechanical aspects of perceptive abilities. They test what the senses perceive, fail to perceive, or perceive that isn't there. If the sense organs are so patently unreliable, how much more so are they when blocked by our emotions, our prejudices, and our desires! It is small wonder that the police and the community see each other in unpredictable ways, and how vital it is that every effort be made to guard against misperceptions that can sabotage the most important programs for enhancing police and community rapport.

The first of these illusions is the classic case of lines of equal length made to look unequal by attaching lines from their ends, or by placing them at right angles to each other, as in Fig. 2–8, left and right respectively.

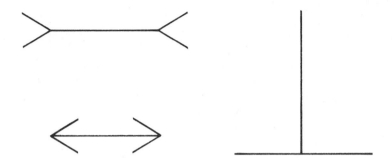

The second illusion is that created by Hadley Cantril, called the trapezoidal window (Fig. 2–9). A trapezoid is a four-sided plane

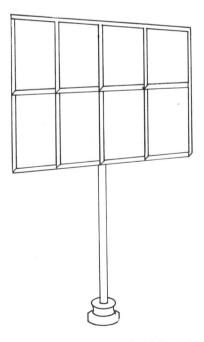

Figure 2–9.   Trapezoidal window

figure, two of whose sides are parallel. This one, simulating a window, consists of a frame cut from very thin metal, painted to look as though it had three dimensions. It does not contain panes of glass. As the window is slowly rotated by a motor at the foot of the stand, the viewer believes he is seeing a rectangular window, and he cannot be sure which way it is rotating. Eugene L. Hartley described the device at the 1965 Institute on Police and Community Relations at Michigan State University in his paper, "Perception as a Psychological Process":

> This is an illusion but calling it an illusion does not explain it. Illusions are really special cases of perception where what we see does not correspond to the true stimulus situation. We like to study illusions because they give a better understanding of how we perceive things, and of just what the perceptual processes are.
>
> This particular illusion seems to be based on your lifetime of experiences with perspective, the way parallel lines seem to meet at a distance, and your lifetime experiences with rectangular windows. The shorter side of the trapezoid is *seen* as being farther away than the longer side. Now notice, even though you *know* that the "window" is rotating a full 360 degrees, going all the way around, you still get the illusion that it is a rectangular window as long as you *see* it as a window. A little bit of information (that it really is a trapezoid) even when you believe it and know it to be true, does not change the perceptual habits that have built up through a lifetime. This is the case with the window, and it is equally true in connection with perceiving ourselves and others.
>
> Change *can* be effected but you have to work at it.

An illusion is also produced with aniseikonic lenses. These are eyeglasses that change the size of images that fall on the two eyes in such a manner that for most people they introduce a slant instead of a simple magnification. In short, distortion is built into the lenses. Hartley explains:

> ... it is interesting to note the latency effects—the length of time between putting the glasses on and when you begin to see the slant. *Physically,* the moment you put them on, the world is hitting your retinas as if it were slanted. But you *know* the object is foursquare, and you resist your eyes, and each person has his own speed for accepting what his eyes tell him. For some it is a few seconds; for others it may be 20 minutes.
>
> Moreover, when we wear the glasses, some things shift faster than others *depending on what they mean to us* ... When I wear such glasses (while teaching), I can go half an hour and the students remain unchanged, although the room develops a bit of a bias. But when I walk down the corridors I have to watch my step. The whole place shifts ... For me, the students are of great importance and maintain their characteristics. *What is important to us, we hold onto—* other things we let slide.

In the next study, "Points on Prejudice," we shall note further instances of discrepancies in perception as they affect our human relationships. But in concluding this study, it is important to stress that accurate consensual perception *is* possible. Indeed, this is the main thrust of our discussion of the fallacies of the perceptive processes: to show that people *can* come to see things as others see them. The purpose here has been to suggest the importance of making the conscious effort to do so.

STUDY 5

Points on Prejudice

People tend to be influenced in their thinking by their backgrounds; for example, in their judgments. Speaking to the National Institute on Police and Community Relations at Michigan State University on "Perceptions as a Psychological Process," Professor Eugene L. Hartley, then of City College, New York City, explained that he and his associates had collected about 90 group psychotherapists' ratings of the seriousness of 14 violations listed below. Their ratings are indicated in the footnote on the following page. Before you check them, however, rate the violations yourself, listed here in alphabetical order. Rate them from #1 as most serious to #14 as least serious:

1. aggravated assault ____
2. cheating on exams ____
3. driving while drunk ____
4. drunkenness ____
5. falsifying tax returns ____
6. forcible rape ____
7. gambling ____
8. homicide ____

9. homosexuality ____
10. narcotics violations ____
11. prostitution ____
12. vagrancy ____
13. violating civil rights of minority groups ____
14. wire tapping ____

Now check the footnote on the following page for the ratings the psychotherapists gave these violations. Who is right?

Prejudice is not necessarily an evil phenomenon. In fact, every decision or judgment we make is based on our tendency to like this more than that. Our responses to the above list of violations are based on our individual experiences, our point of view. Obviously, persons working in crime control would respond differently than liberal theorists. But our backgrounds, being *our* backgrounds, tend to make us consistently see things in predictable ways that can get us into trouble.

Art Buchwald ("The Good Guys and the Bad") tells the following tale:

> One of the major problems facing the United States in its racial troubles is trying to separate the good guys from the bad guys. White

Americans tend to refer to all Negroes as "they," or worse. The Negroes use the term "whitey," or worse, to take in all the white people in the United States.

This becomes a problem, as I discovered not long ago when I had a conversation with a Negro acquaintance named Winslow.

"I see you people tried to burn down Washington last week," I said.

"Yes, but only after you people killed Martin Luther King."

"We didn't kill Martin Luther King. Some white nut did it."

"Well, I didn't burn down Washington," Winslow said. "I happened to be at home holding a bucket of water in case my house caught on fire."

"When I say 'you'," I said, "I don't mean you, Winslow, I mean your people."

"What people are you talking about? I have to walk twenty blocks to buy a loaf of bread now. I can't even collect the insurance on my damaged car; my kids are afraid to go to school. Those cats weren't my people."

"I didn't exactly mean your people, Winslow," I tried to explain. "I meant people that look like you."

"Yeah, and what about your people? The reason we had all the trouble in the first place is that your people don't give a damn about what goes on in the ghettos until you have looting and riots."

"You can't make a general statement like that. A lot of white people care. You got to get it through your head, Winslow, that there are good white people and bad white people."

"Well, why don't you get it through your head that there are good black people and bad black people, and most of the black people don't dig rioting any more than the white people do?"

"If your people would stop supporting Stokely Carmichael and Rap Brown, it would be easier for us to be sympathetic to your problems."

"Then why don't the white people stop supporting Lester Maddox and George Wallace?"

"The white people don't support Maddox and Wallace. It's only a small minority that goes for them."

Ratings by the psychotherapists: 1. homicide, 2. forcible rape, 3. violating civil rights of minority groups, 4. aggravated assault, 5. driving while drunk, 6. falsifying tax returns, 7. wire tapping, 8. narcotics violations, 9. cheating on exams, 10. prostitution, 11. drunkenness, 12. gambling, 13. vagrancy, 14. homosexuality.

If you agree with this rating, is it, "of course I do," or do you think the "headshrinkers" are nuts?

"How many black people do you think are doing cartwheels over Carmichael and Brown?" Winslow asked. "As a matter of fact, it's the white press that made them into our leaders. We never heard of them before."

"You're just trying to confuse me, Winslow," I protested. "I hear all you people have guns now."

"I don't have a gun and I never owned a gun. That's all I need with kids around the house. Whitey's got the guns."

"I don't have a gun either," I said angrily. "I got kids, too."

"I don't know what we're fighting about," Winslow said. "We both want to live in peace."

"Of course we do," I said, grabbing Winslow's hand. "You're a good Negro."

"And you're a good white man," Winslow said.

"You know what I'm going to do, Winslow, to show you how much I like you? I'm going to join the Urban League."

"And you know what I'm going to do in exchange?" Winslow said. "I'm going to join the Sons of the American Revolution. In that way we'll be soul brothers forever."

In our daily living, as we noted in Study II–4, we *see* with our eyes but *perceive* with our brains, as in the case of the three observers in a city street who saw a bank, a clock, or a pretty girl. We select what we *want* to see according to our prejudices, often quite unconsciously.

Professor Hartley illustrated this point in his paper. He described experiments in the use of a stereoscope, the familiar viewer of yester-year that gave the illusion of three dimensions. If two photos are taken with lenses three or four inches apart, the views they record will be slightly different. If we then view the two pictures through the stereoscope, we will see a combination that gives us depth rather than the flatness of two-dimensional pictures.

But what happens if we put two very different pictures in the stereoscope? Sometimes there is a fusion of the two, or an alternation, in which we see first one and then the other picture. It is hard to believe that a man would entirely fail to see something right before his eyes, especially when he knows that it is there. "So I got a slide," said Hartley, "of a Big Alaskan brown bear, and a slide of a nude. When I put these two pictures in the stereoscope, sure enough, I saw the 'bare'—but not the one from Alaska!"

Even after testing for "one-eyedness" (one eye dominates the other) by shifting the pictures back and forth, the principle still holds. An early study used pictures from the Mexican and American scenes that were tried on Anglos and Spanish-Americans in the Southwest.

Each group saw only their own picture—a baseball player or a bull-fighter. Religious symbols were tried on a mixed group in which Catholics saw only a crucifix, and Jews saw only the Star of David. This even worked with typed *words*: Torah and Saint; Cross and Rabbi; Talmud and Novena.

When beginning police trainees were shown pictures—one a scene of serenity and one of violence—they saw only the former. But when the same pictures were shown to third-year students in police administration, they saw only the violent scene. The experiment worked even when a professor of political science actually saw the preparation of two slides—one bearing the word "communism" and the other "democracy"—and then viewed them in the stereoscope. He could see only the latter. Furthermore, experiments have shown that the degree to which people *can* perceive the stereoscopic pictures that are uncongenial to them correlates directly with the results of their tests on openmindedness.

Thus it is clear, as Hartley pointed out, that people behave in a rational, purposeful, logical manner, dependent on the objective world as they perceive it. Each of us sees the world and reacts sensibly in accordance with the way he perceives it. Of course, we do not all perceive the world in exactly the same way, but however we see it, each one of us behaves rationally within *that* framework.

Obviously, we see each other from our own points of view. By way of illustration, you may check on how you see yourself and how others see you by the following simple test: First, write down on a sheet of paper a list of 20 statements under the heading "I Am," in the order in which the ideas come to you; for example, man, policeman, husband, Protestant, grumpy, liberal, tired, etc. Then have some other person do the same about you. To preserve anonymity, have 10 or more persons do this together about themselves and about some other person in the group. Draw lots to see who is to write about whom. It helps if the members of the group are fairly well known to each other. Do not sign the papers, but number them in matched pairs for later comparison. Thus:

(1)   I AM   (1)   HE IS

_____   _____

_____   _____

_____   _____

etc.

Afterward, have the paired sheets (Nos. 1, Nos. 2, etc.) read aloud. This could, of course, be part of an exercise in sensitivity training. But it helps to "see ourselves as others see us." The main point of the exercise is to check the degree to which prejudices enter into the responses. To do it in meaningful depth, the second phase—the HE IS portion—should be done by a number of people in order to compare the responses. It could perhaps be done at the beginning and at the end of a school term for further comparisons.

Another way to check yourself for prejudices (good or bad), and to realize that no one is without them, is to test yourself on the following:

Exercise on Personal Prejudice

Can you think of any area in which you are totally without prejudice? How do you account for your feelings about the following terms?

1. FOODS: cabbage, cauliflower, carrots, parsley, spinach, parsnips; caviar, rattlesnake, snails, raw fish, oysters, lobster; mushrooms, matzoth, unsalted foods, creamed chipped beef, steak, baked beans, caper sauce.

2. CLOTHES: *women:* maxis, midis, minis; pants, topless, nude. *men:* flared pants, love beads, turtle necks, boots, uniforms.

3. FADS: *women:* wigs, smoking pipes or cigars, Women's Lib. *men:* wigs, long hair, sideburns, beards, bare feet.

4. MANNERS: ladies first, knife and fork customs, hats off to ladies, use of "lady" vs. "woman" vs. "babe," saluting, four-letter words.

5. POLITICS: Democrat, Republican, AIP, Communist, Socialist, Independent, Dixiecrat; liberal, conservative, radical.

6. MORALS: marriage and divorce laws (50 sets); homosexuals, free love, Lesbians; abortion, the pill; use of drugs, tobacco, liquor; white lies, lying; petty larceny, murder, civil disobedience, protests, use of violence.

7. CULTURE: movies, plays, radio, TV; *Atlantic, Playboy, Ramparts, Life, Look, Newsweek, True Story, Readers Digest, Ebony, Police. Sports Illustrated, Yachting;* novels, nonfiction, poetry; art and/or science museums; jive, jazz, rock, symphonies, chamber music; pornography.

8. SOCIAL: charity balls, dances, stag parties; cliques, fraternities, unions, service clubs, YMCA, DAR, gangs, bridge or poker clubs; ostracism, integration, mixed marriages, strivers.

9. ECONOMICS: monopolies, poverty, hard-hats, competition, free enterprise, Mafia controls, black businesses.

10. SPORTS: salt water vs. fresh water recreation; hunting, fishing, skiing, golf, croquet, tennis, squash, horseshoes; football, baseball, basketball, bullfighting, auto or horse racing; bowling, billiards, pool; Olympics, World Series.

11. RELIGION: WASPs, Protestants, Catholics, Jews, Christian Scientists, Mormons, Black Muslims, Hindus, Quakers, Amish, Adventists, Dukhobors (doó-ko-borz), Menonites, Islam.

12. PEOPLE: senior citizens, middle-agers, teen-agers, juveniles, college kids; introverts, extroverts; queers, jocks, drips, schmos, oddballs, dudes; hippies, tomboys, sissies; people-on-the-hill or across the tracks; melting pot, pluralism.

13. TRAVEL: mountains, plains, lakes, seas, deserts; England, Ireland, Canada, Mexico, Russia, France, Italy, Greece; South Seas, Iceland, Far North, Bermuda.

Some of the foregoing terms leave one so unmoved that one wonders why they were included. Others stir feelings of warm reminiscences or of revulsion. Our responses reflect our experiences, which thereafter serve as the basis of prejudgments we make for the rest of our lives, unless deliberate efforts to reshape our thinking and feelings are made. Let us be more specific.

Definition: Prejudice is defined by the *Readers Digest Encyclopedic Dictionary* as "a judgment or opinion formed without thoughtful examination of the pertinent facts, issues or arguments; especially an unfavorable, irrational opinion . . . hatred or dislike of particular groups, races, religions, etc."

Concepts Involved in Prejudice

1. Prejudices and attitudes are acquired; we are not born with them.

2. There are no natural antipathies; we are not born warlike, shrewd, etc., although each of us has both "good guy" and "bad guy" impulses very early in life.

3. The sources of prejudice are: (1) *primary groups* (home, early playmates); (2) *secondary groups* (schoolmates, clubs, occupational associates); and (3) larger social groups (community).

4. Ideas such as the following help us to rationalize our prejudices:

   "Human beings, to feel secure, must be satisfied with their place in society: convinced that they are better than some people, and can advance to the level of others."

   "Human beings must have someone to hate and someone to love at all times—even if self is the object of both passions."

5. Science has joined religion in asserting that all men are indeed brothers, deriving from the same creative process, having more common traits than differences evolved through adaptation and survival of the fittest.

6. Prejudices are transient and will last only as long as the problems that seem to give them meaning remain.

7. The challenge is to resolve our prejudices even before the problems that give them meaning are resolved.

Types of Prejudice and Corresponding Stereotypes

1. RACIAL: Most visible: Nego: inferior intelligence; Japanese: warlike; Chinese: laundrymen; Hindu: Caucasian? Expressed as: "Nigger" used derogatively (like "boy" and "Sam") by whites, but affectionately to each other by blacks. Also restrictive covenants and "gentlemen's agreements."

2. RELIGIOUS: gentile vs. Jew; Protestant vs. Catholic. Exploited for ulterior purposes, as by Hitler's persecution of Jews, then Catholics, then Protestants, to divide and conquer. Also in epithets ("Dirty Irish") and derogatory "funny stories" ("D'ja hear about the Jew who—"), and in myths ("The Jews control the nation").

3. ETHNIC: derogation of national origins: Wop or Dago; dumb Swede; Mexicans as villains in movies; areas of cities (Little Italy); migrants.

4. SOCIAL: divorcees, illegitimates, adoptions, manners, "F.F.V.s"*

5. ECONOMIC: "Vanderfeller," material possessions, "two cars in every garage," club memberships; "good, honest working man," etc.

6. INTELLECTUAL: "effete snobs"; comparison of sibs**; "what do you expect with a father like that?"

7. SEX: real vs. fictional superiorities, differences; laws (miscegenation).

8. URBAN VS. RURAL (disappearing): "hick," "rube," "city slicker."

9. RESIDENCE: "goat hill," "across the tracks," "Swedetown."

Samples of Prejudice

Many of our prejudices are based on words or phrases that we have long heard but never examined. We believe them unconsciously or because of isolated instances that seem to support them. Consider the following familiar sayings:

1. You can't change (trust) a _____!

2. You can tell a Methodist by his walk.

3. A _____ will gyp you every time.

4. Give a _____ an inch and he'll take a mile.

5. The rich get richer and the poor get children.

6. Honesty and hard work bring success.

---

*First families of Virginia.
**Brothers and sisters.

7. Gentlemen prefer blondes—but marry brunettes.

8. Opposites attract one another.

9. Better to have loved and lost than never to have loved at all.

10. Damned clever, these Chinese.

11. There is only one true faith.

12. A woman is only a woman but a good cigar is a smoke.

13. A woman's singing is like a dog's walking on its hind legs; not that he does it well, but you're surprised he can do it at all.

14. You never hear of great women musicians (composers, statesmen).

15. A woman's work is never done.

16. The only good _____ is a dead _____.

17. Our country can get along by itself.

18. A child born with a veil will be able to foresee the future.

Stereotypes That Govern Our Thinking

1. Germans are natural scientists.

2. Mohammedans have many wives.

3. The Irish are dirty (have lyric voices, a fine sense of humor).

4. Frenchwomen are beautiful.

5. English have a poor sense of humor.

6. Scots are tight-fisted.

7. Spanish are fickle lovers.

8. Italians are passionate lovers.

9. Jealous Spaniards and Italians will kill the *girl*, but Nordics will kill the other man.

10. Japs have silly grins (because of their teeth).

11. Negroes smell different (have natural rhythm; are prolific).

12. Norwegians are fishermen.

13. Jews are shrewd.

14. Episcopalians are "upper crust" (Catholics are poor).

15. Scientists are atheists.

16. Men are all alike.

17. Irish have red hair.

18. Gypsies will steal.

19. Red-haired people have bad tempers (fat people are jolly).

20. Women are neater than men.

Epithets That Express Our Anger or Derision

1. Shanty Irish.

2. Dirty Dutch.

3. Lousy wops.

4. Proper Bostonians.

5. Lazy nigger.

6. Dumb Dutchman (Swede, Mick, Wop, etc.).

7. Absent-minded professor.

8. Helpless male (or female).

9. Stodgy English.

10. Greasy Greek.

11. Dumb cop.

12. Dirty politician, etc.

Doubtful Facts

We tend to accept without question statements that we've heard often enough, especially if they agree with our moods or prejudices. Following are some examples:

1. The Jews control the nation's finances.

2. The Republicans are always for the rich (are generally upper class).

3. Washington never told a lie.

4. Women don't sleep very well.

5. There are no pianos in Japan.

6. You never see foreigners fishing.

7. Peach ice cream is never as good as you think it is going to be.

8. Gamblers hate women.

9. Dogs know when you're despondent.

10. Cops off duty always shoot somebody.

11. Sick people hear everything.

12. People who like birds are queer.

13. Spinsters don't like children.

14. Distance makes the heart grow fonder.

15. Generals are afraid of their daughters.

16. Intellectual women dress funny.

17. Jewelers never go anywhere.

18. Intellectual people have lofty brows.

19. A growing boy eats like a horse; girls eat hardly enough to keep alive.

20. Trouble always comes in bunches (it never rains but it pours).

21. Men are better drivers than women.

22. Men think better than women.

23. Children resemble grandparents more than their parents.

24. Women are the weaker sex.

25. Jews always study hard (or see what they can get away with).

26. Men are better cooks than women (or milliners, fashion designers).

27. Women gossip more than men.

28. Try hard, and you'll succeed.

29. Pride is at the bottom of all mistakes.

30. The man who can't make a mistake can't make anything.

31. The critics are those who have failed in the art they criticize.

32. If you can't do it, you can always teach it.

33. The best means of obtaining credit is never to ask for it.

34. The only way to get rid of a temptation is to yield to it.

35. They can conquer who believe they can.

36. Who judges others condemns himself.

37. You are what you eat.

38. What once were vices are now the manners of the day.

39. What a man does tells what he is.

40. A woman's way is the other way.

41. Nothing is so useless as a great maxim.

42. There is nothing that is always true, including this.

The human mind is capable of devising all sorts of gimmicks to justify its prejudices. It is refreshing to find some that do just the opposite. The following are good examples:

The Superior Race. In the following table, the assumption is that superiority in men is measured by distance from traits of apes.

Three comparisons of men and apes in this context show a surprising outcome:

SELECTED TRAITS	APES	Nearest	Middle	Farthest	SUPERIOR RACE
Height of brow	low	mongol	Negro	white	white
Nature of hair	curly	Negro	white	mongol	mongol
Distribution of body hair	whole body	white	mongol	Negro	Negro

A Monkey Viewpoint: Three monkeys sat in a coconut tree, discussing things as they're said to be: Said one to the others, "Now listen you two, there's a certain rumor that can't be true, that man descended from our noble race. The very idea is a sad disgrace. No monkey ever deserted his wife, starved her babies or ruined her life. You've never known a mother monk to leave her babies with others to bunk. And another thing, you'll never see a monk build a fence 'round a coconut tree, and let the coconut go to waste, forbidding all other monks to taste. Why, if I'd put a fence around this tree, starvation would force you to steal from me. And another thing a monk won't do—go out at night and go on a stew, and use a gun or club or knife, to take some other monkey's life. Yes, man descended—the ornery cuss—but brother, he didn't descend from us!"

Techniques to Curb Prejudice

1. When you hear a generalization, stop it on its way into your subconscious and examine it: often there will not be enough left of it to bother to throw away!

2. Get the *facts:* e.g., intelligence range is equal in all races.

3. A word, silence, gesture, facial expression can either set a prejudice or prevent its developing.

4. Consider the *positive* about minorities. Get to know people *as persons.* Avoid group labels.

5. See plays, read books, talk with people who "tell it like it is."

6. Support laws and customs that eliminate discrimination, but be sure they actually do or will.

7. Take part in community action programs that are grounded in justice for all people.

8. Remember that in a democracy people will have deep dissatisfactions with things as they are; that citizenship in a democracy is a struggle but, unlike life under other forms of government, it is only in a democracy that we have both the hope and the means of setting things right.

STUDY 6

Points on Rumor

"Where there is smoke there is fire" has prefaced literally millions of ugly rumors throughout the ages; rumors that have been instrumental in wrecking the lives of people, gigantic corporations, large segments of populations, and even nations. To many people, gossip and rumor-mongering appear to be innocent pastimes, simply brushed off as idle conversation, while in fact, the practice can be devastating. Elmo Roper's research has shown that rumors cost our nation millions of dollars annually.

Who is free from the malevolent and destructive effects of vicious rumors? They can be major hazards to efficient law enforcement operations. Consider the numerous cases in recent years in which anonymous phone calls have reported bombs planted in an auditorium where a mass meeting was about to be held, in a plane which was about to take off, in schools packed with children, or in a hospital in which some famous patient was confined. The fact that bombs have actually been found in a few such instances requires that each rumor be checked out, painstakingly and expensively.

Gordon Allport defined rumor as a "specific proposition or belief, passed along from person to person, usually by word of mouth, without secure standards of evidence being present." Rumors may or may not be deliberately created. They are generally of transitory concern and are viable only to the extent of the public interest in their particular subject matter.

Rumormongering ranges from innocent, uncritical repetition of some news item, through the addition of innuendo, to possibly deliberate distortion for the purpose of achieving some dramatic or devastating effect. Rumors often contain partial truth. They cite supposed authority. They are specific in that they mention names of persons, places and

---

This study is adapted from "The Psychology of Rumor," a talk given by Norman J. Schleigh, then a captain in the Baltimore Police Department, to the Institute on Police-Community Relations at Michigan State University, 1959; from *The Proceedings*, Hoyt Coe Reed (ed.)

events. They thrive as well in times of paucity of news as in times of fast-breaking stories of critical events or crises. They may be occasioned by anything from idle boredom to a mass sense of racial guilt or anger.

Rumors embody *fear* or *hope* that something has happened, or that something will or will not happen; the thrill of passing on some juicy morsel. There may be an unconscious projection, into the actions of others, of the repressed desires of one's own inhibitions. *Hatred* may motivate the spreading of untruths, to ruin a person or business or a political competitor. Various degrees or combinations of these may be involved.

Forms of Rumor Circulation

Motivations for creating or repeating rumors take many forms:

1. *Casual conversation* may contain rumors motivated by the simple desire to be the first to pass on the latest news. "They say—." Or one may make a mere observation such as, "I wonder why Mary couldn't come today." The listener might add, when later telling a third person, "I hope she isn't sick." A later spreader of the news might put it, "Mary wasn't there today because she is seriously ill." It might take the final form of, "I better phone and find out when the funeral is to be."

2. *Gossip* might start with the observation, "I saw that insurance man going into Thelma's apartment today," and soon become, "Thelma had another gentleman caller today," and go on from there until Thelma has to leave town.

3. *Mischief* may be the motivation, as when a high school student (in the light of the events of the day) phones the principal that he has heard that a bomb has been planted in the school during the lunch period. Perhaps the student believed the rumor, or he may have done it "just for kicks." But the principal can take no chances with the lives in his charge. He cannot be sure if it is a prank, or a plot of the Weathermen. Action is even more imperative if the phone call is from a mother who "heard it from her boy who heard it from—"

4. *Scandal* differs from idle gossip in that a desire to hurt someone is involved. Psychologists' explanation of the motivation is that the originator or passer of the rumor suffers from repressed desires, which he projects into the person who is the subject of the tale. It is a vicarious type of "sinning" without the penalty of punishment. "Well, I saw them together in the theater myself. They were sitting in the row right in front of me. You'd never mistake *him* with that red hair, and *no* one dresses the way she does."

5. *Scuttlebutt* is the male form of gossip. In a police station, one might hear, "Did you see Tom got promoted again?" The repeater might put it, "Did you hear Tom's rabbi did it again? Got him promoted to—" In the Armed Forces world of "hurry and wait," a rumor might grow

from, "Hey, d'ya see in *The Stars and Stripes* that three more ships are being retired?" to a conclusion affecting the careers of the men, such as, "No chance for promotions now. They've stopped enlistments, promotions—the works!"

6. *Relief from boredom* can motivate passing the latest word about such things as flying saucers, or about neighbors who supposedly have psychic powers, or even the possibility that the Highway Department may want one's land for a new boulevard. These are all subjects of idle interest. However, the hunger for news may well motivate the accceptance of malicious rumors, such as those spread during World War II when long-established German-American naturalized citizens were persecuted by "spy" rumors, and the newly created WACs were accredited with more pregnancies than there were WACs in the Army.

Fabricated Rumors

The most troublesome rumors are those that have been deliberately created to serve some purpose. Some may be innocent at the outset; others burgeon into monumental proportions:

1. *Publicity* "rumors" may be initiated by promotional agencies to create an image for a client. For example, one thinks of Jack Benny (miser) or Dean Martin (toper). This is usually innocent in purpose, but fact and fiction may become difficult to separate.

2. *Business* people start rumors. Newspapers fan readers' suspicions in their efforts to get "scoops," which they hope to be able to confirm in time for the next edition. Criminal suspects are created out of whole cloth (in the need to sell papers), in the hope that one of them may prove to be the guilty person. Such journalism has sometimes necessitated a change of venue to assure the accused of a fair trial.

3. *Political* rumors are timed to ruin the reputation of an opposition candidate. An example would be the wholly fabricated story released to the press on the eve of election—too late for refutation, if that were possible—about the candidate's being a secret alcoholic, or dope addict, or accepting a "fortune" from X corporation so that he would be "their man" when elected.

4. *Panic* rumors are perhaps the most devastating to a community and to the police who must keep the peace. The Detroit race riots of 1943 and 1967 were classic examples because the situation in the city provided the conditions essential for such rumors to have maximum effect: long-seething racial tension, which the smallest incident could ignite. In the case of the 1943 riot, there was mounting competition for jobs, housing, and community services between established citizens on the one hand and in-migrant Southern whites and Negroes seeking economic betterment on the other. Race hatred was palpable.

The initial rumor had it that a traffic snarl on the Belle Isle bridge was caused by a Negro accosting a white woman and the Negro, in turn, being attacked by her white companion. Because of the traffic jam, no one more than a few feet away could get the facts. They could only tell the people behind them what they *thought* the situation was. So the stories grew. The cast of characters changed. By the time the police at the entrance to the bridge got a garbled version, it was, "Blacks and whites are killing each other. They've thrown a baby off the bridge." Panic was a reality (Lee and Humphrey, *Race Riot*).

The rest is history. It was the vague, confused accumulation of rumors compounded by rumors that resulted in blacks and whites attacking each other for days. Autos and streetcars were toppled on people. Perhaps the most ironic tragedy occurred when a white doctor, long a beloved physician to poor blacks, was murdered while trying to reach his patients. Only sheer exhaustion and horror at what had happened stopped the rioting. In the appalled calm that followed, it seemed that such a thing could never happen again. Yet in 1967, we learned that rumors can always ignite a deprived community, whether in Newark, Los Angeles, Philadelphia, or again in Detroit. The conditions were the same. They are little better today.

5. *Propaganda* rumors abound in times of national crises. Propaganda means any organized or concerted group effort or movement to spread particular information. In the present context, it means the deliberate seeding of rumors for an ulterior purpose. After Pearl Harbor, rumors had it that our entire Pacific Fleet had been wiped out. The Government itself, through the Office of War Information (although it had evidence to the contrary), encouraged the public to think we were defenseless. The nation's emotions and manpower had to be mobilized against the enemy. We had to be made to think that all Japanese in the country were suspect, although most of them had been loyal American citizens for generations. So they were all herded into prison compounds and deprived of their property. We were encouraged to think that these people were the crudest barbarians, although we had traditionally looked upon Japan as a citadel of ancient culture. Rumors in the form of cartoons depicted Hirohito with a buck-toothed, assinine grin. We had to be made to believe that these people were beneath contempt; that we could and must defeat them. Here, indeed, was fabricated rumor.

In Europe, at the same time, Hitler was using the genius of his propaganda minister, Josef Goebbels, to bamboozle his own people. The purpose was to thwart the resistance of the intellectuals and other powerful elements in Germany against his insane efforts to bring the Continent under his dominion. The initial rumors had it that the Jews (always the persecuted minority) held the power posts of the nation and that they were therefore responsible for its economic depression. To bring them under even deeper anathema, their racial inferiority was asserted by the Ministry. Only the pure "Aryan"* (tall, blond, robust, white) German should be allowed to survive. Hence, six million Jews were exterminated. This, despite the fact that Hitler himself, *der Fuehrer,* was short, dark, thin, and sallow. The fabricated rumor was supported by the controlled press, the bayonet, and the ovens of Dachau. But even this was not enough to dupe the sophisticated German people. Here was one case where "the-bigger-the-lie-the-more-it-will-be-believed" tactic did not work. Resistance continued to mount to the point where both Catholics and Protestants were eliminated by Storm Troopers, invading their homes in the night. Hitler's genocide finally mobilized world opinion against these perpetrators of outrageous propaganda rumors.

What to Do About Rumors

1. Obtain the facts. Accurate information is the best tool to offset rumor.

2. Don't fall for everything that you hear. Don't repeat the rumor.

3. Quietly endeavor to learn the source, although this may be impossible in some instances.

4. Ridicule sometimes kills rumor. Don't be a dupe to rumor; laugh it off.

5. Report the existence of persistent rumors to authorities who can debunk them.

6. Understand that rumors are symptoms. Discover their causes.

Detroit newspapers, for some months after the 1943 riot, conducted special columns in which current rumors were checked out and relevant facts supplied. Also, The Urban League employed a device for checking on any increase of "funny" stories being told in neighborhoods of the city, which ended with a "kickline" denigrating a particular ethnic or racial group. The League had noted that such anecdotes multiply at a geometric rate when there are rumors that a factory is about to close, or some other development is about to create a shortage of jobs, housing, or services. Such rumors, and the anecdotes that accompany them, herald the building of community tensions that can culminate in riots.

The Urban League therefore established liaison with more than 3,000 citizens of the city, such as bus drivers, cigar-counter clerks, chambermaids, police, and other persons whose jobs placed them in anonymous contacts with the passing public (one does not actually *see*

---

*"Aryan" properly means the Caucasian peoples of the Iranian plateau in South-Central Asia from whom (Monogenetic theory) modern man is said to have descended.

such people as one accepts their services). These correspondents volunteered to phone The Urban League Tension Center when they noted an increase of anecdotes concerning a particular minority group. The Center then checked out the appropriate area and reported the findings to the proper authorities for remedial actions.

An effective tool for training people to detect rumors is an exercise developed during World War II by Gordon Allport and Leo Postman at Harvard University (*The Psychology of Rumor*). They devised an experiment in which an audience is shown a series of one to five slides from a filmstrip* which they prepared. The slides depict line drawings of scenes portraying people in various relationships. The scenes are rich in detail, but ambiguous as to what, precisely, the situations are. A team of six or seven persons is chosen from an audience. All but one are sent from the room. The remaining team member is shown, along with the audience, one of the slides. After he has studied it to note its many details and the general situation shown, he moves to a position where he can no longer see the screen (although the audience still can), and describes the picture to the first of his teammates, now brought into the room. As the successive members of the team each hear the description in turn from the previous member, there is, of course, an attrition and frequently a refabrication of detail.

Two scenes are reproduced in Fig. 2–10 (on the following page) so that the exercise can be conducted in a class, although the experiment is more effective when the slides are projected on a screen. Obviously, team members should not look at the pictures until after the experiment is completed. The effect can be further dramatized by the use of a tape recorder or secretary to take down, and later report, the accounts of the succeeding team members. In analyzing the results, look for leveling (loss of detail), sharpening (exaggeration of surviving details), bias (reflecting the backgrounds of the team members), and the nature of the final details in terms of the interests of the team members and of the audience.

---

*Available from the offices of the National Conference of Christians and Jews, with explanatory text.

Scene 1

Scene 2

From *The Psychology of Rumor* by Gordon W. Allport and Leo Postman. Copyright 1947 by Holt, Rinehart and Winston, Inc. Reprinted by permission of Holt, Rinehart and Winston, Inc.

Figure 2–10.   Scenes for Allport and Postman rumor test

Part Three

Sociological Considerations

Just as psychological forces affect the ways we see, hear, and feel about each other, sociological forces influence how we respond to one another. The impact of social processes and population trends on police and community relations, particularly in police relationships with minority groups, is the subject of Part III of the textbook *The Police and the Community*.

The Studies presented here are designed to give students and workers in the field some insight into how far-reaching are the considerations in modern police work. Study 1 focuses on the black population and the forces affecting its migration. Studies 2 through 5 describe four contrasting minority groups and associated problems: the SAMs from Appalachia, black teen-age gangs, Mexican-Americans, and the Black Panthers. Understanding of these groups has important bearing on matters of race relations, civil rights, collective behavior, and civil disobedience that police must deal with in their relations with the community. Study 6 presents a model for handling citizen complaints to and about the police in the light of their nature, variety, and the social forces that generate the complaints.

It should be clear after reading these Studies how profoundly social forces affect intergroup behavior. But it is encouraging to know that, at least in some instances, adequate relationships have been achieved between some police and some minority groups. Unfortunately, there is no panacea, but some of the methods and solutions contained in these studies may prove helpful elsewhere.

STUDY 1

The Negro Population of the United States

Long-range planning by governments is essential if the diverse needs of citizens are to be anticipated. Provision for adequate employment, education, housing, health and welfare services, and police protection can be realistic only in terms of knowledge of population movements as a whole, and of minority trends in particular. Because Negroes constitute the largest minority group in the nation, the purpose of this study is to present salient information about them.

According to the U.S. Census, the population of the country in 1969 was 204.6 million, including transients and servicemen overseas; Negroes numbered 22.3 million, or approximately 11 percent of the total (*The New York Times Almanac—1971,* pp. 35 and 287). What are the migratory trends in which they were involved, and where do they now live? What socio-economic progress have they made?

Regional statistics show that in the South, the black population has grown only 5.8 percent in the last decade (*U.S. News and World Report,* July 19, 1971, p. 42). It has actually declined in the East South Central states. But the number of Negroes has increased 43.4 percent in the Northeastern states, 32.7 percent in the North Central states, and 56.1 percent in the West.

Six states lost Negro population in the 1960s. West Virginia lost 24.7 percent, Maine 15.6 percent, Mississippi 10.9 percent, Arkansas 9.4 percent, Alabama 7.8 percent, and South Carolina 4.9 percent.

Some 102 Southern counties remained predominantly black in 1970, although all but four of these have smaller percentages of Negroes today than they did in 1960. Mississippi has the most counties where blacks outnumber whites—25. Georgia has 22 such counties, South Carolina 12, Virginia 11, Alabama 10, Louisiana 9, North Carolina 5, Arkansas 3, Florida and Tennessee 2, and Texas 1.

Thirteen cities with large black populations had a net out-migration of Negroes in the 1960s—nine of them in the South. For the most part they moved to the big cities in the North and West. Tables 3–1, 3–2, 3–3 (*from U.S. News and World Report,* July 19, 1971) reflect this migration. The urban centers that experienced the greatest percentage gains in Negro population are listed in Table 3–1.

TABLE 3–1
Gains in Negro Population in Urban Centers

Percent Negro	1950	1960	1970
New York	9.5	14.0	21.2
Chicago	13.6	22.9	32.7
Detroit	16.2	28.9	43.7
Philadelphia	18.2	26.4	33.6
Washington	35.0	53.9	71.1
Los Angeles	8.7	13.5	17.9
Baltimore	23.7	34.7	46.4
Cleveland	16.2	28.6	38.3
St. Louis	18.0	28.6	40.9
Newark	17.1	34.1	54.2

In 1970 there were 16 communities with populations above 25,000 that were more than half black, 10 of them outside of the South (Table 3–2). In 1960, by contrast, there were only three predominantly black communities, and all were in the South.

TABLE 3–2
16 Communities Where Whites Are Outnumbered

Community	Total Population	Percent Negro
Willowbrook, Calif.*	28,705	82.3
Westmont, Calif.*	29,310	80.6
Washington, D.C.	756,510	71.1
Compton, Calif.	78,611	71.0
East St. Louis, Ill.	69,996	69.1
Florence-Graham, Calif.*	42,895	56.0
Highland Park, Mich.	35,444	55.3
Petersburg, Va.	36,103	55.2
Newark, N.J.	382,417	54.2
East Orange, N.J.	75,471	53.1
Gary, Ind.	175,415	52.8
Bessemer, Ala.	33,428	52.2
Greenville, Miss.	39,648	52.0
Atlanta, Ga.	496,973	51.3
Prichard, Ala.	41,578	50.5

*Unincorporated places

In the largest cities of the nation, the percentages of Negro population are below the 50 percent level (except in Washington, Atlanta, and Newark), but the total size of such cities makes the Negro percentages reflect far larger numbers of black people (Table 3–3).

TABLE 3–3
25 Cities That Have 100,000 or More Negroes

City	Negro Population	Negro % of Total
New York	1,666,636	21.2
Chicago	1,102,620	32.7
Detroit	660,428	43.7
Philadelphia	653,791	33.6
Washington*	537,712	71.1
Los Angeles	503,606	17.9
Baltimore	420,210	46.4
Houston	316,551	25.7
Cleveland*	287,841	38.3
New Orleans	267,308	45.0
Atlanta	255,051	51.3
St. Louis	254,191	40.9
Memphis	242,513	38.9
Dallas	210,238	24.9
Newark*	207,458	54.2
Indianapolis	134,320	18.0
Birmingham	126,388	42.0
Cincinnati	125,070	27.6
Oakland, Calif.	124,710	34.5
Jacksonville	118,158	22.3
Kansas City, Mo.	112,005	22.1
Milwaukee	105,088	14.7
Pittsburgh	104,904	20.2
Richmond, Va.	104,766	42.0
Boston	104,707	16.3

*Have black mayors

Political Implications

These statistics have considerable political significance. In the predominantly black counties, more and more Negroes are registering to vote. More than 200 were running for office in Mississippi in 1971. In the North, such heavily black cities as Newark, Cleveland, Washington, and Gary had Negro mayors. All 13 black members of the 92nd Congress—12 representatives and one senator—were from outside the South. Washington has a black superintendent of schools. Cleveland's black mayor was re-elected to his second term. In Michigan, a black candidate for mayor of Detroit, just barely defeated, ran successfully in the next election for secretary of state. The state superintendent of schools and the president of Michigan State University are black. Accession of Negroes to positions of political power is a national trend resulting from their enfranchisement and concentration in urban voting jurisdictions.

... more Negroes than ever are voting, particularly in the South, and the number of elected black officials is growing rapidly. In 1965, when Congress passed the Voting Rights Act, there were only 70 elected Negroes in public office in eleven Southern states. By February 1, 1970, the total [in these states] had reached 565, and the U.S. total was 1,469.

Alabama and Mississippi each had more Negroes in elective office than any one of 36 states outside the South. Nine states had none: Idaho, Maine, Montana, New Hampshire, North Dakota, Oregon, South Dakota, Utah and Vermont.

Black voter registration grew in the South from less than 250,000 in 1944 to over 3.3 million in the Spring-Summer of 1970. [*Reader's Digest Almanac*, 1971, p. 713]

On a national scale, the states with the most black elected officials are: Michigan 110, California 105, Ohio 89, Alabama 86, and Mississippi 81. For the country as a whole, the types of office held by Negroes are: at the city level, 623, including 48 mayors; state legislature members, 169; school board members, 362; magistrates, judges, etc., 213. In spite of the urbanization of the American Negro and his election to important political positions, the proportion of Negroes in police and sheriff's departments is only 3.9 percent (*U.S. Statistical Abstract,* 1971, p. 228).

The New York Times Almanac for 1971 (p. 287) shows that in 1967, 55 of every 100 Negroes lived in central cities, with an additional 15 of every hundred living in suburban areas. By contrast, only 26 of every hundred whites lived in central cities, with 38 of every 100 living in suburbs. There are indications that more and more middle-class Negroes are moving to the suburbs. The Negro population is growing (18.8 percent) faster than is the population of the country at large (10.9 percent). Between 1960–1967, 4 percent of Negroes migrated, of whom 45 percent left the South, but as late as 1969, 52 percent of all U.S. Negroes still lived in the South. The usefulness of this figure depends on what states one includes in "The South." Table 3–4, from the *U.S. Statistical Abstract* for 1970 (p. 27) gives details.

The increase in the total number of Negroes was from 12 to 18 million between 1940 and 1960. Will the rate continue? With this rate of increase coupled with the urbanization trend, it is not inconceivable that many of our major cities will become predominantly black service centers for commuting whites residing in the suburbs and fringe areas. Indeed, this is becoming the case in Washington, Chicago, Detroit, and other large cities. It would seem vital that the personnel of police departments should reflect these trends, and it may be predicted that this will occur with increasing black political power.

TABLE 3–4
Negro Population by Regions: 1940, 1950, 1960

Regions	1940	1950	1960	% of all classes
U.S. Total	12,865,914	15,044,937	18,871,831	10.5
New England	101,509	142,941	243,363	2.3
Middle Atlantic	1,268,366	1,875,241	2,785,136	8.2
E. No. Central	1,069,326	1,803,698	2,884,969	8.
W. No. Central	350,992	424,178	561,068	3.6
South Atlantic	4,698,863	5,094,744	5,884,565	22.5
E. So. Central	2,780,635	2,698,635	2,698,839	22.4
W. So. Central	2,425,121	2,432,028	2,768,203	16.3
Mountain	36,411	66,429	123,242	1.8
Pacific	134,691	507,043	962,446	4.5

Some observers think that the new industrialization of the South will lure Negroes to return "home." It is the young who would be more likely to make such moves, but the young in Northern cities have been born there; the North is *their* home. Thus, only the older generation might consider returning to the South of their birth, but typically, they lack the savings, and they cannot know what welfare arrangements they might be able to make if, on returning South, they could not find jobs.

In this connection, it may be noted that the median age for whites is 29.3 years; for Negroes it is 21.1 (*The New York Times Almanac,* 1971, p. 287). Put more dramatically, only 45 percent of whites are under 25 years of age, whereas 55 percent of Negroes are. Thus the bulk of urban Negroes are "native born." They know no other life, and they are not about to move unless lured by jobs in other urban centers—an unlikely circumstance since all urban ghettos have similar problems.

Group Characteristics

Urban Negroes tend to be immobile, for a number of reasons. In 1968 the average Negro family had 4.35 members as compared to 3.59 for whites. Some 27.3 percent of Negro families are headed by a woman, as against 8.9 percent for whites. The total of 6.08 million families (white and black) headed by a woman made up the majority of the 9.4 million persons receiving welfare under the aid-to-families-with-dependent-children program. Such families must remain near the welfare agencies with which they have established relations and near possible part-time jobs. Often the women lack skills that might be marketable in distant cities, even if they had the funds with which to move their families. Moreover, the number of families headed by a woman is likely to increase: the Negro divorce or separation rate is 18 percent, as against 7 percent for whites.

The marginality in economic status of many Negro families is still a barrier to self-improvement. According to a U.S. Census Bureau report, for those Negro families that *had* employment, the median family income in 1968 was $5,395 as against $8,936 for whites. The same report states that median family income for Negroes had risen to $6,520 in 1970—up 50 percent from 1960. For a family of four or more in times of inflation, this does not allow for self-improvement toward the possibility of better employment.

Progress in Status of Blacks

Progress *has* been made in the field of Negro education. For the country as a whole, the median years of school completed is now 12.5 for whites, 12.1 for Negroes. Over one-half of both groups have completed high school. Of persons aged 25–34, 16 percent of whites and 7 percent of blacks had completed college: the latter figure is growing larger each year.

Remaining in school has its advantages. The lifetime income of persons 25 years old and older is reported by the *U.S. Statistical Abstract* for 1970 as depending on the number of years of school completed (Table 3–5).

TABLE 3–5
Lifetime Income of Males 25 Years or Older by
Years of School Completed

Year	8 years	12 years	College or more
1949	$123,000	$175,000	$287,000
1956	166,000	228,000	359,000
1967	192,000	257,000	437,000
ANNUAL MEAN INCOME			
1949	$ 2,829	$ 3,784	$ 6,179
1956	3,631	5,183	7,877
1967	4,206	5,946	9,917

Northern black children have an advantage over black children in the South because of the lower tax incomes of Southern states. Typically, Northern states are able to pay far more per pupil on education. The range is great: from Alaska's $372, California's $273, and Minnesota's $262 down to Mississippi's $130 and Alabama's $112 per pupil last year (*U.S. Statistical Abstract,* 1970, p. 122). Even taking into account differences in the cost of living, the contrasts are notable.

Figures on illiteracy of persons 14 years of age or older indicate that the gap between white and Negro levels is still significant. The U.S. Office of Education and the Bureau of the Census (1970) report that there are nearly one million people in a dozen Southern states who are unable to read and write in any language. Yet progress is being made, though less for blacks than for whites. Between 1960 and 1970, the number of illiterates decreased by 50 percent for whites, but only by 25 percent for blacks. Race is a factor in the difference: many blacks and whites simply refuse to take the remedial courses together, although their children are doing so (*The New York Times,* July 19, 1971).

Similarly, figures for "families below the poverty level" show over-all progress, with much yet to be done. In 1959, some 18.1 percent of white families were so classed, as against 56.2 percent of Negro families. By 1968, the figures were 10 percent for whites, and 33.5 percent for Negroes—one third of all Negro families (*Information Please Almanac,* 1971, Dan Golenpaul, ed., p. 880).

Unemployment figures tell a like story. Some 3.1 percent of whites were unemployed in 1969, as compared with 6.4 percent of Negroes (*U.S. Statistical Abstract,* 1970, p. 214). The situation subsequently worsened, and in some localities in 1970–71, the Negro unemployment rate exceeded 15 percent.

Andrew F. Brimmer, the only black member of the Board of Governors of the Federal Reserve Board, told a convention of the National Association for the Advancement of Colored People on July 6, 1971 that in the 1960s:

> Negroes left low paying jobs on farms and in households at a rate almost three times as fast as whites. . . . The number of non-whites in high paying professional and technical positions jumped by 131 percent, compared with a gain of 49 percent among whites—and the black share of such jobs rose from 4.4 to 6.9 percent. (*U.S. News and World Report,* July 19, 1971.)

However, Brimmer added: "While nonwhites made substantial progress during the 1960s, the occupational center of gravity remained anchored in those positions that require little skill and offering few opportunities for advancement." Nevertheless, more blacks own their own homes these days. Forty-two percent of homes occupied by blacks in 1970 were owner occupied, compared with 65 percent owned by whites (*State Journal,* July 27, 1971, Lansing, Mich.).

Vital Statistics

Finally, relative socio-economic conditions among whites and Negroes are reflected in Table 3-6 with figures taken from the *U.S. Statistical Abstract* for 1970 (pp. 48, 50, 53, 55).

TABLE 3-6
Vital Statistics

Birth rates per thousand		
	1950	**1968**
White	23.0	16.6
Negro	33.3	24.2
Illegitimate live births per thousand		
	1940	**1968**
White	40.3	155.2
Non-White	49.2	183.9
Expectation of life at birth (years)		
	1920	**1967**
White	54.9	71.3
Negro	45.3	64.6
Death rates per thousand		
	1920	**1967**
White	12.6	9.4
Negro	17.7	9.4
Maternal deaths per thousand live births		
	1940	**1967**
White	319.8	19.5
Negro	773.5	69.5
Infant deaths per thousand births (under one year old)		
	1940	**1967**
White	43.2	19.7
Negro	73.8	35.9

Clearly, these data show that while there has been a little progress in meeting the survival problems of disadvantaged Negroes, there yet remains a long way to go. The depths were deep indeed and progress is still too often merely relative.

Countercultural Conflict:
The Police and Insular Culture Groups

One of the prime problems with which the police in major cities are confronted is dealing with peoples of various cultural backgrounds. Even in rural and small town areas, local police have had to learn to cope with the ways of behaving of the members of insular groups who, of economic necessity, must come down from their mountain fastnesses for goods that they do not themselves produce. Their contacts with the police of established communities range from minimal, where only a few provisions are sought, to maximal, where poverty forces whole segments of such peoples to come to the cities seeking employment. Let us cite a few examples.

On a high plateau of the Alleghenies we came, by accident, on a community of 40 or 50 people who were descendents of 17th century Scotch-Irish-English pioneers, of magnificent physique and keen mentality, all dressed in like clothing. The men wore blue denim bib-overalls, heavy work shoes of good quality, beards massive according to their ages, and carried rifles. The women wore blue cotton waists with large white polka dots, tucked into blue denim skirts that reached to their shoe-tops, and medium-heeled high-top shoes designed for work. One stood on the balcony of her two-story square-built, slant-roofed house, unabashedly nursing her baby as the wind swept through her hair. Their speech was that of Elizabethan England, replete with such oaths as "Zounds" and "Egad." The economy of these people was based on moonshine (made from corn, their only crop), which looked, when distilled, like pure water but corroded our unaccustomed tongue. One man was the absolute patriarch of the community. He alone was privileged to go down the mountain to the village in the valley, where we later saw him pointing to pictures in a Sears catalog so the postmaster could write his order for him. His currency? Good U.S. $5 bills, which, we later learned, were the fruit of their simple economy. Down the wooded mountainside from their plateau, a well-used country road widens at a stop point. A row of demijohns waits the not infrequent customers who place a bill under an "empty" to pay for the full one they take away. They wave vaguely to the forested slope, knowing that three husky mountaineers are sitting up there with their guns across their knees. And the "revenooers"? The sheriff told us that they agree with him that the liquor is darn good stuff! An excellent example of police accommodation. The viewpoint is that if the police pressed too hard on these harmless law violators, there would be unnecessary trouble for all concerned.

The nation abounds with such groups, many of them near our largest cities. A short side trip of five miles off the main highway from Atlantic City to Philadelphia takes one to similar colonies of "Pineies" in the Pine Barrens of Southern New Jersey. Their economy is slightly more complex than the Allegheny clan: they make and sell earthenware containers (collector's items) along with the contents. Even so, the need for supplemental income drives some of the men to work in the shore resorts. One we met at a gas pump told us in deep Cockney accent "I come f'm 'cross the Baye, an'oom caynt wayt to g'back!" The police knew that there were hundreds of such people in the Barrens, in little colonies. They harmed no one. They were not dependent on the state, as they would have been if their moonshine economy had been challenged. So the State Police had an understanding that, again, amounted to social accommodation.

An example of an insular people who do occasionally threaten the communities around them, though mildly, is the "Jackson Whites" (a term deeply resented by their descendents today), about 3,000 of whom occupy the rugged Ramapo Mountains, a 30-square-mile area on the border of New York and New Jersey, 25 miles from New York City. If one turns off the highway at Sloatsburg, N.Y., and bears left up into the hills, one comes to Ringwood Manor, the former estate of the Erskine-Hewitt family. In the 1600s, this property comprised 30,000 acres extending South to include the Erskine Lakes and North to encompass a large part of the Ramapos. The remaining 150 acres, including the mansion, have been turned over to the Interstate Park system on the condition that the Jackson Whites, whom the family has protected through the centuries, will continue to be protected by the two States. And necessarily so.

It is said that these people are the descendents of renegade Indians of American frontier days, of Dutch settlers of the 17th century, of Hessian deserters from the Revolution, and of escaped slaves from the underground railway era. Many of them are degenerate both physically and mentally from constant inbreeding without benefit of clergy, although there are occasional magnificent specimens whom the Erskines have supported through advanced academic degrees on the condition that they return for ten years of service (social, medical, educational) to the less fortunate. Individuals may be pure black, red, brown, white, or—as in the case of Jackson White himself, their prototype, actually dappled in these colors. Through the generations, these people have worked the iron mine located on the estate. They made and transported to the Hudson River, 30 miles away, the huge links of the chain that was stretched across the river to thwart the British. Some of these links have been returned to the terrace of the museum where they may be seen beside the statue of Jackson White himself. Over the years, many of the more moronic of these people have drifted into the villages and towns that have grown around them and, as they do among themselves, have "snitched" whatever struck their fancy. The police of the region, knowing that no punitive measures could possibly change their patterns, simply try to recover the loot and return the offenders to the hills.

Many insular culture groups of the United States, then, are never forced by poverty to come into the cities in such numbers as would create friction. Even in the case of the thoroughly deprived Jackson Whites, whose hunting and fishing economy is supplemented in bad times by state aid and the Red Cross, insularity in and of itself need not cause problems for surrounding communities. On the contrary, insularity may prove a strength for socio-economic growth. Until recently, there were 86 ethnic "pockets" in the State of Michigan, in each of which there were sufficient people of foreign origin to make the learning of English unnecessary, except for those breadwinners going into the larger community to earn a living. Their very closeness to one another has provided the strength to build their own economies to a level that would support them until their children—educated in American schools—grew up, married, and either took over or moved away. In either case, such groups finally become assimilated and their ethnic character fades away. They are ordinarily no problem for the police, but in cities, it can be different.

Not long ago, one could walk across Manhattan Island on 43rd Street, from the Hudson to the East River, and encounter distinct enclaves of Russian, Italian, German, and native-born peoples, each compacted in a few square blocks. Their children played ball in the streets and if a Russian pitch was hit, the ball might be caught by an "Eyetalian" across the avenue. Getting the ball back from "Dago Joe" was an experience to brighten a boy's day. But no sweat—the kids all spoke English, learned in school, together.

In such areas, the chief problem for the police was with the parents—locked in the fortresses of their apartments, insulated from assimilation into the American culture by language, religion, dress, customs, and the isolation imposed by the community because of their alien ways. They were subject to jeers from native youth when they ventured out into the streets. Seen as competitors for jobs or welfare payments by native adults, they have been easy targets for blame for the city's ills, and hence are the butt of verbal and even physical attacks, which eventually involve the police. The food they cook smells "different," even offensive to native Americans. Their gestures irk, their speech grates.

During its history, New York has been able to say it contained more Negroes, more Italians, more Irish, and more Jews than any other city on earth. It has had almost as many Germans as Berlin. Such people, on arrival, settle in the areas where their precursors are. Many never leave, keeping their old country ways until death, while their children grow up, marry, move away and, ethnically speaking, get lost in the larger city or the nation as they find success. But the remaining enclaves of older folks are large enough to support their own foreign language press, as in the Yorktown (German) section of New York.

The wise police administrator has, when possible, assigned officers of German background to Yorktown, Chinese to Chinatown, Jews to Jewish areas, and blacks to black districts—and left them there. To keep the peace by protecting them from hostile neighbors, officers must come to know the ways of these peoples. Colorful and often noisy street festivals are accepted. Accommodation is assumed. Trouble for the police arises chiefly when newcomers are settling in areas where they compete with older inhabitants, until such time as greater familiarity brings greater acceptance.

The Southern Appalachian Mountaineers

But there are some in-migrant culture groups that have had special problems of accommodation. One such group has been the Southern Appalachian Mountaineers (SAMs), many of whom have left their mountain homes as the coal mines have been automated or as their submarginal farms have petered out. One would think that this particular group would have the easiest time being assimilated. They are whites of ancient (from the 1700s) Scotch-Irish-English stock who were not content with the coastal regions of the new world, and pressed on to the sanctuaries of the Blue Ridge and Alleghenies. They speak English adorned with regional accents and colloquialisms. Their Protestant religion is often similar to the broad Pentecostal type that is thriving in our cities. But their character and traditions of 300 years of isolation preclude their adjusting to the ways of the urban people among whom they settle and to whom they often lose in the competition for survival.

Perhaps one reason why they fail to "make it" is that unlike later European immigrants, they never come to think of themselves as citizens of the cities to which they migrate for jobs. As soon as they have a little cash ahead, they return "home" to the emotional security of their impoverished but familiar mountain enclaves, returning to the city only when their funds run out, if at all. Such behavior contrasts, for example, with that of most of the rural southern Negroes who moved North during World War II years. They found jobs, rented or bought houses, but—to satisfy their yearning for fat-back, grits, and familiar herb medicines—would cooperatively send one of their number South to bring back a truckload of such supplies. They did this with decreasing frequency as they became acculturated to Northern ways. The SAMs, however, are a different story.*

Some years ago, the Cincinnati Police Department undertook a special study of the SAMs because Cincinnati receives a great number of these migrants. It was felt that an understanding of their customs and attitudes and the environment from which they come would enable police officers to anticipate and control difficult situations and to function with a minimum of friction. The purpose of the study was *not* to promote brotherly love, but to reconcile the prejudgments of officers' "tunnel" perception of the SAMs with an accurate understanding of the "whole man." Such migrants cannot be fenced out with migration quotas; they are there, and more will come, and each SAM, when he arrives, will have similar ways of behaving and feeling.

General Migration Data

There are certain parallels in all migrations:

1. High visibility: clothing, habits, speech, mannerisms.

2. Magnification: The in-group tends to exaggerate the conditions and problems that arise. In New York, a newspaper article estimated 7,000,000 Puerto Ricans had arrived in a period of several years, when the actual number was 1,650,000.

3. Rhetoric: Each new group of immigrants is the recipient of the same verbal abuse, whether Irish, Germans, Italians, or SAMs.

Both internal and external migrants have in common an economic motivation—job seeking—and most can be characterized by ambition, hope, and the search for betterment of their lot. In the case of many migrants, there is a kinship intelligence system. Early arrivals communicate to those at home as to whether there are jobs. Jobs are the only consideration: poor housing, ill treatment, and limited health facilities will not deter the migration if work is available.

General Observations on Migrants

1. In-groups in any community are likely to believe that their ways are God's ways, and anyone who is different is wrong.

---

*The remainder of this Study is adapted from a unit of instruction developed in 1959 for the Training Division of the Cincinnati Police Department by (then) Lieutenant Robert Roncker. Used by permission of that department.

2. Since all behavior is learned, the migrant must learn new habits to conform to the rules of his new society. Most will learn these from those of his group who came before him.

3. Twenty years is the normal time necessary for an in-migrant to lose his former identity in a new community.

4. The key to our likes or dislikes of a new group is less the characteristics of its individuals than of their total situation. The community of German scientists and their families near Huntsville, Alabama, is a striking example: they had been accepted as good neighbors in a culture very different from their own until, during World War II, they were regarded as a great menace.

5. The characteristics of people are devices we seize upon to manifest our likes and dislikes.

Where Do the SAMs Come From?

The Southern Appalachian region embraces 257 counties and stretches across 9 states: Alabama, Georgia, Kentucky, Maryland, North and South Carolina, Tennessee, Virginia, and West Virginia, through all of which the Blue Ridge or Allegheny Mountains pass. The SAMs from one area or county will all migrate to a particular industrial area, such as Cincinnati or Dayton. They identify with their counties of origin, not their states. Migrants tend to follow the highways constructed through the mountain troughs, which run southwest to northeast, and then spill out toward the industrial centers such as Chicago or Detroit. The midwest industrial axis of Cincinnati-Detroit receives 25 percent of the migrating SAMs; the South Atlantic States receive about 37 percent.

Why Do They Come?

Basically, the SAMs migrate to the city in search of jobs. There has been an annual natural increase of population in the mountain area of about 100,000 a year. The economy of the area cannot support such a population. The decline in the demand for coal, plus the automation of the remaining mines has curtailed jobs. The SAMs, like the rest of us, want *things* they have learned about through the kinship intelligence network: televisions, radios, washing machines. The family that, before World War II, was content with the living standards of 100 years ago is passing from the scene. It has been replaced by the semi-agricultural family in which, often, the husband alone migrates to the city for various periods of time and makes enough money to supply the new wants. When a washing machine is bought and sent home, it is set out on the front porch where, in addition to its normal function, it serves as a status symbol.

Who Are They?

The population of Appalachia is 94 percent white. Primarily, the people are of Scotch-Irish descent. During the years 1714–1720, 54

known shiploads emigrated to the Appalachians. A stereotyped mountaineer would be blond, blue-eyed, tall, lanky, and lean faced, though
many of them in no way resemble this image. There is no such person
as a farming mountaineer. Neither does he want to be classed with the
"branch water" variety of mountaineer, who farms to supply his table
and grows supplemental bean and tobacco crops for cash. Even in communities where most families are linked by kinship ties, there are social
strata (upper, middle, and lower classes) just as in urban areas. The
SAMs became identified as mountaineers only after the Civil War, when
they were ostracized because they were Southerners who joined the
Union army. Thereafter, they were refused help and drifted into ignorance, and have remained unschooled except for brief exposure to the
three R's of education. Fiction about them has helped to perpetuate
their sloven, "hillbilly" image. Picked up in the city by the police and
asked where their home is, they invariably name the county of their
birth. Except for association with a primitive, emotional church
organization, the SAM has no tie to any state, community, or social
group other than kinship.

In the home, the father is head of the household in all matters.
The role of the wife is subservient, as in medieval times. Her duties include cooking, cleaning the house, care of the children, canning, gar-
dening, chopping wood, and drawing water. When the father cannot get
work and the mother becomes the breadwinner, the reversal of roles
is devastating, ending often in his drunkenness. At home in the mountains, the children love their mother and respect their father, and assist
him with the daily chores. In the city, the father is away all day and
this family pattern is destroyed.

It is the accepted practice for relatives to visit one another and
stay for extended periods of time, literally eating each other out of
house and home. This accounts for the practice of city SAMs renting a
room or apartment and having numerous relatives move in with them,
perhaps on a permanent basis. Families crowd into the same urban
neighborhoods to fortify each other against the city ways and people.
Their bare, overcrowded homes are repugnant to native city people; to
the SAMs the electric lights and running water are luxury. To the
police, such overcrowding means unemployed adults and idle children,
with resultant pilfering, at the least.

Character of the SAM

His history has made the SAM an individualist, wholly self-reliant.
In the city, this translates as failing to report to work or getting drunk.
He is sensitive, secretive, furtive, distrustful of the law and of the police.
Intelligent but uneducated, he is shrewd. Retaliation is a personal
matter to him that does not concern the courts or the police. Cruel, he
delights in the suffering of others, yet he will suffer pain without expression. His respect for property extends only to that owned by the kinship

group. Hospitable, he helps his kin in need, without thought of pay. Social but not cooperative, he is extremely loyal to the kinship group.

His religious ties with the Holiness Pentecostal or Independent Baptist churches provide his only social link outside the kinship pattern. A fundamentalist, the SAM is at his crest when he is "right with God," but in the depths when he has "backslid." To follow Jesus means no smoking, drinking, dancing, cutting of hair by women, make-up, jewelry, or movies. (Television is permissible.) Pride or harshness is not as evil as smoking; fornication is not as serious as drunkenness. Church services consist in socializing, singing of gospel hymns, climactic witnessing culminated by "speaking in tongues" and shouting of "hallelujahs" and "Amens." The handling of snakes and the laying on of hands are typical. The SAM churches reflect the characteristics of their members. They have evolved a certain theology, but it applies only to their own economy and society and cannot be transplanted to urban life without loss of the fullness of its ecstacies.

Education of the SAMs

The educational level of the SAMs is low, and the handicaps to be overcome in gaining an education are many, not the least of which is lack of motivation resulting from custom. Major factors that affect their attitudes toward education include:

1. Many homes are inaccessible to school buses.

2. Children may have to walk miles to reach the bus.

3. Parents see no need for learning beyond the three Rs.

4. Parents keep children from school if there is work to be done and are apathetic about attendance in the cities.

5. Ignorance is preached as a virtue by their ministers.

6. Courts refuse to convict parents cited for failure to send their children to school.

7. Dropout rate reaches 75% by the 5th grade; only 10% complete high school.

8. Most teachers have only a high school education.

9. Better-qualified teachers leave for cities and higher pay.

Schools have insufficient plant and equipment. Supplies and textbooks are scant. Absenteeism is high. The disregard for education is suggested by one county where school board members are required to have completed only six years of school; magistrates need not be able to read and write; State Representatives average 5 and State Senators 10 years of school. While some of these details may have changed in the recent past, the basic cultural profile remains the same. With such low standards of education, it is not surprising that public assistance programs are minimal, which further contributes to the emigration of the SAMs to the cities where, if jobs are unavailable, at least welfare programs exist. Local law enforcement is of a primitive type reminiscent of the six-gun era, and officers have no training other than the school of experience. Politics and kinships minimize even this poor system. Bootlegging is tolerated. Murder, sex crimes, and assaults are taken lightly in contrast with breaking and entering, which is dealt with more harshly.

Because of limited education of both the SAMs and their local enforcement officers, restraints are minimal. The SAM is opposed to regulation and limitation of personal inclinations and will violently oppose those who attempt to restrict him. The right to absolute freedom is assumed in the mountains. The regulations and law enforcement he meets in the city are therefore traumatic experiences.

The Police and the SAMs

One of the greatest problems facing urban police in their contacts with these mountain people is communication. How can they explain "trash" to people who have always thrown leftovers out the back door for the hogs and chickens to eat? In the city, the SAM throws it in the alley. How explain the need for innoculations in times of epidemics? Words such as "ambition," "success," and "career" are beyond his vocabulary. Perhaps a recognition and understanding of the following points may assist law enforcement officers in their official contacts with the SAMs:

1. Urbanization is a lengthy process. Police should not expect the same patterns of response from SAMs as they do from city people.

2. Distrust of law enforcement is a heritage of the SAM. This can only be broken down by consistent fair treatment.

3. Because the SAM must cope with a changed environment in coming to the city, a degree of flexibility must be employed by the police and other agencies, to secure compliance.

4. The lowered status of the male in relation to his family in urban areas is a factor leading to excessive drinking and family fights.

5. All SAMs possess very strong family ties. An arrest of one individual when relatives are present may present the officer with forcible interference by the family.

6. The low educational level and lack of urban experience of the SAM present a communication problem. Ignorance may be mistaken for willful resistance to regulation.

7. Bewilderment and fear in the new environment may be mistaken for noncooperation.

8. "Visibility"—clothing, mannerisms, customs, and attitudes—are factors that may contribute to the arrest of SAMs.

9. Many acts that might result in arrest are a function of youth. Seventy-five percent of all SAMs are under age 35. Therefore a greater percentage of them fall in the "arrest-prone age group" and more will be arrested than from the same age group of in-dwellers.

Clearly, the character, traditions, customs, and educational backgrounds of the many kinds of culture groups who immigrate to our cities from abroad, and from within the country, require individual and understanding treatment by enforcement officers. The study of their differences and expectations is an essential part of the training and work of the emerging professional police officer. As it is often said, it is not only *what* police officers do that affects community relations, it is also *how* they do it.

The Police and Black Teen-age Culture

It is necessary actually to experience life in the black ghetto in order to comprehend emotionally and intellectually the unending, day-and-night contest between the police and teen-age gangs. It is a testing process that is frustrating and challenging, depressing and exhilarating for both sides. The struggle is a function of ghetto life itself. Rat-infested tenements with their bare furnishings, bleak walls, often unheated rooms and nonfunctioning plumbing provide no "home" for the young teen-ager in search of adventure and companionship. He takes to the streets to stake out a "private place" with others like him, seeking together some fulfillment of their natural desires. A few rather well-known books provide some sense of what life in this kind of world is like (*The Autobiography of Malcolm X*; Claude Brown, *Manchild in the Promised Land*; William Foot Whyte, *Street Corner Society*).

From such books one can, to a limited degree, experience vicariously the institutionalized permanence of a struggle from which neither side really expects an outcome of more than a temporary nature. As long as boys continue to reach teen-age, and as long as police continue to be assigned to control them in the name of social order, the mutual testing will continue, like boxers in the early stages of a bout, probing each other for strengths and weaknesses.

Since the early 1940s, when thousands of Negroes left the share-cropping, technologically threatened cotton fields to seek jobs in war production cities, a whole generation of native-born, urban blacks has grown up, sophisticated in city ways. The Gospel-shouting ways of their parents are to them a ludicrous anachronism. Their sole standards of conduct, their expectations and their aspirations, are those learned from their peers, who learned them from previous generations of city street kids who long since have discovered that the everlasting grayness of urban life can really be *something* if one deliberately flaunts the laws

This Study is a condensation and adaptation of "Gang Members and the Police" by Carl Werthman and Irving Piliavin, in *The Police: Six Sociological Essays,* David Bordua (ed.). John Wiley & Sons, New York, 1967. Used with permission.

and mores. The more explicit the laws, the more kicks there are in violating them. The thrill of getting away with it is an end in itself. Street fights with other gangs are, of course, a way of establishing one's manhood. If these encounters blossom into a general brouhaha and the police horn in, so much the better. For the younger teen-agers, thefts for today's needs are fun and functional. To steal a lot at one time may preclude the need for stealing again tomorrow, and it also lays one open to attack by others. For older teen-agers who have passed beyond the fun stage, theft becomes a necessity for getting food, gadgets, sharp clothes, "conks," and drugs.

For the individual gang boy, all this provides companionship. Street-corner gangs abound, for their sheer warmth. The need to belong knows no caste. A guy needs a place to go, a place to be, where he can struggle for acceptance by his peers and, eventually perhaps, become a leader. To be a member of an elite gang that dominates the city for blocks around is something, man. Not to mention the club jackets, the "conks" (long, straightened hairdos) with their "mammy-rags" (to hold the hair in place till it sets), and the "bends" (flared pants) and, for the older boys, "finger chains" (wedding rings to make the cops think they are married).

There is the corner itself, the "turf" that is exclusively theirs by grandly won triumphs over rival gangs. The "corner" may be midblock, in front of a doughnut and coffee shop where the guys actually *pay* for what they consume all day long. But it *is* a kind of private place, where the activities that other cultures confine to the bedroom or living room take place, unashamedly. It is their *home,* in spite of the passers-by whom the gang has defined ways of handling when they pass through the territory. "Familiars" are neighborhood residents who, however reluctantly, recognize that this *is* the boys' area by walking by or through as though they didn't see whatever was going on. Strangers are "let pass," or are challenged according to their attitudes or appearances or the mood of the boys at the moment.

And then there are the cops! Yeah, the cops. These are the despised intruders, the symbols of the law, and as such, an extra-special raison d'etre for the gang to exist. They provide the element of conflict that gives zest to gang loyalties and ingenuities. They are the challenge to the violation process, the "salt" without which there would be no flavor in the whole bit. In short, they are "the enemy."

For the police, the gang represents an on-going challenge to their authority as police, and to the individual officer, a permanent dare to prove himself capable of both enforcing the law and recognizing the "right" of the boys to occupy their space, so long as they do not infringe on the rights of others. To enforce the law as written would be to invite all gangs to unite in resistance. To ignore the violations entirely would be to lose face, not only at headquarters but with the gang itself. The proper compromise behavior is elusive, since no two confrontations are alike. The kids *expect* the police to enforce *some* of the laws. If they did not, the contest would lose its savor. But too often, the officer's frustrations make him lose his cool and he becomes brutal, verbally or physically. Then no one wins. The kids are beaten up either on their own turf (and lose face) or, more often, in the station house if they are taken in. If the officer has trumped up the charges (by egging the suspect into resistance), the juvenile division is likely to spring the boy, and the officer loses face among his fellow officers.

When the kids get really wild (and who doesn't get desperate for something different to do?) and ransack a store, the police have a clear-cut case and arrest the guilty. And the boys agree that this is expected police behavior. But when a patrolman accosts a kid merely for being in a strange place (out of his district), or inadvertently near the scene of a recent robbery, or in a middle-class area, the boy often feels he must challenge the officer. If the kids are actually innocent, having only been on their way to look for a job, or visiting a girl friend who is a maid in a white neighborhood, they will probably resist, at least verbally—even if they are alone—even though they know the inevitable outcome.

The outcome is defeat. It is not all fun and games.

Thus far, except for mentioning that the scene is the Negro ghetto, we might have been describing the contest between *any* youth gangs and the police—white, black, Chicano, or whatever. There is a common denominator among all boys seeking something to do—ways to establish themselves as "not chicken," but real guys. But the patterns of this search vary with their place in society. To the police, white kids are white, and that's something in their favor. Chicanos, or Puerto Ricans, may possibly have had some education or breeding before they arrived in the city streets, so there is the hunch that something can be done with them. But in the eyes of the police, the black kids have nothing going for them. They are black, like their parents before them, and the police "know" what *that* means!

The boys' hangout is typically under constant surveillance, and the police stage periodic shakedowns as a reminder to the boys that final authority for their behavior on the streets rests with the public's official landlords. For example:

> One time me and a couple of friends, we came down to the corner because we was supposed to have our meeting . . . Then this cop on a motorcycle pulled over . . . I seen him before. He rides around the neighborhood a lot. He didn't say nothing. He just zipped down his jacket and there was his old billy club. And then he started asking questions, identification, what we were doing and all like that. And

he searched us and got our names down in the book and everything.
We wasn't doing anything except what we usually do on that corner . . . They want us to know they in charge.

The police and the gang boys do not always agree on what rules
the police should enforce and how they should enforce them. The
smoothest course for the officer is to conform to the social organization
with which he is in direct contact, and at the same time try to give the
impression to the outside world that he is enforcing the law . . . The
police must stand for *something;* if they tolerate *all* behavior, they are
likely to be defined by the gang boys as either "chicken" or corrupt.
Example:

> Man, you should have seen them cop out at the Point Saturday night.
> Zeke and Orville and Percy (gang workers) were there. They can
> tell you. Five carloads of cops was there, lights flashing and every-
> thing. And everybody is just standing around after this party. Fights
> going on, girls screaming, everything. And then this cat (one of the
> gang) pulls out a gun and starts firing. Man, he was five feet way from
> them cops and they just stood there! Somebody coulda' got killed or
> something. Maybe they just didn't care. Maybe they was saying, "Why
> not let them niggers go kill each other anyway. They ain't got no
> sense."

The gang boys are not without their own standards of fairness,
and it is these standards that the patrolman must attempt to enforce.
A "good cop" is thus a man who can successfully handle a subtle and
narrowly defined moral challenge. He must try to order the life of an
ethnic lower-class community from within by holding people such as
gang boys to their own ideals, however little these ideals may be reflected in their behavior. In situations involving violence, the good cop
functions as an arbitrator. He does not turn the boys over to the local
school principal or cart them away to the station. He isolates them in
the squad car, talks the situation over with them, and then does what
he can to achieve a semipermanent peace.

> (Have you guys ever met any good cops?) Yeah, there was two studs
> out in Lakeview once, not the regular cops, who was pretty straight.
> Remember when we had that big fight at the playground and those
> guys from Hunters Point got hurt? . . . The cops asked us what we
> was fighting about and why did we fight and could we use boxing
> gloves and did we know that fighting was against the law and all like
> that. But they finally let us go, and they got Willie to take the Hunters
> Point boys home. They was *real* straight, those two. I think they must
> have lived out there or something, or maybe they was in a club once
> themselves.

Police normally look for indicators of possible guilt of people in the areas they patrol.

(Why do you think the cops pick you up all the time?) Why do they pick us up? They don't pick up everybody. They pick up the ones with the hats on and trench coat and conks. If you got long hair and hats on, something like this one, you gonna get picked up. Especially a conk. And the way you dress. Sometimes like if you've got on black pants, or bends or Levi's. They think you gonna rob somebody. And don't have a head scarf ... And the way you walk sometimes. If you walk pimp. Don't try to walk pimp. Don't try to be cool. Like you got a boss (good) high, a fix or something. Last night a cop picked me up for that. He told me I had a bad walk ... He say, "You think you're bad." You know.

Every time an officer makes visible contact with a citizen, the citi- is forced to confront his own status in the eyes of the law. The :e learn to rely on hostile looks and furtive glances as signs of pos- guilt. A policeman's uniform is a potent symbolic device. When ng with people under suspect circumstances, patrolmen may see a vdriver as a "deadly weapon" and a scratch on the neck as evidence pe.

Like you be walking. Just coming from working on the car or some- thing. And if you have a screwdriver in your back pocket, hell, they beat the shit out of you. They talk: you got a burglary tool or a deadly weapon on you. Remember the time we was getting ready to go up to the gym? One guy had some scratches on his neck, and the cop pull over and say, "Turn around!" ... It seem like some girl way over in another district got raped. And the girl say, "I think they live over in Hunters Point (Negro section) and I scratched one of them on the neck." Some stuff like that.

As one might imagine, gang boys tend to regard their more or ess permanent suspect "image" with considerable resentment that quite often spills over into outrage. ... Not all trips to neighboring territories are undertaken for the purposes of attacking rival gangs or pillaging the houses of the white rich, and most of the time, as the boys put it, "we was just mindin' our own business when the cops come along and ..."

As one might expect, gang members make various kinds of attempts to avoid suspicion. Large groups will break up into two's and three's.

Sometimes we jump next to the little ladies. Like one time when we was waiting for a bus and it was after curfew, we saw the heat coming down the street. And there was this ugly old lady walkin' by the bus stop. Well, I just step right up beside her ... you better off walkin' with a woman.

As adolescence wears on, the consequences of being picked up by the police become more serious. Boys begin to alter their appearances in ways that imply ever-increasing compromises with their preferred public identities. The wearing of "finger chains" in order to look married is easy. But the real sacrifices are the things they can no longer risk. The first and most precious article of clothing to disappear is the club jacket. Or at least they will wear it inside out so the club or nickname doesn't show. Last to go is the long hair.

> Our whole club is getting this kind of haircut; short ones. (With long hair) they say, "Conk job! Get in the wagon! You a hood!" I guess they gonna find somethin' else to pick on now.

The police expect law-abiding citizens to show their respect for the law by addressing officers with various gestures of deference. . . . It is desired that the suspect's physical presence will communicate civility, politeness, penitence, and even fear. The use of such terms as "Sir" and "Officer" are expected as indications of the humble status of the juvenile.

> (What responses seem to work for you when the cops pick you up?) If you kiss their ass and say, "Yes, sir, No, Sir," and all that jazz, they let you go. If you don't, they gonna take you in. And if you say it funny, they gonna take you in. Like "Yes, *Sir!* No, *Sir!*"

If an officer is polite, he is vulnerable to a response suggesting his authority is being rebuffed. Most officers decide not to risk this challenge to their honor. They communicate to the gang member that *authority* is not the basis on which the encounter is socially grounded, but rather that the *power to investigate* is being invoked instead. In effect, this move denies the gang member the option of accepting authority as the basis for participating in the exchange. Officers may make their contempt for gang members even more explicit:

> Remember the time we was coming from the show? This cop car pulls up and these two cops jump out quick. The first stud says, "All right, God Damn you! All you black Africans up against the m———f——— wall!" So then they started, "Where all you ignorant sons of bitches coming from? . . . What's your name? Let me see your I.D." Finally this cop's buddy say, "You want to run them in, Joe? They ain't really done nothing." . . . Like that, man. Happens all the time. They ain't a day we don't get rousted like that.

When a gang boy finds himself both suspected and insulted, he must decide whether to swallow the insult by deferring, or to defend his honor by challenging the officer. To display the ritual signs of deference means suffering the private torments of cowardice and losing face. Thus, most gang members prefer to challenge. This gestural rebellion takes a variety of forms. The most passive is a posture of sullenness: body muscles tense, shoulders slightly bowed, eyes averted and cast down or directed blankly at the interrogating officer. Voice tones range from silence to a barely audible, "I don't know." The posture conveys hostility, but the officer can't know whether it has been injected into the encounter as a result of previous experiences or betrays guilty knowledge.

Rather than adopt a posture of sullenness, a gang boy may choose to be insolent, with a straightforward nonchalance or indifference. This requires that the body be relaxed, and the officer is addressed directly with a flat statement, "Leave me alone. I don't know nothing." In a third stance, the boy may glare at the officer, move his arms and legs freely in abandoned gestures of anger, and say things like, "What the hell's wrong now? I ain't done nothing. Why do you guys pick on me?" But by offering to talk, the boy exposes himself to the possibility of being broken down by interrogation. This leaves the police officer with a choice of three alternatives.

First, he can back down, allowing his authority to be dissipated. But any fleeting defeat at the hands of a gang member has the prospect of becoming permanent. In a certain sense, then, gang members have a great deal of power. With a mere hint of impiety, they may strip a patrolman of his authority, symbolically. Or the officer can attempt an arrest.

> One day we were standing about three blocks from the school and this officer comes up. He say, "Hey, you boys, come here!" So everybody walk over. But this one stud made like he didn't hear him. So the cop say, "Hey, punk! Come here!" So the stud sorta look up like he hear him and start walking over real slow. So the cop walk over there and grab him and throw him down and put the handcuffs on him, saying, "When I call you next time, come see what I want!"—Just for standing there looking at him.

On the other hand, there are a variety of curfew, vagrancy, and loitering laws that can be used. The boy may be charged with "suspicion" of practically anything—robbery, rape, and the like. But gang boys are aware that the police have a very difficult time making these illusory charges stick. Most are dismissed on the recommendation of probation officers. More important, the patrolman's sergeant knows this, and puts a premium on ability to command authority without making an arrest. So the policeman may continue to provoke a suspect until the level of belligerence reaches proportions that validate invoking a charge of resistance to arrest:

> So what you do in a case like this is to egg the guy on until he makes a remark where you can justifiably slap him, and then if he fights back, you can call it resisting arrest.

From a gang member's point of view:

Another reason why they beat you up is because they always have the advantage over you. The cop say, "You done this." You say, "I didn't!" He say, "Don't talk back to me or I'll upside your head!" You're always in the wrong.

Unlike encounters between gang members and patrolmen, the confrontations between gang members and juvenile officers rarely end in violence. This is because the ability to command respect is not as crucial to the juvenile officer, who is evaluated largely by his skill at interrogation. But boys continue to believe that patrolmen *should* treat them with respect and that arrests *should* be confined to behavior that is clearly against the law. This is why policemen who treat the boys deferentially may still be considered "good cops."

Gang boys interpret the way the boundaries of their neighborhoods are patrolled as a conscious policy of confinement, and the police are looked upon as a foreign army of occupation. There are limits to what the natives will take from these troops, however, and there are times when more is needed to express rebellion than artful displays of insolence. These boys have been angry, bewildered, and resentful about the police as long as they can remember, and they strike back the only way they know how. As on September 28, 1966, when a white patrolman in Hunters Point (San Francisco) spotted three Negro boys in an approaching car and became suspicious when the boys jumped out and started running away. The officer claimed he fired three shots into the air before hitting one of the boys in the back with a fourth. The boy was 16, and he died on a barren stretch of rocky Hunters Point Hill, just a few feet from his home. The car was reported stolen four hours after the boy was dead. When the gang boys in the area saw the body, they began breaking windows, burning buildings, and looting stores. The uprising went on for 24 hours and stopped only when the National Guard arrived. Some citizens of San Francisco responded by attempting to find jobs for the youth, apparently believing that the cause of the riot was unemployment.

But a life for a stolen car?

Of course, neither the boys nor the police were right.

Nor is a society that ignores the causes of its trauma and fails to train its peace officers to cope with the "dirty work."

Mexican-Americans and the Administration of Justice in the Southwest

Excerpts from a Report of the United States Commission on Civil Rights, U.S. Government Printing Office, March 1970:

The U.S. Commission on Civil Rights undertook this study against a background of written complaints and allegations at Commission hearings and at meetings of the Commission's State Advisory Committees that Mexican-Americans* in the Southwest** were being subjected to discrimination by agencies of law enforcement and in the administration of justice. The alleged discrimination included physical and verbal abuse and harassment by law enforcement officers; exclusion from grand and petit juries; improper and discriminatory use of bail; lack of and inadequate representation by counsel; and employment of disproportionately low numbers of Mexican-Americans in law enforcement agencies—particularly in high ranking positions.

In the course of the study, Commission staff attorneys conducted field investigations (1967–1968) in which they interviewed 450 persons in the Southwest, including law enforcement officers, probation officers, prosecuting attorneys, judges, public defenders, attorneys in private practice, leaders of Mexican-American organizations, and private citizens. Four State Advisory Committee meetings were held, in different States. The Commission also contracted with California Rural Legal Assistance, Inc., for a study of service by Mexican-Americans on grand juries in selected California counties.

In addition, the Report is based on the results of a questionnaire mailed to 793 law enforcement agencies in five states (on the state, county and municipal levels), of which 280 were returned with sufficient information for tabulation.

---

*The term "Mexican-American" refers to persons living in the United States who are themselves of Mexican origin or whose parents or more remote ancestors came to the United States from Mexico or whose antecedents resided in those parts of the Southwestern United States which were once a part of the Mexican Nation. Other designations: Spanish American, Latin, or Latin American.

**Arizona, California, Colorado, New Mexico, and Texas.

Findings of the Report

1. *Police misconduct*

There is evidence of widespread patterns of police misconduct against Mexican-Americans in the Southwest. Such patterns include:

a. Incidents of excessive police violence against Mexican-Americans.

b. Discriminatory treatment of juveniles by law enforcement officers.

c. Discourtesy toward Mexican-Americans.

d. Discriminatory enforcement of motor vehicle ordinances.

e. Excessive use of arrests for "investigation" and of "stop and frisk."

f. Interference with attempts to rehabilitate narcotics addicts.

2. *Inadequate protection*

Complaints also were heard that police protection in Mexican-American neighborhoods was inadequate in comparison to that in other neighborhoods.

3. *Interference with Mexican-American organizational efforts*

In several instances law enforcement officers interfered with Mexican-American organizational efforts aimed at improving the conditions of Mexican-Americans in the Southwest.

4. *Inadequacy of local remedies for police malpractice*

Remedies for police malpractice in the Southwest were inadequate:

a. In most Southwestern cities, the only places where individuals can file complaints against the police are the police departments themselves. Internal grievance procedures did not result in adequate remedies for police malpractice.

b. Some cities in the Southwest have established independent or quasi-independent police review boards but these have not provided effective relief to complainants.

c. Civil litigation by Mexican-Americans against police officers accused of civil rights violations is infrequent.

d. There are few instances of successful local prosecutions of police officers for unlawful acts toward Mexican-Americans.

e. There have been instances of retaliation against Mexican-Americans who complain about law enforcement officers to the local police department or to the FBI.

5. *Federal remedies*

a. Agents of the Federal Bureau of Investigation have often failed to interview important witnesses in cases of alleged violation of 18

U.S.C. 242* or interviewed such witnesses in a perfunctory and hostile manner.

b. More aggressive efforts to implement 18 U.S.C. 242 by the Department of Justice are needed.

6. *Underrepresentation of Mexican-Americans on juries*

There is serious and widespread underrepresentation of Mexican-Americans on grand and petit State Juries in the Southwest:

a. Neither lack of knowledge of the English language nor low-incomes of Mexican-Americans can explain the wide disparities between the Mexican-American percentage of the population and their representation on juries.

b. Judges or jury commissioners frequently do not make affirmative efforts to obtain a representative cross section of the community for jury service.

c. The peremptory challenge is used frequently both by prosecutors and defendants' lawyers to remove Mexican-Americans from petit jury venires.

The underrepresentation of Mexican-Americans on grand and petit juries results in distrust by Mexican-Americans of the impartiality of verdicts.

7. *Bail*

Local officials in the Southwest abuse their discretion:

a. In setting excessive bail to punish Mexican-Americans rather than to guarantee their appearance for trial.

b. In failing to give Mexican-American defendants an opportunity to be released until long after they were taken into custody.

c. By applying unduly rigid standards for release of Mexican-Americans on their own recognizance where such release is authorized.

In many parts of the Southwest, Mexican-American defendants are hindered in their attempts to gain release from custody before trial

---

*The principal Federal criminal sanction against violence or other unlawful action by state and local officials is Title 18, Section 242 of the U.S. Code. It provides:

Whoever, under color of any law, statute, ordinance, regulation, or custom, willfully subjects any inhabitant of any State, Territory, or District to the deprivation of any rights, privileges, or immunities secured or protected by the Constitution or laws of the United States, or to different punishments, pains, or penalties, on account of such inhabitant being an alien, or by reason of his color or race, than are prescribed for the punishment of citizens, shall be fined not more than $1,000 or imprisoned not more than one year, or both, and if death results shall be subject to imprisonment for any term of years or for life.

because they cannot afford the cost of bail under the traditional bail system.

8. *Counsel*

There are serious gaps in legal representation for Mexican-Americans in the Southwest:

a. The lack of appointed counsel in misdemeanor cases results in serious injustices to indigent Mexican-American defendants.

b. Even in felony cases, where counsel must be provided for indigent defendants, there were many complaints that appointed counsel often was inadequate.

c. Where public defender's offices are available to indigent criminal defendants, they frequently did not have enough lawyers or other staff members to adequately represent all their clients, many of whom are Mexican-Americans.

d. In parts of the Southwest, there are not enough attorneys to provide legal assistance to indigent Mexican-Americans involved in civil matters.

e. Many lawyers in the Southwest will not handle cases for Mexican-American plaintiffs or defendants because they are "controversial" or not sufficiently rewarding financially.

f. Despite the enormous need for lawyers fluent in Spanish and willing to handle cases for Mexican-American clients, there are very few Mexican-American lawyers in the Southwest.

9. *Attitudes toward the courts*

Mexican-Americans in the Southwest distrust the courts and think they are insensitive to their background, culture, and language. The alienation of Mexican-Americans from the courts and the traditional Anglo-American legal system is particularly pronounced in northern New Mexico.

10. *Language disability*

Many Mexican-Americans in the Southwest have a language disability that seriously interferes with their relations with agencies and individuals responsible for the administration of justice:

a. There are instances where the inability to communicate with police officers has resulted in the unnecessary aggravation of routine situations and has created serious law enforcement problems.

b. Mexican-Americans are disadvantaged in criminal cases because they cannot understand the charges against them nor the proceedings in the courtroom.

    c. In many cases Mexican-American plaintiffs or defendants have difficulty communicating with their lawyers, which hampers preparation of their cases.

    d. Language disability also adversely affects the relations of some Mexican-Americans with probation and parole officers.

11. *Interpreters*

Interpreters are not readily available in many Southwestern courtrooms:

    a. In the lower courts, when interpreters were made available, they are often untrained and unqualified.

    b. In the higher courts, where qualified interpreters were more readily available, there has been criticism of the standards of their selection and training and skills.

12. *Employment by law enforcement agencies*

Employment of Mexican-Americans by law enforcement agencies throughout the five Southwestern states does not reflect the population patterns of these areas:

    a. Neither police departments, sheriffs' offices, nor state law enforcement agencies employ Mexican-Americans in significant numbers.

    b. State and local law enforcement agencies in the Southwest do not have programs of affirmative recruitment which would attract more Mexican-American employees.

    c. Failure to employ more Mexican-Americans creates problems in law enforcement, including problems in police-community relations.

13. *Courts and prosecutors*

Other agencies in charge of the administration of justice—courts, district attorneys' offices, and the Department of Justice—also have significantly fewer Mexican-American employees than the proportion of Mexican-Americans in the general population.

Conclusion

This report paints a bleak picture of the relationship between Mexican-Americans in the Southwest and the agencies which administer justice in those States. The attitude of Mexican-Americans toward the institutions responsible for the administration of justice—the police, the courts, and related agencies—is distrustful, fearful, and hostile. Police departments, courts, and the law itself are viewed as Anglo institutions in which Mexican-Americans have no stake and from which they do not expect fair treatment.

The U.S. Civil Rights Commission found that the attitudes of Mexican-Americans are based, at least in part, on the actual experience of injustice. Contacts with the police represent the most common encounters with the law for the average citizen. There is evidence of police misconduct against Mexican-Americans. In the Southwest, as throughout the nation, remedies for police misconduct are inadequate. Mexican-Americans have been excluded from full participation in many of the institutions that administer justice; they are underrepresented in employment in police departments, state prosecutors' offices, courts, and other official agencies. Consequently, these agencies tend to reflect a lack of knowledge about and understanding of the cultural background of Mexican-Americans.

The Commission's report shows that Mexican-Americans believe they are subjected to such treatment again and again because of their ethnic background. Moreover, their complaints bear striking similarities to those of other minority groups which have been documented in earlier Commission studies of the administration of justice, namely, that on black Americans (*Justice,* 1961) and Indians (*Law Enforcement,* 1965). Consequently, the Commission's recommendations in this report are designed to be sufficiently broad to be applicable to all minority groups.

The essence of this situation is summed up in the words of a Mexican-American participant in the California State Advisory Committee meeting, who said, "I think that my race has contributed to this country with pride, honor, and dignity, and we deserve to be treated as citizens today, tomorrow, and every day of our lives. I think it is the duty of our Government to guarantee the equality that we have earned."

STUDY 5

The Black Panther Phenomenon

The weeping began quietly: 12 slaves stolen in 1441. Over 400 years, 20 million more were taken, draining Africa. Perhaps one third died marching; another third at sea. They were branded and stuffed on ships so crowded that they couldn't stand, shift or lie down. Africans and Europeans profited from their misery. In 1619, some 20 blacks were sold at Jamestown, Va. About 500,000 made it here. By 1744, 300 ships had sailed out of Liverpool. The Africans fought back. They rebelled in Hispaniola in 1522; in Puerto Rico in 1527; in Panama in 1531. And in America in 1969 they were putting the black fist to our lie.

This quotation (from *Look* magazine, January 7, 1969, p. 28) skips over the American phase of the black struggle. Between 1619 and today, we wrote the institution of slavery into the Constitution when we stipulated that a black was 3/5 of a man—not for his sake, but as a sort of bulk count for purposes of establishing white representation in Congress. Since then, the black contribution to the American economy has been so vast that, after the Emancipation, the South collapsed, as did the world-wide clipper ship trade out of Salem and New Bedford when Yankee owners had to start paying their black crews.

The great lie of America to itself that these were something less than people continues, despite the death of Crispus Attucks (1770) at the Boston Massacre; of white John Brown (1859); the innumerable lynchings of yesterday that have been succeeded by gunnings-down in the streets; despite the careers and dignity of Booker T. Washington, Marcus Garvey, and George Washington Carver. Despite, too, the more recent sit-ins, boycotts, Resurrection City, the riots of 1967–68, and the diverse efforts of Martin Luther King, Jr., Roy Wilkins (NAACP), the late Whitney Young (Urban League), James Forman (SNCC and lately National Black Economic Development Conference); James Farmer (CORE, HEW), and Jesse Jackson (Operation Breadbasket). To name only these few is an embarassment, for the list could be so long. The great lie continues despite the careers of writers, actors, athletes, musicians, and such statesmen as Ralph Bunche, Edward Brooke and Thurgood Marshall. Because we still rationalize such names as Paul Robeson and Marian Anderson as exceptions to the great lie, we are, and will continue to be confronted by the Malcolm X's, Stokely Carmichaels, Rap Browns, Huey Newtons, and Eldridge Cleavers of our time. The problem that has burned in all of these remains: an unequal society that must be set aright.

The 1954 Supreme Court decision on desegregating the schools and new voting rights laws—with their half-hearted enforcement—have done little more than dramatize the need for true solutions. Ghettos and poverty remain. Integration itself is being questioned by many of the concerned, black and white alike. For the Negro, black is still painfully black, although—since Malcolm X—it is becoming beautiful.

Now the "revolution of rising expectations" is really being felt. The totally hopeless and the abject do not despair; they know nothing better. But when, as now in America, the door has been opened a crack so that the repressed can glimpse the vision of the possibilities of the world beyond ("I have been to the mountain . . ;"), there is a surge of hope mounting to a panic of desire. The mockery of "all deliberate speed" enflames the frustrated. A whole new generation of young blacks has grown up since 1954. As many blacks see it, the maddeningly slow, tedious democratic processes have become totally irrelevant as means of realizing equality in our time.

The wonder is that the Black Panther phenomenon didn't develop sooner (although there was, of course, Marcus Garvey) and that the vast majority of American blacks have not joined them. Perhaps the national expectation was that, after the riots of 1967–68, laws would be passed and public acceptance would assure, at long last, the sought-for equality. The laws *were* passed. But you can't legislate good will. You can only pass laws that will give legal support to those who are disposed to practice good will. And these were still too few. White unions still control the labor market. The black sections of our cities and towns are still walled off by "gentlemen's" agreements in spite of the laws. Most white churches are still searching their souls about admitting black brothers. In the South and North, those schools which achieved at least token integration are having a rough time: there are still riots and cuttings. Most of this is unorganized, but the deadly struggle continues in a dull, disheartening monotony that shows little sign of positive outcome.

It is no surprise, then, that out of this hopelessness there should emerge a small band of the new black youth determined to take their stand. Picture the three black young giants in black jackets and black berets standing on the white steps of the white courthouse in Oakland, California: legs spread in a stance of strength, holding three huge and beautifully painted banners bearing the new symbol of black determination—the Black Panther, with the professionally painted words "Free Huey."

This was 1966: the birth of the Black Panther Party.

Huey Newton, along with Bobby Seale, later joined by Eldridge Cleaver, had quietly conceived the party over cups of expresso at Oakland's Merritt College. It was to be, and became, a tightly disciplined organization of chapters across the country dedicated to wiping out "the pigs" by violence; to start the revolution that would knock over "the White Establishment" and bring in a socialist regime. Racism, they knew, was here to stay, but they believed it would be easier to handle it under a socialist system where everyone would presumably have an equal voice. At first, it was an all-black movement, but Cleaver was later to persuade the Panthers that blacks couldn't do the job alone—that alliances with white, disaffected groups should be solicited.

Huey was jailed, to await trial for killing a policeman. This bestowed upon him a martyr charisma with more associated power than would have been the case if he had tried to build the party as a free man. As *Newsweek* (February 23, 1970, p. 29) put it:

> Revolutions create their own mythologies and their own folk heroes. The Panthers' main man is Huey P. Newton. In prison he is like a lost saint, and tales of his wonders sustain the Panthers. Huey could talk down any professor and throw hands with any blood on the block. Huey faced down a whole cordon of cops with his M-1 and his law book. Huey has even beaten his jailers because he knows they have only his body and that he lives in the revolution. Huey was a figure in the days when the Panther Revolution was still romantic, when he and Seale and Bobby Hutton and David Hilliard rode the streets bird-dogging the Oakland police. Cleaver first laid eyes on Huey in those days, standing down itchy-fingered policemen, and thought to himself, "Goddam, that nigger is crazy!" And Seale, in his jail cell, sorts over the memories like fading photographs. "Those were the days, man," he said, staring into a cloud of cigarette smoke. "Dangerous days. Patrolling the police—that was beautiful."

In the years since the heyday of the movement, the lustre has faded. Huey had the misfortune to be freed on bail. Bobby Seale, the organizer, was jailed in New Haven, but this martyrdom—arousing Yale students to his support—faded with their preoccupation with pollution or other causes. Eldridge Cleaver, the party's philosopher, was jailed for rape of white women (perhaps a symbolic gesture on his part!), released on bail, and fled to Algeria where he tried to form alliances with disaffected youth groups of Europe and the Palestinians. For awhile, the Panthers operated clinics for Negro children, ostensibly to feed and tend their health needs, actually for purposes of indoctrination. But this required funds that proved hard to come by, despite gifts from upper-class groups on Park Avenue whose interest waned with expressed white dismay and black ingratitude.

The Panthers and what they symbolized sputtered on, as reflected in these brief excerpts from the *Information Please Almanac* for 1971 (Dan Golanpaul, pp. 70–86), covering events for 1970:

February 1: Pre-trial hearings begin for 16 members of the Black Panther Party in New York, charged with plotting to kill policemen and dynamite rail lines and major department stores.

March 9: H. Rap Brown, black militant, goes on trial in Bel Air, Md., on charges of treason and inciting to riot.

March 10: Two Negro men, including an associate of H. Rap Brown, die in an explosion that demolishes their car in Bel Air. Second victim not identified, and Brown's whereabouts unknown. (He had been out on bail). FBI investigation later showed blast was accidental. (Where had the men been going with the bomb?)

April 6: Two gunmen slay four California patrolmen; one captured, the other shot dead.

April 30: U.S. troops flown to New England for Black Panther rally in New Haven (re: Bobby Seale trial) of 20,000.

May 1: Demonstrators rally on New Haven green opposite Yale buildings to support Black Panthers. Federal troops and National Guardsmen stand by, but rally is peaceful.

May 11: Five Negro men killed in racial rioting in Augusta, Ga.

May 15: Jackson State College, Miss., predominantly Negro, closes after two black students are killed, nine wounded, by police gunfire.

June 19: Black volunteer peacemakers restore temporary quiet in Negro area racked by four days of violence in Miami, Fla.

August 5: Black Panther leader Huey Newton released on bail pending retrial of his 1967 manslaughter conviction in the death of a policeman.

August 15: Angela Davis, former UCLA instructor in philosophy, an avowed Communist, is sought on warrant charging murder and kidnap in connection with courtroom raid in which judge and three others were killed.

August 29: Black soldier from Vietnam is buried in all-white cemetery at Fort Pierce, Fla., by court order. Cemetery manager harried with protests and threats as a result.

December 22: Angela Davis, arrested in New York City in October, is extradicted to California to stand trial.

While some of these 1970 events had no apparent direct connection with the Panthers, they testify that the struggle continued, in spite of the 230 arrests that J. Edgar Hoover reported for the 12-month period ending May 1970 and 28 Panther deaths to that date.

What, specifically, do the Panthers want? A few excerpts from Eldridge Cleaver's *Soul on Ice,* written while he was in Folsom prison shortly before the launching of the Black Panther organization, suggest the philosophical base that Cleaver provided for the Panthers:

page 121:   We live today in a system that is in the last stages . . . of breaking up on a worldwide basis . . . Injustice is being challenged at every turn and on every level . . . around the world. But at home there is a Trojan Horse, a black Trojan Horse that has become aware of itself . . . It, too, demands liberation.

page 123:   Black Americans are too easily deceived by a few smiles and friendly gestures, by the passing of a few liberal sounding laws which are left on the books to rot unenforced, and by the speech-making of a President who is a past master at talking out of the thousand sides of his mouth. The black people must be sure beyond all doubt that the reign of terror is ended . . . What is being decided right now is the shape of the world tomorrow.

After the Civil War, America went through a period similar to the one we are now in. The Negro problem received a full hearing. Everybody knew that the black man had been denied justice. No one doubted that it was time for changes and that the black man should be made a first class citizen. But Reconstruction ended. Blacks who had been elevated to high positions were brusquely kicked out into the streets and herded with the mass of blacks into the ghettos and the black belts.

page 125:   Black Americans number 23 million strong. That is a lot of strength. But it is a lot of weakness if it is disorganized and at odds with itself . . . *The need for one organization that will give one voice to the black man's common interest* is felt in every bone and fiber of black America. [*Italics ours.*]

page 130:   Every city has its police department . . . It would be sheer madness to try operating any American city without the heat, the fuzz, the man. Americans are too far gone, or else they haven't arrived yet . . . Take the cops away and Americans would have a coast-to-coast free for all.

page 133:   In their rage against police brutality, the blacks lose sight of the fundamental reality: That the police are only an instrument for the implementation of the policies of those who make the decisions. Police brutality is only one facet of the crystal of terror and oppression. Behind police brutality there is social brutality, economic brutality, political brutality . . . The real problem is a trigger-happy social order.

These quotations show that Cleaver's rationale for the Panther movement was carefully drawn. But in trying to put the Panther program in operation, frustration and desperation sparked a resort to violence. In 1969, *Time* magazine (December 19, 1969, p. 14) said:

> Their stated aim is to give black Americans full pride and dignity; yet though they claim self-defense, they are committed to organized violence. In a last month issue of *The Black Panther,* Information Minister Eldridge Cleaver wrote: "We call for the violent overthrow of the fascist imperialist United States government."

When the police react, or overreact, to such declarations of intention, as in the raid on the Black Panther Chicago headquarters in which Fred Hampton and Mark Clark were slain (December 1969), other blacks than the Panthers cry "genocide" and claim that the police have a plot to wipe out all Panthers. *Time* continued:

> The Panthers make little secret of stockpiling arms; where it is legal, they brandish them in public. "Off the pigs"—kill the police—is the frequent Panther refrain. (But) what the Panthers view as an extermination plot, says one Federal official, is the human response of a cop confronted by someone who has publicly avowed to kill him. "That's no plot," the official says. "It's a perfectly natural reaction by a policeman facing someone who has boasted that he is prepared to shoot it out." To the Panthers, "violence against the police is not a crime but heroism."

The public was not only alarmed by the Panthers' professed intention of violence, but by their confused ideological verbiage. As the *Time* article put it:

> Much of the Panther rhetoric is couched in Marxist-Maoist terms . . . "We know we can learn from the struggles of China, Korea and Russia. We use it as a guide to action. An ideology has to be a living thing. But the Black Panther Party is not really Maoist."

Cleaver himself, even with the perspective of his long view from his self-exile in Algiers, became more disposed to violence. Sanche de Gramont interviewed him there for *The New York Times Magazine* (November 1, 1970, pp. 30ff) and quoted him:

> All I do is toward the idea of going back, but not to surrender myself to those pigs . . . I find it impossible to relate to the judicial system of the United States. I feel like the young brothers who went into the courtroom and offed the judge. That's how black people should treat the courts in Babylon.

> . . . Reforms are not the solution. Our problems derive from the system itself. We have to completely eliminate the capitalist system and replace it with socialism . . . We accepted the principle of revolutionary suicide . . . but we feel we must place our lives on the line . . . Here

in Algiers we will work on recruiting black G.I.'s who have deserted and are in Europe. During our trip to North Vietnam we learned there were black deserters fighting in the ranks of the Viet Cong . . . It would give me great satisfaction if Richard Nixon should be killed. I would consider that an excellent thing . . . The answer is not black capitalism, or black athletes, or black actors, or blacks in cigarette ads; that is just a way of incorporating black people in a device. The answer is to do away with the device. It's not a question of black studies; it's white studies that have got to be changed.

Perhaps a more realistic and authentic view of what the Black Panthers want can be gained from examining their objectives as they spelled them out at their September 1970 convention in Philadelphia. The convention was called to write a new Constitution for the United States. According to one estimate, 35 percent of those attending were whites—members of The Young Lords (Puerto Ricans), members of the Women's and Gay liberation movements, and other radical leftists. The conference was orderly and productive, despite some harassment by the Philadelphia police in the preceding three days. The meetings consisted of 15 study groups, each assigned to develop recommendations, plus a plenary reporting session at Temple University, which had leased facilities for the purpose. The recommendations of the final day included (Lansing, Michigan, *State Journal,* September 7, 1970):

1. Guarantee rights to national minorities to integrate, segregate, federate, amalgamate, congregate, secede, or do whatever they wished, provided that no group oppresses any other.

2. Guarantee representation for all ethnic groups in whatever government structure is formed in proportion to their numbers at the local level.

3. Free housing, health care, education, and day care centers for children, all paid for by the government.

4. The right and duty for everyone to bear arms, perhaps in the form of a justice-dispensing "people's militia" that would include women.

5. People to be judged only by their peers.

6. Free abortion, sterilization, and contraceptive devices for men and women.

7. Drastic changes in the present family structure, with more emphasis on communal living and men sharing house work equally with women.

8. Both education and art to serve "the people" and assist in teaching revolutionary ideas.

9. All special privileges would be forbidden; there would be no com-

pulsory servitude or domination of one group by another, and people would police and defend themselves.

10. Present political boundaries to be abolished and replaced by an undetermined number of autonomous, continuously evolving, self-governing communities from which political power would flow upward.

11. Evolution of a truly stateless society.

12. Exemption from military service.

The convention was due to reconvene in Washington in late November 1970 to formally draw up the Constitution itself. Confusion in obtaining facilities prevented this, although several thousand delegates appeared. The foregoing list of recommendations for the new document reflects the influences of the various white groups present, but these were approved in the plenary session as part of the Panther program of cooperation with disaffected white groups. Officially, as of this writing, these recommendations constitute the position of the Panthers today. But what do *other* blacks want?

Surveys have revealed that the mass of black people in the United States reject such extremism. On April 6, 1970, *Time* magazine reported the results of a *Time*-Louis Harris poll on black attitudes, based on 1,225 nation-wide responses:

WHOM DO BLACKS RESPECT?

	A Great Deal	Some	Hardly at all
N.A.A.C.P.	75%	18%	3%
S.C.L.C.	73	18	3
Cleveland Mayor Carl Stokes	63	20	5
S.C.L.C. President Rev. Ralph Abernathy	62	27	5
Fayette, Miss., Mayor Charles Evers	61	21	5
N.A.A.C.P. Exec. Dir. Roy Wilkins	55	24	6
National Urban League	54	24	5
Justice Thurgood Marshall	54	17	5
The Rev. Jesse Jackson	51	19	7
U.S. Senator Edward Brooke	49	22	7
N.Y. Rep. Shirley Chisholm	48	15	6
Urban League Dir. Whitney Young	44	24	8
N.Y. Rep. Adam Clayton Powell	43	29	17
CORE	43	28	6
Labor Leader A. Philip Randolph	42	17	6
Boxer Muhammad Ali	33	24	27
Panther Eldridge Cleaver	30	19	23
Militant Stokely Carmichael	26	22	33
THE BLACK PANTHERS	23	18	37
Black Muslim Elijah Muhammad	23	23	26

Negroes in general seem to rate the Panthers low as an agency for change. What do they think about the use of violence as a means of achieving reform? The *Time*-Harris poll reported:

IS VIOLENCE NECESSARY?

	Can Win Rights Without Violence	Violence Probably Necessary
1963	63%	22%
1966*	59	21
1970	58	31
South	64	23
Non-South	50	40
Urban	56	34
Rural	64	23
Age Groups:		
14–21	55	40
22–29	58	31
30–49	55	33
50 and over	65	20
Professionals and managers	53	34
Welfare recipients	58	33
Pro-Panthers	44	51

Again, a substantial percentage of blacks reject the use of violence. How *do* they think they can improve their lot?

HOW WILL BLACKS MAKE REAL PROGRESS?

	Yes	No
Getting more blacks better educated	97%	1%
Through black owned businesses	93	3
Electing blacks to public offices	92	4
Cooperating with helpful whites	83	7
Boycotting whites who discriminate	68	20
Taking to streets in protest	42	41
Supporting militant organizations	41	39

rest not sure

There is unmistakable evidence of black socio-economic progress in recent years, although it is chiefly notable in comparison with former years. But this does not mean that the passions are draining from the struggle.** A *Newsweek* survey (June 30, 1969) of black feelings and opinions showed that over half still preferred to be called "Negro" or "colored," but that more than three-quarters were still striving to enter integrated neighborhoods, where their children could attend integrated

---

*Panthers were founded in 1966.
**The third *Newsweek* (June 30, 1969, pp. 19ff) poll of Black America indicates this.

schools, and over half were opposed to the Vietnam war on grounds that they had less freedom to fight for than did whites.

Has the Panther phenomenon caused moderate Negroes to veer to the radical left? One appraisal of the future is presented by Hilary Ng'weno, a former editor of *The Daily Nation* in Nairobi:

> The irony of the Black Panthers and other militant black groups is that though doomed to fail insofar as their own avowed goals are concerned, they will in the end achieve some of the moderate goals for which less militant civil rights groups have unsuccessfully been fighting during the past decade. They will fail in their own program because . . . they are hopelessly out of touch with political realities in America. (They) continue to behave as if in ignorance of the full capacity for violence which the police possess . . .

> America may be headed for a revolution. But if Kent State, Jackson, and Vice President Agnew's words have any meaning, it will not come from the Left . . . It is safe to assume that the Panthers have now been reduced to two alternative courses: annihilation by police gunfire, jail and enforced exile; or 'respectable' existence devoid of revolutionary pretensions. The former may be heroic, and the latter repugnant; both spell the same fate as far as the Black Panther Party is concerned.

> Nevertheless, the Panthers [have given] the blacks a sense of pride in their own race and heritage . . . that they have not enjoyed for centuries . . . And if it is ironic that the Panthers should perform this service . . . it is tragic that more than a century after Emancipation, America still needs groups such as the Panthers to prod her into granting her black citizens their constitutional rights. ["The Panthers: An African View"]

A less gentle appraisal of the Panthers was provided by Saul Alinsky when he was interviewed by Israel Shenker in connection with the publication of his new book, *Rules for Radicals*:

> When the Panthers began I found myself quite sympathetic. But what's wrong or right about them now is academic. The moment Huey glorified the shooting in Marin County courthouse, they blew it. I think the Panthers are asking for it. They've never been as strong as the press has indicated, and there's a suicidal obsession now.

> A guy has to be a political idiot to say all power comes from the barrel of a gun when the other side has the guns. A lot of their rhetoric has become a bore. You start saying 'whitefascistracistpig' and people turn off. Here's Newton saying he can't get justice in an American court, and all the time he's saying that, he's out on a reversal by a superior court. The Panthers will still get a bubble of publicity, but their days are numbered. ["Organizers Clutch Key to the Future"]

These words may sound like a premature obituary. Surely the Panther organization has an obscure future. But it is a symbol of the burgeoning revolution aptly described by *Ebony* magazine (August 16, 1969):

> The revolution of which we speak is not a violent political revolution aimed at overthrowing the established government. . . . The Black Panthers may seem poles apart from the members of the Urban League or NAACP (but) in their secret heart they share the common blackness which sent them on separate roads toward the same goal . . . "Say it loud, I'm black and I'm proud." . . . The revolution is black engineers, poets, lawyers, artists, inventors, farmers, builders, nurses, philosophers, space travelers, senators, and secretaries and vice presidents and presidents. It is black men finally free to pursue their personal goals secure in the dignity of their manhood.

Some indication of the immediate future of the Panthers may be gained from this quotation by Don McEvoy, editor, *The Hot Line* (July 1971):

> *PANTHER LEADER ANNOUNCES MAJOR POLICY CHANGES:*
> Huey Newton, co-founder of the Black Panther Party, recently announced a major change in tactics for the organization—avoiding confrontation with the police, promoting church attendance, and seeking new support within the black community.

> Speaking to a conference of San Francisco Bay area theological schools, Newton said the party "was very wrong to think that it could change the police forces the way we tried to do it. All we got was war and a lot of bloodshed."

> He also admitted that "we of the Panther Party were arrogant to say 'dump the church.' When we stepped outside the church we defected from the community because the church is the one institution the whole black community is involved in one way or another."

> "We lost the favor of the black community and left them behind," he continued. "Now there has been a change in the make-up of the central committee and a change in thinking. We're going to be going to church and get involved in the church and the black community."

> Newton's mention of a change in the central committee was an apparent reference to the differences between himself and Eldridge Cleaver which have split the party nationally.

> "Our intention to operate within reality does not mean we accept it," Newton declared. "We'll operate within the system so we can change it. It is wrong to say that the system can't give us anything because it is just not true."

> A minister's son, Newton said he hadn't attended church for ten years

until recently, but now he is telling party members to go to services and "experience the church."

Uncle Tom was once the symbol of oppression, but because of his "Yassuh", he has been denigrated to a symbol of fawning compliance, his name anathema to The Movement. Today, instead, we have the symbols of the raised black fist of star athletes who, while they wouldn't join the Panthers, burn just as deeply and fight the fight in their own ways—as do the wearers of dashikis and Afro hair styles. All are symbols. Like the Black Panther phenomenon, they may not prove to be lasting. But they or other symbols will remain until the Great Lie is no longer the rationalization for inequalities in America.

Perhaps Frantz Fanon, the black psychiatrist from Martinique whose brief life was spent in the revolutionary movements of North Africa, said it best. A philosopher of The Movement, his *Black Skin, White Masks* (1952) and *The Wretched of the Earth* (1961) raged at the suppression of the black ethos by colonial Europeans. The message is equally pointed for the post-slavery Negro of America. Fanon called for blacks everywhere to rise again to an awareness of their integrity as a people. Horace Sutton commented:

> He preached the necessity of controlled violence to bring about abrupt change whether it be "national liberation or national renaissance or the restoration of nationhood to the people." He said, "humanity is waiting for something from us other than...an imitation...an obscene caricature...We must try to set afoot a new man." ["Fanon: The Revolutionary as a Prophet"]

Ten years after Fanon's death, blacks everywhere were rediscovering him. The Black Panthers may prove to be a transient phenomenon, but the message of Frantz Fanon will continue to be heard until there is indeed a renaissance of both black and white in attitudes that recognize and accept the dignity of all men.

STUDY 6

A Model for Handling Citizen Complaints

From the citizens' point of view, a problem of municipal bureaucracies is that there is seldom a procedure, in the hierarchy of bureaus, departments, and agencies, through which complaints can be channeled to achieve redress for wrongs suffered from the governmental system. In our time of increasing awareness of ethnicity, when all manner of minority groups are conscious of their rights and potential powers, the pressures for instituting a satisfactory complaint system are multiplying. But the question of how power is to be controlled is an ancient problem of government.

Cries of "police brutality" typify the complaints with which government officials are most familiar. But in researching ways to handle such complaints, students of the problem have become increasingly aware of the fact that police are not the only agency from which citizens feel they need protection: that they need protection as well, from wrongs done by other arms of government. As examples, citizens feel the need for relief from the tax assessor, the zoning board, condemnation authorities, criminal and civil courts, welfare agencies, and others which sometimes inadvertently injure where they are supposed to help. But few of these arms of government have provided adequate means of appeal.

For instance, the police, long confronted with demands for redress procedures, have explored the relative usefulness of internal versus external complaint systems—generally defending the former and resisting the latter. The ombudsman plan, so successful in Sweden and elsewhere, has been held suspect by American police as another external agency threatening the competence and right—they feel—of the police to police themselves. Generally their objections have been based on a paucity of information about how the ombudsman system might operate.

Another aspect of the matter has been the sometimes adversarial nature of the citizen versus the police relationship, apparently inevitable when a claimant demands redress for a wrong suffered at the hands of a particular officer. New York City police felt this adversary aspect when there was brief experimentation a few years ago with a citizen-dominated review board. The feeling was that even though the board received the complaints, processed them and reported findings to the Police Commissioner, the ultimate effect was possible disciplinary action upon an individual officer. There was the feeling, too, that the police department —of all the municipal agencies—was being singled out for discriminatory harassment. So the Policeman's Benevolent Association led police opposition to this board in an expensive referendum that presaged liquidation of the board. The New York City Police Department appeared to have an effective disciplinary system. But in the citizens' view—as with the zoning board or the tax assessor—the agency is either too overwhelming to approach, or results of complaints and investigations—if any—are seldom reported back.

To meet these objections, Walter Gellhorn, professor of law at Columbia University, has been prominent among those who have proposed that municipalities create "an official with authority to examine the entire range of administration," with whom citizens can file complaints from which they would not only be assured a response but also relief, where appropriate ("Police Review Boards: Hoax or Hope"). Equally, if not more important, the adversary relationship between accuser and accused would be obviated, and municipal administration would be given guidance in improving governmental services as a whole.

In our model, let us say that the city of Urbanton is in the process of establishing just such a "Citizens' Appeals Office" to meet its urgent needs. The reasons for this decision require a brief background of information.

The population of Urbanton is 250,000, but its SMSA includes 700,000 people. In 1950, its Negro population was 14 percent of the total; in 1970 it had mounted to 30 percent. But the adjustment problems are worse than even these figures suggest because Urban River, which flows through the city, has been used as a device to confine Negroes in one-third of the city's area—an all black ghetto of de facto segregation. Since the black population is growing (high birthrate and continuing in-migration) twice as fast as the white population, which has twice as much room, tensions have mounted accordingly. There have been three serious disorders in the past 17 months. In addition, there is a relatively minor ethnic problem with the Appalachians (SAMs) in the white sector. While their number is only 10 percent of the total population, their cultural characteristics make them only a little easier to assimilate than the Negroes. (See the foregoing Study 2 on SAMs).

The police department consists of 400 officers plus 60 civilians. It is a closed system in which the chief and ranking officers have been promoted from within. Personnel is 96 percent white, and traditionally Negroes have not been encouraged to apply. Feelings of minority groups in the city are hostile in the extreme. In an effort to establish contacts with the community, a Police-Community Relations unit has been created. In its first year, the unit has developed a number of programs:

1. Created a citizens' advisory group to the PCR unit. This group is broadly representative of the community.

2. Assisted in the formation of a youth patrol in the Negro community to help communicate with minority groups in tension and conflict areas. From the original 14 members, the group now numbers nearly 160. Plans are being prepared to form another youth group in the white area. At a later date, plans call for incorporation of the two groups into a city-wide youth patrol.

3. Instituted a program of school visitation in elementary schools. Officers have made contact with 1900 children and plans are to visit each school in the city and make personal contact with children in the first three grades. This includes involving the beat officers.

4. Prepared open-house brochures and other hand-out materials and arranged for distribution of materials through business and industrial outlets.

5. Attended meetings of civil rights groups, particularly hostile or militant groups, to sound out feelings in the community.

6. Made a pilot showing of a film on morals at one of the larger high schools: 900 girls were in attendance, and the success of this showing will lead to showing it in all other high schools in the city.

The mayor and city manager of Urbanton are aware that the newly created PCR unit is having initial success in making contacts with elements of the community with whom communication has not heretofore existed. They know that the police department has a well-organized internal disciplinary structure and trial board. But these officials are also aware that the city lacks a system through which citizens can file complaints against the police and other departments with assurance that the complaints will be accepted, processed, and acted upon. For this reason, the city commission authorized the city manager to issue the following directive:

TO: All Department Directors and Agency Heads

FROM: Frederick Fredericks, City Manager

SUBJECT: Creation of the Position of Citizens' Appeals Officer

1. CITIZENS' APPEALS OFFICER CREATED

The position of Citizens' Appeals Officer is hereby created and established in the Office of the City Manager. Such Citizens' Appeals Officer shall be a deputy of the City Manager within the meaning of Sec. 95,1,D of the Charter, and in the unclassified service.

2. SALARY

The Citizens' Appeals Officer shall be paid a salary of $18,000 per year.

3. DUTIES

The Citizens' Appeals Officer shall have the following duties, subject to the limitations hereinafter contained:

    a. Receive, record, and evaluate all complaints from any person concerning inefficiency, maladministration, arrogance, abuse, or other failure arising out of the operation of any department, board, agency, or office of the city.

    b. Investigate, in the manner hereinafter provided, any of such complaints as he may deem appropriate.

4. ASSISTANCE OF OTHER DEPARTMENTS

All departments, boards, agencies, or offices of the City responsible to the City Manager shall give assistance and provide such data or other information to the Citizens' Appeals Officer as he may request in the performance of his duties as herein provided.

5. INVESTIGATIONS

The authority of the City Manager to conduct investigations, as provided in Sec. 50 of the Charter, is hereby delegated to the Citizens' Appeals Officer for the purpose of investigating such complaints. The Citizens' Appeals Officer may determine who, in his discretion, may attend any hearing held by him. Any information gained as the result of any investigation, including the identities of any complainants or witnesses, shall be kept confidential by the Citizens' Appeals Officer, except when disclosure is necessary to enable him to carry out his duties and to support his recommendations. Any witnesses appearing at any investigation conducted by the Citizens' Appeals Officer shall be entitled to have counsel present while being examined.

6. POWERS AND DUTIES AFTER INVESTIGATIONS

The objective of the Citizens' Appeals Officer in making any investigation shall be to determine whether the act complained of was any of the following, taking into consideration only the facts and circumstances existing at the time the act complained of was taken, and in no way considering any fact or circumstance occurring thereafter:

    a. Contrary to law.

    b. Unreasonable, unjust, oppressive, or discriminatory.

    c. Was taken in accordance with a rule, regulation, or standing operating procedure of the City that is unreasonable, unjust, oppressive or discriminatory.

    d. Based wholly or partially on a mistake of law or fact.

    e. An arbitrary use of discretionary power.

The Citizens' Appeals Officer shall report the findings of his investigations to the City Manager together with his recommendation as to whether the act complained of should be affirmed, reversed, or modified, together with any recommendations he may make as to the manner in which his findings should be implemented.

7. STUDIES, INQUIRIES, SURVEYS, ETC.

The Citizens' Appeals Officer may, with the approval of the City Manager, undertake any studies, inquiries, surveys, or analyses concerning any department, board, agency, or office of the City which he may deem appropriate, and may, with the approval of the City Manager, cooperate with any public or private agencies including educational, civic, or research organizations, colleges, universities, institutions, or foundations in conducting any study, inquiry, survey, or analysis.

8. REPORTS

The Citizens' Appeals Officer shall make a report of all investigations, studies, inquiries, surveys, or analyses to the City Manager. The Citizens' Appeals Officer, shall, with the approval of the City Manager, report any relevant information in his possession, which, in his opinion, relates to the commission of a crime, to the appropriate authority charged with the prosecution thereof, including malicious complaints.

9. LIMITATIONS

The Citizens' Appeals Officer shall *not* have authority to do any of the following:

   a. Impose any penalty upon any individual officer or employee of the City, other than the authority to render findings as hereinbefore provided.
   b. Investigate any complaint until it has been submitted to the director of the department or head of the board, agency, or office involved, except that, in any case where there is reason to believe such referral would result in harassment of the complainant, the Citizens' Appeals Officer may, with the approval of the City Manager, investigate such complaint as hereinbefore provided.
   c. To investigate any practice or policy which has not resulted in a complaint from a citizen.

Frederick Fredericks
City Manager

The above directive was formally approved by the Commission of the city of Urbanton and the program is now operative, financed initially by a grant from the Federal Office of Economic Opportunity.

Discussion

In recent years, there has been widespread consideration of the merits and demerits of various systems for handling citizen complaints at the level of municipal government. The Urbanton model outlined above has both strengths and weaknesses. The intention in presenting it here is to provide a basis for discussion of various alternatives. Questions that might be raised include:

1. The model is essentially an ombudsman plan, so successful in Scandinavia. Are American metropolitan situations such that the plan can(not) be effective here?

2. Does the model provide realistic procedures for achieving satisfaction in complaints concerning the mayor, the members of the city commission, or the city manager himself?

3. Should the Appeals Officer be appointed by, and be responsible to, the city manager? the commission? the governor? or whom?

4. Does the model provide adequately for handling complaints by:
   a. policeman vs. policeman, or vs. his superiors?
   b. policeman vs. the police department?
   c. citizen vs. a specific policeman?
   d. citizen vs. the police department as a whole?

5. Would a board of three Appeals Officers, of heterogeneous background, be more effective? Why, or why not?

6. How (and why) would the procedures described in the model be viewed by:
   a. a patrolman?
   b. a black citizen?
   c. a SAM?
   d. the county prosecutor?
   e. the tax assessor?
   f. the welfare agencies?
   g. the courts?

7. If you were a graduate student in a university and wished to evaluate the Urbanton model for a master's thesis, what would be the main features of your research design?

Part Four

Special Considerations

Four distinct aspects of community relationships that have direct and indirect impact on the police are:

1. Tensions that develop between police, prosecutors, and the courts.

2. Role confusion that arises from community expectations (or lack of them) regarding the corrections system.

3. Tensions between the police and the media.

4. The power struggle between police and political forces in the community.

Studies 1 and 2 here examine the paradoxes in the police role in relation to the juvenile justice system and misdemeanant probation practices. Recent progress has been shown especially in the latter field. Study 3 looks at police and the press. Study 4, on Blue Power, suggests the growing ability of the police to resist political pressures from both government and the community.

Study 5, an assessment of Attica, not only serves to show the current confused thinking of the nation as to remedies, but also brings into focus the interrelatedness of the police, prosecutors, courts, corrections, the media, and the community itself. All of these have an enormous stake in how we are to define "offenders" and how we are to handle them.

Juvenile Justice: System or Nonsystem?

The focus of this text is on relationships: police-community relationships, police–minority-group relationships, and police-youth relationships, and others within the criminal justice system. The relationships between the police and youth will be best understood by studying concrete situations rather than abstract concepts. For example, to underscore the importance of relationships within the system, and between the system and the public, we will consider the handling of juvenile offenders in the reasonably typical state of Michigan.

The study material describes how this system is *supposed* to function at present in Michigan, from the time the policeman comes in contact with the juvenile until, in some cases, the court takes over. The study is organized by the stages of the process:

1. The juvenile problem today.

2. Procedures of the police in apprehension and referral.

3. Procedures of the juvenile courts.

4. Effects of recent court decisions.

The criminal justice system is concerned with two aspects of the welfare of minors: (1) juvenile delinquency, and (2) child abuse and neglect. Although the problems of juveniles are not new, today's problems are increasingly serious. Because you can find extensive descriptions and analyses on this subject in the library,* this study will not duplicate the research efforts of others. Instead, it will show you how the "system," which society has created to handle juveniles, actually works.

The Juvenile Problem Today

"Our youth . . . have bad manners, contempt for authority; they show disrespect for their elders, and love to chatter in place of exercise.

---

*See Edward Eldefonso, *Law Enforcement and the Youthful Offender;* also Donald H. Bouma, *Kids and Cops.*

They no longer rise when their parents enter the room. They contradict their parents, chatter before company, gobble up their food, and tyrannize their teachers" (Ralph T. Hartell, *Reader's Digest Almanac—*1971, p. 634).

A Victorian complaint? No, it was Socrates speaking more than two thousand years ago. A more recent complaint also gives one a sense of *déjà vu* on an old problem: "One of the juvenile gangs was described as 'Eight young rascals' who had terrorized the city's streets and 'stolen and cut off people's purses.' Another group of young troublemakers included five boys, all between the ages of seven and eleven, who could not be controlled without force even inside the walls of the city jail."

This account did not come from the current press. It is part of a study of the urban ills of Nuremburg, Germany, in the late 1700s, made by Dr. Albert G. Hess of the National Council on Crime and Delinquency during his preparation of *The American Juvenile Court—A Handbook*. According to a review of the study, Dr. Hess is "suspicious" of FBI and other statistics that show "an alarming national increase in juvenile crime in recent years." He says that figures on juvenile crime have been collected only in the last decade; that methods of reporting are improving, and that many "offenses" of children, such as smoking, truancy, and loitering in pool halls, would not be considered violations if committed by adults. Youth rebellion has always been a problem. It may be that the publicity arising from the special systems of courts set up to handle the problems of juveniles adds to the impression that the present generation is a particularly delinquent one.

While it is true that the great majority of children become responsible adults without committing more than the normal childish pranks, it is also true that an alarming proportion of children come before the social agencies and the criminal justice system. Whatever one's appraisal of the FBI crime reports may be, official figures for 1969* showed that:

1. Almost 25% of all persons arrested for any major crime were under 15 years old.

2. Of these, 75% were boys; but the rate for girls is rising at the same rate.

3. Delinquencies in the suburbs are rising at an increasing rate.

4. 49% of all persons charged with a major crime in 1968 were juveniles.

5. The number of juveniles arrested for all offenses (except traffic violations) has doubled since 1960, while the number of adults arrested has increased by only 4%.

---

*James E. Clayton, the Washington *Post,* quoted in Lansing, Mich. *State Journal,* September 4, 1969.

A later study by the FBI (Ralph Hartell, p. 881) shows that arrests of juveniles for violent crimes were 148 percent higher in 1969 than in 1960; and that arrests in those under 18 for property crimes went up 85 percent.

Table 4–1 gives a further idea of the incidence of delinquency. These Delinquency Statistics come from the Probate (juvenile) Court of Ingham County, Michigan (population about 140,000).

In Table 4–2, you will see statistics about child abuse and neglect. Even though all 50 states have legislation in this matter, more than 9,000 such cases were reported in 1967 alone, according to the director of the children's division of the American Humane Association (Lansing *State Journal,* August 22, 1968). And he points out that it will be a long time before our local communities have developed adequate social-police relationships to implement the laws. "We have developed better procedures for protecting animals than for children." The increasing abuse or neglect of children ranges from allowing diaper rash (deliberate neglect) to striking malicious blows with the fist, and homicide, for which sanctions too often remain unimposed for want of adequate agencies, personnel, and courts. The enormous scope of the problem remains beyond the combined efforts of social agencies, volunteers, and the courts to cope with it.

And somewhere between the cases of deliberate juvenile offenders and the cases of neglect and abuse of juveniles are the runaways (Table 4–3). In one recent year a half million youngsters left home. You will see, by looking at Table 4–3, that an issue of *Look* magazine (July 25, 1967) featured a story on "Jimmy the Cop" who was assigned to some juvenile hangouts in Greenwich Village. He said, "Many are here in unwashed defiance of their parents' demands for good marks and proper conduct. They share food, shelter, mattresses and experiences in drugs with friends whose names they don't even know. They try to prove that it's love, not money, that makes the good life."

Police Procedures in Apprehension and Referral

There is no universal system for police procedures in handling juveniles. In a sense there cannot be, because of the varieties of situations from one jurisdiction to another, and because every child is different, and is different at different times, as are the officers in their reactions to them. Like the old song, "You never can tell about a woman/ That's why they're all so nice:/ You never see two alike at any one time/ And you never see one alike twice." The very essence of juvenile apprehension-adjudication-treatment is, to a certain degree, subjective. In that degree, it cannot be systematic. On the other hand, there must be minimal systemic, basic procedures to protect the rights of the child be he offender or offended. Concern for these rights is currently, as we shall see, the primary interest reflected in recent court decisions.

Table 4–1
Delinquency Statistics*
Ingham County, Michigan, Probate/Juvenile Court 1970

	Jan.	Feb.	Mar.	Apr.	May	June	July	Aug.	Sept.	Oct.	Nov.	Dec.	Total	Average
(1) New children petitioned into court, jurisdiction accepted, and processed for further court action	44	29	45	56	34	24	24	29	24	35	31	29	404	33.7
(2) New children petitioned into court, jurisdiction accepted, but matter resolved at intake level	11	9	24	23	17	16	29	15	6	17	31	26	224	18.6
(3) Children petitioned into court, jurisdiction transferred to county of residence	2	7	10	5	13	9	4	0	0	2	7	3	62	5.2
(4) Children petitioned into court, jurisdiction denied	10	0	3	6	2	0	5	3	4	1	3	1	38	3.2
(5) Children petitioned into court, jurisdiction accepted and transferred to S.D.S.S.**	1	2	1	5	3	5	3	1	3	2	4	2	32	2.7
(6) Children under official jurisdiction petitioned for rehearings	18	19	22	45	25	29	20	28	25	25	18	9	283	23.6

*From the *Annual Report*, Ingham County, Michigan, Probate Court, Juvenile Division.

**State Department of Social Services.

Table 4-1 (Continued)

	Jan.	Feb.	Mar.	Apr.	May	June	July	Aug.	Sept.	Oct.	Nov.	Dec.	Total	Average
(7) Supplemental offenses	22	26	19	31	22	23	21	12	10	22	16	9	233	19.4
(8) Rehearing and supplemental petitions contested	0	11	3	6	3	3	6	6	2	8	11	14	71	5.9
(9) New petitions contested	5	2	3	6	2	5	6	10	12	3	10	10	74	6.2
(10) Children dismissed from court jurisdiction returned for new offense	6	5	7	4	4	1	4	6	7	6	0	7	57	4.75
(11) Children under formal court jurisdiction	538	557	545	578	575	509	475	474	450	448	465	458	6,072	506
(12) Boys under formal court jurisdiction	354	365	364	389	386	332	308	315	312	309	321	326	4,081	340
(13) Girls under formal court jurisdiction	184	192	181	189	189	177	167	159	138	139	144	132	1,991	166
(14) Dismissals of children from official court supervision	22	6	58	26	40	86	56	30	48	34	14	36	456	38
(15) Children committed to boys training school													11	.92
(16) Children committed to girls training school													2	.16

Table 4–1 (Continued)

	Jan.	Feb.	Mar.	Apr.	May	June	July	Aug.	Sept.	Oct.	Nov.	Dec.	Total	Average
(17) Children waived to adult criminal court	0	0	0	0	0	0	1	0	0	0	2	0	3	.25
(18) Children placed in private group or institutional care	3	5	4	3	1	5	4	8	9	5	7	2	56	4.7
(19) Children placed in foster homes	2	2	4	4	3	3	10	7	1	1	3	0	40	3.3
(20) Children placed on probation in own home	35	13	34	14	24	21	17	12	3	28	16	19	239	19.9
(21) Children detained in jail	1	0	2	1	2	2	4	1	3	1	1	2	20	1.7
(22) Number of children detained in juvenile home (Ingham County children)	57	69	78	64	86	66	60	48	71	75	74	59	807	67.2
(23) Total days care	375	411	476	416	510	465	354	264	497	507	497	407	5,179	431.5
(24) Children processed for formal court action with no prior offenses	35	25	36	51	28	19	17	29	34	33	34	19	360	30
(25) Children processed for formal court action with one previous offense	19	13	10	15	8	15	9	2	7	14	5	11	128	10.6

Table 4–1 (Continued)

	Jan.	Feb.	Mar.	Apr.	May	June	July	Aug.	Sept.	Oct.	Nov.	Dec.	Total	Average
(26) Children processed for formal court action with two previous offenses	5	7	12	13	10	14	9	20	10	6	8	4	118	9.8
(27) Children with three previous offenses	5	9	12	11	10	8	5	15	4	8	7	4	98	8.2
(28) Children with four or more previous offenses	3	11	6	23	21	9	8	0	7	18	9	10	125	10.4

Table 4–2
Neglect Statistics*
Ingham County, Michigan, Probate/Juvenile Court 1970

	Jan.	Feb.	Mar.	Apr.	May	June	July	Aug.	Sept.	Oct.	Nov.	Dec.	Total	Average
(1) Number of cases active at end of month	194	195	190	176	184	190	177	173	173	168	170	159	2,149	179.8
(2) Total children	342	333	344	326	334	342	325	313	310	299	302	290	3,860	321.6
(3) Boys	181	175	178	169	170	183	175	167	167	160	163	160	2,048	170.7
(4) Girls	161	158	166	157	164	159	150	146	143	139	139	130	1,812	151
(5) New cases	6	7	8	0	11	12	2	4	6	8	8	5	77	6.4
(6) Total children	17	10	26	0	12	23	2	4	8	13	15	5	135	11.2
(7) Boys	5	3	14	0	3	18	2	3	6	7	8	4	73	6.1
(8) Girls	12	7	12	0	9	5	0	1	2	6	7	1	62	5.2
(9) Cases Dismissed from court	7	6	13	14	3	6	15	8	6	13	6	16	113	9.4
(10) Number of children**	7	19	15	18	4	15	19	16	11	24	12	17	177	14.7
(11) Permanent Wardship cases	75	74	74	70	68	68	68	68	68	71	71	70	845	70.4
(12) Number of children**	107	104	98	92	92	92	92	92	92	95	95	89	1,140	95

*From the *Annual Report*, Ingham County, Michigan, Probate Court, Juvenile Division.
**More than one child per case or family.

Table 4-2 (Continued)

	Jan.	Feb.	Mar.	Apr.	May	June	July	Aug.	Sept.	Oct.	Nov.	Dec.	Total	Average
(13) Children made permanent wards	5	2	0	0	0	1	0	0	3	0	3	0	14	1.2
(14) Children supervised in own home	84	87	122	95	97	89	91	78	79	76	80	81	1,059	88.2
(15) Children supervised in relatives home	31	28	30	29	30	29	29	29	32	36	35	35	373	31.1
(16) Children supervised in private agency	58	55	39	48	45	63	55	46	59	48	47	45	608	50.7
(17) Children supervised in foster home	169	163	153	154	162	161	150	149	140	139	140	129	1,809	150.7
(18) Adoptions in progress	404	414	429	431	445	462	425	428	444	454	445	445	5,226	435.5
(19) Adoptions filed	20	32	34	29	33	22	21	39	42	24	18	25	339	28.2
(20) Adoptions confirmed	6	16	31	15	13	56	17	22	31	29	18	16	270	22.5

Table 4–3
1970 Referrals to Ingham County Juvenile Court
for Delinquency Offenses

The following section is an analysis of the nature and number of delinquent offenses brought to the attention of Juvenile Court in 1970.* An analysis of the 1969 statistics shows an increase in 1970 of 170, from 1,142 to 1,312 petitions presented to Juvenile Court.

Offenses	Petitions Presented to Juvenile Court	Petitions Accepted and Processed for Further Court Action	Petitions Accepted but Resolved at Intake Level	Boys	Girls
Runaway	448	345	93	171	267
School Truancy	132	88	39	71	56
Incorrigibility	62	53	7	37	23
Malicious Destruction	26	19	5	23	1
Vandalism	1	0	1	1	0
Disorderly	6	4	2	6	0
Trespassing	1	0	1	1	0
School Law Violation	2	2	0	2	0
Defacing School Property	1	1	0	0	1
Traffic	4	4	0	4	0
Violation of Probation	21	18	3	13	8
Curfew	24	9	11	17	3
Minor in Possession	12	4	6	9	1
Drunk & Disorderly	1	0	0	0	0
Intoxicated	4	3	1	3	1
Loitering	1	0	1	1	0
Begging	1	0	1	0	1
Larceny	128	52	69	84	37
Larceny from Building	19	9	10	12	7
Simple Larceny	9	1	8	8	1
Attempted Larceny	6	4	2	4	2
U.D.A.A.**	58	36	19	55	0
Attempted U.D.A.A.	1	0	1	1	0
Joy Riding	6	4	2	6	0
Breaking & Entering	155	106	45	149	2
Attempted Breaking & Entering	6	6	0	6	0
Entering w/o Permission	14	4	5	9	0
Possession of Stolen Property	5	3	2	4	1

*From the *Annual Report,* Ingham County, Michigan, Probate Court, Juvenile Division.

**Unauthorized driving away of automobile.

Table 4–3 (Continued)

Offenses	Petitions Presented to Juvenile Court	Petitions Accepted and Processed for Further Court Action	Petitions Accepted but Resolved at Intake Level	Boys	Girls
Receiving Stolen Property	3	2	0	2	0
Uttering & Publishing	3	3	0	3	0
Forgery	5	4	1	5	0
Carrying a Concealed Weapon	5	3	2	4	1
Possession of Firearms	1	0	1	1	0
False Report of Crime	1	1	0	1	0
Bomb Threat	4	2	2	2	2
Terror Phone Call	1	1	0	1	0
Glue Sniffing	15	4	9	12	1
Sale of Narcotics	1	1	0	1	0
Sale of Marijuana	1	1	0	1	0
Unlawful Use of Narcotics	3	2	1	2	1
Possession of Drugs	7	4	3	6	1
Possession of Marijuana	18	12	6	10	8
Indecent Exposure	4	1	2	3	0
Attempted Suicide	2	2	0	0	2
Attempted Statutory Rape	1	1	0	1	0
Forcible Rape	1	1	0	1	0
Abduction	1	1	0	1	0
Assault & Battery	28	19	8	20	7
Assault	21	11	10	19	2
Extortion	7	5	2	2	5
Felonious Assault	2	2	0	2	0
Aggravated Assault	1	1	0	1	0
Assault w/Dangerous Weapon	7	7	0	7	0
Assault w/Intent to Rob	2	1	1	2	0
Armed Robbery	2	2	0	2	0
Attempted Armed Robbery	1	1	0	1	0
Unarmed Robbery	5	4	1	4	1
Attempted Unarmed Robbery	3	3	0	0	3
Arson	2	2	0	2	0
TOTALS	1,312	879	383	816	446

Whatever the available facilities for handling juveniles in a given county—special courts, public or private care centers, available legal services—the police are the first arm of the system to be confronted with protecting children from abuse, and protecting the community from errant children. Parents, school officials, the clergy or other complainants may, and often do, take juveniles directly to court. But the greatest number of cases have their initial contacts with the police. In increasing numbers, therefore, cities of significant size are assigning special officers and creating youth bureaus for work with juveniles. In increasing numbers, too, women officers are being detailed to work with girls under 14, and with their families. Ideally, juvenile officers have special educational backgrounds in sociology and psychology or should be subsidized to get such training. Their attitudes toward children have been found to be different from those of the community. William P. Lentz made a study:

> Analysis of data [indicates] that police officers differ from the general public in their attitudes as to how delinquents should be handled. They are less ambivalent and more consistent in their views, and do *not* believe that a strictly legalistic approach should be used. Nor do they want to abrogate their role and have psychologists, psychiatrists and similar experts handle matters . . . The police are more likely to hold views on handling delinquents which are different from those of the older generation and more like those of young adults who are . . . participating in the social and religious affairs of the community. ["Police and Reference Group Attitudes," pp. 27f.]

Ideally, the aim of the juvenile justice system is to get the juvenile back into the community as a functioning member. This can be done at any stage of the process. The police have a significant role in screening children into or out of the system. As Fig. 4–1 shows, they have the most discretion in deciding what to do with a juvenile as the first members of the system to come in contact with him, and they therefore have a great influence on his perceptions of it.

Policewomen, rather than policemen, are assigned to deal with cases of neglect and runaway girls for whom stealing is a common offense of necessity when the girls are on their own. The police try to handle most cases locally, and on an informal level. Only in serious cases is their discretion limited, as in armed robbery or homicide, which would, of course, be crimes if committed by an adult. Such violations must be taken to court. In Ingham County (Michigan), only about 10 percent of juvenile cases are classified as serious. In the remaining percent, the characteristics of the child form the basis for the officer's decision on handling and, in the subjective nature of their work, their decision can be wrong.

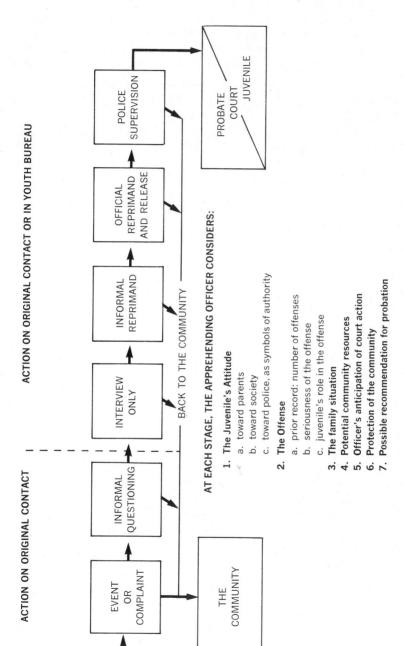

ACTION ON ORIGINAL CONTACT

ACTION ON ORIGINAL CONTACT OR IN YOUTH BUREAU

EVENT OR COMPLAINT

INFORMAL QUESTIONING

INTERVIEW ONLY

INFORMAL REPRIMAND

OFFICIAL REPRIMAND AND RELEASE

POLICE SUPERVISION

PROBATE COURT / JUVENILE

THE COMMUNITY

BACK TO THE COMMUNITY

AT EACH STAGE, THE APPREHENDING OFFICER CONSIDERS:

1. **The Juvenile's Attitude**
   a. toward parents
   b. toward society
   c. toward police, as symbols of authority

2. **The Offense**
   a. prior record: number of offenses
   b. seriousness of the offense
   c. juvenile's role in the offense

3. **The family situation**
4. **Potential community resources**
5. **Officer's anticipation of court action**
6. **Protection of the community**
7. **Possible recommendation for probation**

Figure 4–1.   Decision points in police handling juveniles

In making their judgments of younger juveniles, the policewomen take into account first, the child's attitude toward her parents, society, and the police as symbols of authority. "How does she react toward me?" If the child "gets smart," she'll probably be retained; if sincerely polite (many experienced offenders can pretend remorse), she will probably be released with a reprimand, even if the offense was fairly serious. The officer is alert for emotional problems, signs of contrition, or rebellious attitudes.

Other factors the apprehending officer considers include the number and nature of prior offenses; whether the child is a leader or a follower; the child's home situation; the nature of the available community resources that might prove helpful to the child; whether the child constitutes a threat to the community, and whether it would be helpful or harmful if the case were taken to court. In effect, the officer makes a "social evaluation" of the case, which will be the basis of his or her report (if any) to the Youth Bureau.

As Fig. 4–1 suggests, if the officer takes the case to the Youth Bureau, the officers there have the same discretionary alternatives in disposition as does the original apprehending officer. At any stage of the investigation, they may refer the child back to the parents if this seems appropriate. Referral to the Bureau simply means that more persons will give consideration to the case if the initial contact officer has doubts about it. In addition, the Youth Bureau may refer the child directly to a social agency or volunteer probation officers, rather than take the case on to the juvenile court. It is a function of the Bureau to be familiar with, and have viable contacts with, such agencies as social services, public health, school counselors, special and vocational schools, pregnancy counselors, the Y's boy's clubs, family services, Big Brothers or Sisters, and others that may exist in the community. The presence of these resources influences dispositions, even by the juvenile court itself. A child certainly cannot make an adjustment to the community if he is confined in an institution.

The Youth Bureau has learned that a child with problems frequently comes from a home with problems The Bureau must listen to the child and be prepared, through referrals, to help the whole family if need be. The procedure is to bring in both parents, if possible, and talk with them with the child present, then with the child separately, since he may be afraid to talk before the parents. Some parents may say, "Keep the kid and teach him a lesson!" Others don't know where their children spend their time. "Going to night school?" "Where?" "Studying what?" Other parents are resentful of police interference, believing the child could do no wrong. Mature parents respect the police and try to help.

The Youth Bureau must keep accurate records of all juvenile offenses, partly as a protection against subsequent parental complaints. Parents frequently lie to protect themselves or the child. Public attitudes toward the police vary from "They are not doing enough; get those brats off the street," to "The best place for kids is in the home," which, in many cases, it is not. But the well-trained and motivated officer—particularly policewomen—can create optimum relations with possible offenders. One, who lived in the neighborhood of her beat, reported, "I can be in my levis and sweatshirt, and the kids will come over to talk, bringing their friends. They exclaim, 'Hey, she's a cop,' and they help her find runaways. They seem to feel that this adult doesn't behave like others. 'Maybe she's telling the truth.' "

Her role? "A good police officer can't be a good probation officer too. Let the professionals work on their emotions; we'll work on crime." The job, she feels, is to open communications with families and to help make referrals. But this businesslike attitude is not typical, and is belied by her admission that many juvenile officers set up informal probation schedules in which first offenders are required to report to them personally, with the implied penalty of being processed through the juvenile justice system if they don't. This type of relationship has proved effective with the under-14 age group. But the male members of the Youth Bureau, and the line officers whom they try to help train in handling juveniles, get the worst offenders: recidivists, and those who have committed more serious offenses. If the Bureau feels that it cannot make semi-formal dispositions of such cases, they must refer them to the juvenile court, with which they file a petition.

Thus, the apprehension phase of the juvenile system is highly personalized because it relies on the authorized discretionary powers of the officers. Since most cases are not serious, the police of the original contact are motivated to get the child back into the home and community. If they have doubts, the child is referred to the Youth Bureau which, after further consideration, can also refer the child to the home. The child's experience will have been more impressive, however, because of her experience with the Youth Bureau. But if the Bureau feels that the gravity of the offense necessitates it, the case can be petitioned into juvenile court.

Procedures of the Juvenile Court

As suggested, flexibility in police handling of juveniles is appropriate to the individualistic nature of their contacts. At the court stage of juvenile procedures, however, system is essential to the protection of the child's rights. Unfortunately, no such basic system exists among the juvenile courts of the United States. In *You and the Law**, the chart depicting the varieties of court procedures and requirements takes eight pages to show the different practices in the 50 states in such matters as:

---

*Reader's Digest Association, Pleasantville, N.Y., 1971, p. 432 ff.

1. What court has jurisdiction in juvenile cases?

2. Where may appeals be heard? [e.g., from "no provision" to "directly to the Supreme Court of the state"]

3. Until what age does the court have jurisdiction?

4. Are there provisions for foster homes, institutions?

5. Are fines and restitution used as punishment?

The result of such variations in the protection of children's rights is that in many states the child is actually imperiled. One entirely urban county in Michigan, for example, has only one juvenile judge. Even with the assistance of 14 referees, he can hardly do more than sign their recommendations for dispositions. Here, indeed, is nonsystem where at least basic protections should be a national standard.

> Common law, and the statutes of most states, say that an infant under the age of seven has no criminal capacity . . . and that there is a presumption against criminal capacity of the infant between the ages of seven and fourteen, though the presumption may be proved wrong or rebutted . . . For example, in many states a six-year-old who steals candy from a store may not be charged with the crime of theft . . . even if he is uncommonly bright and knows he has done something wrong . . . His lawyer need only establish that he was under seven. . . . The Congress and the several states have established procedures, although very different ones, for the special treatment of juvenile delinquents.

> The philosophy behind all these statutes is the same: the young offender should not be regarded as a criminal and put behind bars either as a penalty or as a means of protecting society. He should, instead, be regarded as needing protection (from himself) and rehabilitation. Also, to help him get back on his feet and live a normal life, the legal proceedings that follow [his apprehension] should not be made public, and his name should not be revealed. [Ibid., p. 159]

Origins of Juvenile Courts

According to the President's 1966 Crime Commission *Task Force Report on Juvenile Delinquency* (pp. 1–5), some authorities trace the origins of today's juvenile courts to the chancery courts of Feudal England, which oversaw children's property rights and served as *parens patriae* for neglected minors in the name of the king. Others say children's courts are special statutory creations of the American system of jurisprudence. During the great immigrations of the 19th century, concern for children's exposure to tobacco, alcohol, pornography, and street life caused philanthropic organizations to press for separate institutions for children (separate courts in particular) and a new philosophy for handling them. In 1825, New York City's House of Refuge was established to separate young from adult offenders. In 1847, Massachusetts created its first state reform and industrial school and initiated probation as a substitute for punishment in 1880. In the light of the Supreme Court's decision *in re Gault* (1967), which seems to require that juveniles be tried with full adult rights, Massachusetts, interestingly, provided, in 1869, for the presence in court of an agent of the state in cases where a child might be committed to a state reformatory. This agent was also charged with finding foster homes in suitable instances and paying his charges frequent visits.

New York instituted separate trials and records for juveniles in 1892. Rhode Island (1898) started segregating children under 16 while awaiting trial. The concept of the delinquent as a wayward child was established by the Illinois legislature in 1899 with the creation of the first state-wide court especially for children. Hearings were to be informal and private, records kept confidential, and a probation staff appointed. A new vocabulary symbolized the new order: *petition* instead of complaint, *apprehension* instead of arrest, *summons* instead of warrant, *initial hearing* instead of arraignment, *adjudication* instead of conviction, and *disposition* instead of sentence.

Today, there is a juvenile court in every American jurisdiction, with approximately 2,700 courts hearing children's cases, although mere passage of a statute does not automatically establish a tribunal of the sort the reformers had contemplated. In fact, more children's courts than not are staffed by judges and other personnel who spend much of their time on criminal, civil and other nonjuvenile matters. The structure of the juvenile court and its position or status in the jurisprudence system varies widely from state to state. Figure 4–2 shows it to be a division of the probate court in Michigan, and that it ranks low in the hierarchy of courts under the revised Constitution of 1963.

The fact that juvenile courts rank low in the system is doubtless inevitable. Like the police, they must be readily available to their clientele: children are everywhere, and must have ready access to legal relief. But the low rank of children's courts has its disadvantages. They do not attract ambitious young lawyers or social workers. The salary as well as the status is low, and there is often little prospect for working one's way upward in the legal and social work professions. The juvenile court is seen as a dead end. It is typical that its male employees are recent graduates with no experience, who desert the court as soon as possible.

This staffing problem is unfortunate since the need for juvenile courts is so great: preferably separate courts with full-time trained lawyers presiding as judges (not the case in many states), and trained probationary staffs. As far back as 1951, "a million children had contact with police due to delinquencies. About 250,000 of these were

SUPREME COURT (7 justices)
1—Reviews cases from appeals court
2—Does not conduct trials
3—All 7 members rule on each case
4—Chief justice elected by the court
5—Supervises all state courts
    through its appointed administrator

COURT OF APPEALS (9 judges)
1—Reviews cases from circuit courts
2—Does not conduct trials
3—Functions through subdivisions
    of 3 judges each
4—Number of judges may be increased by law

CIRCUIT COURTS (variable number)*
1—Appellate jurisdiction from
    inferior courts
2—Handles major misdemeanors
    (2 years and/or $2,000)
3—May use a 12-man jury
4—Handles all felonies

DISTRICT COURTS*
1—Handles minor misdemeanors**
    (90 days and/or $100)
2—May use a six-man jury
3—Handles examinations for circuit
    courts (reasonable grounds, etc.)
4—Sets bonds

STATUTORY COURTS
(Limited jurisdiction)

PROBATE COURT*
1—**Handles juvenile cases up to 17**
2—Up to 19 under wayward minor law
3—Handles estates, wills, commitments
4—Can order restitution up to $1,500

OTHER STATUTORY COURTS include municipal, police, traffic, etc.,
    as created by law; all having limited jurisdiction.

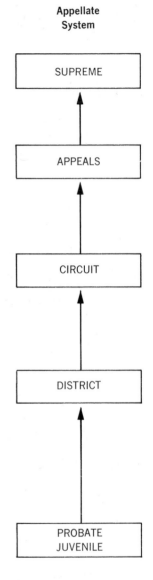

Appellate
System

*Based on county lines and population
**May also handle high misdemeanors in waivers from juvenile court

Figure 4—2.   The Michigan Court System

handled by juvenile courts. An additional 100,000 were *taken* to the courts by parents, teachers and others. Half of the cases were dismissed. About 95,000 were placed back in their own homes under the supervision of probation officers, and 30,000 were committed to institutions ("Juvenile Delinquency," *Encyclopedia Britannica,* vol. 13, p. 229.)

The Process

The need is recognized, but the jurisdiction and patterns of organization are not the same throughout the country.

> In some states juvenile courts have exclusive jurisdiction over all offenses committed by juveniles. In others, over all offenses except those which, if committed by an adult, would be punishable by death or life imprisonment. In the latter, he must be tried in a criminal court. . . . One major exception is the area of traffic violations where, in many states, a minor with a driver's license may be tried in traffic court or before a magistrate, and be fined, or have his license suspended or revoked exactly like an adult. [*You and the Law, pp.* 159, 385]

The Ingham County Probate Court was one of five selected by the Department of Health, Education and Welfare as a model because of its emphasis on community participation, its use of volunteers, and its large number of cooperating agencies; and because of the presence of a long-established state Boy's Training School.* The court also avails itself of many couples who serve as foster parents, by taking newly apprehended children into their homes pending their court hearings and dispositions. The current judge, in office for eight years to date, is committed to the philosophy of developing services and treatment at the community level. He is educating the public to realize that merely placing a child on probation is not going to reform him overnight; and has developed guidelines for the procedures to be followed from intake to final disposition shown in Fig. 4–3. The system aims at returning the child to his parents and the community at the earliest possible stage of the process consistent with the good of all concerned, as in the case of a child's apprehension by the police (Fig. 4–1).

The effort for early release recognizes that a child is more susceptible to being apprehended and charged than is an adult. He may be picked up, for example, for truancy, smoking, running away, incorrigibility or for associating with companions that might endanger his morals. Clearly, such "offenses" are beyond the concern of criminal justice, but the *parens patriae* function on behalf of the child is needed where the home has failed.

Programs Department

In Michigan, this function is supported and enriched by the facilities of the Programs Department (see Fig. 4–4) that have been

---

*Now supplanted by a system of training centers and camps.

Possible Dispositions

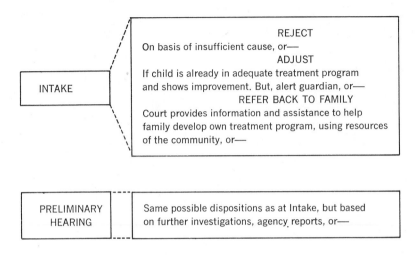

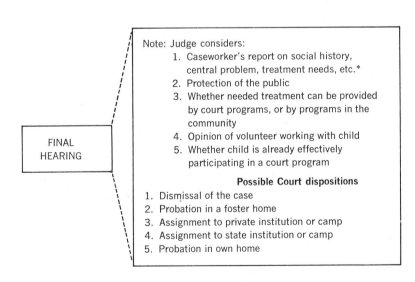

Compare this chart with Table 4–1.

*Caseworker is responsible for providing services to treat and rehabilitate child and family through: (1) psychiatric services, (2) community social agency, (3) court program, (4) observance of probation rules.

Figure 4–3.   Guidelines of procedures of Ingham County
Probate Court Juvenile Division*

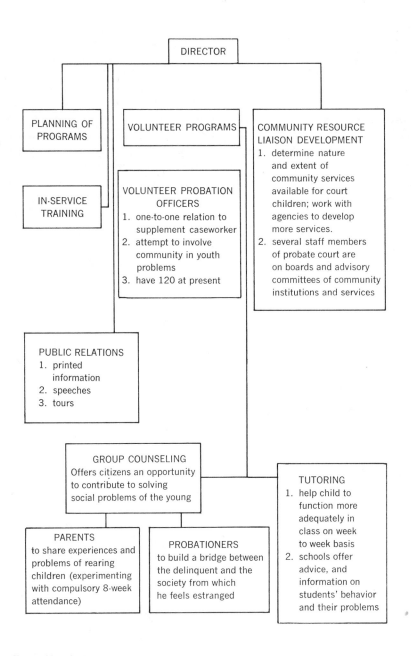

For a description of the use of volunteers in the rehabilitation of young adults (17 years and over) see the discussion of the Royal Oak (Mich.) municipal court program, established by Keith J. Leenhouts, in Study 2, Part Four.

Figure 4–4.　Ingham County Probate Court Programs Department

developed by Ingham County. It was, in part, this complementary dimension of the juvenile court that elicited the praise of HEW, as mentioned above.

As the diagram in Fig. 4–4 makes clear, the chief features of the program are the continuing effort to educate the public and to improve the understanding and cooperation of the public in the treatment of juveniles; and the extensive use of volunteers as foster parents, counselors and informal probation officers. The presence in the community of Michigan State University makes possible the use of volunteer college students in an extensive tutoring program for children who are having trouble in school, or who have "dropped out" in frustration stemming from their home situations. Such pupils would be better characterized as "break-outs." The volunteer college tutors not only help them with the school subjects but establish contacts with their teachers and get the students back into class. Working on a one-to-one basis, such tutors serve as big brothers.

Initiated by Dr. E. L. V. Shelley, a psychologist retired from a career in the state's juvenile and adult corrections departments, the group counseling program for parents consists of voluntary attendance at a series of informal get-together meetings in which common problems and experiences are shared. Group counseling under professional, volunteer leadership allows the probationers to interchange peer-group criticisms (which they can respect) and, perhaps for the first time in their lives, come to realize that other people have problems and valid views too. They find that they are not alone against the world.

An idea of the place of the Programs Division in the Ingham County Juvenile Court in relation to the court's total organization and growth can be gained from a study of Figs. 4–5 and 4–6.

Effects of Recent Court Decisions

Thus far, we have described the guidelines and underlying philosophy of the police, the police youth bureau, and the juvenile court in their handling of delinquents or the abused.* We have suggested that recent court decisions have modified the informality of the proceedings. The traditional pattern of the children's court (sitting around the judge's desk in his chambers, or elsewhere, in which a conversational atmosphere is sought) is threatened, according to some writers.

Informality is all very well, but it can be carried so far that it results in the denial of basic constitutional rights. The U.S. Supreme Court

---

*We are deeply indebted, for their consultation and advice on this section, to Detective Sergeant Ray C. Valley, Assistant Commander, Community Relations/ Juvenile Section, Michigan State Police, and to Robert C. Trojanowicz, Associate Professor, School of Criminal Justice, Michigan State University.

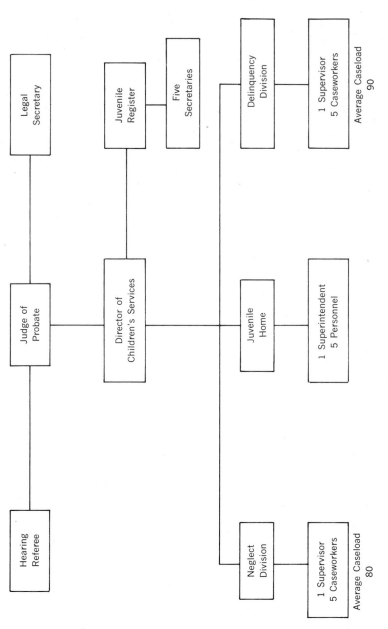

Figure 4–5. Ingham County Juvenile Court organizational—personnel chart, 1963 (28 personnel)

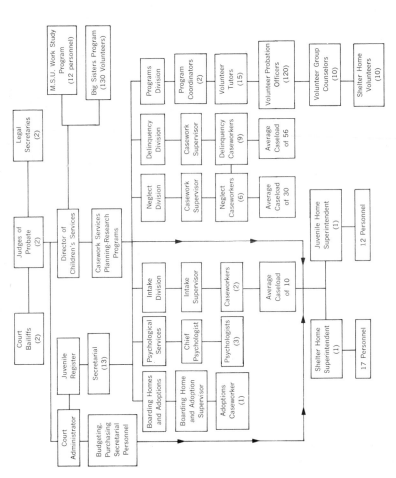

Figure 4–6. Ingham County Juvenile Court
organizational–personnel chart, 1970 (81 personnel)

has ruled that the Constitution requires, in cases involving juveniles as well as in cases involving adults: (a) that the offender must have written notice of the charges against him; (b) that he must be advised of his right to have his own lawyer; (c) that he has a right to meet his accuser and to cross-examine him; (d) that he must be accorded the privilege against self-incrimination ... This Supreme Court decision [*in re* Gault] will go a long way toward protecting the rights of juvenile offenders. [*You and the Law,* p. 159]

The tight legal formalities required under the new rules are suggested by Fig. 4–7, which is based on flow charts prepared for the guidance of police and court officials by Donald Anderson, then of the Center for Children's Court Services, now circuit court judge of Kalamazoo, Michigan.

Judge Anderson pointed out that:

1. For the first time, under the 1969 Juvenile Court Rules, the court can issue a warrant for apprehension and search.

2. If the county appoints an attorney, it may assess the cost against a parent to the extent of his ability to pay.

3. An attorney's written appearance must specifically disclose any representation of other parties to avoid conflict of interest.

4. Waiver of right to counsel by a juvenile must be joined by a parent or guardian.

5. Information or testimony furnished to a court at its request is privileged and the informant is immune from civil or criminal liability.

6. Revocation of parole will be decided in a court hearing (formal docket) without a jury unless the state agency establishes an administrative hearing procedure.

7. Fingerprinting, photographing, and show-ups, or line-ups, may be authorized by the court under controlled circumstances.

Actually, there have been several Federal and state court decisions that tend to restrain the informality of juvenile procedures, all with the purpose of guaranteeing full rights to minors. To cite a few, and suggest their implications:

People v. *Roberts* 364 Mich. 60 (1961): A 15-year-old boy confessed to stabbing a woman to death. Court held confession was voluntarily given, hence valid. *Comment:* The Michigan Supreme Court holds that the Probate Court has exclusive jurisdiction over any juvenile for any offense, but that a juvenile committing an adult offense, if over 14, may be waived to adult court.

COMPLAINT	Without arrest, or arrest with release to parent
POLICE SCREENING	(See Fig. 4–1, "Action on Original Contact")
PRELIMINARY INQUIRY —or—	No "hearing" required (See Fig. 4–1, "Youth Bureau")
RELEASE TO PARENT —or—	Dismiss as unfounded or refer to family or agency on agreement to produce child when requested
APPREHEND AND DETAIN	Grounds: runaway; serious offense endangers community; child imperiled by surroundings; hold for observation, study or treatment

PROCEDURE:

OUTSIDE COURT HOURS	Contact court official for authority to detain pending preliminary hearing within 48 hours
DURING COURT HOURS	**Forthwith** to
PRELIMINARY HEARING	Notify of Miranda, Gault, etc., rights, plus right to bond (in delinquency cases only), plus right to trial by jury **Decisions:** (1) Dismiss as above, (2) authorize petition, (3) detain for further hearing **Record hearing** verbatim or memorandum (secret, to be destroyed at discretion of judge)
IF PETITION AUTHORIZED	Go to **Consent, Formal** or **Waiver** dockets
CONSENT DOCKET —or—	No verbatim record, no **appointed** attorney, no change of custody, no transfer to formal docket after agreement
FORMAL DOCKET —or—	PRELIMINARIES: serve written specific charges on parent and child, plus notice of rights to silence, to attorney (**retained** in offense by child, or **appointed** in offense vs. child), to trial by jury, plus special notice if termination of parental rights is a possibility HEARING: **Notices** and **record** as in preliminaries. ADJUDICATION: Evidence to be relevant, competent and material as in civil cases DISPOSITION: (1) warn and dismiss, (2) supervision or probation in or out of home, (3) private or public institution, or (4) terminate parental rights permanently
WAIVER DOCKET	PRELIMINARIES same as formal docket, plus specific notice of waiver possibility. Attorney must be assured unless expressly refused. HEARING same as formal docket except determine **probable** cause that child committed act in nature of felony, and that child is 15 or over DISPOSITION: Deny waiver, or waive to criminal court.

Based on Donald Anderson

Figure 4–7.   Flow Chart—Juvenile Court
Under Michigan Juvenile Court Rules 1969
(Post Gault)

Gallegos v. *Colorado,* 370 US 49 (1964): Boy of 14 was tried and convicted in adult court of assault on man who later died. Basis of proof, his confession. Conviction reversed on grounds confession was obtained illegally since boy had had no counsel.

Kent v. *US Sup Court* 1045 (1966): Boy confessed to robberies and rapes. Juvenile judge waived case to criminal court refusing to allow defense lawyer access to records. U.S. Supreme Court reversed criminal court conviction on grounds of denial of access to records and denial of hearing on waiver decision.

Miranda v. *Arizona* 384 *US* 436 (1966): Case involved custodial interrogation and its admissibility. Court held that for admissibility, it must be shown that there was proper advice of (1) right to remain silent, (2) that any statement can be used in court, (3) right to retained counsel. That any waiver of these rights must be shown to have been made "voluntarily, knowingly and intelligently."

US v. *Wade* 338 *US* 218 (1967): Indicates that a child has right to presence of counsel in line-up proceedings. No implication that suspect has a right NOT to be viewed in a line-up.

In Re Gault 387 *US* 1 (1967): Gault, on juvenile probation, was charged with making obscene telephone calls to neighbor. He was held in detention. Later, a scrap of paper was left at his home, advising parents that court hearing was to be held. A postponement of the case was made and again there was no formal notice to parents of the charges to be heard at the hearing. Complainant not present. Boy committed to training school. US Supreme Court held proceedings illegal: no formal notice of charges, no confrontation by complainant, no record of hearing and, by Arizona law, no appeal was possible from the juvenile court. (See comments below)

In Re Marsh 237 N.E. 2nd 529 (May 1968): held that juveniles are entitled to protection against unlawful search and seizure, and to transcript on appeal. (Based on 4th Amendment's bar against admission of illegally seized evidence).

In Re Winship, May 1970: U.S. Supreme Court held that due process clause requires that conviction of the criminally accused be based on proof of guilt beyond reasonable doubt; that same standard applies to the adjudicatory stage of juvenile court delinquency proceedings in which a youth is charged with an act that, if committed by an adult, would be a crime.

In sum, the decisions in these cases threaten the informality of juvenile court proceedings. Some lament the effects of this threat on the grounds "that due process of law for a child does not require criminal proceeding in the juvenile court" (Noyes, *Crime and Delinquency,* April 1970, pp. 158 ff). Alfred D. Noyes takes the view:

A child is entitled to more than the bare legal rights afforded an adult. He is entitled to be in custody of someone who cares for him; to have a chance for an education and a job; to be supervised and disciplined; to live in a community that will give him an opportunity to develop into a self-respecting, productive, law-abiding citizen, and to be understood. The Gault decision has given aid and comfort to those who would weaken the juvenile court concept of a non-adversary judicial proceeding in which the judge administers the precept of *parens patriae* . . .

Some courts are appointing defense counsel in every delinquency case even if a child and his parents have not requested representation, and this has slowed down the process to the point where they are months behind in hearing the cases. Some courts are conducting full adversary proceeding in nearly all delinquency cases; and children, through their attorneys, are using every possible technicality to "beat the rap." When the petition is dismissed because of a legal technicality, what has the child gained? Has the court acted in his best interest?

Noyes quotes Justice Stewart's dissenting opinion which, he feels, clarifies the unique function of the children's court:

Juvenile proceedings are not criminal trials. They are simply *not* adversary proceedings. Whether treating with a delinquent child or a neglected child, a juvenile proceeding's whole purpose and mission is the very opposite of the mission and purpose of a prosecution in a criminal court. The object of the one is correction of a condition. The object of the other is conviction and punishment for a criminal act.

Whether the juvenile court as we know it will survive [Noyes warns, in conclusion] will depend largely on the degree of dedication and determination that juvenile court judges are able and willing to muster to preserve America's greatest contribution to the cause of justice for children. [Ibid.]

Charles E. Reasons, writing in the same issue of *Crime and Delinquency* (pp. 163 ff. passim), sees some merit in the increasing legalization of juvenile court proceedings. His views are based on a pre- and post-*Gault* study in which he analyzed a juvenile court's records for a two-year period:

Both quantitative and qualitative changes were discovered, even though no statutory changes occurred. A doubling in the percentage of cases with counsel and a reduction in the total number of cases reflect an increased emphasis upon legal fact-finding. This change in normative emphasis was brought about primarily by changes in the attitude of court personnel and law-enforcement agencies . . .

A reduction in the number of juveniles placed on probation and an increase in the use of fines may indicate less emphasis on treatment. This is not to say that treatment is incompatible with a more legalistic orientation but rather that treatment must be based on an accurate determination of guilt. Indeed, the reduction in the volume of cases handled and in the number of juveniles placed on probation may allow *more* individualized treatment, thereby fulfilling a primary promise of the court.

Reasons' recognition of "the primary promise" of the juvenile court shows he agrees with Noyes as to its purpose. His contention that legalistic protections for juveniles have decreased the number but increased the quality of cases in the court he studied, suggests that under the new procedures two things will happen: (1) more and more cases will be settled in the informal milieu of the judge's chambers when no adult-type crime is involved, and (2) juvenile defendants in serious cases will be assured the full protection of the laws in those fewer cases that are admitted to court. One can see but one possible peril: that court cases under the adversary system are likely to require records which, if not jealously guarded by juvenile court judges, could threaten the future life of the young defendant should he seek a career in political, financial, military, or other field where his past history is of primary concern. Too frequently, a judge must capitulate to requests from military, bonding, or other investigators for access to records. And if he says "Yes, he has a record," and refuses to release it, the investigator can only suspect the worst offense has been committed.

The following case (Fig. 4–8) suggests that *despite* the new emphasis on the legal rights of minors, there remains a clear distinction in the procedures for handling "juveniles" and "young offenders." Let us hope that *because* of the legalistic emphasis, the rights of both will be more carefully protected.

In Conclusion

It seems that two new directions must be pursued in the handling of juveniles. The first is that members of the bar must learn to serve their roles as judge, prosecutor, and defense counsel not only as *parens patriae* but as *paterfamiliae*. They must commit themselves to playing their roles as father figures, not merely as agents of the state, but personally, in the juvenile court tradition, and as they would for their own children. They will find their dual role difficult after years of symbolizing the majesty of the law. But their very legal competence should enable them to bring to the children's court a concerned awareness of the child's need for protection, and a fatherly dedication to achieving that protection for him. This they must do, not through "getting the child off" on legal technicalities—from which the child will gain only his liberty and a contempt for the law—but through assuring the child the greatest benefit and guidance that the court can possibly provide him.

A CASE OF TWO SUBJECTS APPREHENDED IN STOLEN CAR

Juvenile age 15

1. Placed in juvenile facility.

2. Officer contacts probate court; explains case; arranges for custody or preliminary hearing.

3. Boy brought before juvenile section of probate court. Parents must be there. Lawyer optional. Judge releases, or holds for hearing. If held, officer signs petition.

4. Boy appears before juvenile judge on petition. May have an attorney. Parents present. Officer, owner of car, and boy may testify. May have 6-man jury, or judge decides: place on probation, send to training school or other custody, or find not guilty and release.

5. May be waived into circuit court for a felony. If so, follows same route as 17-year-old, entering at stage 6.

Youth age 17

1. Jailed, fingerprinted, photo.

2. Officer contacts prosecutor; obtains authorization for a warrant.

3. Officer takes authorization to arraigning magistrate, swears to complaint, signs it or has owner of car sign it. Warrant issued.

4. Youth brought before municipal or district court. Advised of: charges (warrant read), right to waive or demand examination. Bond is set and, if produced, youth released. Otherwise held.

5. Appears before municipal or district court for examination. Is represented by attorney. Prosecutor presents facts. Officer and owner testify. Establish reasonable grounds. Bound over or released.

6. Youth appears before circuit court for arraignment. May plead guilty or not guilty. Bond may be continued or changed.

7. Youth appears for trial in circuit court. 12-man jury, or judge may hear case if youth wishes. Represented by attorney. Evidence submitted. Testimony taken. Find guilty or not guilty.

8. If convicted, youth later appears for sentence: placed on probation and ordered to pay costs, and restitution or may be sentenced to county jail for short period and spend remainder of time on probation, or sentenced to a term of imprisonment.

From Ray C. Valley: Case Study to appear in Robert

Figure 4–8.   Juvenile process of prosecution

The second direction must be an increased effort of the police, the courts, and the community toward preventing delinquency. Delinquency can be prevented. And it is socially and economically imperative that it be prevented. We simply cannot afford to waste our youth. The cost is compounded: not only may an untreated, aberrant child not develop into a constructively contributing adult member of society, but the expense of handling him when he becomes a criminal adult can be monumental.* And it is unnecessary, as recent data indicate.

The British police introduced in Liverpool in 1951 their first "juvenile liaison schemes" which have proved so successful that they have been adopted by most of the 41 police forces in England and Wales. The schemes are described by Fred Baddeley who says that their "fundamental principle is to provide an efficient personal service for dealing with children and young persons in which it is not considered necessary or desirable that the alleged offender should be prosecuted, and also to prevent juveniles from finding themselves liable to prosecution." He adds, "Experience has shown that 70 percent of first offenders in this country do not commit further offenses no matter how dealt with, and to give such youngsters the stigma of a criminal conviction so early in their lives is socially undesirable." Juveniles can be considered for inclusion in the scheme provided that:

1. The offender is under 17 years old

2. It is a first offense (normally)

3. The offense is not a serious one

4. The offender admits to the offense

5. The parents or guardian agree to cooperate in the scheme.

The schemes, adapted to the local conditions of police forces, advocate a period of comprehensive supervision, including visits to the home, the school, and all places that young people frequent.

During 1969, a total of 10,002 children and young persons were dealt with, and 1,726 juveniles were supervised for varying periods of time. At the close of the year, 1,285 were currently on supervision, giving an average case load of 30 per officer. Scheme personnel made a total of 36,126 visits—18,469 home visits; 4,745 to schools; 12,912 to stores, clubs and coffee bars; and 310 lectures were given which were attended by 11,253. [These figures are for the Lancashire Constabulary alone.] Within the force area there are now eleven youth clubs, staffed on a volunteer basis by police personnel ... The most progressive venture is the three story permanent youth hostel at Farndon (built by community donations) which is an Adventure

---

*Martin Gold, of the University of Michigan, has pointed out, however, that undetected delinquent behavior does not necessarily foreshadow a criminal career: that indeed, apprehension itself may provoke future delinquency.

Center where 400 young people enjoyed long week-ends free, and
from which they were taken on hikes and excursions on the River
Dee. [Baddeley, *The Police Chief*, May 1971, pp. 68 ff.]

The effectiveness of this "Intermediate Treatment" program is
being continuously evaluated. The city of Leeds, for example, has
handled 3,562 juveniles under the program of whom only nine percent
have committed further offenses. This is in contrast to the lack of success of the old training schools and Borstals which in 1969 handled
9,533 children of whom 5,950 absconded, not to mention the wasted
institutional costs.

Anticipating the possible objections of those who believe that the
police should not be social workers, Baddeley says:

Social workers are normally against police officers becoming involved
in any form of social re-education . . . But police juvenile liaison
officers have much to offer . . . Indeed, on this type of basic social
rehabilitation, the juvenile liaison officer really comes into his own,
for by virtue of the position he holds in society . . . he commands a
degree of respect given to few other British social workers. An intimate knowledge of family attitudes and social norms which prevail
in his police division is his stock in trade and a visit from him brings
home to the offender's parents the fact that all is not well in that
household.

In Scotland, six police forces have launched juvenile liaison
schemes, and are experimenting with panels of citizens to counsel
first-offenders as a substitute for court referral. Like the volunteer
citizens in Ingham County, who work with groups of parents and of
probatióners in on-going group sessions, the Scots are pioneering
prevention. The Gluecks' well-known techniques of predicting delinquent tendencies in young children, however reliable, are impractical
for prevention on a massive national scale. The child who has committed his first minor offense, however, is highly visible and accessible
for treatment. Baddeley concludes that the police forces of Britain
and America should exchange juvenile officer personnel for a pooling
of ideas on how to make the "schemes" of both countries more
effective.*

A Suggested Research Project

Study the juvenile justice system as it functions in England (or any
other country). Compare with the situation in the United States. Check
particularly for contrast as to the role of police in the system.

---

*A. F. Brandstatter, Director of the School of Criminal Justice, Michigan State
University, is currently engaged in a study of such programs as police-school
liaison projects in the United States and other countries, with a view to deter-
mining just how effective they have been in preventing crime and delinquency.

Misdemeanant Probation

Because misdemeanants form a far larger group of offenders than juveniles and felons combined (from the number of cases handled by the criminal justice system), the question logically arises whether their number can be reduced and, if so, how. Experimental projects in Royal Oak, Michigan, and Denver, Colorado, and in several hundred other cities, suggest that the number *can* be reduced by preventing recidivism through the proper use of probation: specifically through the use of volunteers as probation counselors.

We shall first examine the scope and nature of the misdemeanant problem, then look at the traditional uses of probation and their apparent lack of effectiveness for this type of offender, and conclude with a description of a few effective programs, stressing that of Royal Oak.

The definition of a misdemeanor varies from jurisdiction to jurisdiction. A misdemeanor is usually an offense carrying a maximum sentence of one year in the local jail instead of in a state prison. Some criminal codes specifically identify certain offenses as misdemeanors or felonies. Other statutes stipulate that all offenses not specifically enumerated as felonies are misdemeanors. Still others distinguish between "high" and "low" misdemeanors, with the former carrying a sentence of more than one year. A study in twelve states revealed that 93.5 percent of persons arraigned in 1962 for offenses other than traffic violations were charged with misdemeanors, although the range is great between states. When arrests for misdemeanors are totaled, the number reaches almost five million a year for the nation.

Normally, the misdemeanant is not less than 17; the great majority fall in the 18- to 25-year-old bracket, but may be any age beyond that. The fact that 73.5 percent of first felony admissions in California, by one study, had a previous misdemeanant record suggests the need for curbing recidivism at the misdemeanant level. In 1965, the cost of maintaining a felon in an institution was $1,966, whereas

The data on misdemeanant probation in this study are drawn from the President's Commission on Law Enforcement and Administration of Justice, *Task Force Report: Corrections,* 1967, p. 72.

the cost for supervising a probationer in the community was only $142. As we shall see, even the smaller figure can be reduced by using volunteer probation counselors. These figures, of course, do not include the greater losses in economic productivity and human dignity of confined persons.

The diversity of the misdemeanant group is great. The municipal courts handle violators of motor vehicle, health, housing, safety, and commercial regulations, most of which are disposed of with fines or suspension of licenses. Drunks comprise almost half of all misdemeanants—if traffic violators are not counted. Even so, as with prostitutes, many don't reach the judge's bench but are referred to social agencies by the police. Because of inadequate agency facilities, they appear again and again in the police station. Drunks are dried out overnight, and the prostitutes get a medical check. Thus they are denied the benefit of probationary guidance that they might have received had they been tried in a court with adequate pre-sentence investigation and probation guidance procedures.

We understand why we need misdemeanant courts when we understand the types of possible offenders. The National Institute of Mental Health cited (1966) the following:

> *The Prosocial Offender.* Normal individual, identifying with legitimate values and rejecting the norms of delinquent subcultures. His offenses grow out of extraordinary pressures. Most frequently convicted of crimes of violence (homicide, assault, or naïvely committed property offenses such as forgery). May be intimidated, disturbed, overinhibited, anxious, depressed, or withdrawn. Frequently no rehabilitative treatment needed at all. The main job is to get him out of the corrections cycle before he is harmed by contact with other offenders and, if incarcerated, should be kept from contact with other prisoners. Has low recidivism rate. Needs psychiatric help outside of the correctional system.

> *The Antisocial Offender.* Identifies with a delinquent culture, rejects social norms. Is primitive, uninhibited, impulsive, hostile, negative, or alienated. Sees himself as a victim of a hostile world. From an unstable family. Needs an environment with clear, persistent, social demands but one where concern for his welfare is communicated to him. Needs a strong role model and enlarged social horizons.

> *The Pseudosocial Manipulator.* Lacks conventional standards, is guilt-free, self-satisfied, power-oriented, non-trusting, emotionally insulated and cynical. Comes from a family whose members are highly competitive, mutually distrustful, exploitive, with inconsistent patterns of acceptance and rejection. Treatment calls for redirection of skills into acceptable social patterns, group therapy to reveal to him his inconsistencies and the need for acceptable choices. Prospects for successful treatment are discouraging.

The Asocial Offender. Acts out his primitive impulses, is extremely hostile, insecure, negativistic; demands immediate gratification. Cannot identify with others, which distinguishes him from the antisocial type who, although committed to delinquent values, is loyal to his peers. Needs elementary training in human relations, but has difficulty in relating to a therapist or the social world. Must first lose fear of rejection before individual or group treatment can succeed.

Public attitudes toward all these offenders tend to reject them as punks and to want them convicted and confined, regardless of their differences. "They're all alike; they deserve what they get." Many are, in fact, victims of their environments. While some are already beyond rehabilitation and must be confined for the protection of society (rather than for punitive reasons), the greatest number of them are susceptible to treatment and can become contributing members of society rather than its parasites. It was to effect just such changes that the concept of probation was conceived in the early 1800s by a humble cobbler, John Augustus, in Boston. Over the many years of his life, he received into his keeping from the criminal justice system literally hundreds of misdemeanants, guided them, and started them on constructive paths. But it was not until 1891 that Massachusetts formally established a statewide probation system, although originally for juveniles. Vermont established probation on a county basis in 1898; Rhode Island on a statewide basis in 1899. During the early twentieth century, the process was slowly adapted to adult needs. But it was not until 1956 that all states had adult probation programs, however ineffective some have proved to be.

Limits of Probation

The outstanding single fact about misdemeanant probation is the paucity of the service, either because of legal restrictions or excessive caseloads of probation officers. The President's Crime Commission said that the ideal standard "should authorize the court to use probation at its discretion, following adjudication or conviction, when it serves the best interest of the offender or society." But in three states, misdemeanants are not eligible for probation; and in two others, certain offenses are listed for which probation may not be used. In one state, a variety of qualifications must be met, such as no prior felony conviction and no imprisonment within five years. About one-third of the 250 counties studied in the national sample had no misdemeanant probation services. As for caseloads for probation officers handling misdemeanants, the over-all average was 114; but in some counties the average load was over 200, and in one county it was over 400. In counties that required probation officers to prepare pre-sentence investigation reports for municipal court judges, this burden ranged higher, sometimes to more than 50 a month. When we consider that the salary of such officers was only $5000 to $6000 a year, we see that the quality and quantity of misdemeanant guidance is limited to the point of almost total ineffectiveness. Such officers have a typical client service that is limited to one phone call or a two- to three- minute contact a month, hardly an effective means of changing the attitudes of complicated offenders.

It is little wonder that, under this system, more than three quarters of first felony arrests involve people who have misdemeanant records. Nor is it surprising that they land in jails where, through their contacts with experienced criminals and despairing persons who for months have been waiting trial, their criminal tendencies are reenforced and refined. Richard A. McGee, in "The Correctional Process," has commented on the jails where misdemeanants are confined: "The county jail (there are over 3000 in the nation) is the lowest form of social institution in the United States. Most of the inmates are still awaiting trial." They are subject to the same, often-vile conditions of those serving time, when they should have been released on bail or on their own recognizance pending their day in court. Even though the rate of failure to appear for trial of those released is minimal, they are herded into facilities (often in the same overcrowded cells) with felons, drunks, drug addicts, or professional criminals who contaminate them morally and physically. McGee says that keeping men in jail, even with eventual release in mind, is a greater crime than that of the criminal's offense, if we do not provide effective rehabilitation to prepare them to return to the community. Further, we know that confinement is no deterrent to recidivism. Jails are simply not equipped for rehabilitation programs; their populations are too great and diverse, their budgets too low, and their personnel too ill-trained. Thus, the only hope of salvaging the socially unacceptable is through *effective* probation—a type of probation unavailable under our, for the most part, traditional procedures.

Misdemeanant Programs

One obstacle to improving rehabilitative programs for misdemeanants is the brevity of the typical misdemeanant sentence, the national average of which is two months—quite a bit less than the 9.3 months for juveniles, and a great deal less than the 20.9 months for adult felons. Eight weeks is too short a time to do much, but the intensive methods used in some recent programs are geared to just such short periods. The Highfields, New Jersey program, for example, aimed at rehabilitating offenders in three or four months, is premised on the belief that *the major correctional impact occurs early in treatment*. The few correctional institutions for misdemeanants that do exist are generally small and located near metropolitan areas, thus facilitating work-release and other programs for the reintegration of offenders in the community. But the great difficulty is that referral sources of the type needed are virtually nonexistent. Nor is there the support for their development that exists for juveniles. However, a few such programs are worthy of note.

The St. Paul, Minnesota, workhouse has in the last eight years developed a broad range of work and educational programs, and augmented professional staff with volunteers. Under the educational aspect of the program, supported by a foundation grant, scores of inmates have obtained high school diplomas. Counseling and guidance for men under 21 are also provided in the program, supported by a grant from OEO. Only 7 percent of the participating offenders have been returned to the workhouse.

The Westchester County penitentiary in New York, staffed by 41 volunteers, has a pilot program for women that offers courses in shorthand, typing, nursing and the like. Multnomah County, Oregon, has a satellite facility to the county jail in Portland to which qualified inmates may transfer for work training—by volunteers—work release, and medical attention. San Diego, California, has established five honor camps for transfers from the county jail, supplemented by a halfway house for individual and group counseling and work-release. The principle is similar to that of the minimum security, conservation-type camps developed some years ago in Michigan and other states, originally for adults and later for young offenders, as a kind of bridging experience between the maximum security prison and release to the community.

The trend today is away from distinctions between institutional and community treatment. More furloughs are being granted, as are passes for weekends at home. Community corrections centers, halfway houses, and rooms at the YMCA are being used. Neighbors of the Michigan camps have inmates as guests during weekends when home furloughs are also granted. Unarmed counselors have replaced armed guards. The only fences are snow fences. Aside from the human rehabilitation factor, programs using the community as the base for treatment cost but one-tenth of institutional treatment, which can run over $3500 a year in addition to a $20,000 capital investment for each bed: an investment which, with more than 50 percent adult recidivism, has not paid off.

The Royal Oak Probation Program

It has been my privilege as Governor of Michigan to see the work of Judge Keith Leenhouts and his citizen volunteers move outward from a successful local program in Royal Oak to a concept that is now operating in over 400 courts around the nation. The idea has spread because it works. The introduction of an inspirational personality into the life of a delinquent or young criminal is not *an* answer to crime—it is *the* answer.

This quotation is taken from a statement made by George Romney, former Secretary of Housing and Urban Development, with reference to a program in Royal Oak, Michigan, pioneered some years ago by then Municipal Court Judge Keith Leenhouts.*

As so often happens in human innovations, the Royal Oak (population 90,000) program was born of the long-time concern of a young lawyer-judge about young people getting into trouble, acquiring prison records, and facing a lifetime of more trouble because of it. To do something about it, Keith J. Leenhouts began working on the problem as soon as he was elected a municipal judge. He knew that eight out of ten major crimes are committed by persons who first appeared for misdemeanors in lower courts such as his. But he also knew that the city could not afford enough probation officers to provide the kind of guidance that could save these first offenders from criminal careers. Further, he knew that he had not had adequate information about his cases upon which to base wise decisions. He sought help in meeting the double challenge.

A month after his first case, Leenhouts sat with eight men around a table to discuss what they could do about the problem. In the group were two Protestant ministers, a Catholic priest, a psychiatrist, a psychologist, a former professional youth worker, and two junior high school assistant principals. They started planning. On April 15, 1960 they received the sanction of the Michigan Corrections Department to institute a new type of probation program.** Each of the eight "counselors" agreed to give a maximum of five hours a month uncompensated time to work with a maximum of five probationers each. One of the assistant principals was appointed chief probation officer, and he agreed to coordinate the program without pay. The hope was to establish an inspirational relationship of trust and confidence between the probationer and an adult in the community who had both the zeal of the volunteer and the training, education, and experience of the expert in a phase of counseling.

By June, it became apparent that the chief probation officer was working many more hours than a volunteer should. He was seeing each probationer once a month. Thus, each probationer had a minimum of two meetings a month, the other being with his volunteer counselor. It seemed then that the chief officer should be paid at least a token amount for his extra time. Consequently, businessmen were solicited

---

*Described by Joe Alex Morris in *The First Offender,* Funk & Wagnalls, New York, N.Y.; and by the same author in "Royal Oak Aids Its Youth Problem," *Reader's Digest,* October, 1965; and in "Big Help to Small Offenders," *Reader's Digest,* April, 1968. Reprints of these articles and other materials pertaining to this program are available from Volunteers in Probation, Inc., 200 Washington Square Plaza, Royal Oak, Mi., 48067.

**Originally called the Project Misdemeanant Foundation, Inc. and later changed to Volunteers in Probation, Inc.

who agreed to pay $25 or $50 a month each. By the end of 1961, seventeen more volunteer counselors had been added, and a staff assistant as well, who, like the chief, worked 25 hours a month. But the program was growing so rapidly that a full-time administrator was indicated.

The City of Royal Oak offered $2,200 a year to help. (Its contributions now comprise 75 percent of the annual budget.) Office work grew. Notices of meetings had to be mailed. Reports from volunteers were being handled monthly on each case. The judge himself—engaged 40 hours a week in court work—could not give enough time to guiding the program. The perfect solution was found when retired professionals volunteered for administrative work, accepting only the maximum salary they were allowed to receive under their Social Security restrictions.

The program grew as dictated by the needs of the court and of the probationers. The greatest need of all was for help in pre-sentence investigations of misdemeanants brought before the judge. This was the point where the nation's typical probation procedures and personnel were most handicapped. Eventually help was volunteered by 25 psychiatrists, 10 psychologists, two staff psychiatrists, and five psychological and psychiatric clinics. All but the two staff psychiatrists, whose fees were greatly reduced, worked without remuneration. Thus, it was possible for the judge to have at hand—when the moment for sentencing arrived— case histories and analyses upon which he could base realistic decisions as to fine, length of sentence, and the subsequent nature and length of the probationary program for each offender.

Sentences could be for as much as 90 days but the typical one was much less. In some cases, the court thought that the shock of brief incarceration was helpful but that, on the whole, its contaminating effects must be avoided. The aim has been to bring the subject under the guidance of an appropriate volunteer as soon as possible, and to keep him or her under such care for as long as two years if need be. To this end, the program has evolved into the organizational pattern shown in the chart in Fig. 4–9.

Some of the items in the chart need a bit of explanation:

Chief Counselors.   When probation is desirable, offenders are assigned to one of twelve professionally trained, part-time staff members who counsel and supervise probationers. The heart of the professional counseling program, these counselors are each responsible for about 15 probationers whom they meet with regularly. They are responsible for coordinating other prescribed services and they supervise the volunteers.

Psychiatric-Psychological Services.   For the offender in need of such assistance, these free services are available: 1—Psychiatric evaluations and psychological testing; 2—Individual treatment by a part-time psychiatrist; 3—Individual therapy on a private basis; 4—Group therapy conducted by staff and volunteer psychiatrists. Thirty volunteer professionals are involved.

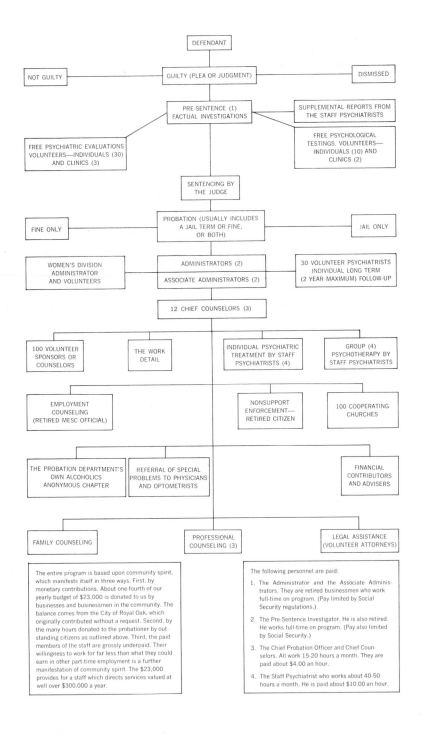

Figure 4–9.   Organization of Royal Oak program:
Volunteers in Probation, Inc.

Volunteer Sponsors. Often a probationer is assigned to one of about 150 volunteer men or women sponsors representing about every sector of the community. Those not trained as counselors are selected with care, receive orientation and are carefully supervised. The sponsor is an inspirational personality with whom the probationer can identify. His main function is to be a friend. It has been said that he is not *an* answer but *the* answer to rising crime and delinquency. He does everything that you would do for a friend.

Other Volunteer Assistance. Professional men including doctors, lawyers and optometrists lend their skills to the program whenever called upon. Volunteer secretaries help out. Businessmen assist through financial contributions and job placements.

Marriage and Family Counseling. Available at no cost. A chief counselor is specifically trained in this area and works solely with cases needing individual or group counseling.

Church Referral Service. If a probationer indicates a desire to have a church "home," volunteer clergy establish contacts for him with one of 90 churches cooperating in the program.

Alcoholics Anonymous. The court has launched its own A.A. program, directed by a retired man with many years of A.A. membership. Referrals are made directly by the court.

Non-support Enforcement and Restitution. A retired senior citizen and the Probation Administrator carry out this important task, without cost.

Employment Counseling. Aptitude testing and placement services are provided by a senior citizen, formerly with the Employment Securities Commission—a great aid in rehabilitation.

A special word should be said about *The Work Detail.* Here the basic idea is to punish without creating a permanent court record for the offender. Worthy defendants without a criminal record are assigned to this detail, in which each works for the city four Saturdays a month for one to six months, doing such work as cleaning city parks, removing snow, collecting litter, painting park tables, etc. They pay the city $48 a month for the privilege of having this way to avoid a jail sentence. They are supervised by a volunteer counselor and must meet all the obligations of a probationer. The Work Detail is ordinarily prescribed only when there is parental concern and police approval. This program by which an offender can *earn* his dismissal has proved most effective.

The Royal Oak program has come far and is still growing. How effective has it been? Out of some 2,000 probationers over the past eight years, more than 90 percent have refrained from committing a second offense in Royal Oak. Seventy percent is conceded a good result by professionals. Less than one percent have gone on to commit a felony—less than a third of the national average (3 percent). To completely change the life of 200 criminal offenders and to control 1800 offenders makes the efforts of the judge and his 500 volunteers not only gratifying, but provides the clue why over 400 other courts in the land have adapted their procedures to those of this program. It should be pointed out that the word was spread through a grant of $24,000 from the Board of Christian Social Concerns of the Methodist Church, which financed the dissemination of literature and travel expenses for the judge and his associates to carry the word to inquiring courts across the country. Recently, Judge Leenhouts resigned from the bench to devote his full time to directing the Royal Oak Program.

In 1966, Judge William H. Burnett in Denver adapted the Royal Oak program to his court, which had eleven judges but no probation officers. By the end of 1967, some 700 volunteers had attended training classes, and up to 50 new volunteers were being trained each month. In Boulder, Colorado, The National Information Center on Volunteers in Courts (NICOVIC) has been established for preparing and distributing publications on the subject, and for providing consultant services.* In April, 1972, a national conference on the subject, sponsored by Volunteers in Probation, Inc., was held in Memphis, Tennessee.

On January 1, 1972, VIPI became an official Division of the National Council on Crime and Delinquency (NCCD), whose headquarters are in Paramus, New Jersey. The growing importance of volunteers in providing relief for overcrowded courts is further evidenced by the facts that:

In 1959, virtually no volunteers were involved anywhere.

In 1967, there were about 2,000 in the United States.

In 1969, about 12,000 volunteers were active in the country.

In 1971, there were 200,000 citizens involved as volunteers.

By 1976, or 1981 at the latest, there should be more than a million volunteers supplementing the staffs of courts, and saving misdemeanants and certain first offenders from having criminal records.

Additional recognition has been given the movement by the insurance now available to protect volunteers against judgments resulting from accidents involving probationers (as while transporting them to sports events in cars, etc.), or judgments for financial losses probationers may suffer as a result of advice given by volunteers.

It is clearly an accepted fact now that volunteers in probation programs offer much for the relief of limited probation budgets** as well as establishing one-to-one programs for the reclamation of early offenders. This is, indeed, a realistic crime prevention approach, with substantial community concern and action.

---

*P.O. Box 2150, Boulder, Colorado 80302.

**The Royal Oak program provides $300,000 worth of services for a cash investment of only $23,000.

STUDY 3

The Free Press—Fair Trial Issue

"A conflict almost as old as democracy itself is raging in Washington these days. The issue is the accessibility of information about government operations." So wrote John L. Steele in *Time* magazine in January, 1971. He was referring to the tendency of the Executive and Legislative branches of the Federal government to classify documents on foreign and domestic affairs.

> Many historians, philosophers and journalists agree [he continued] that there have to be certain checks on the unlimited right of the public to knowledge about its government . . . James Russell Wiggins, former editor of the *Washington Post* writes, "We can give up a little freedom without surrendering all of it. . . . Each added measure of secrecy, however, measurably diminishes our freedom." ["The People's Right to Know"]

Steele suggested a value of the press publicizing government activities:

> Occasionally, the Government's concern for secrecy affects not only the public's right to know, but its own efficiency of operation. . . . Reporters might well remember President John Kennedy's comment to *New York Times* editor Turner Catledge, whose paper had practised a dutiful self-censorship in not reporting the imminence of the Bay of Pigs invasion: "If you had printed more about the operation, you would have saved us from a colossal mistake."

> But excessive secrecy is a contagious disease that could be fatal to the practice of democracy itself. [Ibid.]

In the area of American jurisprudence, the questions of when, how, and to what extent releases to the printed and electronic media are to be made has been gaining increasing attention in recent years. As competition among newspapers, and between them and the electronic media, is intensified in their efforts to scoop each other, the danger

195

increases of irresponsibility in the type of news divulged. Trial by the media—before, during, and after verdicts are announced—imperils the right of the accused to a fair trial. It is sometimes difficult to impanel a jury of venireman who have not read or heard details of crimes (accurate or otherwise) publicized by the media. During trials, publicity given to the more melodramatic aspects has influenced juries that have not been sequestered. After guilt has been established, the media sometimes respond in ways that prejudice appellate procedures.

But the media are not alone to blame. Public officials often have been at fault in the nature of their news releases made under pressure, and even in their handling of the person of the accused, as in the case of Lee Harvey Oswald. The temptation for a sheriff, prosecutor, or counsel to exploit their positions can make them as culpable as reporters who publicize their releases.

Are there no laws to govern the bar, the bench, the prosecutors, the police, and the media in such matters? The answer—for better or for worse—is no. There are only guidelines. On the government side there are the First, Sixth, and Fourteenth Amendments to the Constitution. Their relevant portions are:

> *First Amendment:* Congress shall make no law . . . abridging the freedom of speech or of the press . . .

> *Sixth Amendment:* In criminal prosecutions, the accused shall enjoy the right to a speedy and public trial, by an impartial jury . . .

> *Fourteenth Amendment:* . . . no State shall make or enforce any law which shall abridge the privileges or immunities of citizens of the United States; nor shall any State deprive any person of life, liberty, or property, without due process of law; nor deny to any person within its jurisdiction the equal protection of the laws.

Since Congress can "make no law" defining the rights of either the accused or of the media, the only guidelines have been decisions of the Supreme Court and the decisions and precedents of State and local courts which, in our appellate system, are subject to reversal by higher Courts. These precedents have proved precarious guides, since all courts may reverse themselves, presumably reflecting the tenor of the times.

Traditionally, the only extra-legal guidelines have been the dicta or codes of the American and State Bar Associations. But these can only *recommend* conduct for members of the bar and bench. They are not law. But as codes of ethics, they carry the implied threat of disbarment for those who do not conform. While these codes do not regulate the *media,* they have the effect of cutting off their sources of information.

John D. Molloy has made a study of the free press—fair trial issue. He cites numerous cases in which the role of the media has played an important part in the outcomes of trials.* He points out two types of cases that have produced frictions: those in which the press has criticized the court itself, and those in which a free press may influence jurors, witnesses, prosecutors, and others connected with the judicial process, particularly with peril to the defendant.

Criticisms of the Court Itself

Bridges v. *California*. (*Times-Mirror Corporation* v. *Superior Court of California*) 1941. While a motion was pending for a new trial to adjudicate a dispute between the AFL and a CIO union (Longshoremen) of which he was an officer, Harry Bridges . . . acquiesced in the publication of a telegram that he had sent to the U.S. Secretary of Labor. This telegram called the judge's decision "outrageous" and Bridges threatened that enforcement of the court order would tie up the Port of Los Angeles and perhaps paralyze the entire Pacific Coast. Bridges contended that the Longshoremen did not intend to allow state courts to override the majority vote of union members . . .

Also bearing on the case were editorials in *The Los Angeles Times* that commented on action pending before the same court. Under the headline "Probation for Gorillas?" the *Times* vigorously denounced two members of the Teamsters union who previously had been convicted of assaulting nonunion truck drivers. The *Times* concluded its advice to the court with, "Judge A. A. Scott will make a serious mistake if he grants probation to Matthew Shannon and Kennan Holmes. This community needs the example of their assignment to the jute mill."

Both Bridges and the Los Angeles *Times* were cited for contempt and convicted . . . The Supreme Court of California upheld the convictions on the ground that the editorial had a "reasonable tendency" to interfere with the administration of justice. The U.S. Supreme Court found otherwise (5–4), ruling that the convictions impaired the rights of free speech and press. Speaking for the majority, Mr. Justice Black reasoned that the telegram criticizing the decision of the Court that Bridges sent to the Secretary of Labor was merely a statement of facts that the Secretary was entitled to know inasmuch as action might result in a serious strike:

> Again, we find exaggeration in the conclusion that the utterance ever "tended" to interfere with justice. If there was electricity in the air

---

*John D. Molloy, *Justice and Journalism: The Free Press-Fair Trial Debate,* an address given to the Social Science Colloquium, Michigan State University, Fall, 1967. Much of what follows is adapted from this paper, with Professor Molloy's permission. See also Armand Mergen, *Project Summary: The Sensationalist Trial,* Faculty of Law and Economic Sciences, University of Mainz, Germany. (Project period: 1964–67, Project 314, Council of Europe.)

it was generated by the facts; the charge added by Bridges can be dismissed as negligible.

Considering the impact of the editorial on the situation, Mr. Justice Black said:

> This editorial, given the most intimidating construction it will bear, did no more than threaten future adverse criticism which was reasonably to be expected anyway in the event of a lenient disposition of the pending case. To regard it, therefore, as in itself of substantial influence upon the course of justice would be to impute to judges a lack of firmness, wisdom or honor, which we cannot accept as a major premise.

Speaking for the majority, Justice Black recognized the "clear and present danger" standard as a "minimum compulsion of the Bill of Rights, and not as marking the furthermost constitutional boundaries of protected expression."

Craig v. *Harney,* 1947.   In a similar case, the Supreme Court reversed a lower court decision and stated:

> This was strong language . . . and we assume an unfair criticism. But a judge may not hold in contempt one who ventures to publish anything that tends to make him unpopular or to belittle him . . . The fire which [the language] kindles must constitute an imminent, not merely a likely threat to the administration of justice. *The danger must not be remote or even probable: it must immediately imperil.*

Free Press and the Rights of the Accused

Sheppard v. *Florida,* 1951.   Four Negroes were convicted of raping a 17-year-old white girl. The press reported that the defendants had confessed, though no confession was offered at the trial. The U.S. Supreme Court reversed the conviction on the grounds of discrimination in selection of the jury, but added that they would have reversed anyway on "prejudicial influences outside the courtroom." Justice Jackson said:

> . . . prejudicial influences outside the courtroom, becoming all too typical of a highly publicized trial, were brought to bear on this jury with such force that the conclusion is inescapable that these defendants were prejudged as guilty and the trial was but a legal gesture to register a verdict already dictated by the press and the public opinion which it generated.

> If freedoms of the press are so abused as to make a fair trial in the locality impossible, the judicial process must be protected by removing the trial to a forum beyond its probable influence. These convictions, accompanied by such events, do not meet any civilized conception of due process of law. That alone is sufficient to my mind, to warrant reversal.

Stroble v. *California,* 1952. Defendant Fred Stroble had been convicted of first degree murder of a small girl. Excerpts of a confession had been released to the press by the District Attorney, who also offered the view that the defendant was both guilty and sane, on which basis the press wrote inflammatory stories. The U.S. Supreme Court upheld the decision, but Mr. Justice Frankfurter gave a minority opinion with regard to the District Attorney's role in the publicity:

> I cannot agree to uphold a conviction which affirmatively treats newspaper participation instigated by a prosecutor as part of the traditional concept of the "American way of the conduct of a trial."

With such dissents, the free press—fair trial issue became more noticeable. But it was not until 1961 that the Supreme Court reversed a conviction based solely on pre-trial publicity.

Irvin v. *Dowd,* 1961. In that year, the Supreme Court unanimously struck down an Indiana conviction on the ground of prejudicial pretrial publicity. Nothing happened to the offending newspaper or radio and television stations that blanketed the area with news of Irvin's alleged crime of six murders. Although clearly culpable in imperiling the rights of the accused, *they* were not on trial. But even more important is the fact that the basis for overturning the conviction —prejudicial pretrial publicity—was a technical point by which the accused was freed from charges that he had committed the murders. Mr. Justice Frankfurter wrote a concurring opinion reversing the conviction, in which he pointed out that prejudicial publicity imperiled both the accused and the community:

> ... this is, unfortunately, not an isolated case, nor an atypical miscarriage of justice due to anticipatory trial by newspaper instead of trial in court before a jury . . . But again and again, such disregard of fundamental fairness is so flagrant that the Court is compelled . . . to reverse a conviction in which prejudicial newspaper intrusion has poisoned the outcome . . . This Court has not yet decided that the fair administration of criminal justice must be subordinated to another safeguard of our constitutional system—freedom of the press, properly conceived. The Court has not yet decided that, while convictions must be reversed and *miscarriages of justice result* because the minds of jurors or potential jurors were poisoned, the poisoner is constitutionally protected in plying his trade [italics added].

Here, indeed, was a strong warning to the media, as well as a lament by the Court, that it was not able to base its decision on the guilt of the accused.

Some critics of the American press have suggested that we copy the British system that any pretrial publication of information about a defendant in a criminal case leads to contempt of court. In one case, a Scottish newspaper was fined $21,000 for using a front page picture of a soccer star charged with indecent exposure. "How is a judge or jury to know," asked the presiding judge in the case, "that the witness is identifying the man seen on the occasion of the crime and not the man whose photograph has been blazoned on the front page of a newspaper?"

Perhaps the reason that the American media have not been equally restricted is that the British court system is nationally controlled. With our separation of powers, we have fifty-one court systems; to bring them into alignment, with a central policy, is no small task.

Estes v. *Texas,* 1965. Another important case of a conviction overturned because of prejudicial coverage was that of Billy Sol Estes, Texas financier and wheeler-dealer. During the pretrial hearing, extensive television coverage took place. *The New York Times* reported that the courtroom was "turned into a snake-pit by the multiplicity of cameras, wires, microphones, and technicians milling about the chamber." Estes' appeal to the U.S. Supreme Court alleged denial of his constitutional rights of "due process of law." In its decision, the Court focused on television, excluding consideration of the press:

> The State . . . says that the use of television in the instant case was "without injustice to the person immediately concerned," basing its position on the fact that the petitioner has established no isolatable prejudice and that this must be shown in order to invalidate a conviction; for this the court itself has found instances in which a showing of actual prejudice is not a prerequisite to reversal. This is such a case.

This was a 5–4 decision. In dissenting, Mr. Justice Stewart said:

> The suggestion that there are limits upon the public's right to know what goes on in the courts causes me deep concern. The idea of imposing upon any medium of communication the burden of justifying its presence is contrary to where I had always thought the presumption must lie in the area of First Amendment freedoms.

Considering that six opinions were written in this case, it is little wonder that the free press—fair trial debate continues. The niceties of the law beclouded the issue even more in the following case.

Sheppard v. *Maxwell,* 1966. Perhaps the most highly publicized episode in the recent annals of the free press—fair trial controversy was the case of Dr. Sam Sheppard, Cleveland osteopath (*Time* reported that Sheppard had been called "the Romeo of the rubbing table"), who was convicted of murdering his pregnant wife in a trial in the Cuyahoga County, Ohio, Common Pleas Court of Judge Edward Blythin in 1954. Dr. Sheppard's subsequent legal battles, his personal misfortunes, and his eventual acquittal at a second trial in 1966, make for one of the most dramatic cases in this area.

In the 1954 trial, Sheppard originally offered to submit to a polygraph test, but later refused to do so. There unfolded a chain of publicity by the media virtually unprecedented in the annals of American jurisprudence. The Cleveland newspapers hit at Sheppard's unavailability for questioning (he had not been arrested), and then at his refusal to take the test. Front page editorials said that someone was getting away with murder and asked "Why no inquest?"

Dr. Samuel Gerber, county coroner, called an inquest the same day. This hearing was broadcast from a school auditorium. None of Sheppard's lawyers were permitted to participate; in fact, they were forcibly ejected from the room amid cheers from the audience. Sheppard's illicit love affair with another woman became public. In a front page editorial, the Cleveland *Press* asked "Why isn't Sam Sheppard in jail?" and "Quit Stalling—Bring Him In." He was arrested that evening.

What followed was a flagrant example of trial by newspaper. Sheppard was convicted (of second degree murder) and sentenced to life. After a long legal battle, Sheppard was finally freed from prison in 1964 by U.S. District Judge Carl Weinman on a writ of habeas corpus, on the ground that pretrial publicity had denied Sheppard a fair trial. The U.S. (Sixth) Circuit Court overruled Judge Weinman and later (June, 1966) the Supreme Court accepted the case for review.

Striking down the conviction, 8–1, the Court pointed to reports of "clues" found that, in fact, had never existed; cartoons chiding Sheppard for his reluctance to help solve the case; and, in one instance, a picture that had been edited to imply to the reader that Sheppard was the killer. In the original trial, Judge Blythin (a candidate for reelection at the time) had personally written tickets of admission to nationally syndicated journalists, permitted photographs to be taken during the pretrial period, and posed for pictures on the courthouse steps. He had even authorized installation of telephone lines for the press in the courthouse. The Supreme Court concluded that all this media activity interfered with the trial itself. Said Mr. Justice Clark, for the Court:

> A responsible press has always been the handmaiden of effective judicial administration, especially in the criminal field. Its function in this regard is documented by an impressive record of service over several centuries. The press does not simply publish information about trials, but guards against the miscarriage of justice by subjecting the police, prosecutors, and judicial processes to extensive public scrutiny and criticism. This court had, therefore, been unwilling to place and direct limitation on the freedom traditionally exercised by the news media for what transpires in the courtroom is public property.

The important fact is that despite the behavior of the press, recognized even by the press itself and deplored by the Supreme Court, the decision placed the ultimate blame squarely on Judge Blythin for allowing the situation to exist: that the judge had a duty to maintain control of his courtroom and its area during the trial. The essential issue was clarified by the Court:

> Of course, there is nothing that proscribes the press from reporting events that transpire in the courtroom. But where there is a reasonable likelihood that prejudicial news prior to the trial will prevent a fair trial, the judge should continue the case until the threat abates, or transfer it to another county not so permeated with publicity. In addition, sequestration of the jury was something the judge should have raised with counsel. If publicity during the proceedings threatens the fairness of the trial, a new trial should be ordered. But we must remember that reversals are but palliatives; the cure lies in those remedial measures that will prevent the prejudice at its inception.

Molloy points out that one could argue, as publishers do, that if the Supreme Court considers existing procedural remedies adequate to cope with the unparalleled amount of public attention focused on the Sheppard case, it is difficult to conceive of any situation where those same procedural safeguards would be inadequate to protect any defendant. In any case, Sheppard was given a new trial in an atmosphere strongly contrasting with that of 1954 and was acquitted in November, 1966. But either an innocent man spent 10 years behind prison bars, or a murderer was freed because of trial by newspaper.

The Oswald Case, 1963.   The free press–fair trial dilemma was further inflamed by the murder of President John F. Kennedy and subsequent events at Dallas, Texas in November, 1963. Two weeks after the assassination, the American Civil Liberties Union (ACLU) said that had Lee Harvey Oswald lived, he would have been deprived of all opportunity for a fair trial because of the conduct of law enforcement officers. They were guilty of a tragic error in bowing to the pressure of the media. In arranging Oswald's transfer from the city to the county jail under circumstances to suit the convenience of newsmen, they yielded to insistent demands to publicize the case. It was in the course of that transfer that Oswald was slain, in full view of millions of television viewers. Had the media been controlled and had Oswald been given proper trial so that a determination could have been made of whether he were guilty, whether he acted alone, and whether he acted in connection with some foreign power, the subsequent Warren Commission investigation and the Shaw trial might have been obviated. Not only the facts could have been elicited, but millions of dollars could have been saved. As it was, the matter of free press–fair trial again zoomed into national focus. On December 1, 1963, seven members of the Harvard law faculty, in a letter to the *New York Times* said:

> Precisely because the President's assassination was the ultimate in defiance of the law, it called for the ultimate in vindication of the law. The law enforcement agencies, in permitting virtually unlimited access to the media made this impossible. Not only would it have been virtually impossible to impanel a jury which had not formed its own views on those facts which might come before it, but much of the information released, such as statements by Mrs. Oswald, might have been legally inadmissible at trial....We cannot comfort ourselves with the notion that this could only happen in Dallas. It is too frequently a feature of our process of criminal justice that it is regarded as a public carnival. This reflects our general obsession that everybody has a right immediately to know and see everything... that justice must take second place behind the public's right to be informed about every detail of a crime.
>
> As long as we adhere to that notion, and as long as our legislatures and courts [and police] are unwilling to protect the processes of justice, we must recognize that the lamentable behavior of Dallas law enforcement agencies and of communications media reflect a flaw in ourselves as a society.

The Warren Commission Report (1964) summarized the situation:

> The courtroom, not the newspaper or television screen, is the appropriate forum in our system for the trial of a man accused of a crime... The promulgation of a code of professional conduct governing representatives of all news media could be welcome evidence that the press had profited by the lesson of Dallas. The burden of insuring that appropriate action is taken to establish ethical standards of conduct for the news media must also be borne, however, by State and local governments, by the bar, and ultimately by the public... to bring about a proper balance between the right of the public to be kept informed and the right of the individual to a fair and impartial trial.

Not everyone agreed with the Warren Commission findings. Response took a number of forms, several of which Molloy lists:

1. A Joint Media Committee on News Coverage Problems meeting in Washington recommended a voluntary pooling policy for the "orderly, efficient, and unobtrusive coverage of news events" such as took place at Dallas, Little Rock, Oxford, Mississippi, or during Khrushchev's visit to the United States. Such pooling is standard procedure on presidential trips.

2. Members of the press and bar began to discuss the problem in voluntary seminars throughout the nation.

3. The American Bar Association authorized a three-year, $750,000 study of the responsibility of the bar, police, and press in assuring a defendant a fair trial.

4. The Press-Bar committee of the American Society of Newspaper Editors (ASNE), after a year-long study, rejected the primary assertions of the Warren Report about press performance in Dallas. The press, it said, originated no false reports; what rumors developed came from information made public by law enforcement officers.

5. Voluntary codes of press-bar conduct were worked out in Philadelphia, and in the states of Massachusetts, Oregon, Kentucky, and Louisiana, and bar associations in other states began considering the problem.

There was no trial for Lee Harvey Oswald, but the role of the police in providing a public setting for his murder before TV cameras will be debated for a long time to come.

As part of the $750,000 project to define uniform standards for the administration of criminal justice, the American Bar Association and the American Law Institute created a special free press—fair trial advisory committee headed by Justice Paul Reardon of the Supreme Judicial Court of Massachusetts. In October, 1966, after two years of work, this panel found that most prejudicial material does not result from independent news reporting, but originates with law enforcement officers and lawyers; and it recommended imposing strong controls over participants in criminal cases. The press could be punished for contempt of court only when flagrant abuses occurred that were likely to prejudice a jury's verdict.

The Reardon committee proposed a change in the canons of legal ethics that would prevent lawyers from releasing any information or opinion about a criminal case if "there is a reasonable likelihood that such dissemination will interfere with a fair trial or otherwise prejudice the due administration of justice." Specifically, this would bar lawyers from the following actions:

Before trial: From informing others of defendant's prior criminal record or his character or reputation; the existence or contents of a confession; the performance of any examination or tests or the defendant's refusal to submit to such examination; the testimony of prospective witnesses; the possibility that the defendant will plead guilty, and any opinion as to the defendant's guilt or innocence, although a defense attorney may state that his client denies the charges.

During trial: From releasing or approving any statements relating to the case, except to quote from or refer without comment to public records in the case.

The penalty for violating the canon would be suspension or disbarment. These restrictions are similar to the so-called Katzenbach rules laid down by the Department of Justice in 1965 for Federal prosecutions in which the Attorney General ordered that nothing be given to the press that might prejudice a case. But it is in *state* courts that most crimes of violence are tried and where the worst publicity occurs.

Another Reardon Committee recommendation dealt with preliminary hearings:

> The defense may exclude the public from any pretrial hearing where evidence is heard which could not be admitted at the trial. A record would be kept which would be made public after the trial. This would prevent publicizing inflammatory materials.

The Reardon report also recommended use of the contempt power in narrow and clearly defined situations in two types of cases:

> One, where a person "going beyond public records, makes a statement willfully designed to affect the outcome of the trial and which seriously threatens to have that effect."

This would apply only when a jury trial was in progress, and was considered by some to be inadequate. It would not, for example, cover the type of pretrial poisoning that took place in Dr. Sam Sheppard's case.

> Two, contempt action would be permitted against anyone who violates a judge's order not to release information produced at a closed hearing. This would apply to reporters, who at present can only be urged by the bench to cooperate.

A subsequently published book agreed with the Reardon recommendations in essential details.* The authors advised the press:

1. When all else is done with complete respect for the defendant's right of a fair trial and the press nevertheless publishes information that is deliberately partisan, prejudicial in content, timing, and volume and devoid of redeeming purpose, then the press should not expect to be exempt from contempt proceedings.

2. If all other participants in the judicial process behave with maximum care for the defendant's rights, the public pressure against

*Alfred Friendly and Ronald Goldfarb, *Crime and Publicity: The Impact of the News on the Administration of Justice.* Twentieth Century Fund, New York, 1967, pp. 54–88 passim. See also, for a contrary view, American Newspaper Publishers Association, *Free Press and Fair Trial,* ANPA, New York, 1967, 143 pages.

press irresponsibility on that score will be immense. And contrary
to the usual impression, the public pressure can be effective.

3. The argument of the press that it cannot be blamed for what official
   sources freely disclose . . . is neither foolish nor hypocritical. But in
   a situation where other participants in the administration of justice
   have cleaned their houses, the challenge to the press's own sense
   of decency will come in much more impressive form than now.

The press response to the Reardon report was one of outrage. The
president of ASNE called it "detrimental to society," "selection of news,
suppression of the news, censorship of the news" leading to "abuse and
confusion," encouraging the "police tendency toward secrecy," "misguided, quixotic, unnecessary and harmful to our democratic system."
At the annual meeting of ASNE in April, 1967, a report was presented
by the Freedom of Information Committee, with J. Edward Murray,
managing editor of *The Arizona Republic,* acting as chairman. Referring to the Reardon recommendations, the ASNE report said:

> The mere possibility that the bar's tentative proposals for news restric-
> tions may eventually be formalized is causing almost daily attempts
> to muzzle the press so law enforcement can operate behind closed
> doors.

The ASNE report therefore recommended:

1. Increased contacts between the press and bar at the local level to
   improve understanding on both sides and to evolve working agreements which minimize the problem;

2. Continued efforts by ASNE, in cooperation with other professional
   media groups, to modify the ABA proposals for new restrictions
   before these become final;

3. A vigorous educational campaign by editors to take the case for
   the press to the public;

4. Specific, all-out opposition by individual newspapers to any effort
   to restrict the responsible editor's prerogative to print what he
   thinks the public needs to know about law enforcement.

In contrast to the screening of police and court news recommended
by the ABA, the ASNE report said the press would like:

1. Neither sanctions against, nor interference with, the police at the
   pre-arrest and arrest stages of the criminal process;

2. No closing of public records, neither police blotters nor police
   records of criminals, nor court records;

3. No increase in the use of contempt power against the press or
   the police;

4. A sensible and decent respect for the general public's right to be represented at all times in open court by a responsible press which is not unnecessarily restricted from doing its reporting job.

To alert newspaper readers to all aspects of the problem, ASNE outlined a four-point case for the press:

Impartial Jurors: The general public does not need to be denied the full facts at the time a crime is committed—as to who and what kind of a person is accused, why he is accused and what the police know about the matter—in order to get an impartial jury and have a fair trial. "No matter how often it is denied, it would seem that the bar prefers ignorant jurors . . . Honest facts, information, common sense knowledge, are confused with prejudice, just because they are acquired before trial starts."

Compulsory or Voluntary Controls: The ASNE study reaffirms its belief in the traditional position that the First Amendment will not permit compulsory controls of either the press or its news sources. A committee of the bar of the City of New York, headed by Justice Harold R. Medina, has issued a report which concludes that the Constitution will not permit the bar and bench to censor police on trial news through court order or contempt power, as recommended in the Reardon report.

Threat of Secret Law Enforcement: The bar is seeking what amounts to secret law enforcement because less than 10 percent of the 700,000 felonies committed each year ever come to trial. Given the bar's restrictions, this would mean that the great majority of crimes would never be adequately reported and "crimes would be swept even further under the rug at a time when it is increasing at an alarming rate."

Artificial restriction of crime news encourages police secrecy, weakens the press as the watch-dog of law enforcement, including fair trial, and damages the credibility of the press as a guarantor of public order in times of crisis.

Other Threats to Fair Trial: "The criminal law is in a morass of difficulties which pose a greater threat to equal justice than so-called pre-trial publicity . . . Among the worst of these are the delay of cases in clogged dockets; assembly line justice; plea negotiations which wink at perjury; high-priced technicality justice for some and low-grade unequal justice for others; exclusionary rules of evidence which bar common sense facts; and an overemphasis on the rights of the accused at the expense of the rights of the victims of crime."

The ASNE report summarized its position by saying:

If the rules of evidence are so technical, so deliberate, so fragile that they cannot function properly in the company of the full reporting of the truth by the mass media, then let's not muzzle the press. Instead, let's take a hard look at this tricky house of cards called the adversary system . . . and the rules of evidence. To do this, we need more reporting, not less.

Clearly, the adamant positions taken by the American Bar Association on the one hand and by the American Society of Newspaper Editors on the other revealed not only depths of feeling that blurred judgment, but also unreconciled positions. In September, 1968, as pressures for clarification of proper procedures grew, the Judicial Conference of the United States adopted and released a report that did little to mollify the press. This report was prepared by a committee headed by Judge Irving R. Kaufman of the U.S. Court of Appeals for the Second Circuit, who had been appointed by Chief Justice Earl Warren two years earlier to prepare it. The Judicial Conference is composed of the chief judges of the U.S. Courts of Appeals, the chief judge of every Federal District Court, the chief judge of the Court of Claims, and the chief judge of the Court of Customs and Patents. The body has a quasi-legal status in that its members are all government officials, but its recommendations are those of an association of Federal office holders. Further, its recommendations are primarily significant for Federal jurists; it can only hope that State members of the bar and bench will be guided by their leadership.

The Kaufman report, adopted by the Conference, recommended that courts act in three major areas:*

1. Using their power to control the release of prejudicial information by lawyers under penalty of disciplinary action;

2. Prohibiting prejudicial disclosures by courthouse personnel such as bailiffs, clerks, marshals and court reporters;

3. Providing rules for special orders governing the proceedings in any case in which prejudicial influences might otherwise penetrate into the trial.

But as to press coverage of a trial, the committee said it does not at present recommend any direct curb or restraint on publication by the press of potentially prejudicial materials. "Such a curb is both unwise as a matter of policy, and poses serious Constitutional problems."

It also did not recommend any judicially imposed restriction on the release of information by Federal law enforcement agencies.

Apparently, the jurists did not feel that visual and audio communications systems should enjoy the same privileges as the printed word. The *New York Times* continued:

The committee was adamant in telling the courts to adopt rules prohibiting the taking of photographs, or radio or television broadcasting

---

The New York Times, September 20, 1968, p. 34. See also Spencer A. Gard, *"Free Press vs. Fair Trial: Another Tempest in the Teapot."*

from the courtroom or its environs. The environs might take in an entire courthouse, it suggested.

The recommendations in the three areas first cited were so specific that one wonders why the media resented them. It was said that these recommendations inhibited the "public's right to know"—for example, the recommendations on *Release of Information by Attorneys:*

> From the time of arrest, issuance of an arrest warrant or filing of a complaint, information or indictment of any criminal matter until the commencement of trial or disposition without trial, a lawyer associated with the prosecution or defense shall *not* release, nor authorize the release of any extra-judicial statement, for dissemination by any means of public communication, relating to that matter and concerning:
>
> 1. The prior criminal record (including arrests, indictments, or other charges of crime), or the character or reputation of the accused, except that the lawyer may make a factual statement of the accused's name, age, residence or occupation, and family status, and if the accused has not been apprehended, a lawyer associated with the prosecution may release any information necessary to aid in his apprehension or to warn the public of any dangers he may present;
>
> 2. [Nor] the existence of contents of any confession, admission, or statement given by the accused, or the refusal or failure to make any statement;
>
> 3. [Nor] the performance of any examination or tests or the accused's refusal or failure to submit to an examination or test;
>
> 4. [Nor] the identity, testimony, or credibility of prospective witnesses, except that the lawyer may announce the identity of the victim if the announcement is not otherwise prohibited by law;
>
> 5. [Nor] the possibility of a plea of guilty to the offense charged or to a lesser offense;
>
> 6. [Nor] any opinion as to the accused's guilt or innocence or as to the merits of the case or the evidence in the case.

Because this seemed to leave the lawyer little to release to the media, the recommendation spelled out specifically what he *may* announce:

> This shall not preclude the lawyer . . . from announcing the fact and circumstances of the arrest (including the time and place of arrest, resistance, pursuit, and use of weapons), the identity of the investigating and arresting officer or agency, and the length of the investigation; from making an announcement at the time of seizure of any physical evidence other than a confession, admission or statement,

which is limited to a description of the evidence seized; from disclosing the nature, substance, or text of the charge including a brief description of the offense charged; from quoting, or referring without comment to public records of the court in the case; from announcing the scheduling or result of any stage in the judicial process; from requesting assistance in obtaining evidence; or from announcing without further comment that the accused denies the charges made against him.

[But] during the trial of any criminal matter, including the period of selecting the jury, no lawyer associated with the prosecution or the defense shall give or authorize any extra-judicial statement or interview, relating to the trial . . . except that the lawyer may quote from or refer without comment to public records of the court in the case.

The foregoing defines and restricts conduct of *lawyers* on a case. While it does not regulate the media, it does inhibit their news output by restricting the types of information that lawyers and other courthouse personnel may release. Quite naturally, the media were not about to accept such a situation. In New York state, leaders of the media in cooperation with influential members of the bar and bench set about planning a conference in which they could, together, develop standards for releases.

On September 26, 1969, a New York State Free Press—Fair Trial Conference took place, at which voluntary guidelines were adopted. The Conference, the result of 15 months of planning, was headed by Chief Judge Stanley H. Fuld of the State Court of Appeals, and Clifton Daniel, associate editor of the *New York Times*. State and municipal bar and press associations attended. Judge Fuld said:

The essence of the guidelines is mutual respect to both the basic rights of free press and fair trial. In effect, the responsibility for decisions as to what is to be printed or broadcast is left with the news media with the reminder that the rights of accused persons and civil litigants may be prejudiced by irresponsible reporting. [*The New York Times*, September 27, 1969]

Principles were set forth as follows:

Freedom of the press is guaranteed by the First Amendment . . . the right to a speedy and public trial by the Sixth . . . While the news media recognize the responsibility of the judge to preserve order in the court and seek the ends of justice by all those means available to him, decisions about the handling of news rest with the editors, who, in the exercise of news judgments, should remember that:

1. An accused person is presumed innocent until proven guilty;

2. Accused persons and civil litigants are entitled to be judged in an atmosphere free from passion, prejudice and sensationalism;

3. Readers, listeners and viewers are potential jurors;

4. No one's reputation should be injured needlessly. [Ibid.]

After all the contentions on both sides during the preceding years, Judge Fuld's summary of the conference seemed anticlimactic in its simplicity. In effect, it threw the whole issue back to where it had been before the principles had been adopted. But the statement was made in the light of the preceding controversy which, it was hoped, would deter others from going down the same path. Current situations show some evidence that advances have been made in resolving a conflict of interest inherent in our system.

Molloy sums up the situation well:

Perhaps most significantly, journalism today is showing a new professionalism. As more newspapers realize that great rights demand great standards of responsibility for their moral exercise, the problem may well be on its way toward a solution.

Blue Power

Today the police find themselves confronted with changing functions, in cities presenting bigger challenges with less and less dollars to meet them. The police are part of a criminal justice system more accurately called a nonsystem. Little wonder that their old organizational arrangements no longer meet their needs. They are turning to political power as are other activist groups. In the old days, when the main role of the police was keeping order, when enforcement was the job of detectives or of private agencies, Tammany Hall or other "bosses" provided all the political support patrolmen needed. Their job was to see that needy people received coal, or defense against landlords, in return for votes to keep the Irish Tiger in city hall. As uniformed ward-heelers, the police had little to worry about (and little pay and status), so long as they played big brother to the poor, smiled on wealthy traffic violators, and channeled the proceeds of graft to the "higher ups." But then came Horace Greeley, Jacob Riis, and other reformers. Tammany Hall and Boss Tweed declined and the police were left rudderless—although there are still cities where political machines maintain a firm grip on various aspects of criminal justice processes.

With the influx into big cities of minority populations who were left stranded after the opulent employment of the War years, unemployment and crime have soared. More and more the question is raised of what the police role should be: controlling crime or keeping the peace. Police manpower, heavily drawn from the lower middle class, is inadequate for the former and ill-trained for the latter. Their need to organize for self-defense and for moral support has grown. In larger departments, they first met this need by creating ethnic and racial organizations of a social nature. But these lacked clout against political forces and competing pressure groups. A need for unions has been growing. Private occupational groups organize; why not public servants?

The Boston Police Strike

In Boston, the police organized a union as early as 1919, applied for affiliation with the American Federation of Labor, and sought recognition from the Massachusetts state government. When the state did not respond to their pleas for improved working conditions, they struck. For two days and a night, the suspension of law enforcement resulted in disorder and riots despite the services of volunteer police and the Boston forces of the State Guard, which had been requested by the mayor. Not until the opportune political moment did Governor Calvin Coolidge order the entire State Guard to restore order in the city, and to demonstrate that public servants must not desert their posts. Samuel Gompers, AFL president, futilely appealed to Coolidge on behalf of the policemen. In a tense nation beset, at the time, by a general strike in Seattle and a strike of steel workers, Coolidge's reply received a national acclaim that led him to the Presidency: "There is no right to strike against public safety by anybody, anywhere, at any time" (James Henry Snidler, "John Calvin Coolidge").

For many years, this view was accepted. Indeed, most states passed laws forbidding public servants to strike. But the police have unionized for collective bargaining purposes. While these organizations found themselves weakened without the ultimate threat of striking, they have also found that unions have other ways of exerting power.

For instance, their treasuries grew large and could be used to mount campaigns to achieve some of their ends. Ed Cray tells of one of the most dramatic examples of this in an article he wrote for *The Nation*. The reference is to New York City:

> No sooner had Howard Leary settled into the dreary headquarters on Centre Street [as police commissioner] in 1966 than the Police Benevolent Association (PBA) moved to challenge the [mayor] Lindsay sponsored Civilian Review Board. That board had been in existence since 1955 and, though police mistrusted it, had performed its pittance by authority of the police commissioners. Lindsay, to offer a promise of greater redress to victims of police malpractice, made two changes in the board: he expanded it and installed a civilian majority. That was enough.

> As justification for first, an unsuccessful lawsuit, and then a referendum which would return the board to its former police-dominated status, the PBA insisted it was acting to preserve the commissioner's authority.

> The PBA poured great sums of money into the campaign against the board, its city-wide ads deliberately hinting that rape and pillage would prevail were the Lindsay set-up to continue.

> That November was a turning point. For the first time, police felt a

public support strong enough to mount a counter-attack on the per-
missiveness of parents, courts and miscellaneous do-gooders.

According to former police lieutenant Arthur Niederhoffer, "The
commissioner's power was never the primary concern at all. It was a
fight for PBA power, police power and perhaps Conservative Party
power." Their victory (3–1) was their first political triumph in the
public forum. [Cray, "Politics of Blue Power," p. 493]*

The Right to Strike

Perhaps it was this taste of victory and power that emboldened
the New York City police to test the main issue of the right to strike.
Actually, since 1919, public servants (including police) had organized
unions, affiliated with the AFL, and indulged in slow-downs, "blue flu,"
and actual strikes in Des Moines, Sioux Falls, Sacramento, Battle Creek,
Gary, Kalamazoo, Montreal, and other cities. Theodore W. Kheel, a
labor lawyer and arbitrator since the 1940s, says:

> Last year (1968) saw more strikes by teachers, garbage collectors,
> police, firemen, city hall and statehouse workers than ever before.
> Children in 21 states and the District of Columbia went without
> school as 160,000 teachers walked out of 114 separate work stoppages.
> Citizens of Kansas City and Youngstown have gone without full police
> and fire protection. Few public services remain untouched as welfare
> workers, even doctors and nurses also struck.

> Today, [he continues] virtually everybody is getting into the organi-
> zation act. Tenants and landlords do it, so do clergymen, racehorse
> owners, professional baseball and football players, welfare recipients,
> and students. Add the fact that government is one of the nation's
> fastest growing industries. Some 8,500,000 men and women now work
> for state and city agencies, and this army is expected to swell to
> 14 million over the next decade. Another 2,800,000 work for the
> federal government.

> Public service unions are growing accordingly. The American Fed-
> eration of State, County and Municipal Employees (AFL-CIO) may
> soon dwarf such giants as the Teamsters . . . Moreover, as living costs
> rise and civil service employees' earnings lag behind those of private
> employment, the public employees' unions find cause for militancy.
> [Kheel, Reader's Digest, August 1969]

Kheel shares the view of most Americans that the civil servant's
right to strike must be subordinated to the public interest. But he raises
the question of how to do it. "Antistrike laws not only fail to prevent
a strike; they may actually impede its settlement."

---

*For a fuller account of the New York Civilian Complaint Review Board con-
troversy, see Algeron D. Black, The People and the Police.

Consider New York City's ordeal during the strike of 30,000 transit workers in 1966. When a court injunction was issued to stop the strike, union leader Michael Quill tore it up on television. Quill and his fellow leaders were jailed for contempt. Uncertain of whom to talk with, Mayor Lindsay sent an aide to parley secretly with the incarcerated Quill, but that didn't work . . . Finally, on the 12th day of the strike, a wage increase was granted and the subway and bus men went back to work.

But according to state law, public service workers who struck were denied wage increases for three years, so a judge had to declare the settlement illegal. To prevent a resumption of the strike, Governor Nelson Rockefeller rushed through an amendment to the state's anti-strike law, exempting the city transit workers from the law's penalty provisions—retroactively! That was New York's last effort to combat public service strikes by punitive legislation alone. [Ibid.]

How would Kheel solve the problem? New York state's Taylor law (1967) did not prevent the New York City police strike of early 1971. The law failed to incorporate suggestions made by Kheel:

How do we give public service employees the right to strike that makes collective bargaining work, and still minimize the chances of strike if negotiations break down anyway? We already have the solution. The Taft-Hartley Act of 1947 empowers the President to invoke an 80-day cooling-off period when a strike in the private sector endangers public health or safety. Union leaders and managers continue bargaining. If the cooling-off period ends without agreement, the President refers the dispute to Congress, which can impose arbitration. [Ibid.]

The New York City Police Strike, 1971

With Taft-Hartley provisions on the state level, the governor of New York could have invoked them in the 1971 New York City police strike. But there were none, so he could not. The situation was intricate legally, and emotional to a high degree. Mayor John Lindsay was confronted simultaneously with contract negotiations with sanitary, fire and transit workers, in addition to the police. Moreover, when the police struck (they used the euphemism *job action*), some police officers of the Welfare, Housing and Transit Authorities walked out in sympathy. Also, the mayor had just announced that the City was almost $300 million in the red, the significance of which was apparent in relation to the demands of the Policemens Benevolent Association (PBA).

The strike concerned the relative pay scales of policemen and firemen on the one hand, and of patrolmen and sergeants on the other. Said *The New York Times*, January 16, 1971:

Pay relationships among patrolmen and police officers, and firemen and fire officers, have a long history. Since 1898 policemen and firemen at the entry level have had the same annual salaries. But the first and second promotional ranks of the police—sergeants and lieutenants—had received lower than their counterpart fire ranks. It was this discrepancy that led police sergeants and lieutenants to seek improvements that would give them parity with the fire officers.

The more favorable salary levels of fire officers apparently resulted from steps to equalize weekly hours of work in 1937 during the administration of Mayor Fiorello LaGuardia. In early years, police officers' hours were substantially less than those of the Fire Department. When the hours of fire officers were reduced, however, their salaries continued to be maintained, and afterward they were increased in equal amounts or percentages with those of the police officers . . .

The occasion for the New York City patrolmen's so-called job action on January 14, 1971, was a decision announced that day by the State Court of Appeals that it was asking the State Supreme Court to decide whether an agreement *initialed* on January 29, 1969 by representatives of the PBA and of the city was indeed a legally binding collective bargaining agreement. The city argued that this agreement was simply a preliminary step in negotiations leading to a formal contract, but that there was no such contract.

The agreement—or contract, if such it was—provided that the pay of patrolmen should be maintained at a ratio of 3 to 3.5 with that of police sergeants. In their suit, filed with the Court of Appeals, the PBA claimed retroactive pay of $100 a month to bring patrolmen's pay in line with that of sergeants, who had been raised following the agreement. Said the *Times,* January 15, 1971:

> The dispute between the city and its patrolmen that the Court of Appeals yesterday asked the State Supreme Court to decide concerns the validity of a contract that the patrolmen contend requires the relationship between salaries of patrolmen and sergeants to be maintained at a 3 to 3.5 ratio.

> At present, the base pay of patrolmen with three years' service is $10,950 a year and that of sergeants with the same seniority is $14,235, which is higher than the ratio would allow. To restore the ratio, the patrolmen would have to receive a $100 a month increase, bringing their base salaries to $12,150 a year.

> If this were done, however, it would start a potentially endless spiral of wage increases. The ratio issue arose when sergeants' pay was increased, on the recommendation of a fact-finding panel, so that they would receive the same pay as *lieutenants* in the Fire Department. If the patrolmen won their $1,200-a-year increase, it is likely that the Uniformed Fire Fighters Association would seek a retroactive raise to maintain the traditional "parity," in this case, pay equality between patrolmen and first-grade firemen.

This could be followed by a claim by Fire Department lieutenants that their traditional 3.9 to 3 ratio with first-grade firemen had been upset. And a new cycle could begin.

The decision of the Court of Appeals to refer the matter to the State Supreme Court obviously meant—to the patrolmen—another long and infuriating delay before it would be determined whether the agreement was a contract, and back pay at the new level could be forthcoming. The agreement had been initialed October 1, 1968, so that it would have meant back pay of $2,700 for each patrolman, in addition to the new pay level at the 3–3.5 ratio. Such delay was intolerable. Moreover, the Mayor's Labor Policy Committee announced:

> Regardless of the outcome of the court case, the city cannot under the new contract accede to a situation where relationships are formally defined so that action taken with respect to one contract may in turn require a new round of action with all other uniformed service contracts. Such requirements would present the city with uncontrollable costs.

So the patrolmen struck. There was no general wave of crime, as there had been in Boston in 1919. The mayor made reassuring announcements on the air that supervisory personnel were keeping the peace. Even rookies still in training were pressed into service. *Reported* crimes fell off by half—in view of the fact that crimes are normally reported by patrolmen, 85 percent of whom were taking part in the job action. Governor Rockefeller announced that he was in close touch with the situation and that a liaison officer for the National Guard was already in the city. On the sixth day, the PBA president was finally able to mobilize sufficient votes of the patrolmen's delegates to end the strike. The Police Commissioner ordered immediate suspension of any member of the force who failed to perform assigned duties as of 4 P.M. that day. All reported.

Mayor Lindsay invoked the state Taylor law, saying, "The mandated state law has certain penalties in it and this city has no choice but to follow it."

> Paychecks to be distributed tomorrow to the police [he announced] will carry the notice: "You are hereby notified that pursuant to the provisions mandated on the city by the 1969 amendments to the State Taylor Law, and in accordance with city procedures, subsequent checks will reflect deductions from the pay of those patrolmen who refused to perform their duties during the period January 14–19."

This could, at an average pay of $40 a day, have meant a loss to each patrolman of $480, an amount which—multiplied by the thousands on strike—would have gone far toward meeting the overtime pay of supervisory personnel for the six days. But that is incidental to our interest.

The issue is whether public employees have the right to strike. There seems to be no question today that they may organize unions for collective bargaining purposes. On the matter of striking, there is an implied inconsistency between state and Federal laws that withhold the right to strike while yet guaranteeing equal rights for all citizens. Perhaps even the Taft-Hartley law may one day be declared unconstitutional. Are the penalties of the Taylor law defensible? Certainly, until they are declared not to be, they serve as a deterrent to capricious strikes. But the fact is that public servants *are* striking throughout the country, despite the penalties and sometimes despite "the public interest."

Police Pressure

It is not only through unions and strikes that the nation's police have begun to exert political power in recent years. Police executives have jockeyed successfully with city administrators. One or two have been elected mayors. They have gone directly to the people through the ballot box to kill civilian review boards, as noted, and to win appropriations that city councils have denied them. Their growing union power and lobbying have won successes in state legislatures and in Congress. In many states, they have gained control of state planning agencies in channeling Law Enforcement Assistance funds to local criminal justice projects. Recently, attempts are being made to organize a national police union, the purposes of which are presumably to be different from those of local, state, and national associations of sheriffs and chiefs of police that have traditionally been dedicated to fraternalism and to higher professional standards.

Granted that police have long been denied adequate fiscal support that would enable them to do their job, or laws which would clarify what their job is, they are beginning to win financial gains, and ride the crest of the billowing wave of law and order. Such gains are long overdue. But as civil libertarian Ed Cray says, the major issue has barely surfaced:

> Who is to control the nation's police forces: the police themselves or the community?
>
> From city to city, the authority of elected officials varies inversely with the control maintained by ranking police officers. In Los Angeles, where the late Chief William H. Parker armored his fortress with a moat of pseudo-professionalism, his successors are in full control. The five man board of police commissioners charged by the city charter with responsibility for policy is a complacent rubber stamp for the

current chief. In Cleveland the mayor has had to replace his chief . . .
In New York, the president of the PBA has felt strong enough to
challenge Mayor Lindsay and bid to usurp the authority of the police
commissioner. [Cray, *The Nation*, pp. 493 ff.]

The trend would seem to be contrary to the long established principle that ultimate control of the police should be in civilian hands.
Cray adds:

> In one way or another, city charters provide that the highest authority
> of the department is to be a civilian—a city manager, a mayor or a
> city council. Whatever the final authority, it *is* political, and it *is*
> civilian.

But police have exerted such power of late that some mayors
have felt it judicious to appoint ex-police executives as "civilian" commissioners, as in New York where Mayor Lindsay's last two appointments were those of Howard Leary and Patrick V. Murphy—both police
career men and former commissioners in Philadelphia and Detroit,
respectively. Perhaps police line organizations are exerting increasing
influence in appointments of their own. It puts progressive police administrators under considerable pressure to avoid making organizational
changes that may be urgently needed. Sometimes even the heads of
patrolmen's groups are subject to a form of insurrection. In 1968, a
few "Young Turks" in the PBA—all out for law and order—organized
the Law Enforcement Group (LEG). They were hard liners, many
with John Birch Society connections and extreme rightist inclinations.
"Five weeks after it was formed," Cray says,

> LEG's membership was city-wide. Some members had assaulted a
> group of nine Black Panthers in a courtroom and thereby gained
> special public notice, and the new organization was the talk of the
> precinct houses. [Ibid.]

Police associations have also achieved political power in other
ways. "In Cleveland and Los Angeles," as Cray points out,

> police have gone directly to the ballot for pay raises or retirement
> benefits refused them by the city fathers. In Los Angeles, too, a third
> successive bond issue for more police facilities was approved, while
> voters were turning down school bond measures.

> In the New York state legislature last year, the police lobbied suc-
> cessfully for repeal of a law which more closely defined justifiable
> homicide . . . In legislatures police have found like-minded majorities,
> wary of bucking public sentiment that favors the police . . . With such
> support, the police will push even harder for complete control of law
> enforcement. [Ibid.]

Other Examples of Police Power

Almost daily, the press reports instances of the successful use of political pressure by the police. A few examples are worth noting because of their diversity.

1. A joint committee of police and firemen have been pressing the Lansing (Michigan) city administration to amend the city charter to permit employees of both departments to retire when 50 years old (instead of 55), with full pension benefits if they have been employed 25 years. The city finance director claimed it would cost the city $275,000 in the first year. The proposal lost in public referendum in the spring of 1971 by only a small margin. The point here pertains to political clout, not to the merit of the proposal.

2. Leaders of the Detroit Police Officers Association (DPOA) and the Detroit Detectives Association mobilized support to elect a former sheriff as mayor, and created an association of political pressure (already spread to 38 cities) that is planning to rate state legislators according to the number of bills introduced in the interest of the police. Said the president of the DPOA: "People are beginning to look for police advice. They are more ready to accept our opinion."

3. The emergence of police as a self-conscious political force has lent momentum to separate drives to forge a national police union. The center of one such effort is Boston, where Richard G. MacEachern learned the ways of power by building the Boston Police Patrolmen's Association into a national model of police political militancy. Philadelphian John Harrington is campaigning nationally in a separate effort. Former head of New York's PBA, John Cassese, is said to be working for a similar goal. Although these men may at the moment seem to be working at cross purposes, or even in competition, consolidated efforts are in the long run inevitable. The prospect of a national policemen's union with the power—and perhaps eventually even the legal right—to strike is sobering.

"The really dangerous aspect of all this," says sociologist Jerome Skolnick in *State News,* East Lansing (October 29, 1969), "is that the police take a quite distinct political position. That position is toward the politics of the extreme right."

Police Lobbies

Police pressure to achieve improved wages, working conditions, and equipment—all matters depending on appropriations—are exerted on city fathers and, if need be, on local electorates. The pressures may be made either by police leadership or by unions. But when it comes to changing the laws that affect the work of police (other than local ordinances), pressure must be exerted on state legislative bodies. Preferably this should be done by an organization which represents the maximum number of enforcement-related agencies, so that they can not only afford to maintain a lobby, but also so that their lobby will be seen as speaking for the broadest possible base of voters.

An example of such a lobby is that maintained by the Michigan Sheriffs' Association. It speaks for the sheriff's departments of 83 counties. Since each sheriff is elected, he undertakes to speak for his constituents (in police-related matters) as well as for his own department. The current executive secretary of this association is a former ranking officer of the State Police. In addition to the enforcement contacts he has made through the years, he is careful to invite to weekly association meetings representatives of as many related groups as possible. These may include (depending on the issue then before the legislature) representatives or spokesmen for the Michigan Association of Chiefs of Police, the State Police, the attorney general's office, the state association of prosecuting attorneys, regional councils of county governments, the state crime commission, probation and parole officials, and the like. Since none of these groups is large enough (or deems it appropriate) to maintain its own lobby, cooperation with the sheriffs' association is an important means of communicating with the legislators.

When the need for legislation arises, or when a relevant bill is being considered, the director of the association contacts every sheriff in the state, who, being elected officials themselves, know all elected personnel in their counties. The local sheriffs contact these officials, enlisting their assistance in rounding up contacts and communications with lawmakers. Such pressure can be massive. And it is also highly respected by legislators who depend upon lobbies as a means of learning the facts about an issue. Before they vote, their appropriate committee calls the director of the association to testify, and his influence in their ultimate decisions is a reflection of the thoroughness with which he has prepared his testimony.

But it is not always smooth sailing for police lobbyists. Legislators listen to other segments of the public also. For example, when a bill to require the licensing of snowmobiles was being considered by the Michigan legislature, the sheriffs' association asked that the fees be paid to them to finance a state-wide educational and enforcement campaign on the proper uses of the machines. The governor and state treasurer wanted the fees to accrue to the state's general fund, which badly needed replenishing. The State Conservation Department wanted the fees to finance snowmobile trails and resort developments. All three groups wanted the bill passed, but it was delayed pending an amendment that would determine the allocation of the funds. As usual, a compromise was the result, but the enforcement agencies would probably have had nothing had they not been represented by a strong lobby.

The sheriffs' association lobby maintains a day-to-day posture attuned to the interests of enforcement organizations. But it also is alert to the rights of personnel. To illustrate, a deputy was discharged by a sheriff for reasons that are irrelevant here. The courts ordered the sheriff to reemploy the man. The sheriff protested that the State Constitution stated that a sheriff may hire or fire deputies at his pleasure. The deputy's union brought pressure to bear. So the sheriff rehired the man but assigned him to a different job "more suited to him." The court supported the sheriff.

Commenting on the case, the lobbyist observed: "A union is as good or bad as you let it be." He explained: "They are very good in helping the sheriff get raises for his men, but the sheriff must always make sure that his own disciplinary rights are protected in the union contract."

Lobbies can do much if they represent all segments of enforcement, but to be effective they must be absolutely nonpartisan, and be known to be so. They do not seek to usurp enforcement power. Their sole interest is to make enforcement effective, even if laws must be made more realistic to accomplish this end.

Summary

In the days when police were adjuncts of and protected by city hall, there was little need for them to possess political power of their own. But as departments have become autonomous and professionalized, police officers have felt it necessary to organize to improve their economic position and to work for laws suiting their notions of police work. The Boston police strike in 1919 proved abortive. But Coolidge's flat statement only served to raise the issue of whether police, and other public servants, had the right to unionize for collective bargaining purposes, and to strike if these efforts failed. Did they, in fact, have equal rights with employees in the private sector?

In the years since 1919, unions have been legalized. The New York PBA campaign against the Civilian Complaint Review Board in 1966 demonstrated the power of a police union. As for the right to strike—still technically illegal—the many work stoppages of public employees in the last two decades seem to suggest that there is no way to prevent them. Lee Rainwater has referred to this as "the revolt of the dirty workers." A city administrator simply cannot fire the entire teacher corps, nor all the garbage collectors, transit workers, or police. A penalty system such as that provided by New York's Taylor Law can only hope to deter capricious strikes. But the strike right remains unclear. Either existing laws should be expanded to include Taft-Hartley types of provisions to postpone strikes through cooling-off periods, or strikes must be legalized and adequate machinery for handling them established.

As we view the emergence of police power exercised through unions, through the leadership of police executives, and through lobbies, it seems inevitable that the strike issue must soon be clarified, in response to pressures from the police themselves. The public seems ready and even sympathetic to the modification of anti-strike laws which cannot be enforced.

The recent movements to establish a national police union, if successful through consolidation, appear to be a logical expansion of Blue Power. But the purposes seems awesome when one considers the possibility of a national strike, perhaps joined by AFL-CIO affiliates or the Teamsters in a general work stoppage. A national police union appears to be certain. But a strike need not be.

Questions for Discussion

1. What advantages do you see in the Blue Power movement of recent years from the points of view of (a) policemen, (b) police administrators, (c) departmental morale, (d) public interest?

2. From the same points of view, what disadvantages do you see?

3. How do you assess the trend toward a national police union?

4. As police unionization and other evidences of Blue Power appear to be increasing, the question of public employees' right to strike becomes more heated. What are the arguments for and against such a right?

5. What do you think will be the effects of Blue Power on the professionalization of the police?

STUDY 5

Assessment of Attica ... A Symposium (December 4, 1971)

Participants

ALEX J. CADE—Professor of Counseling, Personnel Services and Educational Psychology and Director of *Upward Bound*, College of Education, Michigan State University; a practicing private psychologist; formerly Chief Psychologist, Reception-Diagnostic Center, Michigan Department of Corrections; Ph.D., Michigan State University and Diplomate, American Board of Professional Psychology.

WILLIAM A. GOLDBERG—Professor of Criminal Justice, Michigan State University; lifetime careerist in the corrections field, primarily in probation; Ph.D., Northwestern University.

PETER K. MANNING—Associate Professor of Sociology and Psychiatry, Michigan State University; special interest in the sociology of criminal justice and in social psychiatry; Ph.D., Duke University.

MARY P. SHARP—Member, East Lansing City Council; Assistant Director, Michigan State University Office of Equal Opportunity Programs; J.D., University of Michigan.

ROBERT H. SCOTT—(See page 468, Volume I, *The Police and the Community.*)

LOUIS A. RADELET

The chapter dealing with corrections in *The Police and the Community* (XVII) was written by the authors during the Fall of 1971, before and after the tragedy at Attica prison. The issues in corrections that Attica headlined are discussed in this chapter, but the authors felt that these were issues recommending a variety of views. With this in mind, a symposium was arranged in which the authors engaged in a dialogue with four professional colleagues whose views on some of the issues were known to be different, with the aim of reflecting the differences as well as the similarities.

The discussion revolved around these points:

The delineation and discussion of the causes. What happened at Attica had a number of causes. Prison conditions might be one. A new kind of problem-prisoner has been suggested as another.

The broader social and moral issues Attica dramatized and underlined.

The specific, critical dilemmas of corrections highlighted by the Attica-type phenomenon.

The lessons of Attica.

MANNING: An implication of each of these questions is that if we can develop an understanding of them, we might assess what can be done to minimize, prevent, or alter the pattern of development of subsequent events of this sort. A related consideration is how, with an understanding of the problems involved, one could modify the decision-making processes of those administering correctional systems.

RADELET: There are some supplementary questions to the broader points, such as:

1. There is the question of goals in corrections. Conflicting community expectations of the correctional system is the basic community relations problem. It is in some ways similar to the police role dilemma. This goal-role hang-up is an important central issue. William Raspberry, writing in *The Washington Post,* referred to a "counter-productive ambivalence" in simultaneous punishment and education: the custody vs. treatment argument. He went on to say that the separation of these functions in the correctional system also entails problems when looked at from the point of view of community expectations. If this is a central problem in corrections, how can it be resolved?

2. In recent years, there has been a shift in mental health treatment in the general field of social psychiatry. This shift has been generally away from institutional treatment toward noninstitutional community treatment. Looking at community mental health, is there a message in this for the field of corrections?

3. Other questions arise regarding the recent emphasis on due process in corrections. In Chapter XVII, we say that in the last ten years, police and the courts have witnessed a new emphasis on due process, which is more recently observable in corrections—particularly in the parole aspects and in custodial institutions, as in advocate programs for inmates who are accused of violating institutional rules. While this new emphasis on due process is widely applauded, what special problems does it create?

GOLDBERG: Curb the lawyer.

RADELET: That's pretty strong language.

GOLDBERG: It *is* pretty strong. But I attended three bar association meetings a few years ago, following the *Gault* decision on juvenile hearings, and all they were saying was, "Lawyers, here is a field that you better get into."

SCOTT: That may be true, Bill, in a limited sense. But I'm seeing a new breed of lawyers who are not interested in a Wall Street practice, but rather in the lawyer's role in social problems.

RADELET: There are several additional questions we may wish to add to our agenda:

1. Attica produces public attitudes that stress toughness. Rehabilitation, therefore, loses public support, at least in the short run. That which is most needed tends to be blighted. Is there anything to do about this?

2. Corrections people are afflicted with a kind of group inferiority complex. Public turbulence tends to have a certain backlash in the field of corrections that contributes further to the basic conservatism of corrections professionals. An occupational shyness on the part of corrections administrators inhibits experimenting with imaginative techniques in treatment and rehabilitation. Is there anything to do about this?

3. There is a need for *wholeness* of perspective in the corrections field. What does this mean to each of you?

4. Finally, who is the client in corrections? This goes back to the goal-role question. Police tend to see their client as society and their adversary as the criminal, whereas corrections people see the client as the inmate, probationer, or parolee and the adversaries as those who oppose treatment and rehabilitation.

SCOTT: That is one way of putting it. In some senses, the public is viewed as an opponent.

RADELET: Right. The "public" in the sense of widespread demands for harsher treatment, immediately following the Attica rebellion.

MANNING: What level of correctional administrators are you referring to?

GOLDBERG: Do you mean the prison guard?

CADE: Or do you mean the counselors, who form a group of significant size. I would not agree with that statement at all if you are speaking about that group.

SCOTT: Yes, it's important to distinguish among them—but by philosophy, not merely by position.

RADELET: But the first question is, with which point do you wish to begin the discussion?

MANNING: I think No. 1 is number one. I think it makes sense to talk first about *causes*. Prison riots, strikes, rebellions, etc., are not new; they have been going on for a long time. I think however, that something has changed—that there is a new set of causal factors.

RADELET: Let's pursue that. Riots in prisons, even to taking hostages, is not a new phenomenon. What is there about Attica that is different?

MANNING: I suggest that we make several assumptions. We have not seen major changes in prison conditions or in the quality of staffing, except that they have improved to some degree. Perhaps prisons have become larger. But changes in the prison as an organization would not account for the pattern of events occurring during the past year or so. As George Jackson pointed out, the changes that we are now able to see more clearly have been going on subtly for at least 10 years in prisons. Change results when people recognize new meanings and take them into account: in this case as a result of a change in the *definition of the situation*. What events are significant in the initial period of prison disturbances? Someone gets roughed up, the food is bad, etc. The food has been similar for years. Roughing probably happens from time to time, even in the finest prisons. What is it, then, that's changed? It's not the structure of the prison nor the attitudes nor quality of the staff. The change has to do with a shift in the definition of the situation: crime and imprisonment are now seen in a political context. I like the phrase—the politicization of crime—the belief on the part of alleged and convicted criminals and segments of the public that *all* crime and *all* punishment is a political act. People within the criminal justice system certainly at least tacitly have always recognized this. But the degree to which this ideology has become shared public knowledge and become part of a political stance has been changing radically. If imprisonment is defined as an arbitrary political act, as a result of "racism" or "class war," it has the effect of linking up diverse events, in prisons and outside of them, that have been seen as isolated. Crime will not be seen as the result of the failures of individual people. If you read Eldridge Cleaver or George Jackson, as examples, you realize that they came to understand that it was not they, as isolated individuals, who suffered these kinds of experiences, but rather that they were experiencing things that others had experienced. Further, they explained their own criminalization as a function of the power of the dominant societal groups: their fate seemed to be accounted for best, not by the vicissitudes of life, nor by their own personal hang-ups, but rather as a result of their class, color, and by the American racist tradition. Once such an explanation for criminal behavior becomes current, the extent to which it can spread further and become a system of extensive and intensive belief becomes much more highly probable. I believe it is this change in belief and in a shared explanation of one's life situation that is a critical new element in prison riots.

RADELET: Alex, do you have a comment at this point?

CADE: Having been involved in corrections for some time, I agree with Peter in the sense that I believe that there isn't too much we can say regarding the internal situation in correctional institutions that would explain the changes in the nature of prison riots. We know that the prison situation is a microcosm of the total society. We understand that the walls of the prison do not separate the "institutional society" (a society embraced by the correctional institution) from the rest of society (society outside the prison). We are aware that inmates know what's going on outside and that politicized attitudes and collective behavior spread by contagion. So here we have the general factors that tend to explain why things are happening in prisons as they are today.

But we must consider other factors that are perhaps more fundamental. All of the factors that would stimulate and nurture insurrections in the world outside of the prison sub-society are intensified in the prison environment. What happens in prisons, then, is an intensified version of what is happening in the larger society. For a moment, I would like to go back to our ideas of an earlier time. A few years ago, we as social scientists were emphasizing concepts of *anomie* and *alienation* as we talked about the ills of the larger society. We theorized that anomie and alienation ultimately resulted from the type of impersonalization and pathological individualism inherent in a highly industrialized and mechanized society of plenty. We do not need to elaborate upon this for our present purpose. By *anomie* we mean the situation where societal norms tend to break down, give way, and we don't have anything with which to replace them at the moment. There is a decided diminution in those socially standardized codes by which individual and group behavior is regulated. In other words, there are no adequate norms. Then we began to study the individual afflictions brought on by this societal condition known as anomie. It was at that time that we revived the concept of alienation. Alienation refers to the negative psychological experiences of the individual who finds himself in the society characterized by the condition of anomie. Alienated individuals feel uprooted. Such writers as David Reisman and Eric Fromm have analyzed this phenomenon quite thoroughly. Today, I think we have gone a step beyond alienation (which is a lack of sense of *personal* power) to a quest for artificial *group* power. Max Weber in the early 1900s, and later Karen Horney upon coming here from Germany, observed that we did not seem to have a meaningful sense of interrelatedness or a sense of interdependence, and these writers assumed that this state of affairs was a natural result of capitalistic society. This notion revived the concept of alienation, the experiencing of individual isolation, aloneness, and powerlessness. Now, I believe a search for secondary power is coming into existence. What we have done, I suspect, is to have unconsciously substituted what I call groupism for relatedness. By *groupism,* I mean the situation where the individual's primary motive for relating himself to some other individual is a conscious and selfish motive to obtain manipulative-type power. The notion is, "I am powerless without you, but at the same time I feel nothing for you." Another way of saying this is that the relationships resulting from this type of motivation are more exploitative than fulfilling. As we see more of this type of behavior in the larger, extraprison society, prisoners (who are, by the way, quite as different from each other as a given prisoner is different from the average nonprisoner) feel freer to use each other for a common purpose. This is exploitation, just as it is in the larger society. Without putting a value on this kind of behavior, that is, without stating whether it is good or bad in some absolute sense, we can say it is functional through the eyes of the alienated inmate, deprived as he is of the "need" to assume responsibility for his acts. The inmate moves from the notion that "alone, I am completely ineffective" to the conception, "when I merge with the group, I am all powerful."

As I see it, this is basically what has happened during the past ten years: the blind insurrections; people following but not knowing why they are really following, not experiencing themselves in the process, and giving reasons for the collective behavior that consumes them and drawing on the available rhetoric that pervades the larger society. These people will die for the "cause" (although the "cause" is seldom really theirs), rather than experience the psychological hell of aloneness and powerlessness.

RADELET: It's a pragmatic, political thing.

CADE: Right. But I think we tend to overlook the major way that politics enters into the situations in the development of the political personality—the need for a groupist approach to life in general. The point is that the increase in prison riots is not a matter of the nature of pathological "prison conditions." To assume this is to miss the essential point of what has actually happened in the past decade and what is continuing to happen now. Therefore, when we talk about how to deal with Attica, we must realize that we are probably not talking about Attica at all.

MANNING: Sociologists have conceptualized what Alex is referring to as the effects of the mass society—the breakdown in previous traditions, values, and patterns of behavior, and a new belief in radical, equalitarian rule. As previous traditions are attenuated and past controls over behavior begin to dissolve, people are left "on their own." What I believe is taking place as a result of the massification of society is the rise in importance of political ideology, a point made by Fromm and associates in the thirties in Germany. The politicization of the prisoners is thus just one indicator of broad societal dissatisfactions with the distribution of power, the opportunity structure, the "freedom to be." The breakdown of consensus affects not only the prisoners, but also the prison staffs (much as it affects university administrators). There is less consensus now among them as to the proper philosophy and policy in the face of the new political nature of events.

One rule of thumb that comes out of studies of mental hospitals and prisons is that when you have a degree of dissensus among those in authority, it is reflected in the behavior of the inmates. A classic case is suicide epidemics in mental hospitals. This is true not only in a prison, of course, but in society at large. The absence of control can be linked at several levels and this potential for social linkage is the reason why things are so very explosive. But at the same time there is a sense of coming together by the prisoners in some prisons. Their perception is that there is a possibility of modifying the situation, and that action may generate power.

RADELET: I must say, Peter, that for a man who says that he doesn't know very much about sociology, Alex has revealed considerable understanding of sociological concepts.

CADE: No, these are *my* concepts. Seriously, there is another point: The most fertile soil for what I call secondary groupism—this coming together out of a feeling of aloneness, worthlessness, and powerlessness —yields a societal condition to which we refer as *normative dissensus.* When inmates perceive that people "out there" are not together, this has two effects on them. First, it gives them justification for failing to develop a sense of integrated purpose of their own, and it makes them feel even more alienated in the sense that there is nothing solid to relate to, even on the outside. They also begin to perceive that they can defeat the disintegrated outside society, and this is a motive for insurrection in its own right. Again, much of the cause for prison insurrection lies on the outside of the prison situation.

RADELET: Bill, you have a point?

GOLDBERG: There is another element here. There is also a certain semantic skill in prisons, particularly with militants. This skill—by contagion, by press coverage, by writings or whatever—is one to which the public has been exposed. Another incidental thing: one of our difficulties, as Alex and Peter have suggested, in finding causes for Attica,

Rahway, etc., is that we blame the prisons. We make the prison the focal point for a lot of things over which it has no control.

RADELET: Just as the police are blamed for many problems not of their making.

GOLDBERG: Exactly. Corrections is hemmed in by police, court and legislative activity of one sort or another, as well as by institutional regulations. How you can handle the institutional part of it without substantial change in these others, I don't know. We've gotten away from physical punishment; we've gone to the psychological. We encourage publicly the quiet running of institutions. One is a good warden or a good administrator as long as there isn't trouble. When there is trouble, he's at fault. I don't see how we can reconcile what the public expects of institutions with what prisoners expect of institutions.

Let me clear that up a bit. The public doesn't really care too much about what goes on in any correctional institution. As long as it's out of sight and there isn't trouble, everything is "fine." Institutions tend to be traditional. Guards, counselors, etc., say "don't stick your neck out, be a good boy, keep on doing things the way they're supposed to be done."

Let me return to the idea of "Let's curb the lawyers." We now have a group of young lawyers who are community-minded rather than pocket-minded. They are taking advantage of the present situation where they go to court for every administrative decision. I for one would refuse to be an administrator where I had a lawyer breathing over my shoulder. This inhibits serious changes within institutions—within the narrow range of changes that an institution can carry out. The only solution that I see in practical terms is that we use the prison as a last resort rather than as a first resort. This is going to take a lot of changing of public viewpoints, and those of judges and police. Maybe we are coming to a court-regulated correctional system, because the system itself doesn't foresee or make the changes that are necessary. In the same vein, correctional institutions encourage secrecy. One can't get to see them or find out what is really going on.

SHARP: When it was revealed that the hostages had been shot rather than stabbed, in the Attica revolt, large numbers of people found it impossible for that to penetrate their consciousness. This same attitude, in reverse, is true of many young people who are so convinced that society is rotten to the core, and that our institutions are out of tune with the time, that for them a crime—even when proven to have been committed—is not the fault of the perpetrator. They say that society failed him by making him live in the ghetto. Therefore it's our fault, not his. They have a tendency to absolve the individual of any responsibility for his acts. They believe that all the black prisoners are right; that they are not bad. They really don't believe that a man is sinful—rather that society makes him sinful. This is society's problem with prisons. We're talking about how the public perceives correctional institutions and I agree with what Bill has said. The public says if everything is quiet, you are rehabilitating the criminal. Don't beat them; I want you to do a good job in the prisons, but don't bother me with it. It's just like I don't let *them* live next door; don't let "housing" come in next door. Don't make me share my land with those unwanted out there simply because we're overpopulated.

CADE: And who do you think is having the greatest influence on the direction of corrections? The public attitude or the people on the inside?

SCOTT: I'd like to come in here for just a minute, with a couple of points, and this is backing up a little bit. There are some significant differences between riots. Compare two riots occurring at approximately the same time: Attica and Rahway. The New York Corrections system is a fairly tight one. I'm not saying that it's inhumane or particularly repressive, but it is a tight ship. There are more squads "east and west," higher walls, more guards, and greater social distance between inmates and staff.

MANNING: What is often meant by "a more professional" system?

SCOTT: By some people's definition, yes. But it is interesting that New York state is (or was) in a process of sharp transition when Attica "blew." The corrections spectrum was reorganized under new leadership. Changes were planned under Commissioner Russell Oswald, who is regarded as a progressive. So in a sense, Attica was ill-timed. It jumped the gun. I think this is often the case in social change. The prospect of change is likely to produce an explosive atmosphere.

   Now the interesting thing to me is that the list of demands by the rebels are believed to have been agreed to, with two exceptions: immunity and sanctuary. These were said to be non-negotiable by Commissioner Oswald. The other element that was involved was the *inviting in* of several well-known radical activists, so that there was an ideological fraternizing between radical elements on the outside and radical leadership designated by inmate rebels. This resulted in identification with radical elements on the outside by rebels on the inside. Support of a radical nature evidenced in recent criminal trials has begun to emerge in corrections process. The presence of such leadership seems to have been absent in the Rahway situation. The public gets confused on the difference between reprisals and responsibility for crimes. The promise at Rahway was that there would be no reprisals. An important difference exists between reprisals and bringing a person to trial on criminal charges. Reprisals include loss of good time, punitive isolation, loss of privileges, and the like. That difference came out more clearly at

Rahway. And no activists seem to have been involved in the negotiations. These distinctions are important.

One further element: as Alex says, the political unrest and change on the outside of prisons is reflected on the inside. There are two types of activists in prison. One uses the techniques of civil disobedience to arouse the conscience of society. The more radical type uses violence to overthrow what is seen as the "total rottenness" of society. To the latter, any degree of force necessary to produce change is justifiable, be it bombing, political assassinations, or the high-jacking and destruction of airplanes.

The radicals on the outside are, by the very nature of their acts, becoming a part of the general population. Therefore they become a rallying point within the institution. This produces an exculpation by prisoners—shedding blame on somebody lese. "It ain't me." Mary was alluding to this when she noted the failure of the young to realize the sinfulness of man. I think that this is a powerful force in an understandable drive on the part of the inmate to *be* somebody—to cease being an "it," a thing, a pawn. So he rallies to any cause which gives him a rationale or justification for who he is and why he is where he is.

CADE: I think we should get into the question of the goals of corrections. If you are thinking about corrections in the sense of rehabilitating individuals (and I am sure that we are all aware of the fact that it's impossible to rehabilitate groups!), then we should focus upon the needs, motivations, and reactions of individuals. We all have a need to fill up the void frequently experienced in our lives, and in the inmate's case, it is far more frequent. When in trying to help inmates we devote all of our attention to the political framework, the conditions that tend to set the boundaries for their experiences rather than their experiences as such, we merely assist them in further escaping from the responsibility or the reality of themselves. Often, as well-meaning humanitarians, we provide a rallying cry for inmates, which tends to consume all of their energies in the process of "pointing the finger" outward from themselves and excusing themselves from becoming involved in the process of their own self-actualization. In other words, any effort which would ultimately take all or most of the individual's attention away from himself and focus it upon the conditions of society, even his prison sub-society, is counter to personal rehabilitation.

This is often a paradox in corrections. No matter how important the cause, how urgent it is to change society, how urgent it is to change prison conditions (and it is indeed urgent), we are never justified in encouraging the individual to reduce his need to look to himself for what is ultimately required for his rehabilitation. The individual should be encouraged always to ask the question, "What do I need? Or what is actually wrong with *me?*" The typical prison inmate should not be saddled with the responsibility for changing society. He probably has far more psychological needs to cope with than most of us will ever have. So we are a bit freer than he is to try to change prison conditions and the factors in society which tend to interfere with his self-actualization and rehabilitation. Fundamental questions we should ask about the goals of corrections are: Is a correctional institution simply a holding situation? Are correctional efforts themselves merely attempts to keep people out of society for a while? Or are we really serious about trying to correct people, not as pawns of society but as human beings who have a right to be self-actualizing and productive?

GOLDBERG: I think the goals of corrections are largely semantic.

CADE: I agree. This is more or less evident from the way employees in correctional work are promoted. If we look at the personalities and values of the persons in certain positions in corrections, we would learn a great deal about the extent to which the goals of corrections are largely semantic. One generalization that can be made, if one takes a brief look at the personalities in certain positions in corrections, is that the basic purpose of most correctional institutions is to detain and keep order.

SCOTT: I would have to agree.

RADELET: What about ". . . the counterproductive ambivalence involved in simultaneous punishment and education . . ."?

CADE: If keeping order and detention are the major goals of corrections, perhaps we should admit this and the problem would be much simplified.

SCOTT: It is not the *major* goal, in my judgment. But I think the sooner we face order and security as a reality, the less confusion will result. Society has the right to be protected against persons who loot, rape, and kill, and has a duty to prevent inmates from harming each other.

CADE: I don't disagree with that, but it is obvious that if our major goal in correction is the keeping of order and the detaining of persons who are dangerous to society, it is logical to emphasize rules and regulations in prisons rather than the understanding of individual criminals within their own right. Thus, the probability is tremendously enhanced that our efforts will tend to bypass the inmate as an important unit within his own right. It seems to me that this approach would be alien to the concept of actually correcting people's behavior.

RADELET: . . . the multiplication of rules in custodial institutions— rule upon rule until, in effect, many things that might be conducive to "correcting" are suppressed.

MANNING: I've read that less than 30 percent of the people in maximum security prisons in California have committed violent crimes. Most people in prisons are not dangerous to society in the sense that they may commit violent crimes against other persons. Most crime (over 80 percent) is property crime. I think that this kind of figure presents the first indication that we can do different things with different kinds of prisoners. We *do* need to protect ourselves from each other. The violent criminals in prison must be controlled. In medicine there is the term *iatrogenic disease,* or something that is induced by the therapeutic process. The crimes committed against humanity and society itself as a result of imprisonment are probably more profoundly damaging to society than the behavior that sent people to prison initially.

SCOTT: Possibly so, Peter. I am arguing for this point only because I think we have a better chance of moving into productive treatment if we recognize the reality of society's insistence upon protection.

SHARP: I don't know whose job it is to educate society in the sense of the community that asks for the prisons and provides for them with its tax dollars. In trying to differentiate between the types of persons who have violated the law, meaning the law under which we are all living together, I'm reminded of a story I read about a society in which the persons who violated the laws were sent across an invisible barrier. They could not cross back over this barrier until they had demonstrated to a group of people that they were again able to live under the rules of the group. They were not put in prison; they simply could not return. This sentence did not fulfill the function of trying to rehabilitate but it did say to the man that he was responsible for himself. Society also wants retribution, because we identify with the *victim* of crime and we want something to happen. But in putting people in prison, we put them so far away that we don't have the satisfaction of "He killed somebody; he has to pay." Because we catch only half of those who commit crime we make them really pay.

RADELET: We have an idea—Bob and I—that this choice between punishment and rehabilitation is complicated by something to which Alex and Peter have referred—an anomie factor. In addition to what might be called the rehabilitative or treatment goal, and in addition to the custodial or societal security goal, we think there is a third factor, represented by society's demand for protection against anomie. Society insists upon the maintenance and safeguarding of some basic, minimum norms of behavior.

CADE: I see prisoners reflecting the same anomie or normlessness that is found in the larger society. They are not the perpetrators of anomie; the fact of anomie in the larger society merely reinforces their tendencies toward criminal behavior and ultimately riot behavior. Anomie reinforces such behavior on the part of inmates and criminals in general from two main points of view: (1) because the norms are not clearly defined and the extent to which so-called noncriminal individuals subscribe to these hazy norms vary tremendously, both permitting and encouraging antisocial behavior and attitudes, (2) because the feeling of alienation, with its associated sense of powerlessness and lack of meaningful relatedness, is born in a society characterized by anomie. And as I have already said, the experience of alienation drives certain individuals to seek significance and relatedness by identifying with the only identifiable group available to them, the antisocial or criminal group.

But there is something else that I think we tend to forget when we are speaking about uniform treatment of people with adjustment difficulties. The fact is that there are significant individual differences among individuals in any setting, the prison situation being no exception. I remember when I began my work in prisons, I had a number of "considered" stereotypes concerning "maladjusted people," mostly growing out of my training in clinical psychology. I was trained to categorize people by "diseased" types and to work with them within the framework of concepts associated with these categorizations. But I really found early in my work in prisons that there was no such thing as a common prison personality. I found overt psychotics, incipient or latent psychotics, psychoneurotics, so-called sociopaths, a variety of personality patterns and trait disorders, and many many people whose motivations, attitudes, values, and behavior defied any attempt at categorizing. What I discovered was that the crimes that individuals often committed actually reflected certain need patterns and behavioral orientations. The crimes they committed, then, were better indicators of the treatment procedures needed than diagnostic categories expounded in text books in abnormal psychology and psychopathology. Of course, it is obvious that there were significant individual variations in terms of psychological needs even when we considered the types of crimes committed. Nevertheless, I noted that individuals who committed thefts had certain basic needs in common, which were categorically different from individuals who committed indecent liberties or incest. Individuals who characteristically committed the offense of armed robbery tended to have certain needs in common which were consistently different from those of individuals who came to prison frequently for involvement with drugs.

The examples can be extended on and on. In addition to the types of prison inmates who seem to have committed these types of crime because of either psychological conflict or insufficient value development, there were the political prisoners who I think were, even then, trying to be catalysts for needed social change. Here were all these people together in one prison. So you ask the question, how should we treat *the* prisoner? In response I ask another question, "Do we treat them all the same?" After all, in addition to these need and motivation differences, some were very intelligent and others were quite the opposite. Some were capable of training for rather sophisticated vocational skills and some were not. Some were capable of understanding the demands of society and the implications of those demands to a much greater extent than others. Another question that is not nearly as academic as it seems is, "Why must we even *call* them all criminals and put them in the same institution?" I think this is the point where the most significant problem lies, when we are really serious about an attempt to treat the difficulties of the individual that have resulted in his "criminal behavior."

SCOTT: Permit me to footnote one thing about these different types of people. There is also the tragic case of the mentally retarded. Let me say also that corrections is often blamed for something that is not altogether its fault, as Bill said earlier. It is the court that goes through the process of identifying; it is the court that imposes the imprisonment set by society, and corrections must move within these limits. There is a great tendency to blame corrections for much that is repressive. There is enough that corrections *can* be blamed for and enough that it can change without being blamed for the things that it cannot change.

CADE: To demonstrate what you are talking about, let's say you get a political-type prisoner who is in prison because he has violated some law in his zeal to change society in some way he thinks it ought to be changed, or even because of his misunderstanding of social phenomena. This individual meets a number of neurotic compulsives, dependent neurotics, or mentally defective persons in his new environment, his new political arena. He has a purpose (and let's not place a value on that purpose at this point) in his behavior aimed at insurrection. He is a leader, let us assume, so he loosely organizes his fellow inmates, a number of whom are in prison for crimes committed because of psychological conflict, limited intelligence, etc. The political-type prisoner has a scheme for changing things and he needs the assistance of these other inmates. When things begin to move, however, the political prisoner loses control simply because his followers are motivated by their own inner drives and conflicts. A riot ensues, a number of people get killed and the political inmate is labeled the ring-leader. Labeling him as the ring leader is not necessarily inaccurate, but what is important is that such labeling is not nearly so bad as the assumption which usually follows, that his personal pathology is responsible for the consequences of the riot, or that all inmates were involved to the same extent and were motivated to do what they did by the same factors. The political-type prisoner had a cause, but perhaps the compulsive neurotic merely had a need to do something extreme, the dependent neurotic followed along because he urgently needed to be accepted, and the mentally defective went along simply because he was suggestible and did not really know what the consequences of his acts would be. This really bugs me. I see this hypothetical situation as being a good example of what actually happens in most prison riots; and such a situation obviously comes about because we have put the wrong people together and we attempt to deal with them as if they were all alike in all significant ways.

GOLDBERG: I want to reenforce what Bob said. We are expecting prisons to do a job that the legislature has fenced in with restrictions. The legislature says that for one offense, there must be a mandatory sentence. How do they determine that? They determine it on the basis of an act and their personal biases, rather than on the basis of an indiivdual's needs. And corrections is supposed to take these people—and often for a long time. We have some people in prisons that we don't *know* what to do with. The question of rehabilitation for them is stupid. They are and they always will be difficult people. In addition to this, and this goes back to the "political" prisoner, we are blaming the prison for a dichotomy in the judicial process. The poor man gets it in the neck, whatever his color, and the rich get away with minor punishment, if any. When the poor see that there are other people who are getting away with mere fines, it becomes *us* against *them.* So when we talk about goals, we must keep this in mind.

Permit me to extend further the point I am making. Prisons, as one segment of the criminal justice system, receive the onus of compounded errors of the other segments: the police, the judge and prosecutor, the legislative definitions of both the crime and the penalty, the money appropriated for the prison and parole operation, as well as legislative acts and parole board rules and decisions. The prisons—to do an effective job—must be relieved of total responsibility for recidivism, for the failures of the community and of the individual prisoner.

Prisons are traditionally operated. Bureaucracy in prisons, as evidenced by several studies of prison rules made by graduate students at our school, perpetuates tradition. Many of the rules governing prisoner conduct are out-dated, old-fashioned, and stupid, and should be thrown out. The traditional administrator hesitates to make serious changes, from fear of inmate reaction and from fear of public reaction.

The militant prisoner, aided by young lawyers of the "liberal" persuasion, has suddenly discovered that he has "rights" which some of the recent court decisions have upheld. Many of the "rights" concern administrative rules governing prisoner conduct. To a large extent, these rules could be changed without legislation, if the administrators had the courage. There has been a rash of appellate court decisions upsetting the harshness of these rules. Apparently, administrators of prisons have been unable or unwilling to modernize their rules, to eliminate the silly ones.

In essence, therefore, the lessons of Attica, Rahway, San Quentin, The Tombs, among others, point to the need for the criminal justice system to upgrade itself, to swerve from legal fiction to reality. This involves a cooperative effort of the police, prosecutor, the courts (of original and appellate jurisdiction), the prison system, the parole board and the legislature. Criminal justice needs a higher priority rating than it enjoys currently. Much of this can be done by administrative action of the original and appellate courts (by means of rules of procedure set forth by the State Supreme Courts), and by the prisons and parole boards, were they willing to do so.

It is sheer nonsense to attribute failure to the prison system or to a particular prison in a specific state when they contain so many un-redeemable prisoners. By suspended sentences, by fines, by probation, the criminal justice system has theoretically "skimmed off" the "better" prisoners and sent to the prisons those residuals who allegedly present the lesser hope for successful community processing.

The blame for failure must rest with the total system, rather than one specific part—the prison.

MANNING: Back to anomie again. There is a distinction between *anomie* which classically refers to disjunction between segments of society and *alienation,* seen as referring to individuals who are lost, feel powerless, or who differ from the dominant social order. A very popular explanation for social problems is to attribute their causes to individual pathology. There is a distinction, however, because social disjunction and individual pathology are analytically separable. In a prison, we find a mixture of these forms of anomie. In some ways, what is happening in our country is not a result of individual alienation but of the changing power relationships among various social groups. There are whole groups of people who feel less powerful than they desire to be, but they are not alienated from a set of norms. They are quite strongly identified with a set of goals and values, and these aims represent a challenge to the going social order and existing distribution of power. I do not attribute this challenge to alienation, or anomie. In fact, the challenge can be seen as a function of organization, coherence, order. Psychological discreditation has been used against people who want to change the distribution of power. "Alienation" has been used to reject and neutralize the political claims of groups of people who challenge the status quo. Sometimes it is used as in connection with recent prison riots, to imply that all prisoners are fanatics, insane, or crazy, or to dismiss real grievances as mere political rhetoric. It's a way of neutralizing the political message.

There's a related point about the psychiatric interpretation of the problems in prisons. It relates to whether we explain these problems as a function of individual pathologies. I think the social sciences have had a great impact on the theory and practice of rehabilitation and the staffs in prisons—social workers, probation, parole, corrections, etc., on up to the highest level of professional administrators. But as this diffusion of information has taken place, a conflict has resulted between the rehabilitative and the punishment functions of the prison. In the psychiatric view, people are a product of group and family experiences, processes of learning about which they, as independent people, had little to say. This theory has had tremendous impact because it eschews the legal notion that Alex and Mary mentioned—that it is the act and intention to commit it that is the classic legal concern. Psychiatry reduces the purity of a purely legal concern with *justice*. The criminal justice system must minimize arbitrary justice—the act and its relation to the law is what ought to be central in legal considerations.

SHARP: Look at how we differentiate the degrees of murder.

MANNING: The bar is now struggling with the intrusion into the law of what Dean Francis Allen calls "the rehabilitative ideal." The rehabilitative ideal argues that some people actually are *not* responsible. To the degree that the rehabilitative ideal—that people are not responsible and ought to be "cured," not punished by the law—gains strength, it breaks down the previous concern for the act. It places responsibility in the hands of "society" not on the individual. Psychiatry has blurred the distinctions between moral and social responsibility. When psychiatry confronts or intrudes into legal settings, one sees a set of interpretive contexts for disposition that are overlapping and noncomplementary. They are used in different points in time for the explanation of illegal acts, and for punishment and rehabilitation of the person.

CADE: I think quite a few of the people that we are talking about are aware that these considerations (and this is what I refer to as groupism) are political considerations. Various people question, from a value standpoint, whether this ought to be. But I think that we are all aware that these people are criminals. Another point is that I think that we do charge the individual with the responsibility for himself, but we do not permit him to really assume that responsibility. Of course, we do this in other institutions of society, even in colleges and universities, but in prisons the contradiction is glaring. We go overboard telling the individual prisoner that he has been irresponsible and that he must be more responsible if he is going to be blessed by society. But let's face it, most experiences encountered in prison by the average inmate are dictated and controlled by custody-minded individuals.

While telling the inmate he must be responsible, custodial behavior reflects the verbalization, "I will decide your destiny, at least while you're here." I do not refer here to only custodial officers and prison officials; prison counselors also tend unwittingly to subscribe to and foster this attitude. I think the psychiatric point of view is very similar to this attitude. Consequently, I think you are wrong about the psychiatric contamination. I feel that the opposite is closer to the truth.

SCOTT: We are dealing with an area that is in a great state of flux. First, parole boards are having to reexamine their roles and procedures, and to sharpen their focus. The central question becomes "parolability," "equity," and the extent to which the crime shocks the public conscience. However, these questions must be answered within a framework that does not violate the right of the offender to even-handed justice.

The second thing is that we have been talking about the theory of criminal justice as though it were a *fact* when there is a very wide discrepancy in the whole plea-bargaining process as to what a man happens to be convicted of and what, in fact, his problem really is. Take the man who breaks into a residence with intent to rape, but who is convicted only of breaking and entering. Or consider the man who commits an armed robbery but pleads guilty to an attempt to receive stolen property. In facing these questions, one must look at the act as well as the conviction. Unfortunately, our rhetoric suggests that the only purpose of sentencing a person to prison is to rehabilitate or correct. This is only part of the picture. The purpose is to protect persons and property *and* to correct the offender.

RADELET: This is what Bill evidently had in mind when he referred to the semantics of it.

SHARP: I think that there is no doubt in the public mind that political reasons explain why Jimmy Hoffa was not paroled earlier. If you want politics, it's going to be there. This could or could not be true, but I'm saying that it is the belief of many—the uninformed public—that Hoffa's parole was delayed purely for political reasons. He was not a threat to society. He may have been seen as a threat to the teamsters union, but they felt able to cope with him. But there was somebody somewhere who did not want him back in the presidency of the teamsters union again.

GOLDBERG: Yes, but it was put on another basis. They are punishing him for tampering with one of the nation's most venerable institutions, the jury.

SCOTT: I think one should define what is meant by the term "political" here. Maybe a less loaded case would be that of Alger Hiss, who was denied parole for a long time apparently because of the repugnance that many people felt for his alleged crimes.

SHARP: His *alleged* crimes. I still say alleged, you note, even though he was convicted. That was a case in which there was a real political division of whether or not he was guilty, even in the face of the evidence.

SCOTT: I was referring to the fact that he was convicted of perjury, not of espionage. Thus, in the one case, the politics applies to conviction and in the other it applied to parole.

GOLDBERG: Of course you have to raise the question, does it really reflect the actual event? We tend to place the most serious charge on a defendant when he is charged initially.

SHARP: I think the defendant should have the option of trading.

CADE: One of our problems is that we don't treat criminal behavior, we treat the motivation and the conflict underlying criminal behavior.

GOLDBERG: This raises the question of how responsive or unresponsive a judge can be to the immediate characterization of an act. It is one facet of what the community thinks, that property must be protected, willy-nilly. Sentences too often reveal only a judge's personal concept of morality and/or bias.

RADELET: What we are doing in this discussion, it seems to me, is dealing somewhat helter-skelter with a whole cluster of questions. We are casting a net over a number of things; and, not surprisingly, some weighty considerations are eluding us. You may wish to switch at this point to a particular focus and stick with it for a few minutes. What do you think, for instance, about the question regarding the clients of a correctional system? Or the question regarding what corrections might learn from the mental health field?

CADE: I don't think that corrections has honestly approached the implications of the concept of morality. One of the main factors underlying the whole correctional concept still seems to be that there is a differential morality involved. "Some people are more moral than other people; criminals are usually less moral than noncriminals." Since the meaning of morality is itself "up for grabs" in today's society, it is not so easy any more for us to deal with morality in the correctional setting. The trend now seems to be toward a concept of internal morality, a morality of the individual's will, in contrast to morality imposed by the ethics of the society. The concept of internal morality implies that functional morality is intrinsic and is a reflection of the real nature of the human being. In keeping with this concept, the moral individual is a fully functioning individual who is true to himself because this is his will and because he is true to himself, he is true to others. He is not inhibited by codes and pressures imposed upon him from the outside; he consciously controls his actions because he deems that it is "good" to do so. Thus, the concept would hold that we should help him to discover what he really is and should trust his ability to control his own actions.

Treatment of the prison inmate, then, becomes synonymous with efforts to draw out that which is in the individual; that which is potentially good, which in a deeper sense is really what he would like to manifest. We have to help the individual grow in intellectuality, emotionality, and in social sensitivity. The humanistic psychologists as a group maintain that man by nature, at the core of his being, does have a primary need for other people. In general, the correctional setting should permit the individual the type of freedom that will help him find himself and so become a socially adjusted person as well. Carl Rogers has said that a personally adjusted individual is a socially adjusted person. The traditional Freudian approach to understanding and dealing with people has been tremendously altered or modified in much of our present-day thinking. Educators are beginning to speak much more about personal development or self-actualizing education than about education for vocational purposes or conditioning people to act a certain way. However, in correctional institutions, we are still trying to educate for control purposes. Very little emphasis is placed upon personal development or self-actualizing experiences in prison.

Again, inmates must never be considered in isolation from the rest of society and the rest of the world. One of the major objectives of correctional institutions should be to keep people who are institutionalized in step with what's going on outside, to the extent possible. The reason we do not do this, I believe, is because we feel that persons in prison must be controlled regardless of what is happening in the outside society.

RADELET: This comes down to what it means to be pro-social vs. anti-social?

CADE: Exactly. And one's point of view can change rapidly.

MANNING: I would like to expand on the need for wholeness of perspective. What I think can be said about needed changes in prisons —changes that will lead to people being treated as whole beings—is that we need to minimize the transition between prison and the outside in order to increase personal growth. One way, of course, would be to follow the model of the "7th STEP" Foundation that Bill Sands developed, or to use more Halfway houses on the Synanon model, and to combine them with self-help programs. A gradual transition to social responsibility is needed, in contrast to being treated as if you were irresponsible within prison, and totally responsible once released. It's frightening enough for those of us who have never been in prison to be totally responsible for our lives. At least we have some discretion and freedom. What happens when a person is thrown out into society and told that he must now be a totally responsible human being, but he must not do a number of things that are normally expected of any man of his age? He must not associate with his old friends; he must not see women that he previously knew; he must not drink or use drugs. In other words, he must not do what he has been doing all his life. Furthermore, we're suspicious and survey him carefully, looking for evidence that he might have done these things.

We must continue to be aware of rehabilitation as a process which incorporates the person's experience, from early socialization through the criminal justice process, and finally through the process of return to society. We must minimize some of the trauma of the transition between being a non-person to becoming a wholly responsible, observed and stigmatized member of the community. This is where I think the political activities of Chicanos and black activists are terribly important. They provide a continuity in the sense of providing channels to help establish where one is going and how one is going to get there. What Chavez, Brown Power people, the Black Congressional Caucus, and others are doing is very significant in spite of the fact that the political dimension adds additional explosiveness. It has important meaning because it represents organization. Black political activism represents the source of an identity that is non-criminal. That is crucial. And it has continuity, outside and inside. You're black. You've got friends and brothers in the same kinds of life situations, and with similar political beliefs. It has positive and negative values, but I see the need to underscore the positive dimensions. A George Jackson or a Huey Newton, in prison, has a significant popular "image" among blacks as a symbol of political and personal identity, and of non-criminal success and respect from white society.

SCOTT: But there are some difficulties here. The first is about the process of the criminal law itself. It is actually a legal fiction. It represents a kind of fantasy of an ideal world to which you expect people to conform. It must be understood *as* a fantasy, with all of its implications and difficulties, because it's a beginning of a process by which society separates the "sheep" from the "goats." The second thing is that corrections, no less than the police, though perhaps in a different context, are the conservators of a certain kind of dominant tradition. They are cast in a role that is an ambivalent one and creates a great many difficulties. The third point is that this prosocializing process we speak of has to counteract an antisocializing process that has been going on for a long time in the lives of these individuals. To counteract and redirect it presents practical difficulties. This does not in any way excuse the corrections worker from having a whole concept and understanding what is positive, but it demands a dual process of education. The client and the worker must both be reeducated.

MANNING: Yes. I think that what has been said about most policemen and that could be said just as well about most corrections workers is that they often have risen from the same social origin as the people they work with, but their social values, experiences and the bases of their rewards have become different. This confronts them with themselves in a direct way, and makes clear the arbitrary fact that one group is on the other side of the legal mirror.

SCOTT: Right. Could I make just one further point. Theoretically, we see progress as a kind of fixed point. That point is usually identified with the most advanced theory and practice. In reality, we are dealing with a long column, the point of which is way up front and the rear guard is a long way back. Not only is its dimension one of length, but it has its breadth as well. As a shoreline, it has its capes and its bays, so that in some areas we are pushing forward and in others we are way behind. I think the kind of input that you are providing in this discussion—the conceptualization theory—is the point at which the corrections worker needs to reflect. The worker needs a house of ideas in which he can live. If he doesn't have some degree of consistency and meaningfulness of his own, he is going to be badly frustrated.

MANNING: I think corrections people *are* badly frustrated.

SCOTT: True. And therefore the exchange between theory and practice, the opportunity to reflect, examine, and evaluate, is a commodity which is badly lacking. However, it is not the corrections worker alone with whom we must deal, but also with a society that places conflicting demands upon corrections.

SHARP: We also need to work with the individual who has been convicted in ways other than committing him to prison—a horrible, huge institution. How many clients can a social worker query, how many can a psychiatrist work with? But if you are going to be effective, people should be grouped in much smaller units—no more than 25 in an institution, if you are going to accomplish something with them. We should separate the types of criminals by the needs of the criminal rather than the needs of society. Whose responsibility is it to educate the public to this kind of change? Many articles say that this should be done by the sociologists or the corrections people or whomever. I read an article in *The Atlantic* about California, by Jessica Mitford, which describes the problems of the correctional system in that state. Yet I had thought of it as quite advanced. The truth probably lies somewhere between.

Somebody experiments and tries something. It doesn't achieve the hoped-for goal. Instead of getting credit for having tried to experiment, there is criticism. In the same way, some have criticized our American political system because we expect government to solve a problem with *a* solution. But on the other hand, we are not going to be in a position to experiment unless we are willing to stand the expense and the hazards of it.

CADE: I remember when I was in graduate school, proposing a research project for myself which was quite ambitious and which deviated considerably from the main line of thought in that particular research area. My advisor strongly suggested that I should not go through with the research because the project was too broad in scope, deviated too far from what other researchers had been doing in the area, and was not adequately geared to "accepted theory." Further, he felt that it would consume too much time to do a "neat job," and he did not believe it would lend itself to statistical treatment. He did not deny that the research I proposed was needed at the time. I feel that we are caught up in such an attitude in corrections. It seems to me that we should do a great deal of exploratory work and brainstorming in the area of corrections, considering all data as potentially valid and meaningful and being extremely idealistic and yet open-minded in our approaches. No existing practice in corrections should be considered sacred because it is obvious that most existing practices are to no real avail.

For example, in recent years we have begun to give much credence to the notion that to the extent ethnic and racial groups experience a sense of togetherness among themselves, the more healthy they will be as a people. I think it is often inferred from this that they will be less likely to misbehave in some gross socially destructive manner. Perhaps we should consider the possibility that this type of togetherness might not be at all fulfilling to the individual, might cause even further conflict, and might result in a much greater degree of polarization in society. It is only through exploring such a possibility that we will be able to discover the truth in terms of the relationship between treatment, conditions of racial ethnic groups, and prison insurrections. It is my personal feeling that at least in some situations, the political attitude blocks the pathway into the inner life of the individual that must be dealt with in any realistic correctional program.

SHARP: I don't think it is immoral to use political leverage like that.

CADE: I agree with you, but suppose I was trying to make the point that I believe polarization is one of our greatest problems in society and anything that aids and abets polarization cannot be the best possible answer.

SCOTT: I understand your diagnosis of the problem, Alex, but I'm not sure that I understand your proposal.

CADE: I don't really have a specific proposal. I'm saying that we should not rely on the nature and reactions of groups internal to the prison situation to solve either the individual problems in corrections or the institutional problems in corrections. I'm saying that this is our responsibility, as professionals in the area of corrections, to set the course of correctional practices, based upon our understanding of these dynamics.

GOLDBERG: But you run into another concept of the community. In theory, parole preparation begins the day the man goes into the institution. This is the ideal; in reality, parole preparation begins about 3 months before a man is released. The other thing is that we have a society which tells us that everybody in Rahway (on a definite sentence) must serve a third of his sentence before he can be released. In some of the intermediate sentence states, it is theoretically one year. So by law and by rule, we deny that we have individuals. This is what society has accepted in this state, in the other 49, and in the Federal government. A possible solution is to take away from the judge the power to specify a particular sentence, and give to somebody the authority to say that John Doe is to be put on probation or given a suspended sentence, etc., and somebody in authority will then say he should serve three months, and we'll let him go back into the community. This is one of the realities. By today's law no matter how much you want to do something for an individual, everybody must serve that minimum prison term.

SCOTT: Two comments. First, what Mary said comes under the heading of historical accidents. At the time that the California system was adopted in 1942, it was considered the best plan available by students in the field. Second, going back to what you were saying, Alex —what you are advocating is a very revolutionary idea, in the best and most positive sense. What you are suggesting is that the Establishment, instead of entrenching itself behind the ramparts of the status quo, should begin to take a much more positive role. But the problems that this poses are enormous.

RADELET: I know a prominent liberal politician who is telling police officers that they should join the civil rights movement. They think he must be kidding. But he reminds them that several years ago, some policemen thought it was O.K. to join the John Birch Society.

MANNING: It is not only a question of mobilizing people to become involved in spreading justice. I think that there is no societal consensus about the changes we want made in any social institution. It is not viable simply to agree that there should be changes made, although at that level nearly everyone might agree. We have a pluralistic society in which there is no avoiding the fact that there are differential group rules, values, and powers, and consequently for at least the next 25 years, we will be engaged in establishing and living with a quasi-legalistic pluralism. The central question in my mind is whether those in positions of power are willing and able to provide the means by which those with less power can contribute to the growth of a strong pluralism. The union-management situation is exactly replicated in the prison. Every union versus management encounter sees unions asking for more power; management replies "you have enough." All the power and authority was originally in the hands of the management. So in any negotiation, it always appears that management, or the powerful, lose. Any changes in prisons are seen as gains on the part of the prisoners, and losses by authorities.

We have to provide two things. We must provide administrators with security in their jobs and in their personal lives. We cannot afford the "you-win-I-lose" feeling and definition of social change in the prison system. That's what happened at Attica, I think. The second thing we need to do is to try to develop means within prisons by which prisoners can represent themselves as members of bargaining groups. We now recognize that living in some black neighborhoods in this country is very much like being in jail. The only way black citizens can alter their situation is by obtaining some of the power that lies solely in the hands of authorities outside their neighborhoods. Powerlessness was at least a part of the dynamic of the riots of the late sixties, and it certainly plays a role in prison riots. Why not provide some power to the powerless and institutionalize its use? This would enable prisoners to present their life situation as human beings realistically, and not as categories of dehumanized robots under control. Sweden has devised ways of representation by prisoners through some kind of bargaining agent. The fundamental cause of violent prison confrontations is a lack of organization—the total fear and degradation that occurs when you reduce a man to looking out solely for himself. Organization within prisons would provide an alternative to violence, which (as Hobbes argued) is the lowest level and most elementary form of social order.

This is what has happened in civil rights. Powerful organizations now bargain and confront the dominant society. We have observed the growth of a Movement that has begun to make profound changes in our laws, to redistribute the means by which the laws become reality. But now we are moving in areas that are much more subtle. We can't be sure that people will "treat me like a human being."

GOLDBERG: We are beginning to see some of this in prisons—for example at Walla Walla in Washington. But it can be carried to a point where administration loses control of the institution.

MANNING: That's a possible outcome. But there are large numbers of people who believe that institutions should not be governed by administrators. Take any institution—a university, a labor union, a police department—the idea of "power to the people" is a slogan that claims that the power to control institutions belongs at least as much in the hands of the majority who are being served by it as it does in the hands of administrators.

GOLDBERG: Which raises another question: if inmates are able to do this, why are they in the institution? We don't permit too much inmate participation in the government of penal institutions. We're afraid of it.

CADE: I think that you're getting close to a very key issue; controversial but extremely important. If, as we have alleged in the civil rights movement (and I believe it is indeed true), the individual does indeed need to experience a sense of power over his own destiny within the guidelines set by his significant society, it would seem to hold that the individual who finds himself in a correctional institution would likewise need to experience this sense of power. Consequently, I would be inclined to work just as hard for individual rights within a prison as I would to work for civil rights on the outside of prison. I think we need to define the "human" status of the prison inmate before we can do much else. The important question is, "How different should the prison inmates' status be in this sense from the status of the individual who is not in prison?" Other very crucial questions are, "To what extent should the prison inmate participate in the governing of his own life?" and "To what extent should the prison inmate participate in the determination of his prison environment?" In other words, how do we bring the need for societal control of misbehavior on the part of the individual and the needs of the individual as a human being in quest of self-actualization into some degree of functional compatibility?

MANNING: A definition of the needs of individuals and of society will always be arbitrary. It is historically true that Western, industrial societies consider criminals to be culpable and responsible and that we consider the mentally sick not to be.

CADE: But don't you agree that more people in the world would think that people in prison are more sick than black people in general?

MANNING: There's no evidence that shows that to be true. What I mean is that we cannot connect personality traits, intelligence, or ability with a propensity to crime. Nor do any of these characteristics distinguish or differentiate prisoners from nonprisoners.

GOLDBERG: All we're saying is that somebody in authority has said that these are different people. There's no logic to it.

MANNING: There's a culturally assigned logic to it.

SHARP: If the prisoner has equal power, he gets his gun back and shoots me up and this I don't like. I do not like people who shoot up other people.

MANNING: It happened in 1776, and the rebels won.

SHARP: That's an entirely different situation.

CADE: Of course, we cannot consider such socially accepted killing as takes place in wars in the same vein. It is obvious to me that killing is bad whether it is sanctioned by society or not. However, as we talk about murders executed by criminals we are, of course, talking about a completely different pattern of motivation. We can't deny the existence of the so-called "psychopathic killer"; we can't deny his disease. We cannot forget that some people kill because they are sick and are in need of help. I cannot agree that a black man is sick because he is black and as a result, he engages in some "not so legal" behavior to ameliorate his undesirable circumstances. As I have said, there are different kinds of people in prison; lawyers, doctors, middle class whites, middle class blacks, lower class blacks, Chicanos, psychotics, psychoneurotics, psychopaths, and so forth.

SHARP: Like Nathan Leopold, for an example.

CADE: Right. I cannot accept the idea that Leopold was an underprivileged person. He certainly was not "hurt" by society in the same sense as the under-privileged black man or woman in the present day society. Again, I think you have to identify your population before making generalizations. I think identifying sub-populations in prison based upon needs and individual circumstances is one of the most important tasks confronting us in corrections at this time.

SHARP: Because there are people who do things who have no business being in prison. Why should an embezzler be in prison? Let him pay it back and learn that way he has to pay for what he did. You have retribution for what happened. Hopefully, it's also a rehabilitative thing.

CADE: A good example can be found in the drug problem as we now think of it. When I was in correctional work, most of the individuals being incarcerated for drug usage and the handling of drugs were black men from the larger cities. For the most part, these were slum dwellers. At that time they were treated as if they were the worst kind of criminals. Subsequent to my work in prison, I started teaching at Michigan State University. I noted that college students were using the same type of drugs, in some cases, very openly and much more extensively. These were mostly white middle and upper middle class students. They were considered "young, misguided citizens," at the worst. And in some cases, good, upstanding, liberal professors fought relentlessly for their cause, giving a positive meaning to their drug practices. During those days, I couldn't help but think of all the years the unfortunate blacks from the slums and ghettos of Detroit spent in prison for the same practice, with no one coming to their rescue and most people not even being aware of their plight. They had the misfortunes of being slum dwellers, black, and less "intelligent" (chiefly because of their circumstances of existence). They could not adequately defend themselves, and they had no one to champion their "cause," so they served time in prison.

SHARP: —because the whites are in on it now!

MANNING: That's what I'm saying about the arbitrary nature of society's rules and definitions of criminal behavior.

SHARP: But you go too far when you speak of giving them power.

MANNING: You see, there are a lot of inconsistencies showing in what people are saying right here—mirroring inconsistencies in society. You argue we should make reforms, treat people as human beings, and give them individualized treatment—all of which requires an alteration in power arrangements. But none of you wants to permit changes in power and authority!

RADELET: There is a particular paradox that may be worth noting. It pertains to the difficulty of individualization of the correctional process. Our credo—the American creed—stresses individualization. But our society has become a vast, complicated, superbureaucracy, including corrections, universities, etc. This carries with it the connotations of dealing with people in categories—through processes that make it technically simple to determine who's in and who's out—data we can process by computer. Our criteria for vital determinations affecting the lives of people lend themselves more to management efficiency than to individualization. To be a policeman, one must be so tall, so old, have an IQ of such and such, etc. All of this, it seems to me, is incongruent with the time and the process, the care, the patience, and the sensitivity to human personhood that is implied in the concept of individualization, whether you're talking about police or corrections or whatever. There must be some limit to how much we can "machine tool" people or "program" them if we are serious about individuality.

CADE: I think that in the last few years we have assumed that society is ruled by groups and it seems that we feel that it must be this way. Consequently, we haven't tried very hard to develop any individual techniques that we can use for the masses of individuals to the end of improved individual social adjustment. We think in terms of groups for political reasons. This is a political value that has been rather gradual in its development, but now seems to pervade the whole of society. It is my feeling that this is the way to the development of automatons. If you are more interested in developing automatons than in enhancing self-actualization and creative productivity on the part of individuals, then it seems logical to take the political route, to think only in terms of groups. But if you are truly interested in the experiences, the feelings, the anxieties, the aspirations and, ultimately, the development of a truly benevolent and humanistic society, I would conclude that we must look for ways to serve the individual and cope with his needs wherever he may be, whether in prison or in so-called free society.

SHARP: It is the same situation in the employment of women. Are they available? What norms are to be established for employing them? And if you do hire them, will they be treated as equals? Or will they get the silent treatment?

CADE: Generally, I feel that there are two revolutions going on; the revolution of the *have-nots* to *haves,* and the revolution of the *haves* to *be.* The haves are empty people whose chief needs are for a sense of personal power, personal autonomy, and fulfillment. To some extent, in this sense, even the prison inmate in the American society would fall within the category of the haves. He, too, is a victim of a society of plenty although he has not, in most instances, been awarded his equal share.

RADELET: And with that comment, we must bring our discussion to a close. We have, I think, at least touched some of the important questions that Attica dramatized. That we have not exhausted the possibilities is an assumption with which we began the discussion. We have agreed on some points, disagreed on a few, and have developed, I hope, a basis for continuing dialogue by others, aimed at action for constructive change.

Points for Discussion

Concluding the Symposium, Radelet said, "We have agreed on some points, disagreed on a few, and have developed a basis for continuing dialogue by others aimed at constructive change." To guide such continuing dialogue, consider these questions about the points made, in the order they were brought out. What are your responses to them?

General

1. Who are the clients of the corrections system?

Causes of the Riot

2. Physical conditions of the prison? The administration of the prison? The belief that crime and punishment are political acts? Are they? Ignorance

of prisoners about events in the outside world? Anomie? "Groupism"? Lack of consensus among prison administrators? Maintaining the status quo by New York wardens? The presence of outside activists?

Goals of Correction

3. Confinement to protect society? Rehabilitation? Group rehabilitation possible? Does society have a right to be protected? Can (should) we ignore the individual inmate? What about the *iatrogenic* effect of prisons? Must the criminal pay? Is there a common prison personality? What can (or does) the intelligent inmate leader do? What can (should) the legislature do? What has it done? How can we minimize "arbitrary justice"? How handle the new "internal morality"?

What Should Be Done?

4. How help prisoners make the transition to the outside world? *Is* the criminal law a fantasy? Who could supply a "house of ideas" that corrections people could live with? What size groups of offenders could be treated effectively? Do we *know* what will work? Is parole preparation adequate? Does the indeterminate sentence help or hinder rehabilitation? Would gains for prisoners be at the expense of warden and staff?

How do we bring societal control of misbehavior of individuals and the needs of individuals for self-actualization into compatibility? What about psychopathic offenders? *Is* there a limit to how much we can "machine tool" or "program" people if we are serious about individuality?

Part Five

Programs

A number of programs in police training in community relations work have been developed by police departments and various types of institutes that have been or are being conducted in the country.

The 16 Studies presented here report on specific programs that have been operating in many parts of the country with the objective of improving police and community relations. From these the student can learn from the experience of others how these action programs can contribute to better understanding on both sides. Study 16 is included to give some insight into the relations of the British police with the people they serve, and to leave the reader with the refreshing viewpoint of a police force whose rapport with their clientele makes their work seem "all quite fun, really."

STUDY 1

The National Institutes on Police and Community Relations

The idea of specialized police training in the psychological and sociological aspects of modern police work goes back about twenty-five years. Its development has been an important phase of the broader context of police professionalization. The National Institutes on Police and Community Relations have been an important part of this development.

The professional concept suggests an interest in understanding *why* problems occur, as well as in *how* to deal with them; an interest in problem *prevention* as well as in tactical resolution. Thus, through specialized training and education, the police learn something of the nature and causes of crime, delinquency, social deviancy, and social conflict and disorder. Lately, the police are asked to do more—to anticipate and head off social dissonance through constructive projects and programs, with the idea that the best way to handle a problem is to prevent it. Preventive policing, in partnership with the community, is a central idea in any Police and Community Relations Institute.

By the early 1950s, numerous major city police departments had some sort of training in human relations, race relations, the police and minority groups, and such. But the term "police and community relations" had not yet been used to refer to such training. The concept of cooperative action of police and community forces to resolve problems had not as yet been formalized. In 1954, the Supreme Court handed down its landmark decision enunciating that schools which were segregated racially were not, in fact, equal. The decision in itself provided no formula for resolving the problem, but it served to crystalize the imperative need for rapid resolution of intergroup problems confronting the public conscience. New approaches were needed.

One such approach was the first National Institute on Police and Community Relations, held at Michigan State University in May 1955. It was a partnership project of the School of Police Administration and Public Safety (now the School of Criminal Justice) at Michigan State and the National Conference of Christians and Jews—an organization established in 1928 to foster cooperative action on community problems of persons dedicated to the Judaeo-Christian tradition, regardless of their denominational affiliations. The Institute was a one-week conference, conducted annually through 1969, which coined the term "police-community relations" (PCR) and set a pattern for similar programs in many places. Over the years, more than 5,000 police and community leaders from 42 states and 15 foreign countries attended the National Institutes in East Lansing. In addition, regional and local Institutes developed across the country, patterned on the national format, and attracted thousands of participants over the years. The National Institutes were endorsed by such organizations as the International Associations of Chiefs of Police, the International City Managers Association, State Associations of Chiefs of Police and of Sheriffs, State Corrections Departments, the National Association of Intergroup Relations Officials, the National Council on Crime and Delinquency, and the United States Conference of Mayors.

The purposes of the Institutes were stated as follows:

1. To encourage police-citizen partnership in crime prevention.

2. To improve police-community relations and, at the same time, to foster cooperative community efforts in problem solving.

3. To assist police and other community leaders in understanding the nature and causes of complex problems in people-to-people relations, and especially to improve police-minority group relationships.

4. To encourage a cooperative relationship between the police and other agencies in the criminal justice system.

5. To help make the principle of equal protection of the law meaningful for the *total* society and to emphasize that law enforcement is a general community responsibility.

The Institutes followed the format of opening Sunday afternoons with registration and a formal opening dinner, and closing Friday mornings with concluding summary panels or addresses. The intervening work days were programmed for presentations and reaction sessions in the mornings and afternoon work group sessions devoted either to assigned subjects or to local problems identified by the work groups. The latter sessions, totaling some ten hours during the week, proved over the years to be the most fruitful and popular aspect of the Institutes, as evidenced in opinionaires that were completed by participants as part of the Friday morning sessions. Each work group filed a report of their discussions and findings, which became the basis for the mimeographed *Proceedings* of the Institutes, along with manuscripts of the presentations.

Participants through the years were typically about 70 percent police or other criminal justice personnel and 30 percent community leaders representing interests of education, religion, social agencies, the media, and the like. Participants were, of course, diversified as to race, religion, economic level, and education and included many students. It was not unusual to have spokesmen for various dissident groups in attendance. Recruitment of those attending was effected largely through the sixty-some regional offices of NCCJ, which often provided scholarships covering housing and meals. Travel costs were paid by groups sponsoring the participants, police departments often paying the total costs of their delegates. Frequently, the NCCJ offices recruited teams of delegates from a particular city or area so that on their return, the members of the teams would have each other's support in undertaking projects.

Planning for the Institutes was originally done by representatives of the University, NCCJ, and local police leadership, but the committee was expanded in later years to include national figures representing many pertinent interests. Planning was done in several meetings in advance of each Institute, and the program finally adopted was a product of considerable give-and-take.

Techniques used in the Institutes included speeches (fewer through the years, in favor of more work-group time), panels, field trips to prisons and correctional camps, films, topical clinics, role-playing demonstrations, and case studies. Speakers included police administrators, PCR officials, editors, mayors, city managers, judges, attorneys, Supreme Court justices, psychiatrists, psychologists, educators, churchmen, corrections officials, probation and parole officers, civil rights and community agency leaders. Topics ranged through "understanding ourselves," "understanding others," "understanding the community," and "marshalling community resources." Included were reports from across the country of successful PCR projects.

The series of National Institutes conducted at Michigan State University terminated with the 1969 meeting. But similar Institutes continue to be held at other universities with the National Conference of Christian and Jews cooperating. At Michigan State, a National Center on Police and Community Relations was established in 1965, growing out of the Institutes. NCCJ publishes a monthly national newsletter called *The Hot Line,** of special interest to PCR program planners.

---

*For information, the address is 43 West 57th Street, New York, N.Y. 10019.

Michigan Institute on Community Relations
and the Administration of Justice

With the discontinuance of the annual National Institute on Police and Community Relations at Michigan State University following the 1969 conference, plans were formulated for a Michigan Statewide Institute on Community Relations and the Administration of Justice. This was undertaken as a cooperative venture of the Center on Police and Community Relations in the School of Criminal Justice of the University, the Michigan Regional Office of the National Conference of Christians and Jews, and the Michigan Office of Criminal Justice Programs. Differing from the national Institutes in several significant respects, this new project was launched in 1970 with a substantial grant under the provisions of the Omnibus Crime Control Act of 1970, with Wayne County (Detroit) Circuit Judge Horace W. Gilmore as chairman.

On April 9th of that year, a planning committee for the initial stage of the Institute met at the University. A statement of Institute purposes was agreed upon:

> To assist task force teams of citizens and law enforcement officers in Michigan cities in developing tangible programs to meet specific problems of their own delineation in their local communities.

The range of the Institute was suggested by its title, broadening the traditional police-community relations compass. Instead of a single annual week-long meeting (like the national program), it was agreed that this Institute would consist of a series of three workshops, the first to be held on June 9th. In this one-day session, plans for future activity would be *developed by the participants*.

Problems

The planners were aware of certain problems that had arisen in the procedures of the National Institutes:

1. Because of the diversity of police and community people attending, ten or twelve types of expectations of outcomes had emerged. No

single Institute could possibly deal with all of these adequately enough to stem frustrations and disappointments among participants.

2. Program evaluation had proved inadequate. *Quantitatively,* the Institutes had seemingly become more popular, measured by the growing number of those wishing to attend. *Qualitatively,* however, evaluation had been confined to post-institute questionnaires and staff evaluation. Too little was known about actual results.

3. There had been inadequate follow-through after the institutes. While some NCCJ offices achieved a multiplication of programs, many merely involved participants in fund-raising or public relations events having little programmatic value.

4. Participants had little involvement in Institute planning, done largely by an elite group. Some participants felt the programs were "rigged" or "not our bag."

5. The Institutes had focused too much on police and on police-minority group relations. Broader problems of the police and "the system," their role quandary in society, and their relationship to other aspects of criminal justice had been slighted.

Philosophy

There was agreement on several philosophical points that should undergird the state Institute:

1. The program should emphasize the interrelatedness of the criminal justice system with governmental and social systems and institutions, to improve coordination in actual practice.

2. *Process* would be at least as important as *product* in the efforts of the task force teams. There is no universal "bag of tricks" in identifying needs or implementing programs. Program evaluation would focus on team process.

3. All aspects of program needs being emphasized by LEAA should be used as guidelines in implementing team projects, such as: programming, planning, and evaluation as a continuing process; adaptation of general improvement standards to a given jurisdiction; recognition of the time needed to evolve quality plans; due attention to both long and short range planning; and the incorporation of explicit program goals and evaluative mechanisms capable of measuring the achievement of these goals.

Workshop I—June 9, 1970

Some 30 cities were represented at this first workshop by two delegates each—one police and one nonpolice appointed to this responsibility by the mayors of their cities in response to Judge Gilmore's invitation. This was the initial session of the Institute: the main idea was to make future program structure in the Institute the handiwork of those for whom it was intended, namely, the participants.

Judge Gilmore opened the meeting with remarks on "Why We Are Here," explaining that this was a planning session for future aspects of the Institute, and that the two-man teams present would be asked to organize larger teams of up to ten members in their home cities. These larger teams would come to a three-day November workshop, prepared to delineate their local problems . in some order of priority and to begin to develop a program to cope with at least one of these problems. Appropriate resources would be marshalled for the November workshop to assist teams in this purpose. At a subsequent two-day workshop in March 1971, teams would reflect their progress and their difficulties in carrying out their projects locally, and additional assistance would be provided.

The director of the National Center on Police and Community Relations provided further background for the new Institute. He dealt with basic concepts and definitions, reviewed the history of such Institutes in the past, and pointed to the need for changing program designs that had seemed satisfactory in the past. The director of the Michigan NCCJ office explained certain procedural matters, including some options for the funding of local projects developed by teams. He proposed a timetable for various steps in preparation for the November Workshop and said that his office would serve as the coordinating center for the Institute.

The two-man teams had an opportunity to meet and discuss what had been proposed and to direct their opinions and suggestions to an ensuing general session. In this way, the total group of approximately 65 accepted the responsibility for planning and began to work at this task. They also acceded to the request that they undertake to develop local teams as they returned to their respective communities.

In a luncheon address, a former administrative assistant to the Detroit Police Commissioner cautioned the participants to be realistic in limiting the scope of their initial projects to what they felt might reasonably be accomplished. Better a success in a modest goal than a failure in a lavish goal! The speaker also stressed the importance, in developing local teams, of including representatives of as many segments of the community as possible, in order to achieve a broad base for action.

In the closing session, the director of the National Center developed "Guidelines for Building Teams" on a blackboard:

1. Teams should reflect a ratio of 2 police to 3 community people, with a total initial team of not more than 10 *active* members, including a racial, ethnic, and political mix of men, women, and youth.

2. Police members of teams should include upper level and line officers, for support and implementation. Community people should include known leaders plus those who have the time to actually work. The media should be involved all the way.

3. City executives should appoint and support the teams, but not have veto power over their membership or programs. Ideally, teams should be concerned with all aspects of the criminal justice system.

4. Team members should be volunteers. Team status in the community will be what teams make it.

5. Ten people should not pretend to "represent" all segments of a community. What these ten do to solicit a wide spectrum of opinion is the important consideration.

The workshop concluded with a statement by the chief of the evaluation team for the Institute (Dr. John H. McNamara of Michigan State University), in which it was proposed that the evaluation would focus during the first year on organizational and procedural processes for each team—*not* on judgments as to the quality of programs developed by the teams. Data would be gathered through periodic questionnaires and field interviews.

Workshop II—November 8–10, 1970

In the interim between June and November, the two-man teams attempted to carry out their responsibilities, as outlined above. Some failed to bring off the larger team, for various reasons, and some cities dropped out of the Institute. Others stayed in, with teams of more than two persons but less than ten. Detroit mounted five teams. Some teams worked hard and made considerable progress in problem delineation in local meetings before the November workshop. Other teams encountered difficulties in getting organized and under way and made less progress.

In attendance at the November workshop were 24 teams from 19 cities, with from 3 to 10 members each—a total of approximately 165 persons. The program began with a representative panel, chaired by Judge Gilmore, addressing itself to the question: What are some of the more serious problems with which the Institute should be concerned? The teams then had their first extended session, meeting separately, with helping consultants available on call—the latter being Michigan State faculty members. An evening session was devoted to a discussion of the topic, "Techniques and Methods of Community Problem-Solving."

The morning of the second day was devoted to both general and team sessions analyzing factors that contribute to the difficulty of solving community problems and factors that facilitate such efforts. A member of the staff of the State Crime Commission, in a luncheon address, identified various possibilities for funding local projects planned by the teams. In the afternoon, the teams—meeting separately again—began work on the development of projects directed to their particular problem delineation and the priorities they had set. An evening session was devoted to discussion of a series of role-playing situations, skillfully directed by an assistant dean of the University of Michigan's School of Education.

The morning of the third day found teams matched according to similarity of problems and meeting in pairs to discuss and evaluate critically, though constructively, each other's plans. Then the teams met separately for a final session. A concluding general session of the workshop aimed at pulling things together and clarifying the steps ahead for teams as they returned home. In essence, the teams were charged to undertake local accomplishment of their projects, requesting assistance, as needed, from the central Institute office.

Workshop III—March 20–30, 1971

The main purpose of the third workshop was to check on the progress of the teams in moving toward the objectives they had set for themselves and to lend help to them. The program began with a spokesman for each team briefly reporting on developments for the team since November. At a noon luncheon, James H. Brickley, the Lieutenant Governor of the State of Michigan—Chairman of the State Crime Commission—spoke on the importance of citizen participation in projects to curb crime. Chief executives of cities with teams were invited to this luncheon session, met privately with the Lieutenant Governor thereafter, and then met for a short time with their respective teams. The teams then went on with their work, in separate rooms. An evening session featured Dr. McNamara, sharing with all participants the results and problems of Institute evaluation to that point. There was considerable discussion, with the participants offering numerous helpful suggestions as to how the evaluation might proceed more productively.

The morning of the second day, paired team sessions were held, and later the teams met individually. The suggestion was made that some teams might be ready for broader problem delineation and broader projects, and for enlarged team membership. The over-all program of the State Crime Commission was reviewed by its director, Bernard G. Winckoski, at the noon luncheon, one objective being to enlarge the perspective of the teams. Also speaking was Dr. Robert Green, the director of the University's Center for Urban Affairs. An afternoon session concluding the workshop again summarized, explained the steps ahead pointing to a November 1971 workshop, and offered the continuing availability of consultant assistance as needed by any team.

Evaluation Aspect

A special word should be said about the evaluation process, because this was a pioneer aim of the Institute. The general purpose of the evaluation was to produce information and guidance for future programs of this type, in Michigan and elsewhere. As mentioned earlier, the thrust of the evaluation in the first year was team process—not attitude or organizational change, nor the quality of projects developed by teams. One member of each team acted as liaison with Dr. McNamara and his associates, specifically for the evaluation. This liaison person was asked to report:

1. The frequency of attendance and dates of meetings of the team.

2. Other local communications relevant to the team's efforts.

3. Changes in the make-up of the team and the reasons for these changes.

4. The emergence of leadership in the group and the manner in which such leadership emerged.

5. The major points of agreement and disagreement regarding the team's activities as expressed by its members.

6. A general description of how the team functioned to achieve the final selection of problem(s) on which the team decided to focus.

7. Identification of events external to the team that influenced the manner in which the team functioned; for example, actions by the mayor, the chief of police, city council, human relations commission, etc.

The evaluation staff announced that reports from the liaison persons would be sought from time to time, either in writing or by telephone, and these reports would eventually be collated and analyzed and the results made available to all teams. By the end of the first year of the Institute (June 1971), the evaluation staff reported that their analysis revealed the following negative and positive elements in team activities:

Factors That Hindered Team Efforts:

1. Getting the cooperation of government, police, and other segments of the community.

2. Changing personnel of teams because of lack of time, fading interest, moving away from district or town, etc.

3. Organizing teams to include necessary representation of varied ethnic, racial, and economic interests.

4. Getting consensus on a project that (a) needed doing, (b) was possible to accomplish, (c) excited cooperation.

5. Lack of team status or political clout due to (a) poor support from government, (b) team personnel who were good workers but were not prominent in the community.

6. Overcoming frustrations such as (a) poor attendance at meetings, (b) personality clashes, (c) red tape, (d) stereotypes of police or of ethnic and racial groups, (e) inexperience, (f) poor communication, (g) apathy.

Factors That Helped Team Efforts:

1. Presence of visible problem or crisis in a community.

2. Having a PCR unit in the police department.

3. Support of police command and line officers.

4. Mayor willing to cooperate regardless of party lines.

5. Support of prominent community leaders and the press.

6. Recognition of the community potential for getting things done.

7. Choosing a project, part or all of which was possible to complete with the dollars and personnel available.

8. Dedication of team members.

Results

Some examples of projects undertaken that were in varying degrees of completion as of June 1971:

Conducting community seminars on the roles of police, the courts, prosecutors, community agencies, and citizens, in a weekly series.

Establishing a liaison group between police and community to accept phone calls from arrested persons to inform them of their rights.

Conducting rap sessions between police and various community groups —especially youth groups.

Establishing a single phone number that citizens could call when in trouble, for referral purposes.

Surveying the attitudes of young people toward the police, parents, etc., and providing help for them when they are in trouble.

Introducing a course in school to help students understand the functions of the police.

Setting up projects for youth and police cooperation in human relations activities.

Getting the PCR unit elevated to division level in a police department.

Setting up a community education program for the prevention of drug use.

Preparing slides and video tapes for schools and model city neighborhoods to explain the criminal justice system, with financial support from the Chamber of Commerce.

Establishing a cadet program for 32 students who meet with and help the police. Hear talks by judges, community leaders.

Circulating a questionnaire to study minority attitudes toward police.

Operating centers for drug education and for runaways, both open 24 hours a day. Installed a PCR library in city hall.

Putting on a talent show in which youth and police officers participate.

Printing instructional materials in Spanish to encourage Latins to register for voting, run for public office, and join their police force.

Completing a series of six police-community-press forums.

Many of these projects were either incomplete at the end of the first year or were designed to be of an on-going nature and needing more time and assistance to get established. Other cities had indicated interest in joining the Institute program. It was therefore decided to apply to the Office of Criminal Justice Programs for an additional grant to continue the Institute for a second year. Although the recycling of a grant was generally discouraged by that Office, an exception was made in this case and a new grant was approved in September 1971, making workshops possible in November 1971 and in March and November 1972.

Rationale for Renewal of Grant

The grant renewal for an additional year was based upon the following considerations:

1. Teams had concentrated on a single problem during the first year to maximize success. Problem conceptions now needed expansion and deepening, building on the first year's work. Only a bare beginning had been made.

2. With such expansion and deepening, teams would see the need for cooperation of more community resources to effectively cope with crime prevention and control.

3. Evaluation results during the first year had been fragmentary; new methods must be tried to achieve effective results in this novel program.

4. Additional cities wished to participate in the Institute.

5. A pattern of consultant assistance was needed to help both the original member cities and the new ones; valuable experience from the former would be available to help the latter.

6. The Institute process required considerably more time to work itself out. Cutting off services at this point would jeopardize the efforts and funds thus far expended.

7. This Institute had some "grand plan" possibilities. It envisioned a state-wide network of locally autonomous programs, engaging citizens of every description in problem-solving endeavors in the criminal justice system. It provided an interacting "we're part of something bigger" perspective, with built-in services and evaluation from the Michigan office of NCCJ and the University.

8. The Institute provided an excellent opportunity to discover what does and does not work, and why, in the State planning of programs such as the LEAA was pledged to facilitate. After one year of the Institute, it was evident that only a beginning had been made.

STUDY 3

The Flint, Michigan, Police-School Liaison Program

New York City, Dec. 6, 1957—Serious trouble in the public schools
. . . delinquency of all kinds . . . 1,280 arrests made on school grounds
this year: 2 for murder, 143 for felonious assaults, 183 for burglaries,
5 for narcotics, 62 for dangerous weapons, 9 for rape, and 45 for other
morals charges. . . . Fear of being assigned to a difficult school has hurt
teacher recruitment . . . Grand jury recommends a uniformed policeman be assigned to each school building to patrol corridors, stairways
and recreation yards as a preventive measure. Reaction of the Superintendent: "Unthinkable. When the schools need police help they get
it promptly and efficiently."—*U.S. News & World Report.*

For years prior to 1957, in New York and other cities, and not just in
ghetto areas, students would not have thought of walking alone to
school lest they be mugged for whatever they had on them. If the New
York School superintendent had been realistic, he would have recognized that calling the police after the fact was no solution. The issue
is one of prevention, not only of law violations, but of situations that
generate delinquency.

One of the more impressive programs in the nation for the prevention of juvenile delinquency is the cooperatively developed police-
school liaison program in Flint, Michigan. Its record of success has
been such that more than 200 requests for information about it are
being received from other cities each year. Mimeographed and printed
materials describing its procedures are available* and visits for observation purposes can be arranged.

While the program is primarily for delinquency prevention, the
assigned officers may make arrests as they would in any other part of
the community. But they may not take part in enforcing school discipline. Their main job as detective liaison officers is to work closely
with students, counseling them (and their parents) with the aim of

---

*From *Police-School Liaison Program.* Flint Police Department, 210 East Fifth
Street, Flint, Michigan 48502.

269

preventing antisocial behavior in the early years of growth and development. Only persons of detective rank or higher may be assigned to the program.

Planning and experimental work for the project took place between 1958 and 1960 with the cooperative efforts of the Board of Education, parents, social agencies, the Probate Court, businessmen, the Charles Stewart Mott Foundation, and the Police Department. Since Flint is an industrial city of great ethnic and racial diversity, a joint effort from the outset was imperative. It should also be noted that Flint schools are organized in the community school pattern. Basic concepts of the program include:

1. The school and the police are the two key agencies in combating delinquency and so must cooperate.

2. Juvenile delinquency is a social ill and, like other diseases, it can be minimized by early treatment. The pre-delinquent child must be reached before he develops an attitude vulnerable to delinquency.

3. First offenders should be directed into rehabilitative programs rather than be removed from society.

4. Parents should be included in the counseling process, especially when custody for diagnostic treatment is indicated.

5. Liaison detectives should be in plain clothes and use unmarked cars while on duty.

6. When possible, records of offenders should be kept in the personal file of the detective liaison officer and not become a part of the police department records. Except in serious cases, they are to be used only as a basis for counseling.

The program was made possible by the offer of the Mott Foundation to pay half of the total cost of each detective liaison officer, his car, and his office space in the assigned school. Other cities have felt that they could not undertake this kind of program because they do not have such a foundation. Flint replies that they were, of course, fortunate in having such a single source of funds, but that most cities can raise funds through community campaigns. At present, too, funds may be available from State planning agencies under the Omnibus Crime Control Act.

Initially, the experiment was started in the junior high schools—locus of most pre-delinquent and delinquent pupils—but it has been expanded to include all junior and senior high schools. A part of each officer's duties is to patrol all the elementary schools that feed his assigned building. This is done daily as school opens, at noon, and after school closes. The purpose is to handle infractions, loitering pupils from other schools, and adults whose behavior may raise suspicion.

The detective liaison officer must earn his acceptance in the school program by making himself known to school personnel, parents, and business and community people. He attends many school functions, and athletic and other events both during and after school hours, in the evening and on weekends, to establish the image of a nonauthoritarian member of the community. He checks out complaints from the downtown Juvenile Bureau, contacting students, parents, and merchants. He makes an endless number of appearances in school classes as an instructor, in assembly programs with slide and other presentations, before service and religious organizations—all to educate students and public on the role of the police and the nature of pertinent laws and ordinances. When he is not in his school, he is in constant radio contact with the principal's office and the police department in case of emergencies or crises.

In addition, he maintains contacts with the courts, social and mental health agencies, his counterparts in other schools, and any other sources that will aid him in his work in counseling or in making referrals.

Counseling of Students

The chief job, for which the foregoing activities prepare him, is the work of the detective liaison officers in counseling students. This is done primarily in conjunction with other school personnel. Each junior and senior high school has a Regional Counseling Team comprising the deans of students and of counseling, a visiting teacher, a nurse counselor, and the detective. If in a given case it is necessary, advisors may be called from Probate Court, child guidance clinics, welfare and mental health agencies, or other sources with which contacts are established for the purpose. The contributions of the detective to this team are that he:

1. Contributes information regarding individual cases and the families and neighborhoods from which they come.

2. Helps make early identification of delinquent behavior.

3. Confers with pupils, parents, and community members on individual cases and delinquent trends in general.

4. Represents the police and the courts as a consultant in law enforcement and juvenile procedures.

5. Presents a more significant and informative petition to the court when that step is necessary.

Because of the increase in offenses by girls, women detective liaison officers have been added to the staff. They wear uniforms and badges to make them identifiable by the younger children as authority figures. In addition to their other liaison functions, they conduct police-cadette units after school to help the girls feel that they are a part of the responsible group in the school. Women officers investigate complaints of sex crimes, lost children, and cases of abuse and neglect. Much of their image-building work is done in the elementary schools.

Favorable Comments

A survey was made of Flint school employees and the liaison officers to elicit their opinions of the police liaison program. The following are excerpts from letters received in reply:

Principals: Today this is a necessary function of our schools . . . I have worked personally with the liaison officers from the start and have nothing but the highest praise . . . The program is a real deterrent to delinquent behavior . . . The program provides a positive image of the police.

Liaison Officers: The relationship has been excellent . . . Tremendous results in preventing delinquent acts. . . . Aids in clearing acts that have occurred.

School Counselor: The program is a MUST.

Teachers: Our officer is fairly unobtrusive and has good rapport with the students . . . The program would fail completely if the officer were asked to enforce school discipline; his function is counseling . . . Gets back to the old policeman on the beat who knew his neighborhood. . . . A marked change in student attitudes toward the police.

Negative Comments

Liaison Officer. We need a different approach for work in the high schools; the philosophy of prevention could be too late.

Teachers: Police liaison officers have no place in the public schools . . . It is a form of intimidation . . . They enforce middle class white ethics and mores . . . We need more officers; they are spread too thin to do the job . . . I do not feel they should be armed on routine school business . . . They need very special training for their work . . . Much depends on the personality of the officers . . . Some are good, some are not.

Statistical Data

In the years (1958–1969) during which the Flint liaison program has operated, juvenile arrests nationally have increased more than 2½ times the rate in Flint (78% vs. 29%). More recent data show that during the period October–December 1970, offender contacts of liaison personnel resulted in only 15.9% being referred to court as against 41% being referred to court by other police personnel. Put another way, liaison personnel were able to counsel and release 84.1% as against 59% released by other police officers. Other figures:

FLINT POLICE ARRESTS FOR SERIOUS OFFENSES

	1958	1964	1969
Juvenile	55%	69%	46%
Adult	45	31	54

(Police liaison program started in 1958–1960)

JUVENILE ARRESTS AS A PERCENT OF TOTAL ARRESTS

	1958	1964	1969
Nation	9.0%	16%	21%
Flint	9.4	14	12

The data show that Flint has made a good beginning. An Institute for Police-School Liaison Officers has been cooperatively established by the Mott Foundation, the Board of Education, and the Mott Leadership Program, in conjunction with several universities.

Opinions on the Merits of the Program

On the Negative Side

Criticisms of police-school liaison programs have arisen on such technical points as whether liaison officers should be armed when on duty in the schools, and whether they should have offices in the school buildings. Agreements on these matters have often been worked out between the police departments and the boards of educations concerned. More philosophical objections to school liaison programs need further consideration. In the April 1971 issue of *Hot Line**, the editor quoted from an article by George Shepard and Jesse James, both former police officers, listing such negative factors as:

1. The lack of officers adequately trained to prevent delinquency in the school setting.

2. The general shortage of manpower in most departments.

3. Possible legal complications.

4. Possible stigma attached to the experimental school.

5. The possibility of the officer being expected to enforce school discipline, thus re-enforcing the image of police officers as repressive rather than helpful.

6. The difficulty of measuring whether attitudes *are* changed by liaison programs.

On the Positive Side

The *Hot Line* editor invited readers' opinions, among which were the following responses quoted from the issues of June and July 1971.

---

*A mimeo newsletter published monthly by the national office of the National Conference of Christians and Jews, 43 West 57th Street, New York, N.Y. 10019.

Carm J. Grande, Community Relations Officer of the San Jose, California, Police Department, stated:

1. Policemen must get involved in the educational process to over-come animosity toward the police.

2. Our problems largely result from the misunderstanding of the police role by youth.

3. Psychologists say that the impressionable age of youth is between five and eleven years; we must reach them then.

4. In San Jose the police have brought all the Administration of Jus-tice agencies into the classrooms of the junior high schools pri-marily, but we work with students at all levels.

5. Anti-police forces are attempting to degrade the police image, but we feel that the students should be the judges.

Sheriff Peter Pitchess of Los Angeles County responded:

1. In 1967 our Department, in cooperation with the Temple City Unified School District, initiated an educational program in the sev-enth and eighth grade levels called "Citizen and The Law," a dynamic approach to educate youth in the problems of law enforcement.

2. The program was an immediate success—five times as many stu-dents wanted to take the course as could be enrolled. We expanded so that we could have four classes per quarter.

3. We have experienced none of the difficulties mentioned by Shepard and James in the April issue.

4. We have further expanded the program to the high school level with a course called "Students and the Law."

5. Instructors are all sheriff personnel with the requisite educational and personality qualifications. They teach during their off-duty hours.

6. We now have 40 instructors in 45 schools reaching 3000 students per semester, plus an adult program.

7. The response has been overwhelmingly favorable.

STUDY 4

Sensitivity Training in Police-Community Relations

Human relations problems invariably prompt "technique-itis"—the illusion that if only a novel, imaginative method can be found, the
method in itself will work miracles. Sometimes the new method is really
an old one rediscovered or an old one applied to new circumstances.
In the last few years, so-called sensitivity training has come to be
regarded as the miracle-worker in police-community relations, with all
sorts of outlandish claims made for it.

The very term, sensitivity training, engenders indignation in some
circles when its use is proposed, because it is so often misunderstood
and confused with other techniques borrowed from it. This is largely
due to a lack of understanding as to what sensitivity training is and
what it is not. The term has become blurred in the public's mind with
"encounter" and "confrontation" groups, "the human potential movement," "synanon games," "marathons," "touch and tell," and labels
expensively publicized by commercial entrepreneurs who offer group
"therapy" at high prices for experiences that are purportedly based on
the sensitivity model. Because some of these methods provide emotional
and erotic binges of body awareness and the joys of touching and
massage in sessions lasting from a day to three weeks (limited only
by the financial and physical endurance of the client), they have sullied
the reputation of genuine sensitivity techniques.

Further confusion has arisen from the adaptations for their purposes made by some religious, educational, and industrial institutions,
which, through group confrontations, aim at bringing participants closer
to God, learning, or interpersonal rapport through processes that are
essentially emotional. Indeed, the one characteristic that all of these
devices have in common is their reliance on emotions. They all
attempt to lift the person out of his normal level of apathy, inhibitions,
awareness, love, or hatred to a point of climax in which he is confronted with the revelation of the reality of himself or of other people.

275

Misuse of Sensitivity Training

The use of ecstacy as a means of human manipulation—for whatever purpose—is, of course, not new. Examples abound in history: Anthony to the commoners, the general exhorting his troops or the coach his team, African and Indian dancers on the eve of tribal wars, the preacher arousing the Holy Rollers or the Shakers in the camp meetings of the old-time religion, the inciting of lynch mobs. The idea is to lift the individual so that he gains the strength of ten, speaks with tongues, or gains courage from the general upsurge of the group. It is the transcendental oversoul of Emerson in which the sum is far greater than the sum of all the parts. It can be power for good or evil. It can raise potentials, and it can destroy. It can be therapy or trauma. Therein lies the danger: it is emotion only. Demagogues through history have made much of it.

As a current example, The Human Potential Movement described by Jane Howard in *Please Touch,* "is a loose chain of several hundred psychological supermarkets in which a customer can buy almost anything his little heart desires: sensitivity training, inter-racial encounters, creative divorce workshops, heterosexual body sandwiches, nude psychodrama, attack therapy or vomit training (*Time,* July 27, 1970). The book is a caustic critique of the more commercial of these enterprises. Some church groups, with sincere motivations, are experimenting with what they call sensitivity training. In one church in San Diego, the congregation is seated in small circles, with everyone clapping hands. They stop, look at, and express their innermost feelings about each other. Then one member allows himself to be passed from person to person, with his eyes closed as a demonstration of trust . . . In Washington, D.C., 500 Catholic nuns and priests gathered in a hotel ballroom to experience a revolutionary liturgical service. In circles of six, individuals exchanged impressions of one another . . . A passage from the Bible was read . . . Before the circles disbanded everyone was instructed to touch one another—shoulder pats, facial touching or hand squeezes—the liturgical kiss of peace, slightly exaggerated (Milton Lounsberry, *Family Weekly,* August 9, 1970).

However sincere its purpose, such a session is not for all. One wonders too, what the aftereffects of encounter groups in industry might be where management personnel of various levels emerge from candid expressions of their feelings about their problems and each other and must resume next day their hierarchical relations with each other. In the field of education, encounter techniques have been employed, sometimes successfully, in groups of administrators and teachers concerned with organization and curricula problems. But sometimes the frictions resulting from such candor have caused resignations of principals or teachers for whom the experience hit too hard and too deep. Teacher-student experiments have sometimes produced similar boomerangs.

But some individuals and groups, hearing about the sometime successes of sensitivity training and desperate for new approaches to solving their problems of alienation, or plain loneliness, keep succumbing to the novelty and the promises of the methods of encounter. Psychologist Bruce Maliver, writing in *The New York Times Magazine* (January 3, 1971, p. 4), said "the encounter cult has grown into a fantastically profitable industry with more than six million customers. This pay-as-you-go intimacy is a response to the alienation felt by so many."

The Real Thing

So much for the peripheral and frequently distorted applications of sensitivity training. What about the real thing? The first training center in group dynamics was established in 1947 at Gould Academy, Bethel, Maine, by Leland Bradford, then director of the Adult Education Division of the National Education Association, with the help of Ronald Lippitt and Kenneth Benne. Theory was based on the work of Kurt Lewin, a pioneer in social psychology. As Max Birnbaum explains it in the *Saturday Review:*

> As the field developed, the T-group (Training group) became the heart of any laboratory or workshop that is devoted to the study of group dynamics or human relations. The traditional T-group consists of, ideally, (the laboratory) for approximately two weeks. . . . The T-group is, because of its intense emotional impact, by far the most significant aspect of any human relations lab.

> The objectives of the T-group are to help individual participants become aware of why both they and others behave as they do in groups. This is accomplished, *with the help of the trainer*, by creating an atmosphere in which the motivations for typical human behavior are brought to the surface *in exaggerated form* ["Sense About Sensitivity Training"]

Birnbaum contends that much of the confusion, even in professional circles, about the technique results from:

> . . . failure to differentiate between those training experiences that are designed to improve an individual's capacity to work effectively as a manager or member of a group . . . and those that are designed to stimulate the individual's personal growth. [The latter] might be labeled paratherapy, in the sense that it is parallel to therapy itself. [Ibid.]

Therapy is the process of healing the unwell, be it mentally or physically. The unwell should never be submitted to the psychic pressures of group experiences without medical supervision. The casualties from commercial group programs have included shock and suicide. Birnbaum states that "the most serious threat to sensitivity training comes first from its enthusiastic but frequently unsophisticated supporters, and second from newly hatched trainers—long on entrepreneurial expertise, but short on professional experience, skill and wisdom."

T-groups are a potent instrument for change in behavior and, for that reason, there are dangers in their indiscriminate use, particularly if the leaders or trainers are not well versed in the problems and difficulties of human adjustment, normal and pathological. Certain guidelines as suggested by Millicent Lane in "Llinas Urges T-Group Safeguards," must be followed:

1. Participation should be strictly voluntary and participants well informed about what the experience will involve.

2. Participants should be carefully screened to eliminate those who may be too vulnerable to the intense feelings aroused in the group.

3. Clear limits should be set regarding acceptable behavior in the group, particularly in reference to physical intimacies.

4. Adequate follow-up of participants should be available.

Unprofessional supervision may result not only in traumatic reactions of the emotionally unstable, as suggested above, but it can result in instances of personality invasion that provoke such resentment as to negate the purposes of the group process. A case in point was a recent instance in a U.S. Department of Agriculture program of T-group sessions from which a resentful worker walked out complaining, "It got down to sex life. It was an invasion of privacy (Carl Craft, "Race Relations Encounter Groups")."

Writing in his syndicated column (Publishers-Hall Syndicate, August 11, 1970), Sydney Harris hit on the proper balance:

We need to understand and use our bodies more effectively, for expression and for communication. We need to become more aware of our sensory needs, and ways of relating more basically and intimately to others. As a whole culture, we are what the youngsters call "uptight."

But—and this is a very important qualification—such bodily awakening and education must be supervised by the most skillful and conscientious of leaders, who are as fully aware of the dangers as they are of the benefits of sensitivity training. When you start messing around with the homeostasis of the human personality, you had better know which buttons to push in case of an emergency.

T-Groups and the Police

Clearly there are pitfalls in sensitivity training, partly because the trainees are so sensitive and partly because some of the trainers have the fast buck as their chief goal. But properly supervised by genuine professionals, it can be made to work. Professor Donald Bimstein, a former New York City Police Academy instructor, feels that sensitivity training is especially helpful for the police:

> Police officers react in anger against the physical and oral abuse to which they are subjected. They sometimes lose control and respond in kind . . . Compounding these difficulties are the problems of built-up prejudices that all officers bring with them when they are sworn into office . . . In the T-group we are dealing with normally adjusted people who are merely seeking to learn more about themselves in their relationships to others, rather than mentally ill people who are trying to find the causes of their ailments . . . It is in this frank and open atmosphere that each can learn about himself and the reactions he produces in others [so that] he can pinpoint those flaws which interfere with proper communication and interaction with other members of society. ["Sensitivity Training for the Police"]

In general, sensitivity training is the meeting together of small groups of people in confrontation situations for the purpose of changing attitudes through catharsis. Paradoxically, the aim is to reduce tensions by temporarily increasing them. Since emotions are stimulated —sometimes to the point of near hysteria—it is vital, as we have said, that the process be supervised by true professionals. It should be kept in mind that the objective is *not* to solve problems, but rather to purge the persons responsible for solving problems of any inhibitions that may have handicapped their doing so. Such inhibitions are typically those which, because of prejudices, biases, and parochial backgrounds, have impeded communication.

Teachers and school administrators have participated for years in variations of encounter groups, drawing on the nondirective counseling philosophy of such authorities as Carl Rogers and derivatives of the group therapy theories of the Esalen Institute. Graduates of the Bethel summer conferences number well into the thousands. T-groups have been used extensively in industry as part of management training. Within the past few years, probably in part because of the sudden availability of Federal and State grants, the police have become a special target of assorted consultant firms with sensitivity training for sale. Resultant projects have been described in LEAA reports and in popular periodicals.*

---

*For example, see Fletcher Knebel, "A Cop Named Joe" and "Doctor to the Cities."

Usually, the participants in such projects are convinced that the experience was beneficial, although they have difficulty in explaining how and why. A few express disappointment that their lives did not change more radically. Little solid research has been done to prove what the effects actually are, beyond an emotional surge. Research does exist showing the effectiveness of group therapy as practiced in hospitals under the direction of psychiatrists. But group therapy is only similar to sensitivity training; it is not the same.

In professional psychological circles during the past ten years, the Association for Humanistic Psychology has gained momentum. It challenges the prevailing schools of thought regarding human behavior—whether behaviorism or Freudian psychoanalysis—arguing that man is uniquely creative, controlled not by outside or subconscious forces, but by his own values and choices. The humanists pay attention to such things as play, warmth, mysticism, joy, Zen Buddhism, and yoga. They have provided the ideological foundation for the human potential movement. Self-actualization and experiential phenomena are emphasized.

What it comes down to is a too-long-delayed recognition—in education, in psychology, in sociology—of the effective aspects of learning, un-learning, and re-learning. But as Birnbaum observes, changing individual behavior and organizational structure are extraordinarily difficult and thorny objectives. So-called planned change is not a product of a bag of gimmicks and a few 33⅓ rpm records. This is simply another way of repeating the most important message to be conveyed about contemporary sensitivity training in police and community relations: check the length, the precise nature, and the integrity of the trainer's experience. But having done this thoroughly and with reassuring results, one should recognize the great need for affective training and its potential values:

1. To develop more fully the qualities of empathy and objectivity in the helping professions.

2. To reduce attitudinal blocks to individual and organizational change.

3. To enhance personality resilience and to improve social intelligence in times of great social tension.

4. To elevate the level of human responsiveness to fellow human beings in need.

STUDY 5

Conflict Management and Crisis Intervention —
Oakland, California

As suggested repeatedly in this text, the term "police and community relations" is a rubric for an infinite number of relationships,
variously organized and having many different emphases as adapted
to local conditions and changing situations. In a letter (September 16,
1971) to Chief of Police Charles R. Gain in Oakland, California,
administrative assistant Raymond Galvin put it this way:

> The department no longer has a police-community relations unit as
> such. The emphasis is on programs which are executed by line officers
> or through temporary specialized units. For instance, we have a
> *Conflict Management Unit* which deals with such matters as problems
> of inter-personal violence, landlord-tenant disputes, and a family crisis
> program. The entire recruit school has been revised to place an em-
> phasis on conflict resolution in Oakland's rather complex environment.
> Further, we are presently considering a consumer fraud effort.

> The emphasis in these programs is to serve the public and maintain the
> peace. In other words, if we do a good police job, we should be able
> to maintain good police and community relationships . . . Our basic
> purpose is to help people help themselves.

The Oakland approach to disturbances is that of problem solving
—usually by referral—and crisis management, rather than necessarily
that of arrest and prosecution. Galvin—who directed the Michigan State
national study of Police and Community Relations in 1966 as a member of the faculty, at that time, of the School of Police Administration
and Public Safety—clarifies the function of the police officer in these
programs:*

> The preferred course inherent in these programs is to enhance the pro-
> fessional competence of the officer and to protect his basic identity as a

---

*The remainder of this study is based on materials available from the Police
Department, City of Oakland, 455 Seventh Street, Oakland, California 94607.

working policeman—*not* to train him as a social worker or psychologist. Police are untrained and ill-equipped to *treat* psychological and social pathology. It is *not*, moreover, our purpose to make them competent in these areas. Officers *can* become competent in identifying a vast range of ills—health problems, employment difficulties, social hardships, and some types of mental illness.

The Oakland Police Department has been "helping people to help themselves" by gradually introducing conflict management programs. In order to deal with problems realistically and effectively, officers must restore order, prevent injury, and at the same time assist the disputants in finding lasting solutions to their problems—solutions that will, hopefully, eliminate the need for repeated police involvement. An example of the introduction of such a project will suggest both the principles and methods used.

Family Crisis Intervention Program

This program was among the first to be initiated. Approximately one-third of all homicides and even more assaults take place in the family. Even more startling, 22 percent of all policemen killed nationally and about 40 percent of those injured meet their difficulty while intervening in a family disturbance situation.* In introducing the program in Oakland, the New York City pilot experience was considered. Morton Bard had trained the first family crisis intervention unit there in 1967, under an LEAA grant, on a two-year experimental basis. In the objective of reducing injuries to officers, their experiment was heartening: during the two year period, not a single injury was sustained by a unit member. By contrast, two members of the regular patrol force and one patrolman were injured in the same precinct while intervening in family disputes.

In the first six months of the Oakland experience (January–June 1970), unit officers responded to more than 16,000 family disturbance calls, with the expenditure of 800 man-hours. Twenty-five percent of the assignments were return calls. The majority of calls for services came between the hours 9 p.m. and 3 a.m., Wednesday through Sunday, primarily from two densely populated districts, heavily black and Mexican-American. In training personnel to respond to such calls, the purposes of family crisis intervention were stated as:

1. To improve police capability of restoring order in family crises.

2. To assist families in resolving the tensions which give rise to disputes by referring them to appropriate helping agencies.

---

*See Morton Bard, "Family Intervention Police Teams as a Community Mental Health Resource," pp. 247–248.

3. To minimize further police involvement by providing solutions before serious physical injury results.

4. To establish liaison between the police and other community service agencies which could provide specialized services in the solution of family crises that would otherwise present a continuing police problem.

5. To enhance police-community relations by making more competent services available to the community.

6. To free beat officers for other police activities by decreasing the number of family disturbances to which they would otherwise respond.

Structure: Field Units.   The field units (FCIUs) of the program are assigned to the Patrol Division and consist of two two-man teams, working in unmarked cars, whose primary responsibility is family crisis intervention but who also respond to other disturbances, especially when not on duty between the hours of 9 p.m. and 3 a.m., Wednesday through Sunday—the time when most family incidents occur. These teams are assigned to the two most troublesome districts. The teams keep careful records of their calls; these are used for study of the effectiveness of the program.

Structure: Staff Unit.   Responsibility for coordinating field unit activities rests with the Experimental Project Coordinator of the Conflict Management Section, whose duty it is to:

1. Implement training programs for unit members.

2. Maintain liaison with referral agencies.

3. Maintain unit records and statistics.

4. Conduct follow-ups with individuals involved in family disturbances to ascertain whether additional services are needed and whether the individual utilized the referral services recommended.

5. Determine the utility and success of agency referrals.

Selection criteria of field unit members include:

1. The member must have volunteered to work in the program.

2. The member must have demonstrated a capability of calming disturbances and maintaining control throughout the call with a minimum of friction between himself and those involved.

3. The member must have demonstrated a willingness to utilize the service and problem-solving approach to family disturbance.

4. The member must have had recent street experience.

Referral agencies cooperating in the program render services in health, welfare, family counseling and assistance, legal matters, emergency finances, and treatment (alcohol, drugs, character disturbances) such as that provided by the Synanon Foundation.

Differences between the New York and Oakland programs may be significant for cities considering FCIU programs. New York provided a one-month intensive training program plus weekly inservice sessions; Oakland relies on the good judgment of the officers recommended by peers and selected through interviews, while holding frequent group meetings for purposes of self-evaluation. Secondly, New York's FCIU members were frozen in the program for two years; Oakland's are requested but not required to remain for six months but can, after consultation, request reassignment. Thirdly, New York considered it an invasion of privacy to conduct follow-up inquiries with the families involved. Oakland considers it in the best interests of the family to inquire about the successes through follow-up, and to determine whether the family needs additional aid. Such data also adds greatly to the evaluation of the program.

Landlord-Tenant Intervention Program

With a similar philosophical approach, the Oakland police have established in their Conflict Management Section a Landlord-Tenant Intervention Program (LTIP), the purpose of which is to achieve settlements of disputes, often by referring the parties to such other agencies as the Small Claims Court. This special unit was set up for an experimental period and directed by a lawyer, the aim being to replace the custom of police rejection of complaints on the grounds that they are civil matters. Landlord-tenant disputes are common in Oakland as in other cities, running to about 90 a month.

Typically, officers are called either by a tenant who has been locked out—with his possessions locked in—or by a landlord seeking payment of back rent. In either case, traditional treatment has been to refer complainants to the court, with the police retiring from the scene, only to be called back hours or days later when tension again reached the violent stage. LTIU officers are trained in knowledge of relevant laws so that they may advise parties to such disputes as to their rights and about the agencies from which they may seek relief. Telling them to get a lawyer—the former practice—was generally futile in view of the poverty or ignorance of the persons concerned. In addition to the referral agencies cooperating in the Family Crisis program, officers are able to refer disputants to the county district attorney's office, the Legal Aid Society, the municipal building and housing department, and the Small Claims Court. From a police standpoint, the main advantage of the LTIU program is that it lets complainants know at once where they may obtain help—free if need be—and relieves officers from the wasteful costs of return calls. Even more important, clients in this program come to see the police as helpful rather than antagonistic—a good way to improve police and community relationships.

Educational Communication

The Department's educational communication programs also are designed to bring police and community closer together. Many brochures are issued advising the citizen "how to prevent" and "what to do in case of" credit card fraud, bad check passing, confidence games, bicycle thefts, home burglaries, robberies, and the like. Pamphlets are also issued as part of the campaign against selling and use of drugs.

A cooperative venture with the community is the "Home Alert" program. This is the use of volunteers who organize block groups, the purpose of which is to acquaint neighbors with each other, who and how many live at each address, what cars they have, etc., so that the appearance of any strange persons or cars in the area can serve as an immediate occasion for alerting residents. Again, pamphlets are issued containing police instructions and suggestions about security in the home.

Emergency telephone numbers are included in all publications, which, in addition, have instructions in Spanish as to the location of the nearest precinct station. While these educational communications serve their obvious purpose, they also have the important function of providing occasions for two-way contacts between police and community, and for bringing people together with each other as they work in the respective programs.

Violence Prevention Unit

The most recent innovation of the Oakland Police Department crisis intervention program is their Violence Prevention Unit. While it is still too early to report any results, its purpose and philosophy merit mention since they constitute a new approach to police service in the community. Heretofore, departments wishing to enhance their community rapport have initiated police-community relations units that have been charged with the whole responsibility of improving community services. Other divisions or units of the departments have remained unaffected and uninvolved.

The new Oakland program is seeking to achieve its purpose by acting on the philosophy that *all* patrolmen who are in contact with the public must be involved in the planning and execution of the project. With the aid of faculty from the School of Criminal Justice of the State University of New York and a grant from the National Institutes of

Health, the planners enlisted the help of seven patrolmen who had had experience in violence situations—an area for which the department had no special procedures. Together they studied the problems, shared their experiences and developed tentative training plans.

Early in 1970, the new Unit selected a number of officers whose histories showed them to be violence-prone in handling conflicts. Eighteen of these officers were taken through a repetition of the training program, led by the original seven officers. It became apparent that changes were needed in departmental organization if more efficient handling of violence were to be achieved. Officers would have to be briefed in the background of violence situations. Recruit and in-service training would have to be developed. To achieve these purposes, the Unit was created in three sections: Action Review, Training Research, and Experimental Projects.

Action Review Section. Since some officers are more apt than others to exaggerate violence situations in the field, the main function of the Action Review Section is to help officers improve their effectiveness. This is accomplished through peer group training sessions in which interaction is frank and open. Experienced patrolmen provide the leadership.

Training Research Section. This section explores aspects of police-citizen violence and devises new training methods in interpersonal relations to enhance officer competence. The coordinator is available to *all* departmental units to assist in human relations training and help in planning programs. Some examples of their work:

> To lead discussion groups focusing on violence prevention and to develop leaders for such groups.

> To refine and implement training suggestions brought to the attention of the Section.

> To develop and evaluate training methods and aids, such as sound-on-sound training tapes.

> To deploy training methods in recruit and line-up training and to test their effectiveness.

> To explore methods for expanding police-citizen violence prevention training for the benefit of community organizations, educational institutions and individuals.

Experimental Projects Section. This Section designs, executes and evaluates experimental projects, particularly of an operational nature, that can improve the department's ability to reduce violence in police-citizen contacts and among citizens. The first project coordinated by the Section was the Family Crisis Intervention Program, described above. A multipronged approach characterizes all activities of this Section. It is responsible for exploring ways of improving police services, increasing safety, and preventing violence through positive interventions. The Section designs and pre-tests pilot programs, plans them in detail, and evaluates their effectiveness. This activity entails the collection of relevant statistics and the collection of new data so that all programs are documented.

The Oakland approach is being watched carefully by many departments and students of police and community relations across the country, in the same fashion as the similar approach in Dayton, Ohio. Just as the Saint Louis pilot was the model for many big-city programs in the sixties, Oakland and Dayton may well be the models for the seventies.

Police Role and Organization for the 1970s

The most critical issue in police and community relations today is the definition of the police role in our modern, urban, democratic society. Until that role is consensually defined, the problem in this field will remain largely unresolved. Historically, the roles of police, even though not carefully or accurately articulated, were nonetheless generally understood and accepted. This is definitely not the case today when we are faced with such questions as:

Are the police to be concerned mainly with peacekeeping or with crime fighting?

Are the police to be blind enforcers of the law or the discretionary agents of a benevolent government?

Are the police to be social workers with guns or gunmen in social work?

Are the police to be facilitators of social change or "defenders of the faith"?

Are the police to be enforcers of the criminal law or society's legal trashbin?

Are the police to be a social agency of last resort after 5:00 p.m., or mere watchmen for business and industry?

If we are to restore public confidence in the police, or of the police in themselves, the police role must be delimited so there are reasonable community expectations as to what the police can and cannot do. When we have done that, we can work on the critical problems of police personnel, training and leadership. As it is, we do not know what we are recruiting and training men for, or what we are leading them to, or what kind of leadership we need to develop, or how to measure police success or failure. Currently, the police are expected to perform two basic roles which are psychologically in conflict: a community service role and a new enforcement role.

The *community service role* is one in which police intervene in

This study is based on addresses by Bernard L. Garmire, Chief, Miami, Florida, Police Department, 1970 and 1971, with his permission.

domestic quarrels, suppress disturbances and riots, handle drug addicts, dependent or neglected children and render emergency medical or rescue services—acting as a social service agency, particularly after 5 p.m., for the impoverished, the sick and the old. The *law enforcement role* includes criminal investigation, collection of evidence, interrogation of suspects, maintenance of order and safety and combating organized crime. Police officers are presently asked to fill both these roles and they are not properly trained or equipped to perform them. Even if the numbers of policemen were vastly increased, their training improved and their resources expanded, they still could not perform both roles effectively—because the roles conflict at points. The situation is complicated by the fact that both the public and the police so strongly perceive their role to be law enforcement *only*. The community service function is, as we have observed, often relegated to secondary consideration—something to do if time and circumstances permit.

To discover the effects on police of the paradoxical role, the Miami, Florida, Police Department and Psychiatric Institute Foundation of Washington, D.C., have collaborated recently in studies from which preliminary results indicate that the multiplicity of roles that officers must fill contributes significantly to fatigue and stress. The ultimate purpose of the studies is to determine if it is possible for policemen to perform two or more somewhat conflicting roles, and what qualities make a good community service worker, a good crime fighter, or a good administrator in police work. One phase of the studies pertains to relations between white policemen and black citizens. Findings include (*The Hot Line,* January 1971):

> A year or two of service in the ghetto inculcates bigotry toward Negroes among white policemen, at least partly because some blacks tend to view the police as their natural enemies. For the same reason, simply donning a police uniform can lead to bigotry if it does not exist already.

> After a few years, a policeman may remain a "hardline bigot . . . and show the black who is boss if he steps out of line." Or, if the policeman feels initially that race is not an issue in his work, it almost invariably becomes one because in a black neighborhood, most of his trouble comes from blacks.

> Rapport is surprisingly good between policemen and black children, the middle aged, and the elderly. The severe hostility is directed principally at teenagers and young adults.

> One of the strong emotions among white patrolmen in the ghetto is fear. The analogy is made to military combat; some speak of their nightly patrols in black areas as ventures into "Vietnam."*

*Sydney Harris has pointed out that their fear is a psychological feedback from pushing lower class Negroes around—a nonverbal "brutality"—*because* of their fear of them.

But more policemen are swinging over to the line: "We have to work with blacks. It's the party line of the department." But it hasn't fully sunk in yet.

The best approach is tailoring the man to the job—rotating men to certain areas from time to time.

Department Organization

In March 1971, Miami Chief of Police Bernard L. Garmire proposed to the City Commission a reorganization of the police department. He prefaced the proposal with this statement:

So long as our community is terrorized by crime and our police officers are threatened by assassination, the *primary* duties of the Miami Police Department will be law enforcement, not community service. We must first seek freedom from fear; then freedom from social deprivation.

The new system of policing he proposed was based on three strategies:

1. The employment of a uniformed *patrol service,* programmatically based and service oriented.

2. The employment of an essentially plainclothes *tactical service,* target-based and mission-oriented.

3. The deployment of the patrol service in a *team policing* concept in both the geographical and functional sense of the term.

Patrol Service

The uniformed patrol service would continue to be the backbone of the police department: patroling, answering calls for service, responding to emergencies, and creating an aura of omnipresence to discourage criminal activities. It would expand its efforts in certain areas. The patrol officer of the future would possess much greater expertise in the handling of social problems. One of his primary, *officially acknowledged* duties would be the initial handling of various social problems. In the past, the police have tended to view their obligation to deal with social problems as a mere irritant that distracted them from their *"real"* work, not realizing that social problems, of which crime is one, *are* their real work. Chief Garmire made it clear that he did not intend that the patrol service should perform the work of social workers or marriage counselors, but that they be "catalytic agents" to bring together people with problems and the professional social agencies capable of handling such problems. On the street, officers would provide something akin to emergency first-aid service until the social agencies could take over.

Therefore, the Miami patrol service officers of the future would be vitally concerned with the community service aspect of policing. They would, of course, continue to handle criminal problems, conduct investigations and make arrests, but they would have assistance in these areas, whereas in the community services area, they would be the *primary* available resource. For such service, the patrol service officers would require an extremely wide base of education and training. They must also possess definite skills in person-to-person relationships and have a highly developed sense of empathy. They would be required to have two years of college minimally to qualify to become patrol service officers. Traditionally, police recruits have always aspired to become detectives. But the future patrol service officers would emerge as the elite of the police, as is now the case with the school resource and the area resident dialogue officers. Garmire added that while the patrol service officer concept is desirable and necessary, the hard facts of crime and violence today require that it remain for the present a desirable, ideal concept. In the meantime, the bulk of police resources would be applied to enforcing the law and establishing safety in the streets.

Tactical Service

The tactical service officers would be primarily concerned with crime and hard-core law enforcement. Their mission would be to apprehend criminals and suppress violence. They would work primarily in plainclothes or any garb facilitating their mission. In effect, the Tactical Service would constitute one (the other being the Patrol Service) of two agencies under one department. The Tactical Service would be supported with computerized information systems and crime analysis services. They would concentrate on likely criminals and places which provide likely conditions for crime.

Tactical officers would also serve as back-up or reserve for the patrol officers. Violators and extremists would come to know that each patrol officer was protected by another who might or might not be visible. The tactical service would also serve as the basic unit to respond to civil emergencies and urban terrorism. The tactical officer, like the patrol officer, would be specifically selected and trained to perform his duties. The present Tactical Operations Platoon, which is the prototype of this service, would be significantly increased in manpower until the present crime situation was brought under control.

Team Policing

The third strategy would be team policing, which originated twenty years ago in England and Scotland. It has since been adapted in several cities in the United States. Team policing has both geographical and functional implications. In the former sense, a team of officers are assigned to a certain area to provide 24-hour service. In the functional sense, the team performs not only regular patrol duties, but also provides virtually all police services to the area, including traffic control, criminal investigations and the like.

Team policing offers several advantages: development of a more intimate knowledge of the area, its residents and problems; officers assigned to the area are fully responsible for and develop an empathy with the people of the area. When the proposal was fully operational, patrol officers would be deployed under the team policing concept and assigned according to their training, skills, compatibility and willingness to serve in an area for a relatively long period of time. Tactical officers would not be assigned to teams because they would be target-oriented rather than program- or service-oriented. But they would work out of administrative headquarters and be available and trained to support team officers if needed. Ultimately, the teams would be comprised not only of patrol officers, but also of trafficmen, detectives and policewomen who, Garmire remarked, have not been as extensively utilized as their skills would allow. Policewomen would be assigned a complete range of police duties so that the department and the community would benefit from their particular aptitudes and abilities.

Making the System Work

The Chief concluded that it would not be possible to put these strategies into effect immediately because:

1. The department's efforts in the immediate future would be primarily concerned with the suppression of the unprecedented high level of lawlessness and violence.

2. It would take two or three years to fully develop and test these strategies under "combat conditions." The target date for full implementation would be that of the completion of the police bond program, i.e., late 1974.

3. It would take two or three years to educate, train and develop personnel so they could effectively respond under the new system.

4. The approval of the proposal and the funds with which to finance it depended on the approval of the City Commission.

Chief Garmire observed, in conclusion:

Although the financial costs may be high, not implementing such a system would result in social costs far exceeding the financial costs. This proposed model for policing Miami responds to the realities of urban life as they exist today and will in the foreseeable future. It is a system that attempts to strike a balance between service to the community and law enforcement. If we provide only service to the community, we could ultimately have anarchy; if we provide only law enforcement, we could have benign repression at best—a police state at the worst. The task is to strike the right balance.

The Saint Louis PCR Program

The Saint Louis police-community relations program was the first to be established in a major metropolitan center. In May 1955, at the invitation of the Missouri regional office of the National Conference of Christians and Jews (NCCJ), a meeting of community leaders was called to hear reports of a National Institute that had been held earlier that month at Michigan State University, at which Saint Louis had been represented by a team of ten members. The 60 community leaders who attended the meeting decided to create a Committee for Better Police-Community Relations. This committee represented a wide range of community agencies, both official and voluntary, as well as the Saint Louis Police Department. The NCCJ director was elected chairman.

A pilot program, initiated by the Committee and approved by the Board of Police Commissioners, was established early in 1956, creating police-community relations committees in three of the city's high crime districts. These three district committees, composed of residents and community relations professionals ,working in these areas, met regularly with the District Commander of the Police Department to discuss problems of law enforcement. The district committees also conducted educational programs for the public on crime prevention techniques and on the work of the beat policeman. The philosophy of the program was expressed as follows: "Whether we like it or not, we are entering a new phase of law enforcement, potentially as significant as the advent of the automobile . . . The traditional role of the policeman as a thief-catcher must be reevaluated in the light of changes in crime patterns and new aspects of social behavior."*

An evaluation of the pilot program in March 1957, listed these accomplishments:

---

*James J. Allman, "Establishing a Police-Community Relations Office Within a Police Department," *The Police Chief,* March 1965, page 11. For details of the Saint Louis organizational experience see this special issue on police-community relations.

1. There appeared to be improved communication between police and citizens through channels other than direct enforcement.

2. There was clearly a growing awareness, by district committee members and citizens, of police problems and the need for the program.

3. The police officials believed they had gained a better appreciation of the importance of consultation with citizen leaders in their districts.

In the Spring of 1957, the Board of Police Commissioners began expanding the program to all nine of the city's police districts—completed in 1965. The membership of the Saint Louis Committee for Better Police-Community Relations voted to become the Saint Louis Council on Police-Community Relations and began work on plans for the expansion of the program. This was followed by the activation within the Saint Louis Police Department of a full-time, professionally staffed Division of Police-Community Relations.

The Saint Louis Program Today

The basic objectives underlying the present Saint Louis program are to reduce and prevent crime in the city through joint police-community cooperation and to improve intergroup relations in the community. The latter goal reflects the recognition by the police department of its responsibility as a community law enforcement agency for aiding in the reduction of racial tensions and in the prevention of racial disorder. In general, the program seeks to achieve its objectives by:

1. Planning and implementing programs to acquaint individual citizens with their responsibilities in the maintenance of law and order.

2. Developing programs to acquaint citizens with the operations of the police department and to gain public support for the department's growing professionalization.

3. Supporting neighborhood organization and responsibility.

4. Conducting continuing surveys of community needs which affect law enforcement activities through regular district committee meetings and regular city-wide meetings with minority group leaders of the city.

5. Publicizing these needs as they are discovered and transmitting them to those in authority, for appropriate action.

Organization

The Saint Louis Council on Police-Communty Relations is a voluntary, independent, and self-constituted body of private citizens responsible only to its constituents and not to the police department.

While the Council cooperates with the Board of Police Commissioners and the chief of police, it does not constitute or represent itself as an official arm of the police department or any other civic body or entity. The primary functions of the Council are two-fold: first, it plans city-wide programs to improve police-community relations and to mobilize community participation in crime prevention efforts; second, the Council serves as a liaison between the district police-community relations committees and the chief of police. Programs originating in the district committees are brought through the Council to the chief and the Board of Commissioners, for review and approval.

The Police-Community Relations Division technical staff administers the programs and activities originating in the Council. The Division is directly responsible to the chief, not to the Council, and its budget is a part of the department's normal appropriation. Aside from the over-all implementation of the Council's programs, the Division has three functions: it assists the Council in developing city-wide programs, it serves as the liaison channel between the district committees and the chief, and it provides professional assistance to the district committees and district police commanders.

The structure of the Police-Community Relations Division has grown from an original staff of one officer and a civilian director to 21 police officers, a civilian director, a civilian manager, nine cadets and a clerical staff of four. Six officers work full-time in a school visitation program, with four serving the primary grades in the Officer Friendly program, and two working with upper grades (4–8) in the *We Elect* program, narcotic programs, etc. Three officers have offices in the district stations, 11 are assigned to store-front centers, and one is a helicopter officer.

In eight districts, officers are assigned full-time as PCR men. They work with district committees on projects; serve as district commanders' PCR representatives; implement the school visitation programs; and conduct special projects assigned by the PCR Division working with all citizens in their districts.

It is important to note that these officers do *not* conduct projects assigned to the district committees, but only offer assistance and guidance. Neither do they serve to substitute for communications between district committees and the PCR Division.

The District Committees are considered to be the heart of the police-community relations program, with approximately 8000 active members currently in the twelve organized groups. These committees are responsible to the Community Relations Division and to the chief. In implementing the Council's programs at the neighborhood level, these committees provide the machinery for active and effective community participation in crime prevention as well as continuing police-citizen communication.

The district committees are composed of police executives in the various districts, and representatives of resident citizens and their organizations. Police representatives include the district commanders, juvenile officers, sanitation officers and others. The citizen membership comes from such organizations as PTA's, churches, businesses, the Urban League, NAACP, CORE, settlement houses, social work agencies and many others. The district committees are in turn divided into eight subcommittees focusing on crime, juvenile problems, auto theft, traffic, sanitation, membership, program development, and public relations. An executive committee of ten members under an elected chairman meets monthly to coordinate the activities of the various subcommittees and outline programs for the district committee as a whole. The district committee meets monthly also, to act on and mobilize support for activities originating in the subcommittees. Each district committee chairman develops a close working relationship with the district police commander so that problems of a local or precinct nature can be resolved quickly, quietly and effectively.

Projects

Store Front Centers are a major effort in this program. Seven locations provide facilities where people can obtain police assistance. They are *not* police sub-stations but—administered by full-time PCR officers—they aid citizens in law enforcement problems and are available for use by local organizations. These centers have become integral parts of the neighborhoods they serve.

The Block Watcher Program consists of citizens from all over the city who are recruited by PCR officers, trained to help reduce crime in such matters as what to look for, how to identify possible suspects, and how to make emergency calls to the special communications center at police headquarters.

Citizen Patrols consist of male tenants of housing projects who assist in patrols, aid firemen, and help in deterring and reporting crimes and enforcing curfew laws. Equipped with two-way radios, they patrol in teams, wearing helmets and uniforms donated by civic groups.

The Clergy-Police Program for improvement of understanding consists of three phases: meetings at the station house to explain police functions; local meetings in which clergy exchange information and program ideas; and a ride-along experience in which clergymen tour their own areas on police patrols.

Self-defense and Canine Demonstrations are given weekly to interested groups by a PCR officer who holds the black belt in karate and judo.

Concerned Citizens meetings are held almost daily throughout the city to explain police policy and procedures and to enlist cooperation.

Pool Room Visitations are constantly being made by **PCR** officers to explain **PCR** programs and to make narcotics presentations.

Block Homes are established through PTA's and Mothers' Clubs for mothers who will be home when children are going and coming from school. Signs are placed in windows to let children know where they may seek help in case of emergency. Training is provided for the mothers.

Brochures on all **PCR** operations are distributed free to provide instruction as to purposes and procedures. These include "Say Hi" and "Citizens Against Crime" cards, and announcements of forthcoming programs.

Headquarters Tours are conducted by police cadets five days a week to explain to interested groups the communications division, detective bureau, laboratories, gun collections, etc.

Youth Programs

Headstart centers are visited frequently by PCR officers who teach pedestrian safety, often showing Walt Disney cartoons for illustration.

The Officer Friendly program of the Sears Roebuck Foundation develops rapport between officers and younger children in elementary schools.

Upper Grade programs (4–8) include instructions about the police department using the "We Elect" textbook, and information about the harmful effects of narcotics.

Assembly programs are provided by PCR officers in high schools which instruct on law enforcement in its various phases.

Explorer Posts of Boy Scouts are taught fingerprinting, identification techniques, first aid, fire alarm safety. Boys wear special uniforms similar to those of the police.

A PCR Youth Council is coordinated by the Division, consisting of students, appointed by their principals in each high school, who represent each class and school newspaper, and who meet monthly at headquarters to serve as liaison between the police and the schools.

Special Youth programs are led by Bill Triplett (Detroit Lions) in the football off-season, for high school hard core youngsters to give them direction, help get them jobs, and provide a big brother image.

Swinging Busmobile programs are provided by the Division for juvenile neighborhood dances, using the amplification equipment of the bus.

Other Youth Programs, such as are found in many cities, include charm and self-improvement clinics, youth employment, Operation Little-Sweep, cruiser tours, community athletic leagues, Christmas programs, and the distribution of Halloween candy.

Awards

Police-Community Relations Assistance Awards are presented each year in a PCR Division ceremony in which the Police Board gives framed letters of thanks to several hundred citizens who have assisted the PCR programs during the year.

Medal of Valor awards are presented by the Chamber of Commerce at a Divisional banquet to honor officers who have exhibited outstanding courage.

Police Human Relations Training

The effectiveness of a formal police-community relations program and its activities depends, to a large extent, on the nature, scope, and depth of human relations training for individual police officers. The Saint Louis program is supported by a comprehensive and thorough police training program in human and community relations for recruits, for in-service personnel and for command executives. The training includes both direct instruction in human relations and broad related training in human behavior.

Recruits presently receive 36 hours of instruction in such diverse subjects as "A Survey of Selected American Institutions and Social Movements," "Historical Change in the Legal Process and the Role of the Supreme Court," "The Negro in the Saint Louis Communty," "Police and the People They Meet," and "The Psychology of Rumor." All recruits are also assigned, for one day, on a one-to-one basis with a PCR officer operating a store-front center. The recruits are introduced to neighborhood residents. In addition each class is lectured on police-community relations by PCR officers, and meetings are held with the staffs of several area universities in attempts to develop better understanding of human relationships.

In-Service and Command personnel are given continuing training in community relations problems. Every officer, upon promotion to the rank of sergeant or higher, enters the Academy for two weeks of pre-assignment training with emphasis on developing abilities in the maintenance of effective relationships with subordinates, peers, superiors, and the community. In addition, six or seven command officers are sent each year to a national institute on police-community relations.

No phase of the Saint Louis recruit and in-service training program is without some indirect as well as direct training in human relations. During the 65-hour criminal law and court proceedings course, for example, stress is placed on American legal philosophy and the concept of individual rights. A major emphasis is how to balance such rights with peace and order. Moreover, in teaching the elements of patrol work, traffic control and criminal investigation, instructors stress the building of effective face to face relationships with merchants, motorists, pedestrians, minority citizens, and even criminals.

Conclusion

In summary, the Saint Louis police-community relations program has resulted in the establishment of a city-wide structure for continuing communication and action. It is supported by a professional staff and extensive police training in human relations. It has produced a basis for mutual cooperation and respect among police and citizens in dealing with difficult and complex problems. The Saint Louis experience is well worth the study of those who are seeking help in developing a positive approach to their communty relations problems.

Community Service Programs

It is, of course, well known that the increasing population of our cities has made a rarity of the once familiar "man on the beat." To respond to the mounting number of calls from extensive areas, motorized patrol has replaced the policeman who knew by name the shopkeepers, citizens, children and even the habitual criminals. His very presence was a crime deterrent, and his knowledge seemed limitless. To replace him, cities—especially those with what are called hard-core districts—are creating "community service units." These often operate in and out of store-front centers, which are strategically placed in the hope that citizens will find them more convenient, less forbidding places to go to with their complaints or their pleas for help.

It is instructive to compare how such community service units are established in larger and smaller cities. As examples, we have selected Chicago and Winston-Salem, North Carolina, each representative of typical situations, proportionately with reference to crime, poverty and social tensions.

Chicago

Reference to the chart in Fig. 5–1 will reveal that the Chicago Police Department has established a full Division of Community Services under a deputy chief, to meet the needs of citizens and to work with them in the prevention of crime.

• The Liaison Officer serves as an aide to the Deputy Chief and is responsible for staff supervision over activities and programs of community service sergeants at each of the outlying districts.

The Coordinator of Community Relations counsels with District Commanders on the programming of PCR workshops. Through his contacts with governmental, business, and social service agencies, he assists the District Commanders and workshop steering committees in the development of timely discussion topics and the selection of speakers. Under the supervision of the Coordinator are the activities of the Officer Friendly assigned to the elementary schools in each of the districts.

The Coordinator of Human Relations heads a unit originally established in 1947. Its officers maintain continuous alert for incidents of racial, ethnic or religious friction and keep open lines of communication between citizens and police personnel at the neighborhood level.

Although the population of Chicago is down almost a quarter million in the last decade (emigrants from the South are going more to other cities now), the current three-and-a-third million people still leaves the police force of 15,000 understaffed. Modern equipment and facilities have enabled officers to respond promptly to citizens' calls for help and, by their conspicuous presence in blue-and-white cars, to deter criminal activity to an unknown extent. But heavy workloads make it impossible for officers to have sufficient opportunity to get acquainted with individual citizens. Lacking such face-to-face contacts, officers often fail to get an adequate understanding of local problems and, in turn, citizens do not learn how they might help officers deal with those problems.

In the late 1960s, the Chicago Police Department set up a number of district-based programs designed to improve communication between police and citizens. Among these, the police-community workshops, school visits by "Officer Friendly," and a wide variety of youth activities have been well received in many neighborhoods. In some areas, however, there has been only limited response to such programs. Residents tend to live in virtual isolation from the larger community surrounding them. Sometimes fearful, certainly uninformed, they are unwilling to call upon those best qualified to help—if, indeed, they know whom to call.

For these reasons, the Division created the Community Service Aides Project in the hope that it would show the way toward building more constructive inner-city relationships, and created many career jobs in the process. The Project, supported by Model Cities funds, brings to four target areas a total of 495 additional personnel (sometimes called subprofessionals), of whom 422 are Community Service Aides, both men and women. All of them reside in the neighborhood in which they work. The Aides are, in effect, the type of community service officers recommended by the President's Crime Commission. Working also in the Project are 69 sworn personnel of various ranks, plus five civilian specialists. Most of the Aides are assigned to foot patrol of area streets. A limited number work in the four store-front community service centers, where they act as receptionists and assist in clerical duties. Aides are also given special assignments such as evening work in police-community workshops, in library branches, or at schools.

The work of the Aides serves several important purposes. They work in a distinctive green uniform. Their presence on the street helps

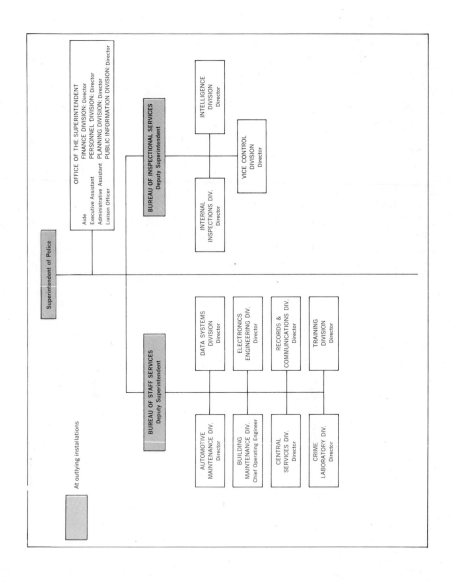

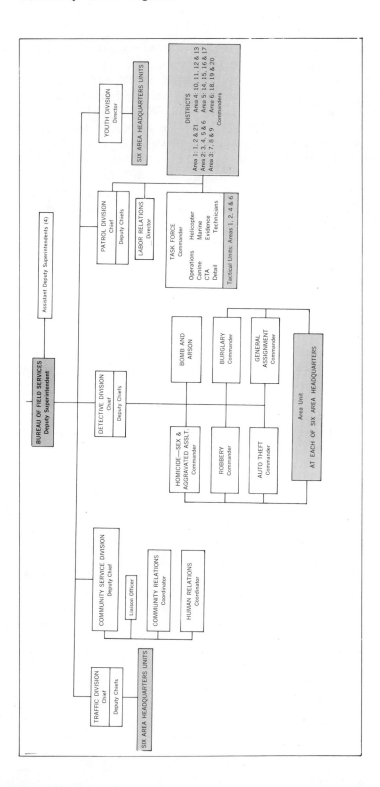

Figure 5–1. Organization of the Chicago Police Department

discourage the commission of crimes and enables the policemen to spend more time on investigation and apprehension. Citizens recognize that police assistance is readily available and learn to participate actively in law enforcement. The Aides are civilians and therefore may not make arrests. They serve in ways not always feasible for sworn personnel. Citizens who are reluctant to report problems directly to policemen welcome the opportunity to talk to fellow residents.

A major aspect of the Aide's duties is to help improve the quality of life in the community. While on patrol, they look for and report on various kinds of adverse conditions such as abandoned cars and vacant buildings. They assist in crowd and traffic control at athletic events or when fires attract large numbers of people. They hear citizen complaints and, in nonpolice matters, provide referrals to appropriate agencies. In the course of rendering such services, the Aides help the police to a better understanding of community needs and, in turn, explain police roles and objectives to the citizens.

Through a variety of special programs, citizens are urged to help themselves. Among the innovations are block clubs organized on each floor of a high-rise housing development, a one-day clean-sweep for a several block area carried out jointly by Aides, citizens and Bureau of Sanitation street sweepers and trucks. For the youngsters there are week-end camping trips—escorted by Aides, supervisory police officers, and area parents—and there are fire hydrants equipped with spray caps for splash parties.

The Community Service Aides project provides employment for community residents at good pay. Aides may continue their education and advance to better positions. The sole requirement is that an applicant must live in the area he serves. Both men and women may apply: men must be at least 17 and women 18 years of age. Salaries start at $445 a month, with increments to $540 after one year. Benefits include one to four weeks vacation depending on length of service; eleven paid holidays a year, twelve days sick leave, free hospital insurance, and uniforms supplied by the Police Department.

Aides receive careful counseling throughout their service starting with thorough pre-service training. They are encouraged to seek higher positions through continued education from whatever their present level may be, including college. They are allowed up to nine hours per week, with pay, to attend school.

Winston-Salem

Case histories of typical contacts of Aides with their community clientele in Chicago are similar to those of such programs in other cities. We shall include some examples at the end of our description of the Winston-Salem experience.

Although Winston-Salem is far smaller (126,000 population) than Chicago, it also has its poverty areas and racial tensions. Yet its police force has proved, thus far, able to man special services for its citizens. The Community Services Unit was formed in June 1966 in the Winston-Salem Police Department by Chief Justus Tucker. It was conceived as having a threefold purpose: to find people in need, to direct them to those agencies or community resources where the need could be met, and to search out factors which are conducive to crime in order to root them out of the community. Features of crime prevention and community service were thus combined. It was felt that the lack of communication between the police and the public reflected other alienations and estrangements in the community. It was the hope of the Department that the Community Services Unit would be able to break the barriers of alienation, to find ways in which the police and the community could help one another.

The Unit assumed that police are called upon to play a dual role: law enforcement and community service, with the latter consuming the major portion of their time. The Unit was created with the aid of a grant from the North Carolina Fund—a private foundation interested in fighting poverty. Under the conditions of the grant, continuous evaluation of the Unit's effectiveness was to be made by sociologists at the University of North Carolina. Their first report, issued in August 1967, after one year of the Unit's operation, stated:

> There is no question that since the establishment of the CSU, the officers' specialized training has resulted in police behavior in the community that has created a positive attitude toward the Police Department and the CSU. This has been found in interviewing social agency personnel, and in an increased awareness in the general population of the necessary functions that the police department as a whole performs.

The report on the first year's work suggested that the Unit should broaden its activities from a focus on poverty problems to include programs for youth clubs and other community organizations. This has since been done, as the following cases suggest.

Typical Cases

Typical of such service units, the CSU in Winston-Salem has put into effect a variety of community projects. After repairing and painting their first community center themselves (other centers have been added since), the Unit has distributed Christmas and Halloween treats to 2000 children each year, in cooperation with churches and boys' clubs. It has established classes for Negroes in subjects ranging from beauty care to football. It has mobilized funds from civic groups to enable the CSU to take groups of poor children to football games. But its special sphere of activity has been in personalized services to individuals and families in poverty areas. In this function, it has been demonstrated again and again that the police are in a unique position to find and help people in need. Their 24-hour availability and their general presence throughout the city make them a resource that none of the "9 to 5" agencies can equal. The following cases illustrate the variety of the referral services the CSU has provided:

Case One: Jealousy?

A 14-year-old boy was found tampering with police call boxes. He explained to the officer that he wanted to be placed in training school rather than live with his mother. Stated his home was never clean, that his mother gave wild parties and had men there. Check-up revealed immaculate home, well-groomed mother who admitted that she had lived that way after her divorce, but not since meeting Mr. C. whom she planned to marry soon. Boy and sisters acknowledged that Mr. C. was kind to them. CSU officers recommended boy stay with his grandmother until able to adjust to idea of forthcoming marriage.

Case Two: Explosion

A family of six was left homeless by an explosion in their house. CSU officers contacted the local radio station to request an appeal for help. Almost immediately the station was flooded with offers of help: food, clothing, and cash for a rental residence. Unit officers collected these and settled the family in new home.

Case Three: Vagrant

An elderly man, arrested for vagrancy, was found to have been living in an abandoned railroad tunnel for several months. CSU investigation revealed he had previously been released from a mental hospital. Taken to the Mental Health Clinic, the doctor found he should be committed. CSU arranged with the Health and the Public Welfare departments to have him placed in the County Nursing Home.

Case Four: Condemned

City Inspection Division condemned the run-down home of an elderly woman. She would have to move unless listed repairs were made. With only $78 monthly pension, she could not afford it. CSU officers obtained an extension on the eviction for 60 days. Welfare Department could not help until certain details of title to house were cleared. CSU procured volunteer legal help which satisfied Welfare and a grant of $30 monthly, till improvement costs were fully paid. CSU procured low bids and volunteers who did the work, painted the house, tore down an outhouse and cleared rubbish from the place. Boy Scouts and neighbors became involved through the intervention of CSU.

Case Five: Homeless

Girl A contacted CSU about Girl B whom she had found destitute and had taken her to her own home. Investigation revealed that Girl B had left her broken home where her step-father had made indecent advances to her. Before Girl A found her, she had been living in a trailer with three men. CSU placed her in a rehabilitation home for wayward girls where she is being cared for, and is arranging a job for her.

Case Six: Conscience

A mother called CSU to report her son had driven home in a stolen car. Boy, 14, explained to officer that he had seen keys in the car on his way home, was overwhelmed with desire to "drive it around the block," but got scared and brought it home. Mother explained privately to officer that boy had displayed emotional instability on several occasions. CSU returned car to owner who after explanation of the case, did not press charges. CSU has placed boy under care of Child Guidance Clinic.

The director of the Winston-Salem Community Service Unit stated, as the above cases would indicate, "that we are trying to reach and help the potential or actual delinquent, the dropout, the frightened housewife, the disturbed, the indifferent, the aggrieved, the concerned principal and clergyman, the troublemaker, the indignant, the harassed social worker, and the idealistically motivated citizen. The CSU job is to bring those who need help, and those who need to help, together."

STUDY 9

Ride-Along Programs

One of the more popular police-community relations programs is the "ride-along" in patrol cruisers. It has proved helpful to the clergy, school principals, lawyers, judges, and others who need to deepen their understanding of police work. It has been used most widely with young people as a means of counteracting parental influences ("I'll call the cops if you don't be good!") that have given them a negative attitude toward the police.

Aside from the thrill in being on the *inside* of a police car as it makes its rounds—sometimes with siren shrieking and lights flashing—rather than on the *outside* watching it go by or fearing it will stop beside you, the experience also gives youth the opportunity to see something of the inside of the police officer himself. Prominent among the objectives is a realistic understanding of why policemanship is so vital a mission in the community. And after the trip is over, the rider not only has his memory of the experience, but in some cities, he may have a blue cap or an arm badge or a framed statement as a souvenir that lets his pals know he has participated in the program.

Model Program

The Los Angeles County Sheriff's Department, aware of the possible hazards, has worked out a careful model for its ride-along project, which includes a legally prepared waiver that the passenger in the police car must sign before the trip. This two-page document—more or less copied in other cities—must be read in the presence of and signed by witnesses. It stipulates the rider's awareness of the enumerated possible dangers and risks, of the liability laws of the state whose protection he is foregoing by signing the waiver, and the fact that he is voluntarily waiving his right to compensation for possible injuries. In the event that he is a minor, the document must be countersigned by the parent or guardian. The risks are real, but should not be exaggerated.

In addition to the waiver provision, the model stipulates:

Who May Volunteer. Local needs and problems should guide, but the opportunity should be afforded to youth, government employees, the clergy, educators, judges, probation officers, prosecutors, law students, and social workers.

Selection of Observers. Volunteers may be recruited through many agencies—schools, service clubs, etc.—but in any case their names, addresses, etc., should be made available to the Community Relations Bureau and the appropriate patrol commanders who will make the final arrangements. The officers with whom the citizens will ride are selected and briefed by the Watch Commander. If possible, the rider should attend the squad briefing prior to the ride, at which time the fact that there will be a rider should be announced.

Dress and Appearance. Riders should wear suitable attire, be clean and neat in appearance. Long hair and beards are permitted if other criteria are met and extremes are avoided.

Identification. Riders are issued pin-on type plastic badges bearing the word "Observer" in large letters, to be worn on the lapel and turned in after the ride. Riders are instructed to remove the badge in cases where mob action might be directed against them.

Females. Under normal conditions, females are permitted to ride the same as males, depending on local department policy.

Juveniles and Minors. High school students (10th to 12th grades) are allowed to participate, preferably in conjunction with other police-school activities such as student-teacher ride-alongs.

Where to Report. The rider reports to the Watch Commander's Office to be introduced to the host officer(s) and, if he has not yet done so, he then signs the liability waiver. In the case of minors, this is done by the observer's parent in the presence of an adult witness.

The Host Officer. The driver-officer instructs the rider: (1) that he not become involved in any investigation by handling evidence, discussion with victim or suspects, or handling of police equipment; (2) that he follow directions of the officer; and (3) that he may indicate at any time a desire to return to the station.

Officers respond to calls in a safe manner and, while en route, attempt to brief the guest as to the information he is hearing on the police radio, procedures being applied and why. The observers are also instructed as to where they should stand or sit on arrival at the call.

Dispatching of Calls. If in the judgment of the officer(s), they are entering a dangerous situation, they may, at their discretion, leave the observer at a safe place. (Experience has shown that in many areas, however, it is advisable to keep the observer with the patrol car. On occasions, the observer has been able to assist the officer.) The dispatcher is notified if the rider is left so that a back-up unit can pick him up. It is intended that the rider witness as much of the activity as possible, therefore he is not restricted to the confines of the unit unless the officer feels that he will be in danger, or that he may interfere.

Arrests-Transportation-Booking. Observers may accompany the officer during the transportation and booking process if, in the officer's opinion, it does not constitute a hazard to the observer or the investigation. During the transport, the prisoner is placed in the caged rear seat, with the observer in the front seat.

Number of Observers Allowed to Ride. The number of observers allowed to ride in any one shift is at the discretion of the Watch Commander or the Chief of Police.

Ending the Tour. After the ride, the guest is brought back to the Watch Commander's office to be thanked for his interest and where he completes an "Observer's Ride-Along Report" form. The officer completes his own report and routes it to the Community Relations Bureau.

Officer's Ride-Along Report. This report includes:

Date and time of ride

Assigned to (name of officer)

Bureau or station

Name of rider: age, sex, address, occupation (if student—name of school and grade)

Special medical information or service requested (if any)

Space for "any unusual activity" which might be of later significance such as major crimes, comments of rider or problems

Number of hours and time of day rider was in unit

Space for "did the rider interfere with your duties?" How?

Officer's signature

The Observer's report is headed with the notation:

Dear Observer—The Department hopes that your Ride-Along has been informative and has given you an insight into the problems facing law enforcement, your policemen and your community. Any comments you have, positive or negative, will be most welcome.

The form has spaces for name and age of rider, followed by three questions: (1) What impressed you most? (2) In what way did this experience affect your attitudes? (3) Relate any suggestions for or criticisms of the program. If the rider wishes more time to complete the form, he is given an addressed envelope for mailing to the Community Relations Bureau.

Questions That Come Up

Ride-alongs have provided many a thrill to kids (of all ages) and have enabled young and old alike to learn much more about the police role, and the other side of life in their cities. Undoubtedly, too, the program provides many occasions for the host officers to see their own roles and their communities more objectively as they explain to their guests what they are seeing and doing. But there are certain questions about the program which should be raised, especially when the rider is a minor.

What should the officer do, for example, when his rider is a 10th-grade high school girl and, during the cruise, the radio snaps out a call to proceed to an address where a family disturbance is in progress? Knowing the high incidence of violence in such cases, the officer asks himself whether he should drop the girl off at a corner drug store a block from the scene—if there *is* one—or whether he should leave her alone in the car in this seamy neighborhood while he mounts three flights to the apartment. There may not be time to call for a back-up car to pick up the girl or to assume responsibility for the case. He is driving as fast as the traffic permits, his attention divided between the safety of the girl, the possibility of hitting someone, and estimating what he is likely to find at the scene of the disturbance. It is little help to him to know that the girl has signed a paper waiving himself, the Department, and the city from liability. After all, she is a *girl,* a youngster. What would the public think if—? How could he live with himself afterward if—?

What should he do? Should the ride-along program have permitted such a possible situation to develop? Should there be two officers on such an assignment? What about manpower? Where would the other officer sit in the car: in the back or would all three sit in the front seat? And what would the street people at the scene think of the police riding their patrol with a girl in the car?

Another type of question arises in deciding what types of persons should *not* be allowed on ride-alongs. Clearly, every effort should be made to eliminate anyone who is emotionally unstable. But how is the Department to know who may be? Ask them? Require a medical statement? Hardly a way to build good public relations. One city refuses to take high school dropouts on rides. May they not especially need help in career motivation?

If manpower shortages preclude having a second officer along, perhaps the answer lies in having an adult citizen along if the rider might constitute a particular problem by reason of age, sex, or some other characteristic. Certainly the answer does not lie in junking the ride-along program. Too much good has apparently come from it—as in the case of the Kirkwood, Missouri, "Police Junior Aide Program," which has been commended in a special letter from President Nixon (Kathy Yount, *Police,* July/August, 1971, p. 35).

The climax of the Kirkwood week-long program of auxiliary work for the police department is a ride-along program in which the youth were able to observe the myriad details and duties of the policeman's day. In their written comments at week's end, the only major criticism was in the form of a backhanded compliment—they liked the ride-along program so much that they complained because it could not be greatly expanded.

Project PACE: San Francisco

Project PACE (Police and Community Enterprise) was a Ford Foundation funded, police-community relations training, education and action program designed to improve relationships between policemen and minority residents in the City of San Francisco. What makes the project unusual is that it has been an attempt to change the attitudes of the police and the community toward each other by the application of proven techniques.

Much of the program model is based upon experiences of the American Institutes for Research in research dealing with crosscultural relationships overseas between South Korean soldiers and citizens and American troops stationed in Korea in the aftermath of the Korean war. In a description of the project as originally proposed, Project Director Terry Eisenberg explained (*Crime and Delinquency,* July 1969):

> The increase we have seen in crime rates, riots and community indifference makes it appear that basic values have deteriorated. The attempted remedy in the form of more law enforcement personnel, better physical equipment, and implementation of a "crack-down" philosophy has been and will continue to be self-defeating; it only produces a vicious cycle. Violence generates more violence.
>
> As an interesting parallel, Americans overseas . . . coming as they do from a comparatively wealthy, literate and sanitary society, tend to be confused, frightened, annoyed, and frustrated when they encounter poverty, illiteracy, stench, filth and strange customs in poorer societies . . . Certainly it must be recognized that one American may very well feel discomfort with or express hostility toward another American whose values and traditions differ from his own . . . The job of the policeman becomes tremendously complex when he misunderstands

This study is based on *Project PACE: Police and Community Enterprise—Performance Statement, August 1970,* by Terry Eisenberg, Ph.D., Project Director; now Research Scientist, Professional Standards Division, International Association of Chiefs of Police. Used with the author's permission.

and is indifferent to variations in subcultural conditions . . . Physical and verbal mistreatment of citizens contributes to citizen mistreatment of the police.

The resemblances between soldier-community and police-community relationships suggested that the concepts and procedures that had been applied successfully by the U.S. Army in Korea, in collaboration with the American Institutes for Research, could be adapted to reducing police-community tensions in large cities in the United States. Americans in Korea came to realize that they were at least in part to blame for anti-Americanism, that some Koreans actually like them, and that the prime reason for poverty was the environment rather than the shortcomings of the people. Improved mutual attitudes resulted in decreases both in stolen property and in hostile actions against the Americans.

In San Francisco, the PACE model consisted of four components:

1. A survey to determine the critical issues bearing on the police-community relationship, and development of a curriculum to shatter misconceptions and myths held by police and by citizens.

2. A training and education program disseminating information to a selected number of policemen and residents.

3. An action phase to implement various "bright ideas" proposed during phases 1 and 2, with a focus on those endorsed by both police and citizens.

4. An institutionalization phase designed to provide continuity to the program beyond the initially funded 2-year period.

The Northern Police District (population 50,000, with high crime rates and abrasive police-community relations) was selected for the pilot program. Three distinctly different groups of residents were consistently included: (1) a group of homophiles (homosexuals, lesbians); (2) 10 adult probation officers; and (3) 15 black teen-agers representing three different youth organizations. Approximately half of the total group were black. They participated in 14 two-hour *separate* sessions and 7 two-hour *mixed* sessions, representing a total of 480 man-hours of training and education.

In addition, three groups of policemen were involved: one day-watch and two night-watches. About 50 officers consistently participated, including a number of sergeants and lieutenants. They attended 12 two-hour separate sessions and 7 two-hour mixed sessions for a total of 640 man-hours of training and education, for which each received one point of college credit.

Although the quantity of consistent resident and police participation was below expectations, the quality of discussion surpassed the leaders' hopes. Indeed, the longer the participants engaged in dialogue, the better the quality of the discussions. Throughout the training, pairs of discussion leaders were used—persons trained by the project for this work. During separate sessions (police only or residents only), two police discussion leaders would be used with police groups and two resident leaders with resident groups. During mixed sessions (police and residents), the two leaders would be a black resident and a white policeman, their performances being privately critiqued by PACE staff. Mutual understanding developed to the point where, during breaks, blacks and whites paired off for further talk on a one-to-one basis.

Attitudinal Changes

Three separate appraisals were made. Police responses to 20 questions before and after training showed:

A change from 22% (before training) to 42% (after) of officers expressing positive feelings toward black people.

A change from 71% (before) to 83% (after) of officers expressing more respect for black people in the district.

A change from 47% to 57% of officers agreeing to the statement, "It would help police-community relations if police mixed more in social, cultural, and athletic functions with blacks."

Police responses to questions asked after training was completed showed:

PACE came out second of some seven formal police-community relations activities which policemen considered to be the most valuable and meaningful to them personally and to the San Francisco Police Department. It is interesting to note that the SF PCR Unit rated lowest.

Some 72% of the policemen said they learned *something* from their participation in the PACE program.

Resident responses to 12 questions *after* training included:

PACE came out first of seven formal police-community relations activities that residents considered to be the most valuable and meaningful to them personally;

And 51% of the residents stated that they changed their minds about *something* because of participation.

In areas where the project fell short of expectations, curricula were revised. It should also be noted that "difficult" participants had been selected deliberately. Almost half of the police were from the day-watch—a group of older men who represented a disproportionate number who were set in their ways. It was necessary to deal early in the training with comments like: "Why do *we* have to do all the changing?" "Why were *we ordered* to attend these b— sessions?" "Why are so many Negroes on welfare?" "Why don't you go talk to the criminals?" Black participants were selected from members of an organization (Youth for Service) one of whose members had recently been killed by an off-duty policeman. A member of the homophile group was chosen *because* he was an outspoken critic of the department. It was encouraging that it was possible to persuade police and citizens alike that the project was not just another study, pacification program, or "snow job."

Behavioral Changes

Evidence emerging from the project showed:

Awareness by policemen of the importance of police-community relations in police service.

Attention by police to what constitutes harassment.

Some effect in improving the breach between the SF PCR Unit and Patrol Force Personnel (See Study 6, Part One.)

Overt and recorded expression by the District captain of the value and importance of Project PACE.

Explicit expression by a black critic of PACE that the project had accomplished some significant things.

Action Programming

In connection with the action phase of the project, a number of programs were planned to complement the project itself. These included:

A series of radio talk shows, sponsored by Kaiser Industries, to reach a broader audience about PCR issues in the city.

Training police to use alternatives to incarceration for drug, alcohol, etc., cases.

Preparation and distribution of a pamphlet "Police and You" to inform citizens of their rights, the role of the police, protecting their homes and how to get police help. This pamphlet has been copied by other cities, with adaptations.

Providing consumers with information on purchasing products and services and facts about fair prices and price gouging.

Training police to cope with residents who are troublesome by word or act at times of arrest.

Exploring, with Youth for Service and the Law Students Civil Rights Council, establishment of a half-way house for juveniles.

Programs already under way included:

Project "PAIRS" (Police Academic Instruction Reaching Students) was started with six volunteer police tutors and six 4th and 5th grade students on a one-to-one basis to help them in English and math. It is hoped that it will expand to become an educational counterpart to PAL.

A Drug Seminar, in cooperation with the SF PCR Unit.

A Jail Reform Conference in cooperation with Citizens Alert, to implement recommendations of the San Francisco Committee on Crime.

A total of 10 two-hour discussion sessions on PCR for 260 patrolmen and sergeants with three or more years of experience, totaling 520 man-hours of training, apart from that included in the regular PACE project.

Similar sessions for 90 police recruits: two two-hour sessions for a total of 180 man-hours of PCR training.

Two three-hour sessions were conducted for the SF PCR Unit and Northern Police District Patrol Officers to reduce the eight-year-old breach between these two police units and to improve communications and understanding of the PCR function.

Establishment of a program through which memos with suggestions for improving police service to the community can be forwarded directly to the chief, during and after the completion of the project.

Media Promotion

A total of 11 radio and television programs were promoted as part of the PACE project by the time it was three-fourths completed. These were included in existing city programs, for the purpose of publicizing and explaining the PACE program. In addition, there were 17 newspaper stories on aspects of the project that appeared in 5 publications, including the minority press. All these accounts were supportive. As a result, there have been inquiries about the project from many cities and government agencies, police and sheriff departments and community groups. Universities have sent investigators from their research centers. Project personnel have mounted workshop conferences in four cities and read papers in other states in connection with contemplated legislation.

Preliminary Results

In addition to the preceding findings, opinions of the participants were reflected in these comments:

Police: We need longer mixed sessions and more of them; brought to light wrongs on both sides; abolished some of the things

I believed about homosexuals; there was a sincere attempt to solve problems jointly; we need a wider representation of the black community; I learned not to provoke people by my manner; we have values in common with the residents; people are as ignorant about us as we are about them; am more able to approach a person in conversation, and the program should certainly be continued after the formal project ends.

Citizens: Not enough mixed sessions; police are people, not pigs; began to work on my prejudice toward police; we realized that most of us are wrong; more citizens and *all* policemen should attend; police are human too; I'll try to be more tolerant; police are not really hostile; we can only solve our problems jointly, and we have a real chance to improve police-community relations.

In spite of the fact that all those who were closely connected with the PACE program felt, as the preliminary report suggested, that it had been a worthwhile undertaking and that it should be continued, the Final Report *Project PACE* (Eisenberg, Fosen, and Glickman), issued in November 1971, shows that it was not. The explanation is best given in the words of the report:

City Support for the PACE Program
As described earlier in this report, the City and County of San Francisco assumed a number of commitments to the PACE program in receiving the grant from the Ford Foundation. All commitments were met.

Interest taken in the PACE program by the Mayor's Office and the Board of Supervisors during the two-year life of the program may be described as representing approval in principle, but nevertheless casual. This is understandable in light of the absence of profound program accomplishments, the absence of explosive neighborhood incidents which often provoke interest in police-community programs, and cities' predispositions to react rather than play; to contain rather than prevent.

Institutionalization Conclusions
It is difficult to speculate on the reasons why the PACE program apparently will not be continued or institutionalized. The same applies to the proposed follow-on program. However, a number of factors appear to have played a significant role in the ultimate disposition of the PACE program.

First, greater effort might have been made in more effectively keeping the traditional establishment informed of the program's operations and progress. Although written progress reports were distributed to many city officials and key police administrators, the absence of their active participation or, at least, personal observation of the PACE program perhaps resulted in a lack of "feel" for what the program was really about. Related to this factor may have been the inadequate use of the mass media including the press and television. A newspaper article captured the essence of this issue when it stated:

> Although it has operated in something of a vacuum, a two-year program aimed at achieving some recognition between police and people who are not ordinarily friendly to lawmen is nearing its end after achieving some modest but real results.

Secondly, two years is indeed a short time to effectively deal with an area as volatile and complex as police-community relations. To a large extent, the PACE program ran out of time at a critical juncture; at a time when community support was just beginning to take on notable proportions. Another six to twelve months may have made a big difference.

A third factor, which has already been alluded to, was the absence of profound accomplishments. Modest and real accomplishments *were* made but perhaps lacked the impact necessary to command the attention of the city's power structure.

Fourthly, it is believed that the absence of a crisis or an explosive police-community relations incident tempts a judgment among city and police administrators that everything is OK; a situation that is not to be messed with or disturbed. As a consequence, progressive and innovative police-community relations activities currently have a low priority in San Francisco.

Finally, the value of police-community relations activities, especially in city governments and police departments which do not incline toward innovative interests and programming, is likely to be appreciated by a relatively small proportion of the people; the progressive, the poor, and the young. Improving the police-community relationship when "the community" is defined in terms of the poor and the young, is perceived to be of little importance and value to the majority community whose members predominate in the local government structure and determine whether programs like PACE are to be implemented, continued or institutionalized.

STUDY 11

Crisis Intervention: Dayton

Stories about the techniques of the community-oriented police of Dayton, Ohio, have been making national headlines. One, accompanied with pictures, showed a detail of officers wearing large plastic daisies and broad smiles as they "kept the kids cool" at the annual State Fair, a scene of youth riots in previous years. Another tells of the Chief (white) and the head of his Conflict Management Program (black) rapping with college students to offer them help in getting their off-campus ramshackle housing (college-owned) rehabilitated in return for their giving up their bonfires in the streets—clearly a trade-off, rather than risking student riots by *ordering* them to cease this traditional practice. Other headlines were made when the Chief announced that henceforth officers could use their own discretion about carrying guns—on or off duty— since these might prove barriers to communication in investigations, or embarrassments socially. The story of the Chief's general order that drunks were henceforth to be treated as medical cases and taken to the city treatment center instead of to the lock-up (unless they were guilty of other offenses) was further evidence that the police of Dayton are "swinging" (one paper said) away from traditional toward innovative, humanized approaches to peacekeeping.

Like Oakland, Miami, San Jose, Charlotte, N.C., and New York —to mention only a few—Dayton has introduced programs that involve team policing, conflict management, generalist/specialists, and community service officers in a new approach to police and community relations. Chief of Police Robert M. Igleburger, Tyree Broomfield (head of the conflict management program), and John Angell (head of the Police Academy) found that traditional methods simply were not working in their "border" city with its "representative" population and problems. In 1968, the department experimented with preventive patrol, but found that while it did decrease street crime, there was at the same time a significant increase in such property crimes as residential burglaries. But more important, the relationship between the police department and some segments of the community deteriorated since residents saw the intensified police actions as repression rather than protection. Officers were repeatedly stopping citizens because they were simply unable to distinguish between suspicious and cultural behavior.

At the same time, the department came to recognize that the very structure of the police organization often prevented effective performance by beat patrolmen. Being very specialized, the department was unable to place responsibility for any action on anyone but the chief. When a beat officer came upon a crime, he was expected to turn the investigation over to a specialized detective. If juveniles were involved, the juvenile officers got the case. Such bureaucratic structure did not allow development of responsible police performance. Moreover, specialization worked against many of the concerns of minority people in times of community unrest.

Police must be responsive to their clientele while maintaining community respect. If crime is a concern in a neighborhood, so are the methods utilized by the police to combat crime. Placing a police officer on every street corner may dramatically reduce crime, but it is neither economically nor politically acceptable to do so, since it creates an image of an "army of occupation."

Team Policing

Through its new team policing program, the Dayton Police Department is attempting to achieve three major goals:

1. Test the effectiveness of a generalist approach to police service as opposed to the specialist approach used by most police organizations.

2. Produce a community-centered police structure that is responsive to neighborhood concerns and which is based upon an understanding of neighborhood life styles.

3. Alter the bureaucratic structure of the police organization, away from the militaristic model toward a neighborhood-oriented professional model. The overall goal is to provide effective police service while establishing a positive relationship between neighborhood residents and the police.

The development of the crisis intervention program has involved: (1) decentralization of the police function, (2) improvement of police attitudes toward the community and vice versa, and (3) increase of police responsiveness to neighborhood concerns.

1. *Decentralization of the Police Function.* All policing is the responsibility, in each area, of one command officer with rank of lieutenant. Applicants for these posts initially applied in writing for the position and were interviewed by a joint neighborhood-police council. Similarly, 18 patrolmen were selected, and approved by the lieutenant.

These patrolmen were not police officers in the traditional sense. Rather, they were "generalist/specialists," responsible for all policing in their districts. No specialized units (detective, juvenile) were allowed to operate in their districts unless specifically requested by the team to do so in emergencies. Under the generalist/specialist concept, each of the 18 officers is trained in general police techniques, but is, in addition, trained for competence in a special field (detection, juvenile work, etc.), so that under normal conditions, the team as a whole is able to handle all police responsibilities in their area. Their policies and objectives are guided by their local Neighborhood Council although, of course, they are under the administrative direction of the chief of police through the lieutenant. These generalist/specialist positions attract college graduates who are "turned off" by the prospect of merely riding cruiser cars all day and never having the chance to see their cases through in ways that fully draw upon their training and creative abilities. This new type of officer (1) investigates those crimes that have occurred recently, (2) assists members of the neighborhood with their problems, (3) answers calls for citizen service, and (4) assists the community to maintain order. When a particular officer needs technical help beyond his general or specific training, he calls upon the member of his team who has the appropriate competency. Allocation of duties is made by team sergeants who have been chosen by the team members themselves, with the approval of the chief. These sergeants work as team leaders rather than as supervisors. They, too, must have volunteered for their assignments.

The work of the teams is complemented by that of the *Community Service Officers,* comparable to the Community Service Aides in Chicago. These are civilians from the local communities, employed by the Police Department. Their dual function is to advise the sworn officers as to community needs and problems, and to do much of the time-consuming work that would otherwise fall on the members of the police team. There are three grades of Community Service Officers. Grade I is composed of individuals who lack the educational background to qualify for the position of patrolman. They are accepted regardless of juvenile arrest records and are encouraged to continue their education so that they may qualify for the next grade.

Grade II Community Service Officers are those who have the educational background to be police officers but are too young, or have not yet met the Civil Service requirements for patrolman. This position serves as an intermediate stage for those with arrest records, providing a period for personality stabilization and evaluation. The Grade III position is composed of persons who have the educational background and have passed the Civil Service test for patrolman. They are required to remain in the position for six months (or longer if they wish), to acclimatize them to community service. Thus, in addition to providing teams with their service assistance and interpretation of community needs, the

Community Service Officers constitute a recruiting and training resource for the police department.

2. *Improvement of Police Attitudes.* Because today's typical police officer is little more than a motorized call answerer, he has little opportunity to understand the neighborhood he serves or to become involved in it. He has little appreciation of its needs. To improve this situation, a number of special projects have been undertaken in Dayton. The District Director is now assisted by a Community Coordinator, an individual with community organization skills, to develop in the community an understanding of what the police are doing, to interpret policy, and—most important—to assist the community in resolving its problems. A resident of the community himself, he helps the community develop defensive security tactics, concern, and action. Since the role of the team members is primarily that of *managing* conflict, it is recognized that conflict is not always destructive, but rather sometimes a constructive means of effecting social change. The Community Coordinator also functions as head of a neighborhood-oriented police auxiliary.

To facilitate communication between the neighborhood and the team members, a Citizens' Assistance Council has been formed, which uses the executive board of the police auxiliary as its base. The District Director has frequent meetings with this Council, which interviews all new officers assigned to the neighborhood on a permanent basis. The Community Coordinator serves as secretary to this Council. This liaison enables the Council and the teams to jointly sponsor coffees and other meetings to seek solutions to current neighborhood problems.

It is very important that each officer be aware of the life-styles of his district. To further this, each officer is required to live with a sponsor family, in the neighborhood he serves, for three to five days, unless excused by the police-neighborhood council. His hosts introduce him to the neighbors and acquaint him with their concerns, in return for which they are compensated. Officers are paid overtime for this period.

3. *Increase Police Responsiveness to Neighborhood Concerns.* It was to further enable the police officers to respond to community concerns that the Community Service Officers were created under the program. Three are assigned to each team. Being residents of the area, they are able to acquaint the police with local problems and leaders. For example, in dealing with juveniles, the Community Service Officer and the team member work closely together.

The very nature of the police team member's selection, a process in which the neighborhood auxiliary participates, makes for choice of more responsive police personnel. In addition, the teams have established arrangements with local social agencies to have at least some of their personnel available after hours in cases of need. Finally, the paramilitary structure of the police department is giving way to the practice of having officers work either in pairs or alone on assignments. There are no ranks in the district; civilian titles are used. The generalist/ specialist structure allows the police officer initially answering a call to follow through on the complaint until it is disposed of. Perhaps most important, employee rewards are now based on success and quality of disposition of cases rather than on quantity of arrests, as is generally the practice. The officer is further encouraged to improve the quality of his responsiveness by being allowed 12 hours of college credit for each year he serves in the program, provided he regularly attends seminars on conflict management at a local community college.

Training Program

The training program for Dayton's crisis intervention program was developed by Harvey Carocas and Myron L. Katz of the Psychology department of Baruch College, City University of New York, and by John Angell, head of the Dayton Police Academy:

> Initially, forty-three patrolmen, four sergeants and a lieutenant were assigned to a mixed ethnic and socio-economic experimental district where team policing had been introduced. The officers, selected via depth interviews, were provided a three-week training period on a full time basis, including one week of police investigative training, one week of exposure to the community and its service agencies, and a one week group workshop experience highlighted by a crisis intervention training laboratory.

> Laboratory demonstrations consisted of dramatized youth, family, and community conflicts role-played by professional actors with improvised police interventions. [Carocas and Katz, *The Police Chief,* July 1971, p. 20]

Since the actors are selected from the Dayton community, they are able to create some realistic situations to which the police can respond. Each situation is role-played twice to enable different teams of officers to intervene and compare their techniques. Each incident is video-taped for later study and criticism by both the original and later trainees. After initial resistance to the device, the participants are able to see themselves "as others see them." During a 15-week follow up period in the field, under trained observers, the officers meet to discuss their handling of crisis situations for two hours each week, in small discussion groups.

During this training course, three problems have emerged that indicate the need to keep the training process flexible:

1. Officers have difficulty in seeing their new role as interveners in social crises and situations, as distinct from the role of sociologists and psychologists in solving situations. They fear and resent having to play the latter role, and need much help to understand the limits of the former role. Emphasis is needed to help them see that their

job is to arrest and cool crises and refer citizens to other agencies for solutions.

2. Officer trainees find that the crisis intervention technique requires so much more time per case (while hearing the "barking" of the dispatcher to get on to the next call) that they tend to give only summary treatment to it. Clearly, they must be protected from headquarters if they are to do the job right.

3. Closely connected with this is the resistance of the Department to changes away from traditional procedures, resulting in frictions which must be resolved at the command level.

Training for Community Service Officers is action oriented in order to maintain the interest of the officers who are recruited from the urban poor. Each of these officers spends one and a half hours of each work day in training at the Police Academy. The remainder of his day is spent in the field working with a selected police generalist/specialist. Much of his training involves gaining an understanding of his community's attitudes and problems in regard to housing, jobs, schools, religion and the like. Community Service Officers, during the action-oriented portion of their training, work basically in three areas. For example:

1. Twelve Community Service Officers are assigned to Community Centered Team policing, financed by LEAA funds.

2. Twelve are assigned to the Conflict Management Team (also financed by LEAA money), concerned with dealing with possible violence in the community.

3. The remainder of the Community Service Officers are utilized in prison processing, traffic control, towing abandoned cars, etc.

A necessary part of the Community Service Officers Program consists in conducting a job analysis study. This includes developing new areas for utilization of such officers in the Department. This has resulted in a re-evaluation and modernization of the Civil Service merit system to develop a new career ladder, with the help of a team of consultants.

Outcomes

It has been said that during a time of crisis, the potential for change is great. The change, of course, can be for better or worse. Which it will be depends largely on the authorities and the community. Hans Toch has said that authorities have frequently triggered more violence than they subdue because of their stereotypic reactions. Communities have been no less guilty, for the same reason. In Dayton, both the police and the community leaders, starting in one experimental district and now broadening their efforts to other parts of the city, are trying to breach their stereotypes in order to work together in keeping the peace. It is yet too early for statistical reports of the outcomes of the new approaches. But some indication is suggested by the words of one police officer in the program—a 17-year veteran on the force:

> This is a great thing for a policeman. I've never experienced such co-operation. It's more than 100 percent. Everybody passes on information, really policing as a team. Morale is so high it's almost unbelievable. There's a pretty good work load, but what I like is the way you get to follow through on your cases.

> Every contact I make, I explain team policing to people and show them how they'll get better protection because of it. We're all talking it up, and people are responding. They're beginning to realize that the neighborhood cop is coming back. And they're cooperating. Have you noticed how attitudes toward police have changed? They used to say, "Man, have you got an easy job!" Now they say, "Man, I wouldn't have your job for NO amount of money!" But I like it.

STUDY 12

Prosecutors, Courts, and Community Relations

The public tends to see prosecution and adjudication as a single functional entity in criminal justice. While this may be somewhat of a misconception, it suggests that prosecutors and courts should seek cooperatively to clarify their relationship in order to improve their services through a better understanding of their roles by the public. To the extent that such cooperation is lacking, the case for the utmost community cooperation in the prosecutorial-judicial process is correspondingly weakened.

This became apparent in the course of two successive sessions of a graduate class at Michigan State University's School of Criminal Justice which was studying the community relations aspects of the criminal justice system. In one session, two county prosecutors were invited to speak on and to respond to questions about their concepts of the community relations functions of their offices. In the second session, two judges (from circuit and district courts) were asked to comment in person on a questionnaire sent to them and to 12 other judges in advance.

The responses of both prosecutors and judges reflected great differences in their perceptions of the functions of the offices to which they had been elected. It is not surprising, therefore, that—as with the police and corrections—the public has diverse concepts of their functions. Indeed, the need for community relations programs to clarify the roles of prosecutors and judges was underscored when it became clear that there was a great difference between the prosecutors themselves and among the judges as to their understandings of the need to assist the public in comprehending their roles.

For example, one prosecutor was deeply committed to public education and had instituted many programs to that end, while the other prosecutor sincerely felt that his duty was more limited in that area. Similarly, one judge had achieved international renown with his innovative programs to develop community understanding of and cooperation with his court, while several other judges were content to preside on the bench, with only a concern for efficient administration of the law. Such differences in the several officials' interpretation of their roles are apparent in their responses to questions asked in the two sessions. Their views are synthesized here.

Q. 1. *What do you see as the role of your office in regard to community relations?*

Prosecutor #1: It is a part of the community relations function of a prosecutor to explain *why* a man was or was not convicted. The public does not understand the legal system and often suspects one or more of its agencies of hanky-panky, especially in the matter of reduced pleas. Or, take the example of a father who refused to let his daughter testify in her rape case lest it prove a permanent embarrassment to her. Result: no evidence and no conviction. Should the court have subpoenaed the girl at her jeopardy? The offender goes free and the public wonders why. Even the prosecutor may be frustrated by events over which he has no control. Clearly, the public must be educated to understand such procedures so it will not lose faith in the system because it suspects bribery or corruption.

Prosecutor #2: I agree that the prosecutor has the burden of guarding the public's faith in the system. But he must be neutral. I won't even have lunch with a defense attorney during a case: it might undermine public faith in my office through suspicion of collusion. And we must be very careful what we say to the media: they might misquote, and then we'd have to smooth things out with other agencies of the criminal justice system. Good performance on the bench is the best community relations.

Judge #1: I don't think the judiciary should be concerned with "community" relations. It's more a matter of *public* relations. But first, let's ask why we should be interested in our image. Under the elective system of choosing judges, it is a matter of self-preservation. Of course a good image is gratifying. But I think the only legitimate answer to having a good image is to more effectively perform my role. It's tough to create meaningful public relations programs. We have only three people in our office compared to the probate judge's staff of 50. I believe that for a court, public relations is a personal matter, on a one-to-one basis with counsel, the jurors and the parties. We must treat people with respect— even criminals—maintain a quiet courtroom, not be pompous, and smile when we can.

Judge #2: In regard to the image matter, I've recently been pressured into ordering a robe. The District Court has already acquired them. But it is a new practice at our level of courts. I think it is a good trend if it will increase respect for the court. But even so, the judge must be warm in explaining his procedures and the laws to those before him. This is not incompatible with wearing a robe, having everyone rise when the judge enters, and with maintaining decorum.

Judge #1: I'm not sure about that. Perhaps robes are all right for serious moments, such as sentencing. Personally, I don't fit the stereotype of a judge anyway. But informality should be retained in chambers. Your image would be pretty stuffy and self-defeating otherwise.

Q. 2. *Is there a problem in your community in regard to the entire criminal justice program?*

Prosecutor #1: The people are not even sure what criminal justice is. Does it mean that a man who kills *should* be charged with "murder one"? Or with manslaughter, which is more often appropriate since it was probably done while drunk or in a rage, or without premeditation? The public does not understand that the law provides for consideration of the circumstances of homicide. By reducing pleas in less important criminal cases, we get time for the trial of more important ones which might otherwise be put over to the next term, when there'll be fewer witnesses available and the case will be harder to try than in the term before. But we don't communicate these things to the public.

Then there is the backbiting between the criminal justice agencies. This further causes lack of public faith in the system. Other problems the public doesn't understand include the drunk driver who wants a trial. Even with only 6% of all cases coming to trial at all, it will take a year to reach his case on the docket. If the other 94% demanded jury trials, we would be out of business. There is obviously a defect in the system. We try 50 drunk driver cases a week, along with all the other cases. In addition, prosecutors must appear in many nonjury cases where there is not even an attorney present. We get farther behind each week. It is our function to help the public to understand all this so they'll press the legislature for more money for more judges and prosecutors, etc., but this would mean more taxes, and the public would, of course, complain about that. If we even had enough police in the streets to deter crime, it would help a little, but we can't get the funds for that either. These are just some of the problems in our community.

Prosecutor #2: And there's the problem that victims of crimes file complaints only to see the accused walking out of the courthouse ahead of them, which tees-off the victims because they don't understand the bail system of our courts. The media don't bother to investigate and explain the situations to the public.

And we have a guilt complex about reduced pleas in many instances. Some 88% of all cases that reach the circuit court are never tried, either because of reduced pleas or dismissals. So we get flack from the police, who see their cases get reductions by the prosecutor's office. And often we can't get warrants because the probability of conviction on the evidence presented is not strong enough. Again, the problem is mainly an economic one.

Judge #1: The courts are frustrated, too, by new prosecutors with little experience, and by new police officers and young lawyers with heavy case loads. There is no solution for this except more money from the Board of Commissioners or Board of Supervisors whose attitude, unfortunately, is, "As long as we can hire new men, we won't raise salaries."

Judge #2: We were talking the other day about how young lawyers can get experience. I think all professionals vary in their abilities, regardless of their ages. We just aren't all created equal. I think the circuit court judges in this county do appoint good people to serve poverty clients. Of course they only get $250 a case, and I know some of the assigned lawyers aren't so good. But I don't know any good answer for the problem. As for the victim who demands strict disposition of the offender—well, the judiciary as such is not responsible for our social problems! And if you set higher bail or hold a man in jail pending trial, it could be considered (perhaps by the press) "cruel and unusual punishment." High bail prostitutes both the judge and the purpose of the system.

Judge #1: And as for the habitual criminal, we are not supposed to look at a man's propensity to commit crimes, at least not during the trial. When it comes to sentencing, of course, we should look at the man's record. Today's judge has available to him the expertise (psychologists, social workers) plus pre-sentence investigation reports to guide him in sentencing. But even supposing the judge has adequate diagnostic resources available to him in a case, what good is it if the rehabilitation programs of our prisons are inadequate?

Judge #2: I'm for consultations, etc., but I feel the judge should do the sentencing. I sincerely believe that in some cases a prison experience is the best way to help a man.

Judge #1: I'm never prepared to say when a man will be rehabilitated. But if we give an indeterminate sentence, it leaves the matter up to corrections. The Michigan Supreme Court is very interested in this dilemma of sentencing. It is considering whether to require local judges to give the defense counsel the pre-sentence investigation reports, and whether or not sentences should be reviewed as well as the facts of the case during the appellate process. This could have great impact on the criminal justice system. And the death penalty is now before the Supreme Court being tested as to whether it is cruel and unusual punishment. I think we must also ask whether it is cruel and unusual to lock up a man for 50 years for *any* crime. Or even for ten years, as in the Sinclair case—for possessing drugs. Is it cruel and unusual punishment to lock a man up at all for possessing drugs? So, getting back to the question, you can see that there are many problems in our community with regard to the criminal justice system.

Q. 3. *Do you believe there should be a closer interrelationship between your office and other criminal justice agencies as an aid in improving community relations?*

Prosecutor #1: Yes. They should meet periodically—officially and socially—so they can come to understand each other's problems better. I get a great deal out of listening to police officers explain their points of view. In our metropolitan police concept, we meet at least every two weeks and we even try to anticipate problems together. Communications with the court is more difficult, but we do meet to discuss our problems. This makes for a more efficient system.

[*Prosecutor #1* might have added that among the programs he has instituted for improving communications with other criminal justice agencies and with the public are:

1. Creation of a metropolitan plan to coordinate such police activities as investigation, intelligence, and training of 22 local police departments.

2. Organization of a rumor control clinic in his office to provide the public with prompt, current and factual information during a crisis.

3. Establishing the first Prosecutor's Consumer Protection Commission in the nation to evaluate citizen complaints of fraud in business practices.

4. Establishing a county Citizens Probation Authority, which in its first three years has guided 2,000 people through probation programs that saved them from criminal records for their offenses.]

Prosecutor #2: I won't let my staff people criticize the police. It doesn't help, and it destroys enforcement. We work with various law enforcement agencies, for example, with the B and E Tri-County Squad, and the Metro Squad on drugs, who have a man in our office to assist us. We also furnish a sheet of telephone numbers of all the criminal justice agencies in case we need help from each other. We meet with the sheriff's department people from the townships. We provide the forms they need. We also meet with the command officers in the county. We tried to get the courts to meet with us but it didn't work out: apparently they don't want to get too closely involved with enforcement agencies. But they do call me by phone sometimes.

Finally, we maintain relationships with the jails and probation people to encourage rehabilitation programs such as vocational education and the use of clinical psychologists to help prisoners immediately on their commitment—before they are contaminated by the incarceration process.

Judge #1: I see the duty of the court as (1) to protect society from criminal elements, (2) to protect one individual from another, and (3) to protect the individual from society and from government. An example of the last is the case of a teacher who joined the armed forces but was eventually denied his teacher's retirement pension on the technicality that he had not taught within three months either before or after his service.

Judge #2: The district court in this state is a volume court, particularly in traffic cases. My philosophy is to try to find out a little about each person—spend three or four minutes with him—in order to provide a safety valve so he'll feel better about it all. One shouldn't just slap a fine on him. It helps if he understands his situation in relation to the laws concerned.

Neither judge referred to cooperation with other criminal justice agencies. But compare this apparent unconcern with the cooperative programs of the judge referred to in Part Four, Study 2. However, further insight into the judges' attitudes toward their community relations role can be derived from their responses to questions put only to them, not to the prosecutors—because of the nature of the questions—such as those following.

Q. 4. *Do you believe that trials should be videoed?*

Judge #1: It depends on the case. There's nothing wrong with video *per se.* But if a judge thinks it might add confusion or disturb the parties in a given case, he should forbid it. I see it as possibly accelerating the appellate system—to give higher court personnel, out of session, a quicker review of the proceedings of the lower court trial.

Judge #2: I can't see how it would help. It could lead to overdramatization by the press.

Q. 5. *How can you get fair reporting on similar cases when the first defendant gets a prison term and the second is let off?*

Judge #1: I try to explain it to the people involved at the time of sentence. But the press most often isn't even there. I've only felt the need to explain to the press once—in a case where an aunt killed her niece. There were psychological factors in that one. In general, I just don't feel the need to explain. But I answer all questions politely, even crank letters.

Q. 6. *With 14 judges in the county, why don't we have more black judges?*

Judge #2: The governor has been working on this, particularly in Detroit where they have a heavy black population. I think we should not only have more black judges, but more black personnel in all judges' offices.

Judge #1:   We can't get them to run for election in this county. They are making too much money in private practice to be able to afford it. One black judge in Detroit is well known for his impartiality: he is strict with both black and white defendants—so much so that they say the appeals courts even enjoy reversing some of his black cases.

Questions for Discussion

1. Judging from their responses to Question 1, which of the four men seems most sensitive to the public need for clarification of their roles?

2. Is there more consensus (or less) among the respondents in their replies to Question 2? Or do they pair off by roles?

3. How do you account for the cleavage by roles in the responses to the third question? Are judges more insensitive to the needs of their clientele? (Consider the replies to Questions 4, 5, and 6 in making your judgments.)

4. On the whole, does the evidence suggest that prosecutors are "liberals" and judges are "conservatives"? What are the implications of your conclusions?

The POST Leadership Training Program: California

The California State Legislature, through actions in 1968 and 1969, charged the Commission on Peace Officer Standards and Training (POST) in that state to develop and implement a statewide community relations training program. After examining several proposals, the Commission selected three institutions—The University of California at Los Angeles, San Diego State College, and San Jose State College—to collaborate in developing the course. The major responsibility for its development was assigned to UCLA, which retained James G. Fisk to direct the project. Mr. Fisk had just completed 30 years in the Los Angeles Police Department, during the last five of which he directed its Community Relations as a Deputy Chief. The curriculum was designed so that the three institutions could follow the same general outline but could also adapt it to stress those problems peculiar to their own areas. The initial Institutes were held in November and December of 1970, lasting for six weeks. Participants' expenses (approximately $2000 each) for tuition, lodging, meals and transportation were covered by POST. The police and sheriffs' departments which sent trainees continued to pay their salaries during the training period.

Objectives of POST

The stated objectives of the training program were to:

1. Teach officers how to analyze communities and identify present and emerging problems of law enforcement.

2. Impart knowledge and develop analytical skills for examining responsibilities of law enforcement agencies during a period of rapid social change.

3. Develop new approaches to community-police relations based on the knowledge, skills and perceptions gained from the course.

4. Develop methods for implementing these approaches and adapting them to the needs of particular police departments.

333

A cursory investigation of law enforcement agencies in California revealed that most community relations officers had little or no training in this field. The POST approach provided an opportunity to study the interrelationships between social control and social change and to examine the extent to which divergencies between these two processes become open and visible sources of friction and conflict between the police and the subgroups of society. The concern is to find the proper role of enforcement in a society where the formal institutions and processes of facilitating changes in values (through the courts, legislatures and executive) are functioning badly, or when societal mechanisms of social control (family, school, church, volunteers) seem to be breaking down. A second concern is to understand the conditions promoting conflict between subcultures, and between subcultures and the larger political system.

The POST Program

The program is offered five times in nine months for periods of six or seven weeks each. A total of 100 California city police and county sheriff officers (20 of the latter per class), drawn from the entire state, participate. During the course, they reside at the university and in the community where they are studying in field projects, for a total of 90 hours of classroom work and 180 hours of field experiences which are designed to reenforce each other. In a variety of lectures, seminars, workshops and small discussion groups, students not only become familiar with the literature but participate in the design of projects, instruction, selection of field activities and in a continuing evaluation of the entire process. The assumption is that the student is his own best instructor and that the faculty role is guidance and direction.

Since heavy emphasis is placed on first-hand information, students live in the community, for example, while serving a week-long internship in a local social organization. They live in and observe neighborhoods with and without the guidance of formal and informal community leaders. To supplement these experiences, students view and react to films and video-tapes and engage in role playing, simulations and case study analyses. The central organizing feature of the training program—the means of integrating field work and classroom—is the development of *community profiles* by groups of four or five trainees. The communities they analyze are different from those they have previously been familiar with in order to prevent prejudgments based on previously formed stereotypes. The profiles seek to answer three questions:

1. What is there about a community which a police department should try to understand and to which it might adapt its style and method of law enforcement?

2. What might a community learn about its police department and the problems and dilemmas of enforcement in that community?

3. How can a community profile be organized and developed as a meaningful aid to policy makers and patrolmen in a particular police department with individual concerns and problems?

Training begins before students arrive on campus. Several weeks in advance, they receive a required reading list covering theory, practices and trends in police and community relations. During the course, trainees explore three major topics, the understanding of which is vital to effective performance in police-community relations:

1. *Subcultures:* their composition, characteristics, values, problems and consequent behavioral implications.

2. *Police:* their roles and their relationship to the complex system of justice and social control.

3. *Social change:* its causes, problems and implications for police.

Subcultures. Students spend 30 classroom hours and 50 field work hours examining American subcultures—homogeneous groups formed on the basis of age, religion, occupation, political tendencies, race, economic status, etc. Through lectures, seminars and discussion groups of varying size, they examine the implications of extended family units among Mexican-Americans, the matriarchal structure of Negro families, and the deference to age and its effect on relationships within Japanese-American families. While in the field, they eat a meal with a family and spend an afternoon visiting in their home. Another afternoon is spent in a ghetto area trying to find a job while dressed in old clothes and pretending to have no skills. They have the experience of buying $5.00 worth of food in a ghetto community and later comparing the experience with other students. Trainees also write required short, analytic papers about one of these experiences and, together, evaluate how the activity relates to information given in class.

Finally, students compare the evidence of class, readings, special films, tapes, and field trips taken with guides (government employees, older police, local leaders) as a basis for writing the first section of their community profiles.

Police as Participants in a System of Social Control. Again, during 30 class and 50 field work hours, students examine four roles which the police perform and how they relate to each other and to the requirements they bring to bear on the officers performing them—order maintenance, law enforcement, service, and crime prevention—and how these functions relate to other agencies in the criminal justice system. Do they support, duplicate, or conflict with one another? Techniques for such study are similar to those used in the study of subcultures, but instead of visiting neighborhoods, students spend several days at other criminal justice agencies, observing and gathering data about them. Answers are sought to such questions as:

1. Would changes in representation on the city council facilitate or impede crime prevention?

2. What efforts are made by city government to deal with poverty, poor housing, unequal education, and the like?

3. How can (or should) styles of enforcement be adapted to the needs of individual communities?

4. Has the effort to professionalize the police separated them from the communities they are intended to serve?

5. What factors influence the patrolman's reactions to the community he serves and to specific situations that arise? Do these include his partner, the watch commander, his training, the paramilitary nature of the police organization, departmental policies, or what?

6. How much diversity in police role requirements is functional for optimum role performance? What is the effect of the uniform?

7. How can positive contacts with citizens be built into police incentive systems?

8. What are the effects of differential law enforcement?

Social Change and Its Implications for Law Enforcement. This section of the training course serves to integrate all materials previously covered. The same ratio of 30/50 hours of class and field work is devoted to discovering the factors precipitating change and their implications for the police. Technological social and economic factors are considered, such as increased specialization and the consequent interdependence of society. The effects of legislation and court decisions in the areas of civil liberties, drugs, the draft, and voting ages are examined. Questions are raised as to the effectiveness in achieving change of voting, strikes, boycotts, protests, riots and legal suits, for examples. In small discussion groups, the students discuss these points in the light of their own experiences and those of more experienced officers. Related issues are the effect on community relations of the use of search warrants, stop and frisk and informer systems. Students discuss these points with different citizen groups including Mexican-Americans, liberal students, a lower-middle class white group, and upper-middle class, white, Protestant and Jewish groups. As in the cases of the other units of study, students continue working on the appropriate portions of their profiles of the neighborhoods they are studying, preparing these in teams of four or five students, and later presenting reports to the entire class for reactions.

Evaluation Criteria

Several evaluation criteria are used throughout the program. The primary concern is the extent to which the course developed existing skills and builds new ones for analyzing a community's law enforcement problems and how well it prepared community relations officers to initiate changes in the departments that result in improved police-community relations. Measuring devices are developed from the literature and from consultation with other agencies (criminal justice, social), community groups, faculty, and from preceding classes of students. Evaluation occurs before, during, and after the training periods.

Two kinds of evaluation are conducted. Students are asked periodically to evaluate the relevance and benefits of activities and the quality of instruction. They, in turn, are evaluated by their peers and the faculty in a number of different ways:

1. Through written assignments, projects and tests such as:

   a. Preparing short analytical papers on specific topics and readings to measure learning and perception.

   b. Planning a community relations program component to meet a specific community need, or changing an operational procedure in their department to correct a way of responding to a community problem.

   c. Preparing draft legislation to change outmoded laws and discriminatory or unfair laws and to reflect changes in values or the need for employing different police practices.

2. Through observation of behavior during role-playing, simulation, guided tours, and the period of internship.

3. Through preparation of the profile, revealing how well trainees worked together to synthesize and analyze information gained from class and field experiences.

A number of post-course measures are used to evaluate the overall program. The profile, in addition to assessing trainee performance during the course, measures the extent to which the profile helps to develop innovative police practices to meet community needs. Also, some of the pre-course measures are repeated immediately following the program. The survey of trainees, taken at the time of recruitment, is repeated, and is repeated again six months later.

In addition to the evaluation techniques already mentioned, two weekend reunions are scheduled at six-month intervals after each program. They are held at UCLA's Lake Arrowhead facility where trainees have the opportunity to discuss what they have done to implement programs in their departments, as well as the problems and successes they have experienced. Thus, they are able to evaluate each others' projects and exchange constructive criticism. These sessions provide feed-back information on the validity of criteria used in constructing the community profiles during the formal program. They also serve motivational purposes by providing new incentives to implement changes in the trainees' departments which will benefit police-community relationships. Finally, the meetings provide a measure of the long-term effects of the program on trainees' knowledge and perceptions.

Results and Recommendations

According to the final report (Michael K. Brown, et al.) on the POST training program:

> In terms of the objectives we originally set for ourselves, we can say that our data and impressions indicate we largely accomplished the first three, and the fourth to a lesser extent . . . [For example in one] police department an effect of the program has been the phasing out of the community relations bureau and its replacement with a number of programs attempting to involve the *whole department* in community-police relations.

> It is in regard to the fourth goal . . . that the results of our efforts were unsatisfactory . . . [There was ample] evidence that many officers were experiencing great difficulty in effecting changes in their departments.

> In the light of the difficulties of implementation . . . if POST continues to support these training programs without coming to grips with the implementation problem, the money will be largely wasted . . . Upgrading community-police relations involves substantial reorientations in attitudes and perceptions to which there is significant resistance by both police and community. Furthermore, it is clear that to be successful, community-police relations must involve the whole department, particularly the patrolmen . . . Specialized training programs for policy makers such as chiefs may help.

> In supporting these training programs, POST is coming to grips with an important problem facing the peace officers of California. However, it is only a beginning and, as this report indicates, a much greater effort will eventually be required. [*Evaluation of the UCLA Community-Police Relations Training Program 1970–71*, pp. 12–14.]

STUDY 14

The North Philadelphia Program

The police-community relations program mounted by the North City Congress of Philadelphia provides an example of such ventures being initiated by the *community*, rather than by the police. Its philosophical approach was the reverse of that generally made: it was based on the concept that there is an inverted power structure in which urban low-income citizens are unable to "control the police" or successfully to negotiate with other municipal agencies. This perspective flows logically from the fact of community sponsorship of the project. Its suggestion of community control of the police was explicit, and this may have been a factor in the failure of the project to perpetuate itself under autonomous community management, after funds for a professional administrative staff were exhausted. But a description of the project should precede an analysis of it. We mention these points at the outset as a rationale for including a study of the experiment in this text.

Background

This account is based on a summary of three major final reports on the North City Congress (NCC) Police-Community Relations Program: The Final General Report, the Final Periodic Effectiveness Report, and the Training Manual.*

The North City Congress Police-Community Relations Program operated in a North Philadelphia target area involving six police districts. In 1960 there were approximately 460,000 people residing in the area, 71 percent of whom were nonwhite (black and Puerto Rican). Of these families, 74 percent had annual incomes of less than $6000. About 47 percent had incomes of less than $4000. In this socio-economic ghetto, the crime rate was the highest in the city. Poor housing and edu-

---

*Copies of the three full reports may still be available from the Office of Juvenile Delinquency and Youth Development, U.S. Department of Health, Education and Welfare, Washington, D.C. 20201, or from the North City Congress offices, 1438 North Broad Street, Philadelphia, Pa., 19121.

cation, and lack of recreation and sanitary facilities were typical. Many of the residents were frustrated, alienated and hostile. By contrast, many were earning livable wages, owned their own homes and were "getting ahead." The greatest number of residents, regardless of income, were law-abiding citizens who were concerned with improving their environment through legitimate means. It is in reference to these people that the word "community" is used in the reports. The program was simply unable to reach those alienated individuals among them who felt no involvement in the community.

The 1964 disturbances in North Philadelphia were but one extreme manifestation of the resentments which the police and the community felt toward each other. The citizens saw the police as an occupation force; the police saw the citizens, collectively, as criminals and sub-humans. The imbalance of power in favor of the police only accentuated the community's distrust. "This power imbalance is an artifact of racism, and any means for its redress [depend] on removing racism from the American scene," the report observes. But citizens demanded assistance in improving their treatment at the hands of the police, and the police participated in the hope of receiving help in the improvement of the community image of themselves. The program tried to meet these two needs.

Organization

North Philadelphia had had for some time a host of independent, self-developed neighborhood organizations—the bedrock of social initiative in the ghetto. Unfortunately, they had little strength in their competition for limited support. In 1963, these organizations federated to form the North City Congress in a demonstration project funded by the Philadelphia Council for Community Advancement. The Congress thus became a tax-exempt, non-profit, corporate entity comprised of 250 organizations including 10,000 individuals. Its functions of education, organization, facilitation, and innovation for betterment were managed by a professional staff. Its Police-Community Relations program was designed by the members in cooperation with the Police Department, to reduce tensions and develop mutual understanding.

The program was functionally divided into two parts: a Training Component and a Demonstration Component. The latter was subdivided into two units: The Community Organization Unit and the Research Unit. The Program Director was primarily responsible for the coordination of all units and served as director of the Community Organization and Research units as well. The Training Component had its own director and specialized staff. A Chief Investigator supervised the Research Unit. Thus there were three administrative elements, each having a major program objective. The Training Component was responsible for the development and administration of an educational program to build civic skills among citizens, to build humanitarian attitudes among policemen, and to promote mutual understanding and communication on a direct, informal basis between citizens and police.

The Community Organization Unit created District Committees in each police district, most of whose members had participated in an educational program under the Training Component. These were the indigenous leaders who were expected to continue the program after the paid staff was withdrawn.

The Research Unit maintained and interpreted records, evaluating the program as it progressed and making recommendations for improvements. To give some idea of the scope of the contacts made by the program during its two years of existence, there were:

107 police institutes held, attended by 1,332 officers

383 community workshops attended by 4,551 residents

197 intergroup sessions attended by 2,319 police/residents

250 special interest group meetings attended by 4,921 people

All told, 830 program-conducted and program-sponsored meetings were held, with a total attendance of 11,791, from 193 North Philadelphia neighborhood organizations and institutions. These figures include 1,591 students who participated through in-school workshops.

The funds provided for the program by the U.S. Department of Health, Education and Welfare included grants of $284,872 for the first year and $311,437 for the second, a total of $596,309 over a thirty month period.

The Program

The Police-Community Relations aspect of the project was not intended to be a permanent organization. It was a demonstration program, and the staff function was primarily in organizing an initial support activity. Resources of indigenous leadership in already existing agencies were used in the target districts to "infect" their own circles of influence by spreading the program among their friends, relatives and neighbors. The District Committees were to become autonomous bodies capable of self-support and continuance. Surveys revealed participant characteristics:

Community Participants. Typically a Negro female, aged 30–49; married, with income from semi-skilled or unskilled labor; resident for five years. Participation high at outset, but leveling off as program neared its known date of termination. As few as ten percent felt the effort had improved police-community relations. Hoped-for continuing interaction did not materialize. Felt that major problems were unchanged, including police disrespect, gangs, poor housing, sanitation, services, etc.

Police Participants. Typically patrolmen, aged 20–40, born in city, married, high school education, two out of three being white, on force either one or two years or more than five but less than 15; had employment prior to police service, and a veteran. Only 1/3 attended *intergroup* sessions. Some felt they had learned something positive; the rest confirmed their beliefs that the "public" didn't understand them and were "ignorant," "gripers," or "narrow minded." Some 83 percent felt the experience had not been helpful. Most of those who did feel it was helpful were black. Most felt that the public did not understand their role as police.

As the list of types of meetings above suggests, the programs consisted of efforts to bring police and community people together for purposes of dialogue from which mutual understanding and greater respect would develop. But no significant changes resulted. The program as implemented was not the solution to the problems at hand, although it helped to clarify the issues. Moreover, during the period of the experiment, Black Power, cultural nationalism, and other militant minority thrusts had emerged as the new ways to organize the ghetto. Such groups rose briefly and then faded away. As the report puts it: "The quest for power needed to *make* change was proscribed on the genteel battleground defined by the existing social order."

Misconceptions

The North City Congress discovered that it had based its program on certain misconceptions. According to the summary of the Reports, they learned that:

> Groups organized on the basis of neighborhood identification and problems did not necessarily create a new power source.

> Political power does not automatically flow from organized numbers of people.

> That community organization (non-electoral democracy) does not always generate sufficient power to cope with the "Establishment."

Conclusions of the Reports

Some of the "Major Findings of Program Analysis and Evaluation" bear critical examination. Beginning with the statement that "the program ended as it began—with a significant number of policemen and members of the community perceiving each other as the enemy," the Reports candidly declare:

The violence and danger generated by bad police-community relations is dysfunctional in a society seeking stability. But the causes of that bad relationship are functional extensions of the social order which the police are organized to protect.

A major element of the police function is to maintain the value structure of the prevailing social order.

Police identification with prevailing values prevents their understanding of the need for socio-economic change . . . and prevents their joining ghetto residents to effect change.

Changing police-community relations for the better will require a transfer of some power from the police to the community.

There is urgent need for a redefinition of the police role. Program experiences showed that both police and community were confused as to what it should be. Most of police work is related to social service functions (marital arbitrator, life-saver, counselor), yet police prefer to see themselves in the more "masculine" role of law enforcers.

Even if the role of the police is redefined to emphasize the social service function, policemen will still be unable to solve social problems which are the proper province of other arms of government and society.

Police processing of citizen complaints, except on the local level, is unsatisfactory because of organizational procedures which preclude complainants learning of the outcomes.

Police-community relations are guided by larger socio-economic forces, and are not susceptible to major improvement without fore-running social change of some sort.

Critique

The description of the North Philadelphia Program in the Summary of the three Reports suggests a realistic sense of failure in improving police-community relations. The listed conclusions, however, do not seem to be based upon realities. They do not, for instance, include the possibility that one basic objective of the program may have been the cause of failure—namely, to have the community gain control over the police. While it is certainly true that the base of police authority is in the community, the phrase "community control" has assumed threatening implications to police officers who see themselves *as the authority,* and the notion that they could possibly be brought under the control of ghetto people for whom they traditionally feel a fear-based contempt was repugnant to them. The facts that only a third of the police attended the *intergroup* meetings, and that (except for the black officers) those who did attend seemingly failed to have their prejudices modified as a result of such meetings suggest a defensive hostility against what they perceived as a threat to their authority posed by the "community control" slogan itself. The idea of the sponsors that the community was suffering from a "power structure inversion" must have been inflammatory to the police.

The admission "that the program ended as it began"—with a failure of the leaders to maintain community-police contacts, and the collapse of contacts briefly made with other agencies—is hardly justification for the conclusion that "police-community relations cannot be changed without prior social changes." The evidence from other cities is strongly to the contrary. However, this does not deny the intimate connection that does exist between police-community relations and the larger context of social justice.

The North Philadelphia program technique was essentially *dialogue—not service*. Propinquity in itself does not spawn understanding. Quite the contrary is often true. Even sensitivity training assumes more than a reliance simply on "bringing people together." There must be a sense of cooperative achievement to produce change.

The fallacy lay in the failure to provide service; service to the community and to the police. There were no improvements in street lighting, sanitary conditions; no counseling of juveniles, pressuring of landlords nor building of useful contacts with other agencies. All of these are achievements of programs in cities where police-community partnerships have focused on *getting things done*—together.

But in one rather remarkable sense, the North Philadelphia project stands out. After investing more than half a million dollars in a program reflecting what seemed to be the best that was then known about how to improve police-community relations in such a social setting, there was a frank admission of failure—and a very valuable indication of some of the main reasons for it. This is worth far more, probably, than any number of less-than-frank reports of similar projects that also fail, but which undertake to delude the observer into the fatuous belief that any project that expends public funds must be made to appear successful, even when it isn't.

STUDY 15

Job Description:
Police and Community Relations Coordinator

In 1967, the National Center on Police and Community Relations at Michigan State University developed the following job description for a Police and Community Relations Coordinator.

This summary of the Responsibilities, Duties, and Qualifications of Police and Community Relations Coordinator is written for the department which is only large enough to assign one person to perform the activities discussed. In larger departments the same activities should be performed but the personnel performing them should be part of a unit under the direction of the Coordinator.

Responsibilities

1. The Coordinator is responsible directly to the Chief of Police as a staff person.
2. He is responsible for the overall coordination and planning of the following activities:
   a. Tension and Conflict Identification
   b. Community Relations Programming
   c. Public Information

Duties

1. *Tension and Conflict Identification.* Through use of all communication channels available, the Coordinator should identify areas of conflict and tension within the community, between community groups themselves, and between such groups and the police. A few available sources of information are:
   a. Complaints Against Police Officers. Such complaints are made when there is a conflict between a citizen and the police depart-

ment. The Coordinator should receive summaries of all complaints and case histories of complaints involving racial, ethnic, or religious factors. Careful consideration should be given to unfounded complaints because the complainant probably still believes his complaint is valid.

b. Attitude Survey. The department should obtain the services of a competent sociologist or social psychologist on a consulting basis to carry out attitude surveys of community attitudes, opinions, tension points in the community, and generally advise the Coordinator on intergroup relations.

c. Assaults on Police Officers. The assault on a police officer is a hostile situation and usually is indicative of tension and conflict. Report summaries should be received by the Coordinator, who should analyze to determine if patterns of conflict exist.

d. Line Personnel. One of the major means of conflict and tension identification should be from the line personnel. *Each* member of the force should watch for tension points, activities of demagogic groups, overt expressions of racial, ethnic, or religious hostilities, and an increase in the speed of rumor circulation of a sensational nature. All such symptoms should promptly be reported to the Coordinator.

e. Community Organizations. The Coordinator should attend as many community organization meetings as possible to provide a source of communication between the department and the community. At all meetings he attends he should attempt to discover where there is conflict existing.

The Coordinator should compile data on types of conflict existing and the causes of this conflict.

2. *Community Relations Programming.* The Coordinator should design programs aimed at reducing conflict and tension. He should report to the Chief his recommendations for programs to be implemented by the line personnel. Following are a few selected programming formats which should be considered:

a. District Committees. Neighborhood Citizen Councils should be formed as a means of focusing community resources on problem areas. The Committee should include membership from *all* segments of the community, including those groups in specific tension and conflict with the police. The Coordinator should serve as consultant to the Committee in developing programs for line implementation at the neighborhood level.

b. Operation "Crime Stop" Activities. These programs should be designed by the Coordinator but carried out by line personnel. They involve issuing cards to as many community members as possible enlisting their aid in reporting crimes they see and serving as witnesses in such cases.

    c. Youth Programs.   The Coordinator should design programs for the education of youths in school. He should appear at schools and give speeches on the functions and operation of the department and should work toward inclusion of lessons on law observance in the school curriculum.

    d. Procedure Evaluation.   The Coordinator should recommend to the Chief changes in operating procedures which have an adverse effect on the police and community relationship. This might include, for example, methods of field interrogation which are least offensive to the community.

    e. Human Relations Training.   The Coordinator should participate in departmental training activities or recommend to the Chief areas in which human relations training is needed.

3. *Public Information.*   The Coordinator should be responsible for police contacts with the press, for the release of information to the public and the press, for conducting tours of police facilities, for providing speakers on department activities to interested groups, and for the design and publication of informational brochures and sheets on departmental activities and problems.

Qualifications

1. The position of Police and Community Relations Coordinator should be an assigned exempt position with rank and authority equal to that of a superior staff officer. The person appointed as Coordinator should clearly be the best man available for that position, without regard to his *present* rank.

2. The Coordinator can be either a civilian or a sworn officer. He should be thoroughly familiar with department activities, rules, and procedures.

3. He should be versed in any minority-group language predominant in the community.

4. He should be able to clearly convey his ideas, both in public and in private.

5. He should have a good understanding of community problems and specific problems of minority groups in the community.

6. He should be a person well respected by minority group members in the community and by police officers in the department.

7. Racial, ethnic, or religious characteristics should be among several factors considered in reaching a determination of desirable qualifications for the position of Coordinator. He should not be assigned solely because of these characteristics, but, if such characteristics will allow him to work most successfully with groups involved in conflict and tension, this should be an important consideration.

Police-Community Relations in Britain

The news from Britain during the last three years has been filled with scare headlines about the rising crime rate in general, the new type of armed criminals, and the activities of colored peoples, particularly of the Black Panthers. While all three of these trends are minimal in comparison with their counterparts in the United States, they are nevertheless surprising since Britain—and especially London, which is most visible to tourists—has for over a century been known to the world as a haven of social tranquility. It has been so since Sir Robert Peel established the Metropolitan Police with the fiat that "the constable will be civil and obliging to all people of every rank and class. He must remember that there is no qualification so indispensable to a police officer as a perfect command of temper."

Through their history, the British police are—as Sydney Harris has pointed out—"courteous beyond belief; they are trained to respect the law in a way that American police are not; they have a long tradition of warning suspects about their civil rights, and they cannot even carry a gun without requesting a special permit to do so." They have been, it would appear, the quintessence of police-community relations at its ideal best. The question is whether their approach to enforcement will prove adequate to meet the new challenges mentioned above.

Rising Crime in General

In the British and American press, these recent items have appeared about England:

Youthful demonstrators have taken to hurling insults ("pig") at policemen.

Officers have been kicked and bitten and gouged in the head and face by muggers.

The crime rate has doubled in the past five years.

Low pay and an inflationary economy have forced hundreds of bobbies to quit, leaving the national police understaffed by 17,000.

Law and order has become a main issue in Parliament. Some 84 percent of polled voters objected when hanging for murder was abolished (1965).

British police still object to being armed. "The result would be shoot-ups, with bystanders and police getting killed."

Nine policemen have been murdered since capital punishment was abolished as against 28 in the previous 50 years.

New Type of Armed Criminals

English police seized arms in 50 coordinated raids in London and throughout England last night. Acted under the Firearms Act of 1968, and the Explosive substances Act of 1883 which forbid possession without a permit. Appeared with warrants at private homes, hotels. Found light weapons and sub-machine guns. Fear their possible use in insurrections, as in Ireland.

Britons seek to cope with new, alarming violence in underworld. In Blackpool, thieves escaping with $125,000 in jewels opened fire on pursuing police; killed superintendent; funeral attended by 100,000 shocked citizens. Chairman of Police Federation says, "The war against crime has become a vicious war. This is no longer a gentle-manly game of Bill Sikes against the Bobby." Not even the Great Train Robbers used guns.

Scotland Yard Commissioner complains, "A criminal used to be sent to Dartmoor, where he was flogged (illegal since 1948), had to break stones and sew mailbags. Prison was a real deterrent."

Manchester *Guardian* reacts: "It is hard to believe that harsher sen-tences would make a difference in present trends." London *Times:* "If the penalty for robbery were increased, it would come perilously close to that for murder, offering little extra penalty to the criminal who chooses to shoot."

Once cosh*-carrying gangs specialized in daytime holdups; now heavily armed, very young four- or five-man gangs are using armed violence against banks, post offices, etc. Why not? Police estimates show the criminal has only a 40 percent chance of being caught, and if appre-hended, has a 40 percent chance of acquittal.

Passersby no longer help the police against persons resisting arrest: they might be armed.

The Activities of "Colored People"**

. . . "RACE RIOT DANGER IN BRITAIN" . . . "17 PC's HURT IN BLACK POWER FIGHT" . . . "PIG'S HEAD ON A STICK WAVED IN FACE OF POLICEMAN" say the headlines.

---

*similar to a blackjack

**In British usage, includes West Indians (about half the total), Afghanistanis, Pakistanis, black Africans, and immigrants from India.

But the London *Evening News,* August 14, 1970, saw nothing like the street scenes of Chicago and Detroit—yet. After a survey, it reported:

> Black Power in Britain consists mainly of two organizations: The Black Panthers (British branch of the American group), and The Racial Adjustment Action Society (RAAS). Out of an estimated 500,000 colored in London, the full-time number of Panther workers is between 30 and 40. RAAS works from a welfare house with many colored coming and going, but with no more workers than the Panthers. But Black Power funds could easily total $250,000. The potential for action is there. However, replies to interviews of various types of colored persons suggested no imminent crises.
>
> "Came to this country for a better life and education for our children" . . . "Want nothing to do with violence and demonstrations" . . . "We want what everybody else wants—a bit of money for the supermarket, perhaps a new car, a week at Butlin's" . . .

The head of Scotland Yard's Community Relations Branch says that figures prove there are no more lawbreakers proportionately among the colored than among the white. "I believe that the Black Power people have very little support, but when people feel they are deprived, you can expect trouble." The British Security Department (for subversive activities) reports learning of talks among Black Power extremists suggesting plans for adopting South American tactics of kidnapping VIP's and of another organization for attacking police. But they see no point in the former since Britain has no political prisoners. As for the latter, they do not foresee bloodbaths in the streets. "British common sense and stability will prevent that. What needs constant watching is the fact that the great majority of colored is silent."

To meet the numerical increase in crime, Scotland Yard has reopened the old Vine Street Station. Established in 1829 with the founding of the Metropolitan Police, it was converted to an alien registry office in 1940 when the West End Central Headquarters took over its functions. But by 1971, supplemental facilities were needed. The Vine Street building, with its white porcelain brick cells, is particularly appropriate for the posh Mayfair district which it serves. Other evidences of the rising crime rate include the increasing amount of overtime officers must put in due to lack of manpower, and the low pay scales, which, even with overtime and some living allowances, still give an officer so little that resignations continue to increase.

Scotland Yard is known to feel keenly that the law is too soft on criminals. There appears to be a tenacious hanging on, by substantial elements of British society, to ideas of vengeance and the antiquated notion that, against all evidence, the harsher the punishment the less the crime. Seemingly forgotten is the memory of pickpockets flourishing in the shadow of the gallows.

Police-Community Relations

The most significant change made to meet the rising crime rate and the possibility of growing tensions with the colored is the new emphasis on police efforts to get closer to the people. Until recently, the London Metropolitan Police have relied chiefly upon Peel's principles of consistently maintaining the best possible rapport between the police and their citizen clientele. Until the introduction of motorized patrols, this proved to be enough. But the person-to-person contacts were threatened, as officials and the public were already beginning to recognize, when the new quality and quantity of crime and the changing nature of the population in parts of the cities demanded a new approach. In brief, it became evident that the traditional police-community relationships needed reinforcing.

The Unit or Home Beat System

The result was the restitution (1967) of the old bobby-on-the-beat plan. Of the 21,000 Metropolitan London policemen who cover a 788-square-mile area in which about 12 million people live, about seven to eight thousand work a unit beat system.

Bernard Weinraub wrote in *The New York Times* (March 3, 1970):

> These men operate from their homes and work alone in a one-square-mile area near their homes. They work at the most critical times of day and they are responsible for that single neighborhood. The officer knows everyone and everyone knows him. He knows who are the trouble-makers, the petty thieves and who is having wife troubles. He knows whom to watch and the neighborhood knows whom to call.

By 1969 Scotland Yard was able to report that the annual rate of the most severe crimes had dropped slightly; five fewer murders, and 34 fewer cases of manslaughter and infanticide, in spite of the increase in the new type of gun-carrying criminal. The Commissioner of the Metropolitan Police, Stanley Johnson, expressed the hope that the unit beat system would become even more effective:

> Basically it's the village constable such as operates in the country, brought into the urban area. If we ever lose that common touch, we shall lose the respect of the public and furthermore we shall lose our information and the intelligence on which we live. [Lansing *State Journal,* April 1, 1971]

The Commissioner explained that this intelligence enabled them to know in advance who the instigators of the Viet Nam demonstrations were in 1968. "Once we knew who they were, we just surrounded them and cut them off from the others—and the crowd fell away."

One constable who is a unit beat officer in the Brixton area of London explained:

> It's an area that can be a regular headache. There are 300 active known criminals on my beat. They're known to me. Now 300—1 might seem considerable odds and, indeed, if it weren't for a very fine back-up team [motorized squad] supporting me, things could be far worse. The home beat system is a great success.

> Juvenile crime on my beat has been reduced 50 to 60 percent, purely because I know every school child. . . . I can talk to them all and every youngster feels that he knows me and that I know what they are doing. It has a very great deterrent effect. [Ibid.]

A well-written description of a typical British bobby on a home beat appeared in *The New Yorker* for August 14, 1971, authored by John Bainbridge and entitled, "Profile of a British Constable." The picture drawn of the six-foot-four, meticulously uniformed and helmeted officer as he makes a near social occasion of his rounds is almost pastoral. To be sure, his beat includes the Victoria and Albert Museum, Harrods, the Royal Court Theatre, the Royal Hospital and part of Kensington Gardens—all of which he pauses to appreciate—but it also encompasses an adjacent seamy neighborhood with its full quota of potential offenders. On his rounds he carries ball-point pens, matches and penknife in case anyone should need them ("One always likes to oblige"); a two-way radio for communication with headquarters or, if working with a partner on a pursuit into a building ("I'm in the back yard, Ron; if chummy makes a break out the back door, he'll see me waiting and grinning all over"); a "Nicholson's Guide to London" (which he has memorized), and a concealed truncheon. But no handcuffs ("I think they're rather primitive, really").

"If chummy gives you a clout behind the ear, you give him a real solid clout back. Funnily enough, that doesn't cause any rancor. Chummy thinks, well, he's not such a bad bloke. But if you were to draw the truncheon, everything would change instantly for the worse. And people would say, 'Look at the big bully!'"

Most of the day is spent answering questions on how to get to - -, where to buy - -, unsnarling traffic and the like. He stops a woman backing into a one-way street: "Pull over to the side, luv," and points out her error. The reply, "How *could* I have been driving against the traffic when I was backing up!" He admitted he had to think about that one.

"Only a tiny fraction of our time is spent catching law-breakers. But the actions of the men on the beat determine what the public thinks of us."

Asked about handling demonstrations: "The first aim of the policeman is to take the heat out of the situation, whether two people or 200. He must never show himself as an authoritarian individual but as a human being. You don't have to be officious to make a point. These young demonstrators have more energy than they'll ever have again. They want to blow off steam. If they want to have a go at us, fair enough. That's better than having them in the back alleys beating up innocent people. Of course, if they get a bit naughty, deliberately trying to hurt, then we'll have to take them into custody."

Perhaps the central issue of police-community relationships in Britain is best suggested by the constable's explanation of why, even now, the police do not wish to carry arms: "It would antagonize the public. As it is, when the butcher and the greengrocer see old chummy having a go at you, they say, 'Well, look at old Tom. He's having a bit of a punch-up. Let's go along and give him a hand.' It's all quite fun, really."

Works Cited

Alinsky, Saul. "Organizers Clutch Key to the Future." *The New York Times,* January 2, 1971, p. 33.

Allman, James J. "Establishing a Police-Community Relations Office Within a Police Department." *The Police Chief,* March 1965.

Allport, Gordon W., and Leo Postman. *The Psychology of Rumor.* New York: Russell & Russell, 1965.

American Newspaper Publishers Association. *Free Press and Fair Trial.* New York: American Newspaper Publishers Association, 1967.

Baddeley, Fred. "British Police Juvenile Liaison Schemes." *The Police Chief,* May 1961.

Bainbridge, John. "Profile of a British Constable." *The New Yorker,* August 14, 1971.

Baldwin, James. *Nobody Knows My Name.* New York: Dell Publishing Co., 1962.

Bard, Morton. "Family Intervention Police Teams and Community Mental Health Resources." *Journal of Criminal Law, Criminology, and Police Science* 60 (1969).

Biderman, Albert, and associates, Bureau of Social Science Research, Inc. *Report on a Pilot Study in the District of Columbia on Victimization and Attitudes Toward Law Enforcement.* Report submitted to the President's Commission on Law Enforcement and Administration of Justice. Washington, D.C.: U.S. Government Printing Office, 1967.

Bimstein, Donald. "Sensitivity Training for the Police." *Police,* May–June 1970.

Birnbaum, Max. "Sense About Sensitivity Training." *Saturday Review,* November 15, 1969.

Black, Algernon D. *The People and the Police.* New York: McGraw-Hill, 1968.

Bordua, David J., ed. *The Police: Six Sociological Essays.* New York: John Wiley & Sons, 1967.

Bouma, Donald H. *Kids and Cops.* Grand Rapids, Mich.: William B. Eerdmans Publishing Co., 1969.

Brown, Claude. *Manchild in the Promised Land.* New York: Macmillan, 1965.

Brown, Michael K., et al. *Evaluation of the UCLA Community-Police Relations Training Program 1970–1971.* Institute of Government and Public Affairs, University of California at Los Angeles, 1971.

Buchwald, Art. "The Good Guys and the Bad," in *The Establishment Is Alive and Well in Washington.* New York: G. P. Putnam's Sons, 1969.

Burnham, David. "Police Violence: A Changing Pattern." *The New York Times,* July 7, 1968.

Carocas, Harvey, and Myron L. Katz. "Dayton's Pilot Training Program: Crisis Intervention." *The Police Chief,* July 1971.

Cleaver, Eldridge. *Soul on Ice.* New York: Delta Book, Dell Publishing Co., 1968.

Craft, Carl C. "Race Relations Encounter Groups Under Investigation." Lansing *State Journal,* September 3, 1971.

Cray, Ed. *The Big Blue Line: Police Power Versus Human Rights.* New York: Coward-McCann, 1967.

———. "The Politics of Blue Power." *The Nation,* April 29, 1969.

Davis, J. C. *Human Nature in Politics.* New York: John Wiley & Sons, 1963.

Eisenberg, Terry, Albert S. Glickman, and Robert H. Fosen. "Action for Change in Police-Community Behaviors." *Crime and Delinquency,* July 1969.

Eisenberg, Terry, Robert H. Fosen, and Albert S. Glickman. *Project PACE: Police-Community Enterprise—A Program for Change in Police-Community Behaviors, Final Report.* American Institutes for Research, Silver Springs, Md., November 1971.

Eldefonso, Edward. *Law Enforcement and the Youthful Offender.* New York: John Wiley & Sons, 1967.

Foster, Lee, and Morris Heath, eds. *The New York Times Almanac—1971.* The New York Times Educational Books.

Friendly, Alfred, and Ronald Goldfarb. *Crime and Publicity: The Impact of the News of the Administration of Justice.* New York: Twentieth Century Fund, 1967.

Gard, Spencer A. "Free Press vs. Fair Trial: Another Tempest in the Teapot." *ABA Journal* 54 (1968): 669-671.

Gellhorn, Walter. "Police Review Boards: Hoax or Hope." *Columbia University Forum,* Summer, 1966.

Golenpaul, Dan, ed. *Information Please Almanac—1971.* New York: Dan Golenpaul Associates, 1970.

Hartell, Ralph T. "American Youth: Are They Really Different?" In *Reader's Digest Almanac—1971.* Pleasantville, N.Y.: Reader's Digest Assn., 1971.

Hartley, Eugene L. "Perception as a Psychological Process." In *Proceedings of the Eighth Annual National Institute on Police and Community Relations, May 1965,* Hoyt Coe Reed, ed. Michigan State University.

Howard, Jane. *Please Touch.* New York: McGraw-Hill, 1970.

Kheel, Theodore W. "Can We Stand Strikes by Public Employees?" *Reader's Digest,* August 1969.

Knebel, Fletcher. "A Cop Named Joe." *Look,* July 27, 1971.

———. "Doctor to the Cities." *Newsweek,* September 1, 1971.

Lane, Millicent. "Llinas Urges T-Group Safeguards." Lansing *State Journal,* January 5, 1970.

Lee, Alfred McClung, and Norman D. Humphrey. *Race Riot.* New York: Dryden Press, 1943.

Lentz, William P. "Police and Reference Group Attitudes Toward Delinquency Control." *Police,* March–April 1971.

Lohman, Joseph D. *The Police and Minority Groups.* Chicago: Chicago Park District, 1947.

Lynden, Patricia. "Why I'm a Cop: Interviews From a Reporter's Notebook." *Atlantic Monthly,* March 1969, pp. 104–108.

Malcolm X, with the assistance of Alex Haley. *The Autobiography of Malcolm X.* New York: Grove Press, 1966.

Marshall, Thurgood. "Racial Factors in Law Enforcement." In *Police and Community Relations: A Sourcebook,* A. F. Brandstatter and Louis A. Radelet, eds. Beverly Hills, Calif.: Glencoe Press, 1968.

Matthews, Linda McVeigh. "Chief Reddin: New Style at the Top." *Atlantic Monthly,* March 1969.

McGee, Richard A. "The Correctional Process." In *Police and Community Relations: A Sourcebook*, A. F. Brandstatter and Louis A. Radelet, eds. Beverly Hills, Calif.: Glencoe Press, 1968.

Ng'weno, Hilary. "The Panthers: An African View." *The New York Times*, October 2, 1970, p. 35.

Niederhoffer, Arthur. *Behind the Shield*. Garden City, N.Y.: Doubleday & Company, 1967.

Noyes, Alfred D. "Has Gault Changed the Juvenile Court Concept." *Crime and Delinquency*, April 1970.

Pepitone, A. "Self, Social Environment, and Stress." In *Psychological Stress*, M. H. Appley and R. Trumbull, eds., pp. 182–208. New York: Appleton-Century-Crofts, 1967.

Preiss, Jack J., and Howard J. Ehrlich. *An Examination of Role Theory: The Case of the State Police*. Lincoln, Neb.: University of Nebraska Press, 1966.

Radelet, Louis A. *The Police and the Community*. Beverly Hills, Calif.: Glencoe Press, 1973.

Reader's Digest Almanac–1971. Pleasantville, N.Y.: Reader's Digest Assn.

Reiss, Albert J., Jr., and associates, University of Michigan. *Studies in Crime and Law Enforcement in Major Metropolitan Areas; Field Surveys III*. 2 vols. Report submitted to the President's Commission on Law Enforcement and Administration of Justice. Washington, D.C.: U.S. Government Printing Office, 1967.

Seeman, Melvin. "On the Meaning of Alienation." *American Sociological Review* 24 (1950): 783–791.

Skolnick, Jerome H. "Police and the Urban Ghetto." *Research Contributions* of the American Bar Association, no. 3 (1968): 10.

Snidler, James Henry. "John Calvin Coolidge." In *Encyclopedia Brittanica*, 1964, vol. 6, p. 446.

Steele, John L. "The People's Right to Know." *Time*, January 11, 1971, p. 16.

Sterling, James W. *Changes in Role Concepts of Police Officers During Recruit Training*. Washington, D.C.: International Association of Chiefs of Police, June 1969.

Strecher, Victor G. "When Subcultures Meet: Police-Negro Relations." In *Science and Technology in Law Enforcement*, Sheldon Yefsky, ed. Chicago: Thompson Co., 1967.

Sutton, Horace. "Fanon: The Revolutionary as a Prophet." *Saturday Review*, July 17, 1971, p. 16.

Toch, Hans. "A Note on Police Experience." *Police*, March–April 1967.

Turner, William W. *The Police Establishment*. New York: G. P. Putnam's Sons, 1968.

U.S., President's Commission on Law Enforcement and Administration of Justice. *Field Surveys II. Criminal Victimization in the United States: A Report of a National Survey*. Prepared for the Commission by the National Opinion Research Center, University of Chicago (Philip Ennis). Washington, D.C.: U.S. Government Printing Office, May 1967.

U.S., President's Commission on Law Enforcement and Administration of Justice. *Task Force Report: Corrections*. Washington, D.C.: U.S. Government Printing Office, 1967.

U.S., Department of Commerce. *U.S. Statistical Abstract*. Washington, D.C.: U.S. Government Printing Office, 1970.

Watson, Nelson A., and James W. Sterling. *Police and Their Opinions*. Washington, D.C.: International Association of Chiefs of Police, 1969.

Whyte, William Foote. *Street Corner Society*. Chicago: University of Chicago Press, 1943.

Wilson, James Q. "Police and Their Problems: A Theory." In *Public Policy* (Year book of the Harvard University Graduate School of Public Administration), 1963.

––––––. *Varieties of Police Behavior: The Management of Law and Order in Eight Communities*. Cambridge: Harvard University Press, 1968.

––––––. "What Makes a Better Policeman." *Atlantic Monthly,* March 1969.

You and the Law. Pleasantville, N.Y.: Reader's Digest Association, 1971.

Yount, Kathy. "Kirkwood Police Junior Aide Program." *Police*, July–August, 1971.

Bibliography

Items listed are primarily recent titles (since 1967) but also include a few classic works.

Adams, Thomas F. *Law Enforcement: An Introduction to the Police Role in the Community*. Englewood Cliffs, N.J.: Prentice-Hall, 1968.

Abrahamsen, David, M.D. *Our Violent Society*. New York: Funk & Wagnalls, 1970.

Ahern, James F. *Police in Trouble: Our Frightening Crisis in Law Enforcement*. New York: Hawthorne Books, 1972.

Aichorn, August. *Wayward Youth*. New York: Viking Press, 1969.

Alex, Nicholas. *Black in Blue: A Study of the Negro Policeman*. New York: Appleton-Century-Crafts, 1969.

Alexander, Rae Pace. *Young and Black in America*. New York: Random House, 1970.

Altshuler, Alan. *Community Control: The Black Demand for Participation in Large American Cities*. New York: Pegasus, 1970.

American Bar Association. *Drug Addiction: Crime or Disease?* Bloomington, Ind.: Indiana University Press. 1970.

American Civil Liberties Union. *Fifty Years of Civil Liberties: The Annual Report of the American Civil Liberties Union*. New York: Arno Press, 1970.

American Friends Service Committee. *Struggle for Justice: A Report on Crime and Punishment in America*. New York: Hill & Wang, Inc. 1971.

Anderson, Stanley V. *Ombudsmen for American Government?* Englewood Cliffs, N.J.: Prentice-Hall Spectrum Books, 1968.

Answers to Your Questions About American Indians. Washington, D.C.: U.S. Government Printing Office, 1969.

Anthony, Earl. *Picking up the Gun: A Report on the Black Panthers*. New York: Dial Press, 1970.

Anti-Defamation League, et al. *Negro History and Literature: A Selected Annotated Bibliography*. New York: Anti-Defamation League, 1969.

Aptheker, Herbert, ed. *Documentary History of the Negro People in the U.S. From Colonial Times to the Founding of the NAACP in 1910*. New York: Citadel Press, 1969.

Arens, Richard. *Make Mad the Guilty: The Insanity Defense in the District of Columbia*. Springfield, Ill.: Charles C. Thomas, 1969.

Arnold, William R. *Juveniles on Parole: A Sociological Perspective*. New York: Random House. 1970.

Asch, Sidney H. *Police Authority and the Rights of the Individual*. New York: Arco, 1968.

Ashley, T. Ludlow, et al. *The Quality of Inequality: Urban and Suburban Public Schools.* Chicago: Center for Police Study, University of Chicago, 1969.

Asinof, Eliot. *People vs. Blutcher.* New York: Viking Press, 1970.

Astor, Gerald. *The New York Cops.* New York: Scriber's, 1971.

Baehr, Melanie E., John E. Furcon, and Ernest C. Froemel. *Psychological Assessment of Patrolman Qualifications in Relations to Field Performance.* Washington, D.C.: Office of Law Enforcement Assistance, U.S. Department of Justice, 1968.

Bagdikian, Ben H. et al. *The Media and the Cities.* Chicago: Center for Policy Study, University of Chicago, 1969.

Baltimore Committee on the Administration of Justice Under Emergency Conditions. *Report,* Baltimore, May 31, 1968.

Banfield, Edward C. *The Unheavenly City: The Nature and Future of Our Urban Crisis.* Boston: Little, Brown, 1970.

Banton, Michael. *Race Relations.* New York: Basic Books, 1968.

———. *The Policeman in the Community.* New York: Basic Books, 1964.

Barbour, Floyd B. (ed.). *The Black Power Revolt.* Boston: Porter Sargent, 1968.

———. *The Black Seventies.* Boston: Porter Sargent, 1970.

Bassiouni, M. Cherif. *Criminal Law and Its Processes: The Law of Public Order.* Springfield, Ill.: Charles C. Thomas, 1969.

———. *The Law of Dissent and Riots.* Springfield, Ill.: Charles C. Thomas, 1971.

Bayley, David H., and Harold Mendelsohn. *Minorities and the Police: Confrontation in America.* New York: Free Press, 1969.

Becker, Harold K. *Issues in Police Administration.* Metuchen, N.J.: Scarecrow Press, 1970.

Becker, Howard S., ed. *Campus Power Struggle.* Chicago: Aldine, 1970.

Bedau, Hugo Adam. *Civil Disobedience Theory and Practice.* New York: Pegasus, 1969.

Bell, Daniel, and Irving Kristol. *Confrontation: The Student Rebellion and the Universities.* New York: Basic Books, 1969.

Bellush, Jewell and Stephen David. *Race and Politics in New York City: Six Case Studies in Policy Making.* New York: Praeger, 1970.

Berger, Peter L. and Richard J. Neuhaus. *Movement and Revolution.* Garden City, N.Y.: Doubleday, 1970.

Bergman, Peter N. *Chronological History of the Negro in America.* New York: Harper & Row, 1970.

Berkley, George E. *The Democratic Policeman.* Boston: Beacon Press, 1969.

Bersani, Carl A. *Crime and Delinquency: A Reader.* New York: Macmillan, 1970.

Berube, Maurice R., and Marilyn Gittell. *Confrontation at Ocean Hill-Brownsville: The New York School Strikes of 1968.* New York: Praeger, 1969.

Bibliography on the Urban Crisis. Washington, D.C.: U.S. Government Printing Office, 1969.

Bichel, Alexander M. *The Supreme Court and the Idea of Progress.* New York: Harper & Row, 1970.

Bierstedt, Robert. *The Social Order* 3d ed. New York: McGraw-Hill, 1970.

Birmingham, John. *Our Time Is Now.* New York: Praeger, 1970.

Bittner, Egon. *The Functions of Police in Modern Society.* Chevy Chase, Md.: National Institutes of Mental Health, 1970.

Black, Charles L. *Structure and Relationship in Constitutional Law.* Baton Rouge, La.: Louisiana State University Press, 1969.

Block, Herbert A., and Gilbert Geis. *Man, Crime, and Society.* New York: Random House, 1970.

Bloom, Leonard. *The Social Psychology of Race Relations.* Morristown, N.J.: General Learning Press, 1972.

Blumberg, Abraham S., ed. *Law and Order: The Scales of Justice.* Chicago: Aldine, 1970.

Bonger, Willem (Abridged by Turk, Austin T.) *Criminality and Economic Conditions.* Bloomington, Ind.: Indiana University Press, 1970.

Booth, Alan, and John Edwards. *Social Participation in Urban Society.* Cambridge, Mass.: Schenkman, 1970.

Bopp, William J. *The Police Rebellion.* Springfield, Ill.: Charles C. Thomas, 1971.

Bordua, David J., ed. *The Police: Six Sociological Essays.* New York: John Wiley & Sons, 1967.

Boskin, Joseph. *Urban Violence in the Twentieth Century.* Beverly Hills, Calif.: Glencoe Press. 1969.

Bosmajian, Haig, ed. *The Principles and Practices of Freedom of Speech.* Boston: Houghton Mifflin, 1970.

Bottomley, A. Keith. *Prison Before Trial.* London: G. Bell, 1970.

Bouma, Donald. *Kids and Cops.* Grand Rapids, Mich.: William B. Erdmans, 1969.

Bouma, Donald and James Hoffman. *The Dynamics of School Integration: Problems and Approaches in a Northern City.* Grand Rapids, Mich.: William B. Erdmans, 1969.

Bracey, John H., Jr. *Black Nationalism in America.* New York: Bobbs-Merrill, 1970.

Bracey, John H., Jr., August Meier, and Elliott Rudwick, eds. *Black Nationalism in America.* New York: Bobbs-Merrill, 1970.

Braden, William. *The Age of Aquarius: Technology and the Cultural Revolution.* Chicago: Quadrangle Books, 1970.

Bragdon, Henry, and John C. Pittenger. *The Pursuit of Justice.* New York: Macmillan, 1969.

Braly, Malcolm. *On the Yard.* New York: Fawcett World Library, 1969.

Brandstatter, A. F., and Allen A. Hyman. *Fundamentals of Law Enforcement.* Beverly Hills, Calif.: Glencoe Press, 1971.

Brandstatter, A. F., and Louis A. Radelet. *Police and Community Relations: A Sourcebook.* Beverly Hills, Calif.: Glencoe Press. 1968.

Brazier, Arthur, et al. *Black Self Determination: The Story of the Woodlawn Organization.* Grand Rapids, Mich.: William B. Erdmans, 1969.

Brennan, James, and Donald W. Olmstead. *Police Work With Delinquents: Analysis of a Training Program.* East Lansing: Social Sciences Research Bureau, Michigan State University, 1965.

Bromley, David G. and Charles F. Longino, *White Racism and Black America.* Morristown, N.J.: General Learning Press, 1972.

Brown, Michael. *The Politics and Anti-Politics of the Young.* Beverly Hills. Calif.: Glencoe Press, 1969.

Buckman, Peter. *The Limits of Protest.* New York: Bobbs-Merrill, 1970.

Bullock, Henry Allen. *A History of Negro Education in the South From 1619 to the Present.* Cambridge, Mass.: Harvard University Press, 1969.

Bundy, McGeorge. *Reconnection for Learning: A Community School System for New York City.* New York: Praeger, 1969.

Burby's Law Refresher Series. *Criminal Law and Procedure,* 4th ed. St. Paul, Minn.: West Publishing Co., 1969.

Burma, John H., ed. *Mexican-Americans in the U.S.: A Reader.* Cambridge, Mass.: Schenkman, 1970.

Burris, Donald S. *The Right to Treatment.* New York: Springer, 1969.

Burpo, John H. *The Police Labor Movement: Problems and Perspectives.* Springfield, Ill.: Charles C. Thomas, 1971.

Caffi, Andrea. *A Critique of Violence.* New York: Bobbs-Merrill, 1970.

Cahn, Edgar S., ed. *Our Brother's Keeper: The Indian in White America.* New York: World Publishing Co., 1969.

Califans, Joseph A., Jr. *The Student Revolution: A Global Confrontation.* New York: W. W. Norton, 1970.

Canton, Norman F. *The Age of Protest: Dissent and Rebellion in the Twentieth Century.* New York: Hawthorne Books, 1970.

Capaldi, Nicholas, ed. *Clear and Present Danger.* New York: Pegasus, 1970.

Carmichael, Stokely, and Charles V. Hamilton. *Black Power: The Politics of Liberation in America.* New York: Vintage Books. 1967.

Carney, Frank J., Hans W. Mattick, and John A. Callaway. *Action on the Streets: A Handbook for Inner City Youth Work.* New York: Association Press, 1969.

Carter, Robert, and Leslie T. Wilkins. *Probation and Parole: Selected Reading.* New York: John Wiley & Sons, 1970.

Center for the Study of Democratic Institutions. *The Establishment and All That.* Santa Barbara, Calif.: The Center for the Study of Democratic Institutions, 1970.

Cerrantes, Lucius F. *The Dropout: Causes and Cures.* Ann Arbor, Mich.: University of Michigan Press, 1969.

Chace, William, and Peter Collier. *Justice Denied: The Black Man in White America.* Chicago: Harcourt, Brace & World, 1970.

Challenge of Crime in a Free Society. President's Commission on Law Enforcement and Administration of Justice. Washington, D.C.: U.S. Government Printing Office, 1967.

Chambliss, William J. *Crime and the Legal Process.* New York: McGraw-Hill, 1968.

Chametzky, Jules, and Sidney Kaplan. *Black and White in American Culture.* Amherst, Mass.: University of Massachusetts Press, 1970.

Chevigny, Paul. *Police Power.* New York: Pantheon, 1969.

Chitty, Elizabeth N., and Ben Arthur. *Ely: Too Black, Too White.* Amherst, Mass.: University of Massachusetts Press, 1970.

Cicourel, Aaron V. *The Social Organization of Juvenile Justice.* New York: John Wiley & Sons, 1968.

Civil Disorders After Action Reports. Washington, D.C.: International Association of Chiefs of Police, Professional Standards Division, 1968.

Clark, N. Terry. *Community Structure, Power, and Decision-Making: Comparative Analyses.* San Francisco: Chandler, 1968.

Clark, Ramsey. *Crime in America.* New York: Simon & Schuster, 1970.

Clark, Thomas D. *The Emerging South.* 2d ed. New York: Oxford University Press, 1969.

Clarke, John Henrik. *Malcolm X: The Man and His Time.* New York: Macmillan, 1969.

Clavir, Judy, and John Spitzer, eds. *The Conspiracy Trial.* New York: Bobbs-Merrill, 1970.

Cleaver, Eldridge. *Soul on Ice.* New York: McGraw-Hill, 1968.

Coffey, Alan, Edward Eldefonso, and Walter Hartinger. *Human Relations: Law Enforcement in a Changing Community.* Englewood Cliffs, N.J.: Prentice-Hall, 1971.

————. *Police-Community Relations.* Englewood Cliffs, N.J.: Prentice-Hall, 1971.

Cohen, Bruce J., ed. *Crime in America.* Itasca, Ill.: Peacock, 1970.

Cohen, Nathan, ed. *The Los Angeles Riots: A Socio-Psychological Study.* New York: Praeger, 1970.

Cohen, Stanley A. *A Law Enforcement Guide to United States Supreme Court Decisions.* Springfield, Ill.: Charles C. Thomas, 1971.

Cole, Jonathan O. and J. R. Wittenborn. *Drug Abuse: Social and Psychopharmacological Effects.* Springfield, Ill.: Charles C. Thomas, 1969.

College Volunteers, A Guide to Action: Helping Students Help Others. Washington, D.C.: U.S. Government Printing Office, 1969.

Comer, James P., M.D. *Beyond Black and White.* New York: New York *Times* Co., 1972.

Commission on Community Interrelations. *Survey on Preparations for Urban Violence and Appendix: Special Study on Preparations fc Urban Violence.* New York: American Jewish Congress, 1968.

Commission on Human Rights. *To Continue Action for Human Rights: Federal Report.* Washington, D.C.: U.S. Government Printing Office, 1969.

Committee for Economic Development. *Training and Jobs for the Urban Poor.* New York: Committee for Economic Development, 477 Madison Avenue, New York: 10022, 1970.

Conant, Ralph W. *The Prospects for Revolution.* New York: Harper & Row, 1971.

Conant, Ralph W., and Molly Apple Levin, eds. *Problems in Research on Community Violence.* New York: Praeger, 1969.

Connery, Robert H. and Caraley Demetrios, eds. *Governing the City: Challenges and Options for New York.* New York: Praeger, 1969.

Conrad, Earl. *The Invention of the Negro.* New York: Paul S. Erickson, 1969.

Correctional Institutions, vol. 2. Washington, D.C.: U.S. Government Printing Office, 1969.

Corson, William R. *Promise or Peril: The Black College Student in America.* New York: W. W. Norton, 1970.

Cousens, Frances Reissman. *Public Civil Rights Agencies and Fair Employment: Promise and Performance.* New York: Praeger, 1969.

Cray, Ed. *The Enemy in the Streets: Police Malpractice in America.* New York: Doubleday Anchor Books, 1972.

Cressey, Donald R., and David A. Ward. *Delinquency, Crime, and Social Process.* New York: Harper & Row, 1969.

Crime Commission of Philadelphia. *Attack on Crime: Design of a Regional Approach to Law Enforcement in the Delaware Valley.* Philadelphia: Crime Commission of Philadelphia (mimeo), 1969.

Crime Commission of Philadelphia. *Violence Today: A Judicial Concern (Proceedings of the 4th Judicial Sentencing Institute, Redford, Pa., 1968).* Philadelphia: Crime Commission of Philadelphia, 1969.

Critchley, T. A. *The Conquest of Violence: Order and Liberty in Britain.* New York: Schocken Books, 1970.

Cruickshank, William M., James L. Paul, and John B. Junkala. *Misfits in the Public Schools.* Syracuse, N.Y.: Syracuse University Press, 1969.

Cumming, Elaine. *Systems of Social Regulation.* New York: Atherton Press, 1968.

Dawson, Robert O. *Sentencing.* (From American Bar Association Administration of Criminal Justice Series). Boston: Little, Brown, 1969.

Deloria, Vine, Jr. *We Talk, You Listen: New Tribes, New Turf.* New York: Macmillan, 1970.

Dentler, Robert A. *American Community Problems.* New York: McGraw-Hill, 1968.

DeTocqueville, Alexis. *Democracy in America.* 2 vols. New York: Schocken Books, 1970.

Detroit Urban League. *A Survey of Attitudes of Detroit Negroes After the Riot of 1967.* Detroit: The Detroit Urban League, 208 Mack Avenue, Detroit, Michigan, 1967.

Dinitz, Simon, Russell R. Dynes, and Alfred C. Clarke, eds. *Deviance: Studies in the Process of Stigmatization and Societal Reaction.* New York: Oxford University Press, 1969.

Dinitz, Simon and Walter Reckless. *Critical Issues in the Study of Crime.* New York: Little, Brown, 1968.

Downs, Anthony. *Who Are the Urban Poor?* New York: Committee for Economic Development, 1970.

Draper, Theodore. *The Rediscovery of Black Nationalism.* New York: Viking Press, 1970.

Dressler, David. *Practice and Theory of Probation and Parole.* New York: Columbia University Press, 1970.

Drucker, Peter F. *The Age of Discontinuity: Guidelines to Our Changing Society.* New York: Harper & Row, 1970.

Drug Dependence—Youth in Rebellion. Washington, D.C.: U.S. Government Printing Office, 1969.

DuBois, W.E.B. *Dusk of Dawn: An Essay Toward an Autobiography of a Race Concept.* New York': Schocken Books, 1969.

Durham, Lewis E., Jack R. Gibbs, and Eric S. Knowles. *A Bibliography of Research —Explorations in Human Relations Training and Research.* Washington, D.C.: National Institute for Applied Behavioral Science, 1967.

Dymally, Mervyn M. *The Black Man in American Politics.* New York: Praeger, 1970.

Earle, Howard H. *Police-Community Relations: Crisis in Our Time,* 2d ed. Springfield, Ill.: Charles C. Thomas, 1970.

————. *Student-Instructor Guide on Police-Community Relations.* Springfield, Ill.: Charles C. Thomas, 1970.

Edwards, George. *The Police on the Urban Frontier: A Guide to Community Understanding.* New York: Institute of Human Relations Press, The American Jewish Committee, 1968.

Eisner, Victor. *The Delinquency Label: The Epidemiology of Juvenile Delinquency.* New York: Random House, 1968.

Eldefonso, Edward. *Youth Problems and Law Enforcement.* Englewood Cliffs, N.J.: Prentice-Hall, 1972.

Eldefonso, Edward, Alan Coffey, and Richard C. Grace. *Principles of Law Enforcement.* New York: John Wiley & Sons, 1968.

Elliott, J. F. and Thomas J. Sardino. *Crime Control Team: An Experiment in Municipal Police Department Management and Operations.* Springfield, Ill.: Charles C. Thomas, 1971.

Ellis, William W. *White Ethics and Black Power: The Emergence of the West Side Organization.* Chicago: Aldine, 1969.

Emerson, Robert E. *Judging Delinquents: Context and Process in Juvenile Court.* Chicago: Aldine, 1969.

Empey, LaMar T. *The Silverlake Experiment: Testing Delinquency Theory and Community Intervention.* Chicago: Aldine, 1971.

Empey, LaMar T. and Steven G. Lubeck. *Delinquency Prevention Strategies.* Washington, D.C.: U.S. Government Printing Office, 1970.

Endleman, Shalom. *Violence in the Streets.* Chicago: Quadrangle Books, 1970.

Epstein, Charlotte. *Intergroup Relations for Police Officers.* Baltimore, Md.: Williams and Wilkins, 1962.

Epstein, Jason. *The Great Conspiracy Trial.* New York: Random House, 1970.

Equal Opportunity: A Bibliography of Research on Equal Opportunity in Housing. Washington, D.C.: U.S. Government Printing Office, 1969.

Erber, Ernest, ed. *Urban Planning in Transition.* New York: Viking Press, 1969.

Etzkowitz, Henry, and Gerald M. Schaflander. *Ghetto Crisis: Riots or Reconciliation?* Boston: Little, Brown, 1969.

Evard, Franklin H. *Successful Parole.* Springfield, Ill.: Charles C. Thomas, 1971.

Eyman, Joy S. *Prisons for Women: A Practical Guide for Administrative Problems.* Springfield, Ill.: Charles C. Thomas, 1971.

Fager, Charles E. *White Reflections on Black Power.* Grand Rapids, Mich.: William B. Eerdmans, 1968.

Fantini, Mario, Marilyn Gittell, and Richard Magat. *Community Control and the Urban School.* New York: Praeger, 1970.

Finn, James, ed. *A Conflict of Loyalties: The Case for Selective Conscientious Objection.* New York: Pegasus, 1969.

Flammang, C. J. *The Police and the Underprotected Child.* Springfield, Ill.: Charles C. Thomas, 1970.

Foley, James A., and Robert K. Foley. *The College Scene: Students Tell It Like It Is.* New York: Cowles Book, 1970.

Forer, Lois G. *No One Will Listen: An Indictment of the Juvenile Court System.* New York: John Day, 1970.

Fort, Joel. *The Pleasure Seekers: The Drug Crisis, Youth and Society.* Indianapolis, Ind.: Bobbs-Merrill, 1970.

Fortas, Abe. *Concerning Dissent and Civil Disobedience—We Have an Alternative to Violence.* New York: Signet Books, New American Library, 1968.

Fox, Vernon B. *Guidelines for Corrections Programs in Community and Junior Colleges.* Washington, D.C.: American Association of Junior Colleges, 1969.

Frazier, Thomas R. *Afro-American History.* Chicago: Harcourt, Brace & World, 1970.

Freeman, Howard, and Norman R. Kurtz, eds. *America's Troubles: A Casebook in Social Conflict.* Englewood Cliffs, N.J.: Prentice-Hall, 1969.

Freeman, Linton C., and Morris H. Sunshine. *Patterns of Residential Segregation.* Cambridge, Mass.: Schenkman, 1969.

Friendly, Alfred, and Ronald Goldfarb. *Crime and Publicity: The Impact of News on the Administration of Justice.* New York: Twentieth Century Fund, 1967.

Galarza, Gallegos, and Samora. *Mexican Americans of the Southwest.* New York: Anti-Defamation League, 1969.

Ganz, Alan S., Hans W. Mattick, Kenneth J. Northcott, and Jerome H. Skolnick. *The Cities and the Police.* Chicago: The University of Chicago Round Table, 1968.

Garabedian, Peter G., and Don C. Gibbons, eds. *Becoming Delinquent: Correctional Process and Delinquent Careers.* Chicago: Aldine, 1970.

Gardiner, John A. *Traffic and the Police: Variations in the Law Enforcement Policy.* Cambridge, Mass.: Harvard University Press, 1969.

Gardner, Erle Stanley. *Cops on Campus and Crime in the Streets.* New York: William Morrow, 1970.

Garn, Stanley M. *Human Races.* 2d ed. Springfield, Ill.: Chares C. Thomas, 1969.

Gawthrop, Louis C., ed. *The Administrative Process and Democratic Theory.* Boston: Houghton Mifflin, 1970.

Gayle, Addison, J. *The Black Situation.* New York: Horizon Press, 1970.

Gaylin, Willard, M.D. *In the Service of Their Country (War Resistors in Prison).* New York: Viking Press, 1970.

Gellhorn, Walter. *When Americans Complain: Governmental Grievance Procedures.* Cambridge, Mass.: Harvard University Press, 1966.

George, B. J., Jr. *Gault and the Juvenile Court.* Ann Arbor, Mich.: Institute of Continuing Legal Education, 1967.

Germann, A. C., Frank D. Day, and Robert G. Gallati. *Introduction to Law Enforcement.* rev. ed. Springfield, Ill.: Charles C. Thomas, 1969.

Gibbons, Don C. *Delinquent Behavior.* Englewood Cliffs, N.J.: Prentice-Hall, 1970.

————. *Society, Crime, and Criminal Careers: An Introduction to Criminology.* Englewood Cliffs, N.J.: Prentice-Hall, 1968.

Gibson, William M. *Lessons in Conflict: Legal Education Materials for Secondary Schools.* Boston: Boston School of Law, 1970.

Gilbert, Ben W. and The Staff of the Washington Post. *Ten Blocks From the White House: Anatomy of the Washington Riots of 1968.* New York: Frederick A. Praeger, 1968.

Gittell, Marilyn and Alan G. Hevesi. *The Politics of Urban Education.* New York: Frederick A. Praeger, 1969.

Glaser, Daniel, ed. *Crime in the City.* New York: Harper & Row, 1970.

Gold, Martin. *Delinquent Behaviors in an American City.* Belmont, Calif.: Brooks-Cole, 1970.

Goldberg, W. A. *Guide to Corrections.* East Lansing, Mich.: (mimeo) Available Gibson's Book Store, 128 W. Grand River, 1969.

Goldman, Nathan. *The Differential Selection of Juvenile Offenders for Court Appearance.* Paramus, N.J.: National Council on Crime and Delinquency, 1968.

Goldman, Peter. *Report from Black America.* New York: Simon & Schuster, 1970.

Goldstein, Joseph E., ed. *Crime, Law and Society: A Collection of Essays on Insanity as a Legal Defense.* Detroit: Detroit Free Press, Oct. 1970.

Gossett, Thomas F. *Race, The History of an Idea in America.* New York: Schocken Books. 1969.

Gourley, G. Douglas, *Effective Municipal Police Organization.* Beverly Hills, Calif.: Glencoe Press, 1971.

————. *Public Relations and the Police.* Springfield, Ill.: Charles C. Thomas, 1953.

Grad, Frank P. *Alcoholism and the Law.* Dobbs Ferry, N.Y.: Oceana Publications, 1970.

Graham, Hugh Davis and Ted Robert Gurr, eds. *The History of Violence in America—Historical and Comparative Perspectives.* New York: Frederick A. Praeger, 1969.

Green, Robert L., ed. *Racial Crisis in American Education.* Chicago: Follett, 1970.

Greenberg, Harold. *Social Environment and Behavior.* Cambridge, Mass.: Schenkman, 1970.

Grier, William H., and Price M. Cobbs, *Black Rage.* New York: Basic Books, 1968.

Griffin, John Howard. *The Church and the Black Man.* Dayton, Ohio: Pflaum, 1970.

Grimshaw, Allen D., ed. *Racial Violence in the United States.* Chicago: Aldine–Atherton, 1971.

Grosman, Brian A. *The Prosecutor.* Toronto: University of Toronto Press, 1970.

Grupp, Stanley E. *Theories of Punishment.* Bloomington, Ill.: Indiana University Press, 1972.

Hacker, Andrew. *The End of the American Era.* New York: Atheneum, 1970.

Hadden, Jeffrey K., Louis H. Masotti, Kenneth Seminatore, and Jerome Corsi. *A Time to Burn? An Evaluation of the Present Crisis in Race Relations.* Chicago: Rand McNally, 1969.

Hannerz, Ulf. *Soulside: Inquiries Into Ghetto Culture and Community.* New York: Columbia University Press, 1970.

Hansen, David A., and Thomas R. Culley. *The Police Leader.* Springfield, Ill.: Charles C. Thomas, 1971.

Hapgood, Hutchins. *The Spirit of the Ghetto: Studies of the Jewish Quarter of New York.* New York: Schocken Books, 1970.

Hare, Nathan. *The Black Anglo-Saxons.* New York: Macmillan, 1970.

Harris, M. A. (Spike). *A Negro History Tour of Manhattan.* Westport, Conn.: Greenwood, 1969.

Harris, M. A. and Morriss Levitt. *Teachers Guide to a Negro History Tour of Manhattan.* Westport, Conn.: Greenwood, 1970.

Harris, Richard. *Justice: The Crisis of Law, Order and Freedom in America.* New York: E. P. Dutton, 1970.
————. *The Fear of Crime.* New York: Frederick A. Praeger, 1969.
Haskins, James. *Diary of a Harlem Schoolteacher.* New York: Grove Press, 1970.
Hazard, Geoffrey C. *Law in a Changing America.* Englewood Cliffs, N.J.: Prentice-Hall, 1969.
Heidt, Sarajane and Amitai Etzioni, eds. *Societal Guidance: A New Approach to Social Problems.* New York: Thomas Y. Crowell, 1969.
Helfer, Ray E., M.D. and Henry Kempe, M.D. *The Battered Child.* Chicago: University of Chicago Press, 1968.
Henderson, David: *De Mayor of Harlem.* New York: E. P. Dutton, 1970.
Hendin, Herbert. *Black Suicide.* New York: Basic Books, 1969.
Hentoff, Nat, ed. *Black Anti-Semitism and Jewish Racism.* Woodbury, N.Y.: Barron's Educational Series, 1970.
Hernandez, Lu's F. *The Forgotten American.* New York: Anti-Defamation League, 1969.
Hersey, John. *The Algiers Motel Incident.* New York: Alfred A. Knopf, 1968.
Hewitt, William H., and Charles L. Newman. *Police-Community Relations: An Anthology and a Bibliography.* Mineola, N.Y.: Foundation Press, 1970.
Heyer, Monte. *Am I a Racist?* New York: Association Press, 1970.
Hill, Albert Fay. *The North Avenue Irregulars.* New York: Cowles, 1968.
Hirschi, Travis. *Causes of Delinquency.* Berkeley: University of California Press, 1969.
Hofstadter, Richard, and Michael Wallace, eds. *American Violence: A Documentary History.* New York: Alfred A. Knopf, 1970.
Holcomb, Richard L. *The Police and the Public.* Springfield, Ill.: Charles C. Thomas, 1969.
Hook, Sidney. *Academic Freedom and Academic Anarchy.* New York: Cowles Book, 1969.
Hoover, J. Edgar. *Communism—History and Evaluation in the U.S.* New York: Random House, 1969.
Hormachea, C. R., and M. Hormachea. *Confrontation: Violence and the Police.* Boston: Holbrook Press, (Allyn & Bacon), 1971.
Horwitz, John J. *Team Practice and the Specialist: An Introduction to Interdisciplinary Teamwork.* Springfield, Ill.: Charles C. Thomas, 1970.
Howard, John R., ed. *The Awakening Minorities: American Indians, Mexican-Americans, and Puerto Ricans.* Chicago. Aldine Publishing Co., 1970.
Iannone, Nathan F. *Supervision of Police Personnel.* Englewood Cliffs, N.J.: Prentice-Hall, 1970.
Inbau, Fred E., and James R. Thompson. *Administration of Criminal Justice.* Mineola, New York: Foundation Press, 1970.
Indian Education: A National Tragedy–A National Challenge. Washington, D.C.: U.S. Government Printing Office, 1969.
Institute for the Study of Crime and Delinquency. *The Non-Prison: A New Approach to Treating Youthful Offenders.* St. Paul, Minn.: Bruce Publishing Co., 1970.
Institute for Training in Municipal Administration. *Municipal Police Administration (A Manual),* 6th ed. Washington, D.C.: International City Management Association, 1969.
Institute of Criminal Law and Procedure. *Rehabilitation Planning Services for the Criminal Defense.* Washington, D.C.: U.S. Government Printing Office, 1970.
Institute of Social, Economic and Government Research. *Survey Manual for Comprehensive Urban Planning: The Use of Opinion Surveys and Sampling Tech-*

niques in Planning Process. Fairbanks, Alaska: University of Alaska Press, 1969.

Jackson, Percival E. *Dissent in the Supreme Court*. Norman, Okla.: University of Oklahoma Press, 1969.

Jacobs, Paul. *Prelude to Riot: A View of Urban America From the Bottom*. New York: Random House, 1968.

James, Howard. *Children in Trouble*. New York: David McKay, 1970.

————. *Crisis in the Courts*. New York: David McKay, 1968.

Janowitz, Morris. *Social Control of Escalated Riots*. Chicago: The University of Chicago Center for Policy Study, 1968.

Jemilo, Robert F. *A Ten Point Program on Police-Community Relations: Planned Aggressive Prevention*. Chicago: The Young Men's Christian Association of Metropolitan Chicago, 1966.

Johnson, Elmer Hubert. *Crime, Correction and Society*. rev. ed. Homewood, Ill.: Dorsey Press, 1969.

Johnston, Norman, Leonard Savitz, and Marvin E. Wolfgang, eds. *The Sociology of Punishment & Corrections*. New York: John Wiley & Sons, 1970.

Jordan, Philip D. *Frontier Law and Order*. Lincoln, Neb.: University of Nebraska Press, 1970.

July, Robert W. *A History of the African People*. New York: Charles Scribner's Sons, 1970.

Justice, Blair. *Assessing Potentials for Racial Violence*. Houston: Rice University, 1968.

Kahn, Roger. *The Battle for Morningside Heights: Why Students Rebel*. New York: William Morrow, 1970.

Kain, John F. *Race and Poverty: The Economics of Discrimination*. Englewood Cliffs, N.J.: Prentice-Hall, 1969.

Kavolis, Vytautas. *Comparative Perspectives on Social Problems*. Boston: Little, Brown, 1969.

Kay, Barbara A., and Clyde B. Vedder. *Probation and Parole*. Springfield, Ill.: Charles C. Thomas, 1969.

Keating, Edward M. *Free Huey! The Murder Trial of Black Panther Leader Huey Newton*. New York: E. P. Dutton, 1970.

Keller, Oliver J. Jr., and Benedict S. Alper. *Halfway Houses: Community-Centered Correction and Treatment*. Lexington, Mass.: D.C. Heath, 1970.

Kelman, Steven. *Push Comes to Shove: The Escalation of Student Protest*. Boston: Houghton Mifflin, 1970.

Kenney, John P. *Police Administration*. Springfield, Ill.: Charles C. Thomas, 1972.

Kenney, John P., and Dan G. Pursuit. *Police Work With Juveniles*. Springfield, Ill.: Charles C. Thomas, 1969.

Klein, Herbert T. *The Police: Damned If They Do—Damned If They Don't*. New York: Brown Publishers, 1969.

Klein, Malcolm W., and Barbara G. Myerhoff, eds. *Juvenile Gangs in Context: Theory Research and Action*. Englewood Cliffs, N.J.: Prentice-Hall, 1967.

Klotter, John C. *Constitutional Law for Police*. Cincinnati: W. H. Anderson, 1970.

Knight, Etheridge. *Black Voices From Prison*. New York: Pathfinder Press, 1970.

Knopf, Terry Ann. *Youth Patrols: An Experiment in Community Participation*. Waltham, Mass.: Brandeis University, the Lemberg Center for the Study of Violence, 1969.

Knowles, Louis, and Kenneth Prewitt. *Institutional Racism in America*. Englewood Cliffs, N.J.: Prentice-Hall, 1969.

Knudten, Richard D. and Stephen Schafer. *Juvenile Delinquency: A Reader*. New York: Random House, 1970.

Kobetz, Robert W. *The Police Role and Juvenile Delinquency*. Gaithersberg, Md.: International Association of Chiefs of Police, 1971.

Kruger, Daniel H., and Charles T. Schmidt, Jr. *Collective Bargaining in Public Service*. New York: Random House, 1969.

Kurland, Philip. *The Supreme Court Review 1969* (Decisions of the year with analyses). Chicago: University of Chicago Press, 1970.

Lambert, John R. *Crime, Police and Race Relations*. New York: Oxford University Press, 1970.

Lansberry, J. Robert. *Introduction to Criminal Justice*. Santa Cruz, Calif.: Davis Publishing Co., 1968.

Lasch, Christopher. *The Agony of the American Left—Protest Without A Problem*. New York: Random House, 1969.

Laurence, John. *History of Capital Punishment*. New York: Citadel Press, 1932/1969.

Law Enforcement Assistance Administration, U.S. Department of Justice. *A Look at Criminal Justice Research* (technological). Washington, D.C.: U.S. Government Printing Office, 1971.

Law-Medicine Institute, Boston University. *Police-Community Relations Project*: *Pilot Project*. Boston: Boston University, Law-Medicine Institute, Training Center in Youth Development, 1966.

Lawler, Irvin D. *Training Program in Human Relations for Cadet and In-Service Officers*. Detroit: Detroit Police Department, 1952.

Lecky, Robert S., and H. Elliott Wright. *Black Manifesto*: *Religion, Racism and Reparation*. New York: Sheed & Ward, 1970.

Lee, Alfred McClung, and Norman D. Humphrey. *Race Riot*: *Detroit, 1943*. New York: Octagon, 1968.

LeMelle, Tilden J., and Wilbert J. LeMelle. *The Black College*: *A Strategy for Relevancy*. New York: Praeger, 1969.

Leonard, V. A. *The Police Communications System*. Springfield, Ill.: Charles C. Thomas, 1970.

———. *Police Crime Prevention*. Springfield, Ill.: Charles C. Thomas, 1971.

———. *The Police Enterprise*: *Its Organization and Management*. Springfield, Ill.: Charles C. Thomas, 1969.

———. *The Police, the Judiciary, and the Criminal*. Springfield, Ill.: Charles C. Thomas, 1969.

Lerman, Paul, ed. *Delinquency and Social Policy*. New York: Praeger, 1970.

Liebow, Elliot. *Tally's Corner*: *A Study of Negro Streetcorner Men*. Boston: Little, Brown, 1968.

Lincoln, C. Eric, ed. *Martin Luther King, Jr*. New York: Hill & Wang, 1970.

Lincoln, James. *Anatomy of a Riot*. New York: McGraw-Hill, 1968.

Lindesmith, Alfred R. *The Addict and the Law*. Bloomington, Ind.: Indiana University Press, 1970.

Lipset, Seymour Martin. *Rebellion in the University*. Boston: Little, Brown, 1972.

Lipset, Seymour Martin, and P. G. Altbach, eds. *Students in Revolt*. Boston: Houghton Mifflin, 1970.

Lipsky, Michael, ed. *Law and Order*: *Police Encounters*. Chicago: Aldine, 1970.

Locke, Hubert G. *The Detroit Riot of 1967*. Detroit: Wayne State University Press, 1969.

Lofland, John. *Deviance and Identity*. Englewood Cliffs, N.J.: Prentice-Hall, 1969.

Lohman, Joseph D. *The Police and Minority Groups*. Chicago: Chicago Park Police, 1947.

Lohman, Joseph D., and Gordon E. Misner. *The Police and the Community*: *The Dynamics of Their Relationship in a Changing Society; Field Surveys IV*. Vols. 1, 2. Washington, D.C.: U.S. Government Printing Office, 1967.

Lohman, Joseph D., James T. Carey, Joel Goldfarb, and Michael J. Rowe. *The Handling of Juveniles From Offense to Disposition*. 7 vols. Berkeley, Calif.: University of California School of Criminology, 1965.

London *Times* News Team. *The Black Man In Search of Power.* Camden, N.J.: Thomas Nelson, 1969.

Ludwig, Frederick J. *Supreme Court Decisions and Law Enforcement.* Dobbs Ferry, N.Y.: Oceana Publications, 1969.

Lystad, Mary H. *The College Scene and Changing Social Values.* Morristown, N.J.: General Learning Press, 1972.

Mack, Raymond W. *Prejudice and Race Relations.* Chicago: Quadrangle Books, 1970.

MacNamara, Donal E. *Perspectives on Correction.* New York: Thomas Y. Crowell, 1971.

Mapp, Edward C. *Blacks in American Films: Today and Yesterday.* Metuchen, N.J.: Scarecrow Press, 1972.

Martin, John M., Joseph P. Fitzpatrick and Robert E. Gould. *The Analysis of Delinquent Behavior: A Structural Approach.* New York: Random House, 1970.

Masotti, Louis H. and Don R. Bowen. *Riots and Rebellion: Civil Violence in the Urban Community.* Beverly Hills, Calif.: Sage Publications, 1968.

Masotti, Louis H. and Jerome Corsi. *Shoot-Out in Cleveland: Black Militants and the Police,* July 23, 1968. New York: Praeger, 1969.

Matthiessen, Peter. *Sal Si Puedes: Cesar Chavez and the New American Revolution.* New York: Random House, 1970.

———. *The New American Revolution.* New York: Random House, 1970.

Matza, David. *Becoming Deviant.* Englewood Cliffs, N.J.: Prentice-Hall, 1969.

Maxwell, James A. *Financing State and Local Governments.* Washington, D.C.: Brookings Institution, 1969.

Meier, August, ed. *Black Experience 2: The Transformation of Activism.* Chicago: Aldine, 1970.

Messner, Gerald. *Another View: To Be Black in America.* Chicago: Harcourt, Brace & World, 1970.

Methvin, Eugene H. *The Riot Makers.* New Rochelle, N.Y.: Arlington House, 1970.

Meyerson, Martin, ed. *The Conscience of the City.* New York: George Braziller, 1970.

Middleton, John. *Black Africa: Its People and Cultures Today.* New York: Macmillan, 1970.

Milio, Nancy. *9226 Kercheval: The Storefront That Did Not Burn.* Ann Arbor, Mich.: University of Michigan Press, 1970.

Miller, Derek. *Growth to Freedom: The Psychological Treatment of Delinquent Youth.* Bloomington, Ind.: Indiana University Press, 1970.

Miller, Kelly. *Radicals and Conservatives and Others on the Negro in America.* New York: Schocken Books, 1970.

Milner, Neal A. *The Court and Law Enforcement: The Impact of Miranda.* Beverly Hills, Calif.: Sage Publications, 1971.

Minton, Robert J. *Inside: Prison American Style.* New York: Random House, 1971.

Mitchell, J. Paul. *Race Riots in Black and White.* Englewood Cliffs, N.J.: Prentice-Hall, 1970.

Momboisse, Raymond M. *Blueprint of Revolution: The Rebel, The Party, the Techniques of Revolt.* Springfield, Ill.: Charles C. Thomas, 1970.

———. *Community Relations and Riot Prevention.* Springfield, Ill.: Charles C. Thomas, 1970.

———. *Riots, Revolts and Insurrections.* Springfield, Ill.: Charles C. Thomas, 1970.

Moore, Chuck (As told to). *I Was a Black Panther.* New York: Doubleday & Co., 1970.

Morgan, John S. *The Negro Breakthrough.* New York: Macmillan, 1970.

Morison, Samuel Eliot, Frederick Merk, and Frank Freidel. *Dissent in Three American Wars.* Cambridge, Mass.: Harvard University Press, 1970.

Morris, Joe Alex. *First Offender: A Volunteer Program for Youth in Trouble With the Law.* New York: Funk & Wagnalls, 1970.

Morris, Norval, and Gordon Hawkins. *The Honest Politician's Guide to Crime Control.* Chicago: University of Chicago Press, 1970.

Moynihan, Daniel Patrick. *Maximum Feasible Misunderstanding: Community Action in the War on Poverty.* New York: Free Press, 1969.

―――. *Toward a National Urban Policy.* New York: Basic Books, 1970.

―――. *Violent Crime: The Challenge to Our Cities. The Report of the National Commission on the Causes and Prevention of Violence.* New York: George Braziller, 1970.

Murphy, Thomas P., and F. Gerald Brown. *Emerging Patterns in Urban Administration.* Lexington, Mass.: Heath Lexington Books, D. C. Heath Co., 1970.

Murray, Albert. *The Omni-Americans: New Perspectives on Black Experience and American Culture.* New York: E. P. Dutton, 1970.

Murton, Thomas, and Joseph Hyams. *Accomplices to the Crime: The Arkansas Prison Scandal.* New York: Grove Press, 1969.

Muse, Benjamin. *The American Negro Revolution: From Non-Violence to Black Power 1963–1967.* Bloomington, Ind.: Indiana University Press, 1970.

Mushkin, Selma J., and John F. Cotton. *Sharing Federal Funds for State and Local Needs: Grants-in-Aid and PPB Systems.* New York: Praeger, 1970.

McCord, William, et al. *Life Styles in the Black Ghetto.* New York: W. W. Norton, 1969.

McLennan, Barbara N. *Crime in Urban Society.* New York: Dunellen, 1970.

McPherson, James Alan. *Hue and Cry.* New York: Fawcett World Library, 1970.

National Advisory Commission on Civil Disorders. *Report* (A Bantam Book: QZ4273). New York: New York *Times* Company, 1968.

National Advisory Council on Economic Opportunity. *Continuity and Changes in Anti-Poverty Programs.* Washington, D.C.: U.S. Government Printing Office, 1969.

National Center on Police and Community Relations of the School of Police Administration and Public Safety, Michigan State University. *A National Survey of Police and Community Relations—Field Surveys V.* Washington, D.C.: U.S. Government Printing Office, 1967.

National Commission on Causes and Prevention of Violence. See under U.S. listings.

National Commission on Reform of Federal Criminal Laws. *Final Report: A Proposed New Federal Criminal Code* (Title 18, United States Code). Washington, D.C.: U.S. Government Printing Office, 1971.

National Council on Crime and Delinquency. *Juvenile Justice Confounded: Pretentions and Realities of Treatment Services.* Paramus, N.J.: National Council on Crime and Delinquency, 1972.

National Criminal Justice Reference Service. *LEAA Reference List of Publications* (free) Washington, D.C.: U.S. Department of Justice, 633 Indiana Avenue, Washington, D.C. 20530, 1971.

National Institute of Mental Health. See under U.S., Department of Health, Education, and Welfare.

National Institute of Law Enforcement and Criminal Justice, U.S. Department of Justice, LEAA. *Police Training and Performance Study.* Washington, D.C.: U.S. Government Printing Office, 1970.

National School of Public Relations Association. *Black Studies in Schools,* no. 2. Washington, D.C.: National Education Association, 1970.

Nearing, Scott, *Black America.* New York: Schocken Books, 1970.

Negro and the City: Adapted From a Special Issue of Fortune On: "Business and the Urban Crisis." New York: Time–Life Books, 1968.

Neighborhood Youth Corps. Washington, D.C.: U.S. Government Printing Office, 1969.

New Jersey. *Governor's Select Commission on Civil Disorder: Report for Action.* Trenton, N.J., 1968.

Newman, Charles L. *Personnel Practices in Adult Parole Systems.* Springfield, Ill.: Charles C. Thomas, 1971.

Niederhoffer, Arthur, and Abraham S. Blumberg. *The Ambivalent Force: Perspectives on the Police.* Waltham, Mass.: Ginn & Co., 1970

Nielsen, Swven C. *General Organizational and Administrative Concepts for University Police.* Springfield, Ill.: Charles C. Thomas, 1971.

Ng, Larry, ed. *Alternatives to Violence: A Stimulus to Dialogue.* New York: Time-Life Books, 1968.

Norrgard, David L. *Regional Law Enforcement.* Chicago: Public Administration Service, 1969.

O'Connor, George W., and Nelson A. Watson. *Juvenile Delinquency and Youth Crime, the Police Role. An Analysis of: Philosophy, Policy, Opinion.* Gaithersberg, Md: International Association of Chiefs of Police, 1965.

Olson, Bruce. *Regional Law Enforcement Training.* Detroit: Metropolitan Fund, 1968.

O'Neill, William L., ed. *American Society Since 1945.* Chicago: Quadrangle Books, 1970.

Operation Open City, New York Urban League. *Enforcing Open Housing.* New York: Friends of Operation Open City, 1970.

Oppenheimer, Martin. *The Urban Guerilla.* Chicago: Quadrangle Books, 1970.

Oppenheimer, Martin, and George Lakey. *A Manual for Direct Action.* Chicago: Quadrangle Books, 1969.

Ornati, Oscar A. *Transportation Needs of the Poor—A Case Study of New York City.* New York: Praeger, 1970.

Ovington, Mary White. *Half A Man: The Status of a Negro in New York.* New York: Schocken Books, 1970.

Packer, Herbert S. *The Limits of the Criminal Sanction,* Stanford, Calif.: Stanford University Press, 1968.

Patrick, Clarence H. *The Police, Crime and Society.* Springfield, Ill.: Charles C. Thomas, 1971.

Paynton, Clifford E. and Robert Blackey. *Why Revolution?* Morristown, N.J.: General Learning Press, 1971.

People of Watts. *The Aftermath.* New York: Grove Press, 1969.

Perkins, Rollin M. *Criminal Law.* 2d ed. Mineola, New York: Foundation Press, 1969.

Perlman, Harvey S., and Thomas Allington. *The Tasks of Penology: A Symposium on Prisons and Correctional Law.* Lincoln, Nebraska: University of Nebraska Press, 1969.

Perucci, Robert. *The Triple Revolution: Social Problems in Depth.* Boston: Little, Brown, 1969.

Petroni, Frank A., Ernest A. Hirsch, and Lillian Petroni. *Two, Four, Six, Eight, When You Gonna Integrate?* New York: Behavioral Publications, 1971.

Pickett, Robert S. *House of Refuge.* Syracuse, N.Y.: Syracuse University Press, 1969.

Pilisuk, Marc, ed. *Poor Americans: How the Poor White Live.* Chicago: Aldine, 1970.

Police and the Civil Rights Acts. Gaithersberg, Md.: International Association of Chiefs of Police, 1965.

Police, the Community, and You. Washington, D.C.: Women's International League for Peace and Freedom, 120 Maryland Avenue, N.E., 20002, 1968.

Poston, Richard W. *The Gang and the Establishment.* New York: Harper & Row, 1971.

President's Commission on Law Enforcement and Administration of Justice; Prepared by The Institute for Defense Analyses. *Task Force Report: Science and Technology.* Washington D.C.: U.S. Government Printing Office, 1967.

President's Commission on Law Enforcement and Administration of Justice. *Task Force Report: The Police.* Washington, D.C.: U.S. Government Printing Office, 1967.

President's Council on Youth Opportunity. *Manual for Youth Coordinators.* Washington, D.C.: U.S. Government Printing Office, 1969.

President's Task Force on Prisoner Rehabilitation. *The Criminal Offender—What Should Be Done?* Washington, D.C.: U.S. Government Printing Office, 1970.

Probation/Parole, vol. 1. Washington, D.C.: U.S. Government Printing Office, 1969.

Puzo, Mario. *The Godfather.* New York: Fawcett World Library, 1970.

Quinney, Richard. *Crime and Justice in Society.* Boston: Little, Brown, 1969.

————. *The Social Reality of Crime.* Boston: Little, Brown, 1970.

Radano, Gene. *Walking the Beat.* Cleveland: World Publishing Co., 1968.

Radzinowicz, Sir Leon and Marvin E. Wolfgang, eds. *Crime and Justice.* 3 vols. New York: Basic Books, 1972.

Rainwater, Lee. *Behind Ghetto Walls: Black Family Life in a Federal Slum.* Chicago: Aldine, 1970.

Rainwater, Lee, ed. *Black Experience I: Soul.* Chicago: Aldine, 1970.

Rapoport, Roger, and Laurence J. Kirshbaum. *Is the Library Burning?* New York: Random House, 1970.

Rathbone, Josephine L., and Carol Lucas. *Recreation in Total Rehabilitation.* Springfield, Ill.: Charles C. Thomas, 1970.

Reasons, Charles E. and Jack L. Kuykendall, eds. *Race, Crime and Justice.* Pacific Palisades, Calif.: Goodyear, 1972.

Reid, Tim, and Julyan Reid, eds. *Student Power and the Canadian Campus.* Toronto: Peter Martin Associates, 1970.

Reich, Charles A. *The Greening of America.* New York: Random House, 1970.

Reiss, Albert J., Jr. *The Police and the Public.* New Haven: Yale University Press, 1971.

————. *Studies in Crime and Law Enforcement in Major Metropolitan Areas.* vols. 1 and 2, *Field Surveys III.* Washington, D.C.: U.S. Government Printing Office, 1967.

Report (and Appendix) of the President's Commission on Crime in the District of Columbia. Washington, D.C.: U.S. Government Printing Office, 1966.

Report of the Advisory Panel Against Armed Violence. Washington, D.C.: U.S. Government Printing Office, 1969.

Report of the National Advisory Commission on Civil Disorders. Washington, D.C.: U.S. Government Printing Office, 1968.

Richette, Lisa A. *The Throwaway Children.* Philadelphia: J. R. Lippincott, 1968.

Roberts, Albert R. *Sourcebook on Prison Education: Past, Present and Future.* Springfield, Ill.: Charles C. Thomas, 1971.

Robinson, Armstead L., Craig C. Foster, and Donald H. Ogilvie. *Black Studies in the University: A symposium.* New Haven: Yale University Press, 1970.

Rogan, Donald L. *Campus Apocalypse: The Student Search Today.* New York: Seabury Press, 1970.

Rolph, C. H. *Law and the Common Man.* Springfield, Ill.: Charles C. Thomas, 1968.

Rose, Thomas. *Violence in America.* New York: Random House, 1969.

Rosenquist, Carl M. and Edwin I. Megargee. *Delinquency in Three Cultures.* Austin, Texas: University of Texas Press, 1969.

Ross, H. Lawrence. *Settled Out of Court.* Chicago: Aldine, 1970.

Risso, Peter H., ed. *Ghetto Revolts.* Chicago: Aldine, 1970.

Rubin, Jerry, *Do It!* New York: Simon & Schuster, 1970.

Rubin, Sol. *Crime and Juvenile Delinquency.* 3d ed. Dobbs Ferry, N.Y.: Oceana Publications, 1970.

Rubin, Ted. *Law as an Agent of Delinquency Prevention.* Washington, D.C.: U.S. Government Printing Office, 1971.

Rubington, Earl and Martin S. Weinberg. *Deviance: The Interactionist Perspective.* New York: Macmillan, 1968.

Saint Louis Council on Police-Community Relations. *Police Community Relations 1966–1967 Program.* Saint Louis: Saint Louis Metropolitan Police Department, 1967.

Sanders, Marion K. *The Professional Radical: Conversations With Saul Alinsky.* New York: Harper & Row, 1970.

Saunders, Charles B., Jr. *Police Education and Training: Key to Better Law Enforcement.* Washington, D.C.: Brookings Institution, 1970.

Saunders, Charles B. *Upgrading the American Police.* Washington, D.C.: Brookings Institution, 1970.

Sauter, Van Gordon and Burleigh Hines. *Nightmare in Detroit: A Rebellion and Its Victims.* Chicago: Henry Regnery, 1968.

Sayler, Richard H., Barry B. Bayer, and Robert E. Gooding, Jr., eds. *The Warren Court.* New York: Chelsea House, 1969.

Scammon, Richard M., and Ben J. Wattenberg. *The Real Majority.* New York: Coward-McCann, 1970.

Schafer, Stephen. *Compensation and Restitution to Victims of Crime.* rev. Montclair, N.J.: Patterson Smith, 1970.

————. *Juvenile Delinquency: An Introduction.* New York: Random House, 1970.

Schanche, Don A. *The Panther Paradox: A Liberal's Dilemma.* New York: David McKay, 1970.

Schlesinger, Arthur M., Jr. *The Crisis in Confidence: Ideas, Power and Violence in America.* Boston: Houghton Mifflin, 1969.

Schreiber, Flora Rheta. *A Job With a Future in Law Enforcement and Related Fields.* New York: Grosset & Dunlap, 1970.

Schuchter, Arnold. *Reparations: The Black Manifesto and Its Challenge to White America.* Philadelphia: Lippincott, 1970.

Schultz, John. *No One Was Killed: Documentation and Meditation: Convention Week, Chicago—August 1968.* Chicago: Big Table Publishers, 1969.

Schur, Edwin M. *Narcotic Addiction in Britain and America.* Bloomington, Ind.: Indiana University Press, 1970.

————. *Our Criminal Society: The Social and Legal Sources of Crime in America.* Englewood Cliffs, N.J.: Prentice-Hall, 1969.

Schwab, Joseph J. *College Curriculum and Student Protest.* Chicago: University of Chicago Press, 1970.

Schwartz, Louis B., and S. R. Goldstein. *Law Enforcement Handbook for Police.* Saint Paul, Minn.: West Publishing Co., 1970.

Schwartz, Richard D. and Jerome H. Skolnik. *Society and the Legal Order.* New York: Basic Books, 1970.

Scott, Benjamin. *The Coming of the Black Man: Manifesto on Black Power.* Boston: Beacon Press, 1969.

Sears, David O. *The Politics of Violence: The New Urban Black Man and the Watts Riot.* Boston: Houghton Mifflin, 1970.

Select Committee on Crime, U.S. House of Representatives. *Juvenile Justice and Corrections.* Washington, D.C.: U.S. Government Printing Office, 1971.

Seligman, Ben B. *Permanent Poverty.* Chicago: Quadrangle Books, 1970.

Selznick, Gertrude J., and Stephen Steinberg. *The Tenacity of Prejudice: Anti-Semitism in Contemporary America.* New York: Harper & Row, 1969.

Servin, Manuel. *The Mexican-Americans: An Awakening Minority*. New York: Macmillan, 1970.

Shaw, Clifford, and Henry D. McKay. *Juvenile Delinquency and Urban Areas: A Study of Rates of Delinquency In Relation to Differential Characteristics of Local Communities and American Cities*. rev. Chicago: University of Chicago Press, 1969.

Shapiro, Martin M., ed. *The Supreme Court and Public Policy*. Glenview, Ill.: Scott, Foresman, 1969.

Sheldon, Charles. *The Supreme Court: Politicians in Robes*. New York: Macmillan, 1970.

Shepard, Harold L., ed. *Poverty and Wealth In America*. Chicago: Quadrangle Books, 1970.

Shepardson, Mary, and Blodwen Hammond. *The Navajo Mountain Community*. Berkeley, Calif.: University of California Press, 1970.

Sherwood, Norman. *The Youth Service Bureau: A Key to Delinquency Prevention*. Paramus, N.J.: National Council on Crime and Delinquency, 1972.

Shiloh, Ailon. *Studies in Human Sexual Behavior: The American Scene*. Springfield, Ill.: Charles C. Thomas, 1970.

Short, James F., Jr., ed. *Modern Criminals*. Chicago: Aldine, 1970.

Sinclair, Ian. *Hostels for Probationers*. London: Her Majesty's Stationery Office, 1971.

Skolnick, Jerome H. *Justice Without Trial: Law Enforcement in Democratic Society*. New York: John Wiley & Sons, 1966.

————. *Professional Police in a Free Society*. New York: National Conference of Christians and Jews, 1968.

Skolnick, Jerome and Elliott Currie. *Crisis in American Institutions*. Boston: Little, Brown, 1970.

Slough, M. C. *Privacy, Freedom and Responsibility*. Springfield, Ill.: Charles C. Thomas, 1969.

Smith, Alexander B. and Harriet Pollack. *Crime and Justice in a Mass Society*. Waltham, Mass.: Xerox College Publishing Corp., 1972.

Smith, R. Dean, and Richard Kobetz. *Guidelines for Civil Disorder and Mobilization Planning: Prepared for the President's Advisory Commission on Civil Disorders*. Gaithersberg, Md.: International Association of Chiefs of Police, Research, Development, and Planning Division, 1968.

Solomon, Arthur, Perry Steven, and Robert Devine. *Interpersonal Communication: Cross Disciplinary Approach*. Springfield, Ill.: Charles C. Thomas, 1970.

Spender, Stephen. *Year of the Young Rebels*. New York: Random House, 1969.

Spiegel, John P. *The Tradition of Violence in Our Society*. Waltham, Mass.: Lemberg Center for the Study of Violence, Brandeis University, 1968.

Stavis, Barrie. *John Brown: The Sword and the Word*. Cranbury, N.J.: A. S. Barnes & Co., 1970.

Stein, David Lewis. *Living the Revolution: The Yippies in Chicago*. Indianapolis, Ind.: Bobbs-Merrill, 1969.

Steiner, Stan. *La Raza: The Mexican Americans*. New York: Harper & Row, 1970.

————. *The New Indians*. New York: Dell, 1969.

Steinfield, Melvin. *Cracks in the Melting Pot: Readings in Racism and Discrimination in American History*. New York: Macmillan, 1970.

Sterling, James W. *Changes in Role Concept of Police Officers*. Gaithersberg, Md.: International Association of Chiefs of Police, Research, Development and Planning Division, 1968.

Stone, Chuck. *Black Political Power in America*. New York: Bobbs-Merrill, 1969.

Stratton, John R., and Robert M. Terry. *Prevention of Delinquency: Problems and Programs*. New York: Macmillan, 1968.

Strecher, Victor G. *The Environment of Law Enforcement: A Community Relations Guide*. Englewood Cliffs, N.J.: Prentice-Hall, 1971.

Supplemental Studies for the National Advisory Commission on Civil Disorders. Washington, D.C.: U.S. Government Printing Office, 1968.

Susman, Jackwell, ed. *Crime and Justice 1970–1971*. New York: 56 E. 13th St., New York 10003: AMS Press, 1972.

Sutherland, Edwin H., and Donald R. Cressey. *Principles of Criminology*. 8th ed. Philadelphia: Lippincott, 1970.

Suttles, Gerald D. *The Social Order of the Slum: Ethnicity and Territory in the Inner City*. Chicago: University of Chicago Press, 1968.

Sykes, Gresham M. and Thomas E. Drabek. *Law and the Lawless: A Reader in Criminology*. New York: Random House, 1969.

Szurek, S. A., and I. N. Berlin, eds. *The Antisocial Child: His Family and His Community*. Palo Alto, Calif.: Science and Behavior Books, 1970.

Taylor, Karl K., and Fred W. Soady, Jr., eds. *Violence: An Element of American Life*. Boston: Holbrook Press, 1972.

Terry, Robert W. *For Whites Only*. Grand Rapids, Mich.: William E. Eerdmans, 1970.

Thurow, Lester C. *Poverty and Discrimination*. Washington, D.C.: Brookings Institution, 1969.

Toch, Hans H. *Violent Men: An Inquiry Into the Psychology of Violence*. Chicago: Aldine, 1969.

Towler, Juby E. *The Police Role in Racial Conflicts*. 2d ed. Springfield, Ill.: Charles C. Thomas, 1969.

Treanor, Gerald F. Jr. *Riots and Municipalities*. Report no. 152. Washington, D.C.: National Institute of Municipal Law Officers, 1968.

Tresolini, Roco J., and Martin Shapiro. *American Constitutional Law*. rev. New York: Macmillan, 1970.

Trubowitz, Julius. *Changing the Racial Attitudes of Children—The Effects of an Activity Group Program in New York City Schools*. New York: Praeger, 1969.

Tucker, Sterling. *Beyond the Burning: Life and Death of the Ghetto*. New York: Association Press, 1970.

————. *Black Reflections on White Power*. Grand Rapids, Mich.: William B. Eerdmans, 1969.

Tumin, Melvin M. *Comparative Perspectives on Race Relations*. Boston: Little, Brown, 1969.

————. *Research Annual on Intergroup Relations—1970*. Chicago: Quadrangle Books, 1970.

Turk, Austin. *Criminality: A Sociological Perspective*. Chicago: Rand McNally, 1969.

Turner, Kenneth A. *Juvenile Justice: Juvenile Court Problems, Procedures and Practices in Tennessee*. Charlottesville, Va.: Michie, 1969.

Turner, William W. *The Police Establishment*. New York: G. P. Putnam's Sons, 1968.

Tussman, Joseph. *Experiment at Berkeley*. New York: Oxford University Press, 1969.

Ulmer, S. Sidney. *Military Justice and the Right to Counsel*. Lexington, Ky.: University of Kentucky Press, 1970.

Urban Outlook, Bibliography of Films, Filmstrips, Etc. Washington, D.C.: U.S. Government Printing Office, 1969.

U.S., Advisory Panel Against Armed Violence. *Report of the Advisory Panel Against Armed Violence*. Washington, D.C.: U.S. Government Printing Office, 1969.

U.S., Commission on Civil Rights. Reports listed are available from the U.S. Government Printing Office, Washington, D.C.

Racism in America and How to Combat It, 1970.

The Unfinished Education: Outcomes for Minorities in Five Southwestern States. Mexican-American Education Series Report 2, 1971.

U.S., Commission on Human Rights. *To Continue Action for Human Rights: Federal Report.* Washington, D.C.: U.S. Government Printing Office, 1969.

U.S., Congress. House. Select Committee on Crime. *Juvenile Justice and Corrections.* Washington, D.C.: U.S. Government Printing Office, 1971.

U.S., Congress, Senate. Committee on Labor and Public Welfare. *Indian Education: A National Tragedy—A National Challenge.* Washington, D.C.: U.S. Government Printing Office, 1969.

U.S., Department of Health, Education, and Welfare. National Institute of Mental Health. Reports listed are available from U.S. Government Printing Office, Washington, D.C.

Civil Commitment of Special Categories of Offenders. Public Health Service Publication no. 2131, 1971.

Community-Based Correctional Programs: Models and Practices. Public Health Service Publication no. 2130, 1971.

Diversion From the Criminal Justice System. Public Health Service Publication no. 2129, 1971.

Graduated Release. Public Health Service Publication no. 2128, 1971.

The Juvenile Court: A Status Report. Public Health Service Publication no. 2132, 1971.

U.S., Department of Housing and Urban Development. *The Model Cities Program: A History and Analysis of the Planning Process in Three Cities: Atlanta, Ga.; Seattle, Wash.; Dayton, Ohio.* Washington, D.C.: U.S. Government Printing Office, 1969.

U.S., Department of Justice. Reports listed are available from U.S. Government Printing Office, Washington, D.C.

Psychological Assessment of Patrolman's Qualifications in Relation to Field Performance. Report Prepared by Melanie E. Baehr, John E. Furcon, and Ernest C. Froemel, Industrial Relations Center, University of Chicago, for the Office of Law Enforcement Assistance, November 1968.

Correctional Institutions, vol. 2, 1969.

A Look at Criminal Justice Research (Technological). Law Enforcement Assistance Administration, 1971.

Police Training and Performance Study, PR 70-4. National Institute of Law Enforcement and Criminal Justice, Law Enforcement Administration, 1971.

U.S., National Advisory Commission on Civil Disorders. Reports listed are available from U.S. Government Printing Office, Washington, D.C.

Report of the National Advisory Commission on Civil Disorders, 1968. (Kerner Report.)

Supplemental Studies for the National Advisory Commission on Civil Disorders, 1968.

U.S., National Advisory Council on Economic Opportunity. *Continuity and Changes in Anti-Poverty Programs.* Washington, D.C.: U.S. Government Printing Office, 1969.

U.S., National Commission on Causes and Prevention of Violence. Reports listed are available from U.S. Government Printing Office, Washington, D.C.

Assassination and Political Violence, 1969.

Criminal Justice, 1969.

Mass Media and Violence, 1969.

Miami Report, 1969.

Political Assassination, 1969.

The Politics of Protest: Violent Aspects of Protest and Confrontation, 1969.

Progress Report of the National Commission on the Causes and Prevention of Violence, 1969.

Rights in Concord: The Response to the Counter-Inaugural Protest Activities in Washington, D.C., 1969.

Shoot-out in Cleveland, 1969.

Shut It Down! A College Crisis (San Francisco State College, October 1968– April 1969), 1969.

To Establish Justice, To Insure Domestic Tranquillity, 1969.

Violence in America: Historical and Comparative Perspectives, vols. 1 and 2, 1969.

U.S., National Commission on Reform of Federal Criminal Laws. *Final Report: A Proposed New Federal Criminal Code* (Title 18, United States Code). Washington, D.C.: U.S. Government Printing Office, 1971.

U.S., President's Commission on Crime in the District of Columbia. *Report of the President's Commission on Crime in the District of Columbia.* Washington, D.C.: U.S. Government Printing Office, 1966.

U.S., President's Commission on Law Enforcement and Administration of Justice. Reports listed are available from U.S. Government Printing Office, Washington, D.C.

Challenge of Crime in a Free Society, 1967.

Field Surveys IV. The Police and the Community: The Dynamics of their Relationship in a Changing Society, 1967.

Field Surveys V. A National Survey of Police and Community Relations, 1967.

Task Force Report: The Police, 1967.

Task Force Report: Science and Technology, 1967.

U.S., President's Council on Youth Opportunity. *Manual for Youth Coordinators.* Washington, D.C.: U.S. Government Printing Office, 1969.

U.S., President's Task Force on Prisoner Rehabilitation. *The Criminal Offender— What Should Be Done?* Washington, D.C.: U.S. Government Printing Office, 1970.

U.S. News and World Reports. *Communism and the New Left.* Washington, D.C.: Books by U.S. News and World Reports, Inc., 1969.

Vedder, Clyde B. *Juvenile Offenders.* Springfield, Ill.: Charles C. Thomas, 1969.

Vedder, Clyde B., and Barbara A. Kay. *Penology.* Springfield, Ill.: Charles C. Thomas, 1969.

Vedder, Clyde B., and Dora B. Somerville. *The Delinquent Girl.* Springfield, Ill.: Charles C. Thomas, 1970.

Vietroisz, Thomas, and Bennett Harrison. *The Economic Development of Harlem.* New York: Praeger, 1970.

Von Hoffman, Nicholas. *We Are The People Our Parents Warned Us Against.* New York: Fawcett World Library, 1969.

Voss, Harwin L. *Reader in Juvenile Delinquency.* Boston: Little, Brown, 1970.

Wade, Richard C., et al. *Urban Violence.* Chicago: Center for Policy Study, University of Chicago, 1969.

Wagstaff, Thomas. *Black Power: The Radical Response to White America.* Beverly Hills, Calif.: Glencoe Press, 1969.

Walker, Daniel. *Rights in Conflict: The Violent Confrontation of Demonstrators and Police in the Parks and Streets of Chicago During the Week of the Democratic National Convention of 1968.* New York: Bantam Books, 1968.

Wambaugh, Joseph. *The New Centurions:* A novel about police work as an intimate social function. Boston: Little, Brown, 1970.

———. *The Blue Knight.* Boston: Little, Brown, 1972.

Wasserman, Miriam. *The School Fix, N.Y.C., U.S.A.* New York: E. P. Dutton, 1970.

Watson, Nelson A. *Attitudes—A Factor in Performance*. Gaithersberg, Md.: International Association of Chiefs of Police, Research, Development and Planning Division, 1968.

―――. *Human Relations Training for Police: A Syllabus*. Gaithersberg, Md.: International Association of Chiefs of Police, Research and Development Division, 1968.

―――. *Improving the Officer-Citizen Contact*. Gaithersberg, Md.: International Association of Chiefs of Police, Research, Development and Planning Division, 1968.

―――. *Issues in Human Relations: Threats and Challenges*. Gaithersberg, Md.: International Association of Chiefs of Police, Research, Development and Planning Division, 1969.

―――. *Police-Community Relations*. Gaithersberg, Md.: International Association of Chiefs of Police, Research, Development and Planning Division, 1966.

―――. *Police Procedures in the Handling of Juveniles*. Address before the American Bar Association, Family Law Annual Meeting, 1966.

―――. ed. *Police and the Changing Community: Selected Readings*. Gaithersberg, Md.: International Association of Chiefs of Police, Research, Development and Planning Division, 1965.

Watson, Nelson A., and Robert N. Walker, eds. *Juvenile Delinquency in Police Education: Proceedings of Workshop for Police Professors, Michigan State University, 1966*. Gaithersberg, Md.: International Association of Chiefs of Police, 1966.

We the Black People of the United States. Washington, D.C.: U.S. Government Printing Office, 1969.

Weaver, James, and Gary Weaver, eds. *The University and Revolution*. Englewood Cliffs, N.J.: Prentice-Hall, 1969.

Weinreb, Lloyd L. *Criminal Law: Cases, Comments, Questions*. Mineola, N.Y.: Foundation Press, 1969.

Weinstein, Allen, and Frank Orro Gatell. *The Segregation Era: 1863–1954*. New York: Oxford University Press, 1970.

Weinstein, James, and David W. Eakins. *For a New America*. New York: Random House, 1970.

Wells, Ida B. *Crusade for Justice*. Chicago: University of Chicago Press, 1970.

Westley, William A. *Violence and the Police*. Cambridge, Mass.: M.I.T. Press, 1970.

Wheeler, Stanton, ed. *Controlling Delinquents*. New York: John Wiley & Sons, 1968.

Whisenand, Paul M. *Police Supervision: Theory and Practice*. Englewood Cliffs, N.J.: Prentice-Hall, 1971.

Whitehead, Donn. *Attack on Terror: The FBI Against the Ku Klux Klan in Mississippi*. New York: Funk & Wagnalls, 1970.

Whittemore, L. H. *Cop*. New York: Fawcett World Library, 1970.

Who Will Listen If You Have a Civil Rights Complaint? Washington, D.C.: U.S. Government Printing Office, 1969.

Wilkins, Leslie T. *Evaluation of Penal Measures*. New York: Random House, 1969.

Wilson, James Q. *City Politics and Public Policy*. New York: John Wiley & Sons, 1968.

―――. *Varieties of Police Behavior: The Management of Law and Order in Eight Communities*. Cambridge, Mass.: Harvard University Press, 1968.

―――. ed. *The Metropolitan Enigma*. Garden City, N.Y.: Doubleday & Co., 1970.

Wittenborn, J. R., Henry Brill, and Sarah A. Wittenborn. *Drugs and Youth: Proceedings of the Rutgers Symposium on Drug Abuse*. Springfield, Ill.: Charles C. Thomas, 1969.

Wolf, Kurt. *Patterns of Self Destruction: Depression and Suicide*. Springfield, Ill.: Charles C. Thomas, 1970.

Wolfgang, Marvin E. *The Culture of Youth*. Washington, D.C.: U.S. Government Printing Office, 1968.

Wolfgang, Marvin E., and Bernard Cohen. *Crime and Race*. Rev. New York: Institute of Human Relations Press, The American Jewish Committee, 165 E. 56th St., 1970.

Wood, Forrest G. *Black Scare: The White Racist Response to Emancipation and Reconstruction*. Berkeley, Calif.: University of California Press, 1970.

Wright, R. Gene, and John A. Marlo. *The Police Officer and Criminal Justice*. New York: McGraw-Hill, 1970.

Yablonsky, Lewis. *The Hippie Trip*. New York: Pegasus Publishing Co., 1969.

Young, Whitney. *Beyond Racism: Building an Open Society*. New York: McGraw-Hill, 1970.

Yuan, D. Y. *The Chinese-American Population: A Study of Voluntary Segregation*. Morristown, N.J.: General Learning Press, 1972.

Zarr, Melvyn. *The Bill of Rights and the Police*. Dobbs Ferry, N.Y.: Oceana Publications, 1970.

Zimmerman, Joseph F. *Subnational Politics: Reading in State and Local Government*. 2d. ed. New York: Holt, Rinehart & Winston, 1970.

Zinn, Howard. *The Politics of History*. Boston: Beacon Press, 1970.

Zuk, Gerald H. *Family Therapy*. New York: Behavioral Publications, 1972.

Index

Name Index

A

Abernathy, Ralph, 140
Agnew, Spiro T., 142
Ali, Muhammed (Clay), 141
Alinsky, Saul, 142
Allen, Francis, 240
Allman, James J., 293
Allport, Gordon, 92, 97
Anderson, Donald, 177 ff.
Anderson, Marian, 134
Andreotti, Dante, 29, 30
Angell, John, 319, 323
Anthony, Mark, 276
Attucks, Crispus, 133
Augustus, John, 187

B

Baddeley, Fred, 183, 184
Bainbridge, John, 352, 353
Baldwin, James, 27
Banton, Michael, 54
Bard, Morton, 282
Becker, Howard S., 55
Benne, Kenneth, 277
Benny, Jack, 94
Biderman, Albert, 19
Bimstein, Donald, 279

Birnbaum, Max, 277, 280
Black, Algernon D., 214
Black, Hugo, 197, 198
Blau, Peter M., 54
Blythin, Edward, 200, 202
Bordua, David, 55, 119
Bouma, Donald H., 153
Bradford, Leland, 277
Brandstatter, A. F., 184
Bridges, Harry, 197
Brimmer, Andrew F., 107
Brooke, Edward, 133, 140
Broomfield, Tyree, 319
Brown, Claude, 119
Brown, H. Rap, 134, 136
Brown, John, 133
Brown, Michael K., 338
Buchwald, Art, 80 ff.
Buckley, William, 63
Bunche, Ralph, 134
Burnett, William H., 193

C

Cade, Alex J., 224 ff.
Cahill, Thomas, 28, 30
Cantril, Hadley, 77
Carmack, William R., 76
Carmichael, Stokely, 134, 140

Carocas, Harvey, 323
Carver, George Washington, 133
Cassese, John, 220
Catledge, Turner, 195
Chavez, Cesar, 244
Chisholm, Shirley, 140
Clark, John P., 54
Clark, Mark, 138
Clark, Tom C., 201
Clayton, James E., 154
Cleaver, Eldridge, 134–143, 227
Coolidge, Calvin John, 17, 213, 222
Craft, Carl C., 278
Cray, Ed, 213, 218, 219

D

Daniel, Clifton, 210
Davis, Angela, 136
Davis, J. C., 51
Dewey, Thomas E., 63

E

Ehrlich, Howard J., 51, 55
Eisenberg, Terry, 312, 317
Eldefonso, Edward, 153
Emerson, Ralph Waldo, 276
Ennis, Philip, 20
Estes, Billy Sol, 200
Evers, Charles, 140

F

Fanon, Frantz, 144
Farmer, James, 133
Fisk, James G., 333
Forman, James, 133
Fosen, Robert H., 317
Frankfurter, Felix, 199
Fredericks, Frederick, 147, 149
Freud, Sigmund, 54
Friendly, Alfred, 205
Fromm, Eric, 228, 230
Fuld, Stanley H., 210, 211

G

Gain, Charles R., 281
Galvin, Raymond, 281
Gard, Spencer A., 208
Garmire, Bernard, 290, 292
Garvey, Marcus, 133, 134
Gellhorn, Walter, 146
Gerber, Samuel, 201

Gilmore, Horace W., 260, 262
Glickman, Albert S., 317
Glueck, Eleanor, 184
Glueck, Sheldon, 184
Goebbels, Joseph, 95
Goldberg, William A., 224 ff.
Goldfarb, Ronald, 205
Gold, Martin, 183
Goldwater, Barry, 63
Golenpaul, Dan, 136
Gompers, Samuel, 213
Gorer, Geoffrey, 54
Gramont, Sanche, 138
Grande, Carm J., 274
Greeley, Horace, 212

H

Hampton, Fred, 138
Harrington, John, 220
Harris, Louis, 140
Harris, Sydney, 278, 289, 348
Hartell, Ralph T., 154, 155
Hartley, Eugene L., 78, 80, 82
Hess, Albert G., 154
Hilliard, David, 135
Hirohito, 95
Hitler, Adolf, 95, 96
Hobbes, Thomas, 248
Hoffa, Jimmy, 241
Holmes, Kennan, 197
Hoover, J. Edgar, 137
Horney, Karen, 228
Howard, Jane, 276
Humphrey, Norman D., 95
Hutton, Bobby, 135

I

Igleburger, Robert M., 319

J

Jackson, George, 227, 244
Jackson, Jesse, 133, 140
Jackson, Robert H., 198
James, Jesse, 273
Johnson, Donald M., 69
Johnson, Stanley, 351
Jones, Geronimo, 72

K

Katz, Myron L., 323
Katzenbach, Nicholas deB., 205

Kaufman, Irving R., 208
Kennedy, John F., 195, 202
Kheel, Theodore W., 214, 215
Khrushchev, Nikita, 203
King, Martin Luther, Jr., 81, 133
Knebel, Fletcher, 279

L

LaGuardia, Fiorello, 216
Lane, Millicent, 278
Lawler, Irvin D., 3
Leary, Howard, 213, 219
Lee, Alfred McClung, 95
Leenhouts, Keith J., 172, 189, 190, 193
Lentz, William P., 164
Leopold, Nathan, 250
Lewin, Kurt, 277
Lindsay, John, 63, 217, 219
Lippitt, Ronald, 277
Lohman, Joseph D., 10, 11, 13
Lounsberry, Milton, 276
Lynden, Patricia, 61 ff.

M

MacArthur, Douglas, 76
MacEachern, Richard G., 220
Malcolm X, 119, 134
Maliver, Bruce, 277
Manning, Peter K., 224 ff.
Marshall, Thurgood, 31, 32, 134, 140
Martin, Dean, 94
Matthews, Linda McVeigh, 26, 27
McEvoy, Don, 143
McGee, Richard A., 188
McGuire, Carson H., 45, 47
McLuhan, Marshall, 76
McNamara, John, 55, 263, 264, 265
Medina, Harold R., 203, 207
Mergen, Armand, 197
Merton, Robert K., 54
Miller, Martin G., 49 ff.
Mitford, Jessica, 245
Molloy, John D., 196, 203, 211
Morris, Joe Alex, 190
Muhammed, Elijah, 140
Murphy, Patrick V., 219
Murray, J. Edward, 206

N

Newton, Huey, 134–136, 142, 244
Ng'weno, Hilary, 142

Niederhoffer, Arthur, 56, 58, 59, 214
Nixon, Richard M., 139
Noyes, Alfred D., 180 ff.

O

Oswald, Lee Harvey, 196, 202, 204
Oswald, Mrs. Lee Harvey, 203
Oswald, Russell, 232

P

Parker, William H., 25, 26, 30, 218
Parsons, Talcott, 51, 54
Peel, Sir Robert, 348, 351
Pepitone, A., 52, 53
Pierce, Chester, 54
Piliavin, Irving, 55, 119
Pitchess, Peter, 274
Postman, Leo, 97
Powell, Adam Clayton, 140
Preiss, Jack J., 51, 55

Q

Quill, Michael, 215

R

Radelet, Louis A., 224 ff.
Rainwater, Lee, 222
Randolph, A. Philip, 140
Raspberry, William, 225
Reardon, Paul, 204–206
Reasons, Charles E., 181
Reddin, Thomas, 26, 27, 34
Reed, Hoyt Coe, 92
Reisman, David, 228
Reiss, Albert J., Jr., 22, 25
Riis, Jacob, 212
Robeson, Paul, 134
Rockefeller, Nelson, 215, 217
Rogers, Carl, 243, 279
Romney, George, 190
Roncker, Robert, 113
Roper, Elmo, 92
Russell, Bertrand, 47, 48

S

Sands, William, 243
Saxe, John Godfrey, 71
Schleigh, Norman J., 92
Scott, A. A., 197

Scott, Robert H., 224 ff.
Seale, Bobby, 135
Shannon, Matthew, 197
Sharp, Mary P., 224 ff.
Shelley, E. L. V., 174
Shenker, Israel, 142
Shepard, George, 273
Sheppard, Sam, 200–202
Skolnick, Jerome H., 26, 28 ff., 55, 220
Snidler, James Henry, 213
Socrates, 154
Steele, John L., 195
Sterling, James W., 14, 33, 37
Stevenson, Adlai, 63
Stewart, Potter, 181, 200
Stinchcombe, Arthur L., 54
Stokes, Carl, 140
Strecher, Victor G., 56
Stroble, Fred, 199
Sutton, Horace, 144

T

Toch, Hans, 54, 72 ff.
Trojanowicz, Robert C., 174
Tucker, Justus, 305
Turner, William W., 34
Tweed, William M., 212

V

Valley, Ray C., 174

W

Warner, W. Lloyd, 45
Warren, Earl, 203, 208
Washington, Booker T., 133
Watson, Nelson A., 14
Weber, Max, 54, 229
Weinman, Carl, 201
Weinraub, Bernard, 351
Werthman, Carl, 55, 119
Westley, William A., 54, 55
White, Jackson, 111
Whyte, William Foote, 119
Wiggins, James Russell, 195
Wilde, Oscar, 47, 48
Wilkins, Roy, 133, 140
Williams, Robin, 50
Wilson, James Q., 25, 37, 38, 41, 49, 55
Wirths, Claudine Gibson, 54

Y

Young, Whitney, 112, 133, 140
Yount, Kathy, 311

Subject Index

A

American Bar Association, 196, 204, 206, 208
American Society of Newspaper Editors, 204, 206–208
Attica prison riot, assessment of, 224–253
    causal factors of riot
        alienation, 228, 230, 236, 239
        anomie, 228, 235, 236, 239
        breakdown of consensus in administration, 230
        collective behavior, 228, 229
        disintegrated outside society, 230
        groupism, 229, 230
        political-type prisoner as ringleader, 237, 238
        politicization of crime, 227
        politicized attitudes, 228, 230
        powerlessness of prisoners, 248
        radical leadership, 230, 232, 233
        society at fault, 231, 232
    comparison with Rahway riot, 232
    corrections system dilemmas
        alternatives to prison, 250
        community expectations, conflicting, 225, 231, 245
        corrections worker, problems of, 245
        due process, emphasis on, 225
        goal-role aims, 225, 226, 233–235, 238
        indeterminate sentence, 247
        multiplicity of rules, 234, 238
        order and detention vs. correction, 234
        parole board role, 241
        parole preparations, 247
        plea-bargaining, 241
        political considerations, 240, 241, 246, 251, 252
        prison personality variations, 236, 237, 250

385

Attica prison riot (*Cont.*)
    public attitudes, 226, 231
    restrictions on prison system,
        231, 237, 238
    retribution vs. rehabilitation,
        234, 235, 240
    societal security, 235, 249
    imprisonment as crime against
        society, 235
    inmate participation in prison
        government, 249, 251
    institutional society as microcosm,
        228
    lessons of Attica and other riots,
        239, 248
    participants in, 224
    purpose of, 224, 225
    rehabilitation, ideal aims of
        cure, not punish, 240
        individualized treatment, 233,
            236, 237, 243, 245, 251, 252
        morality in, 242
        needs of inmates, 233, 236–238,
            245, 249–250
        prison as last resort, 231
        prosocializing vs. antisocializing,
            244, 245
        transition between prison and
            outside, 243, 244
    rights of prisoners, 234, 238, 241, 249

B

Black Panther party
    aims of, 135, 138
    alliances with whites, 135, 139, 140
    appraisals of future of, 142
    attitudes of other blacks toward, 140,
        141
    black revolution and, 143
    chronology of 1970 events relating
        to, 136
    convention, 1970, recommendations
        for new Constitution, 139, 140
    founders of
        Cleaver, Eldridge, party
            philosopher, 135, 137, 138,
            140
        Newton, Huey, party leader,
            135, 136, 142, 143
        Seale, Bobby, party organizer,
            135
    origins in black struggle, 133, 134

    philosophical base of, 137
    police and, 135, 137–139, 142
    policy changes for future, 143
    socialist ideology, 135, 138
    violence tactics, 135, 138
Black population. *See* Negro population,
    U.S.
Black teen-age culture, 118–126
    gang psychology of, 120
    gang standards in, 122
    ghetto origins of, 119
    police and, 120–126
        as authority, 121, 122, 124, 125
        as enemy, 120, 126
        juvenile officers, 126
Blue Power, 212–223
    Boston police strike (1919), 213
    New York City police strike (1971),
        215–218
    pay-scale bargaining, 215–217
    police lobbies, 220–222
    political pressure, uses of, 218–220
    public work stoppages, 214, 215
    right to strike issue, 214, 218, 220
    unionism, 212–214, 218, 220, 223
Boston police strike (1919), 213
Bridges v. California (1941), 197
Britain, police-community relations in,
    348–353
    armed criminals, 349
    Black Power organizations, 350
    colored people's activities, 349–351
    home beat system, 351–353
    juvenile crime, 352
    rising crime rate, 348, 349
    unarmed police, 348, 349, 353

C

California POST training program,
    333–338
Census tract maps, analysis of, 11
Chicago division of community services,
    300–304
Citizen complaint procedures
    adversary relationships in, 145, 146
    model of, 145–150
        background of model city, 146,
            147
        citizens' appeals officer, 147
Civil liberties vs. "law-and-order," 21, 37
Civilian police review board, New York
    City, 145, 146, 213

Community. *See also* Police-community
relationships
definition of, 51
effects on police morale, 49–52
elements of
diagram of, 46 (fig. 2–1)
institutions, 45
life styles, 45
social status, 45
visible differences, 47
police subculture and, 48 (fig. 2–2)
profiles of, 334, 335
social mobility in, 47
Community service programs
Chicago division of community
services, 300–304
community service aides (Chicago
program), 301
community service officers (Dayton
program), 321, 322
typical case histories of service,
305–307
Winston-Salem community services
unit, 304–305
Conflict management programs, 281, 319,
324
Coordinator, police and community
relations, job description, 345–347
Corrections. *See* Attica prison riot,
corrections system dilemmas;
Misdemeanant probation
Countercultural conflict. *See* Insular
culture groups
Courts and community relations, 326–332
Craig v. Harney (1947), 198
Crimes without victims, 39, 40
Criminal justice and community relations,
326–332
Crisis intervention programs, 282–284,
319–325

D

Dayton crisis intervention program,
319–325
community service officers, 319,
321, 322, 324
conflict management, 319, 322, 324
generalist/specialists, 319, 321, 323,
324
results, 324, 325
team policing, 319–323
training program, 323, 324

E

Estes v. Texas (1965), 200
Ethnic. *See* Minority groups; Subcultures

F

Federal Bureau of Investigation (FBI),
154
statistics on juvenile crime, 154, 155
Flint, Michigan, police-school liaison
program, 269–274
concepts, 269, 270
counseling of students, 269, 271
delinquency prevention, 269, 270,
272, 273
detective liaison officer, duties of,
270, 271
merits of program, opinions on,
272–274
statistical data, 272, 273
Free press—fair trial issue, 195–211
British court restrictions, 199, 200
Constitutional Amendments,
related, 196
criticisms of the court, 197, 198
Fuld's, Judge, principles, 210, 211
judges' responsibility, 202, 210
Katzenbach rules, 205
Kaufman committee report, 208, 210
news restrictions, 196, 204, 208–210
Oswald, Lee Harvey, case, 202, 203
prejudicial pretrial publicity, 196–203
press responsibility, 201, 207, 210,
211
public's right to know, 195, 200,
203, 207, 209
Reardon committee report, 204–206
remedial measures
American Bar Association
proposals, 204–206
American Society of Newspaper
Editors proposals, 206–208
Judicial Conference of U.S.
proposals, 208–210
New York State Conference
guidelines, 210, 211
rights of the accused, 196, 198, 203,
205, 209, 210
rights of the media, 196
Sheppard, Sam, case, 200–203
Supreme Court decisions, related,
197–202

Free press—fair trial issue (*Cont.*)
    trial by media, 196, 199, 201
    Warren Commission report
        summary, 203

I

IACP 1969 survey of police role concepts,
    14–18
In-migrant culture groups. *See* Insular
    culture groups
Institute for police-school liaison officers,
    273
Insular culture groups
    immigrants, 112
    Jackson Whites, 110, 111
    migrant characteristics, 113, 114
    migration data, 113
    Pineies, 110
    police and, 109, 111, 112, 117
    Southern Appalachian mountaineers,
        109, 112–118
Irvin v. Dowd (1961), 199

J

Juvenile justice
    British juvenile liaison schemes,
        183, 184
    child abuse and neglect statistics,
        155, 160–161 (table 4–2)
    court decisions on juvenile proceed-
        ings, 174, 177, 180
    delinquency offenses, 155, 162–163
        (table 4–3)
    delinquency statistics, 155, 156–159
        (table 4–1)
    father figure role of members of bar,
        168, 171, 182
    informal vs. adversary proceedings,
        174, 177, 180, 181, 182
    discretionary power of officers, 164,
        166, 167
    juvenile courts
        origins, 168, 169
        procedures, 167
        status in jurisprudence, 169
    juvenile crime rates, 154, 155
    juvenile officers, 126, 164, 184
    Michigan (Ingham County) court
        system
        juvenile division, 169, 170
        (fig. 4–2)

    juvenile court rules (1969), 177
    programs department for
        juvenile treatment, 171–174
    police procedures, 155, 164–167
    preventing delinquency, 183, 184
    probation, 167, 169, 171, 174, 181,
        182
    recidivism, 167
    rights of minors, 155, 168, 177,
        181, 182
    welfare of minors, 153
    youth bureaus, 164, 166

L

Landlord-tenant intervention program,
    284, 285
"Law-and-order" vs. civil liberties, 21, 37
Lohman training texts. *See* Training
    courses for police

M

Marginality of minority police, 60
Mexican-Americans
    administration of justice for, study
        of, 127–132
    attitudes of, 130, 132
    bail abuses, 129
    discrimination against, 127
    lack of legal representation for, 130
    language disability of, 130
    police misconduct against, 128
    underrepresentation of
        on juries, 129
        in law-enforcement and related
        agencies, 131
Miami, Florida, proposed new model of
    policing, 289–292
Michigan Institute on Community
    Relations and Administration of
    Justice, 260–268
    grant renewal rationale, 267, 268
    philosophy, 261
    problems in procedures, 260
    purposes, 260
    task force teams, 261–264
    team effort evaluation, 265, 266
    results, 266, 267
    workshops, 261–264
Michigan Sheriffs' Association, 221
Minority groups
    American, 335

attitudes of, on functions and
  methods of police, 19–21
Black Panthers, 133–144
black teen-age, 119–126
ecological factors affecting, 11
police attitudes toward, 64, 65
police training for work with, 10–13
Mexican-Americans, 127–132
qualitative factors influencing
  behavior of, 12
Minors, rights of, 155, 168, 177, 181, 182
Misdemeanant probation. *See* Probation,
  misdemeanant
Misdemeanants
  age bracket of, 185
  confinement of, 187, 188
  diversity of, 186, 187
  probation programs for, 188–194
  recidivism of, 185, 188
  rehabilitation of, 187–189
  sentences of, 188
Misdemeanors
  definition of, 185
  leading to major crimes, 185, 190
Morale, police, 49–55, 60
  alienation and, 51
  community effects on, 49
  model of, theoretical, 49 -54
    model terminology, 50
  personality system vs. social system,
    51–54
  psychological stress and, 52
  role relationships and, 51, 52
  self-esteem, status and, 50–54
  systemic model of, 52 (table 2–1)
  study references, 54, 55
Mott Foundation, 270

N

National Conference of Christians and
  Jews, 3, 28, 257, 260, 293
National Council on Crime and
  Delinquency, 154, 193
National Information Center on
  Volunteers in Courts, 193
National Institutes on Police and
  Community Relations, 257–260
Negro population, U.S.
  census figures, 101
  economic data on, 106
  gains in urban centers, 102, 103, 104
  group characteristics of, 105–106

progress in status of, 106, 107, 141
  by regions, 105
  vital statistics of, 108
New York City police strike (1971),
  215–218

O

Oakland, California, police-community
  relations programs
  conflict management, 281
  educational communication, 285
  family crisis intervention, 282–284
  landlord-tenant intervention, 284,
    285
  violence prevention unit, 285, 286
Ombudsman, 145
Oswald, Lee Harvey, case, 196, 202, 203

P

PACE (Police and Community
  Enterprise) project, San Francisco
  action programming, 315
  media promotion, 316
  model, 312, 313
  pilot district, nature of, 313
  results
    attitudinal changes, 314
    behavioral changes, 315
    participants' opinions, 316–318
  soldier-community precedents (in
    Korea), 312, 313
  training sessions, 313, 314
Patrol service officer, 290
Perception
  aids to, 75
  effect of experiences on, 69, 72
  of meanings, 73, 75
  nature of, 69
  point of view in, 71
  prejudgments in, 69, 82
  stereotyping in, 72
  techniques for testing, 76–79
  through word-symbols, 72, 73
Philadelphia (North) police-community
  relations program, 339–344
  analysis and evaluation, 342, 343
  background, 339, 340
  community control of police, 339,
    343
  community-initiated, 339
  community participants, typical, 341

Philadelphia (North) police-community
relations program (*Cont.*)
    critique of failure, 343, 344
    funding, 341
    misconceptions as basis, 342
    organization, 340–341
    police participants, typical, 341
Police
    attitudes toward minorities, 64, 65
    behavior of, toward citizens, 22, 23,
      38–41
    brutality, 137, 145
    citizen complaints and, 145–150
    department organization, model of
      (Miami, Florida), 290–292
    discretionary powers of, 38–41, 164,
      166, 167
    generalist/specialists, 319, 321,
      323, 324
    insular culture groups and, 109–118
    job attitudes of, 57 (fig. 2–4), 60, 63
    marginality of minority, 60
    morale, 49–52, 60
    political attitudes of, 62, 63
    political power of (*see* Blue Power)
    problems, analysis of, 17, 18
    professionalization of, 22, 23, 26
    public attitudes toward, 60
    role (*see* Role, police)
    social life attitudes of, 65, 66
    societies, 58, 212
    Southern Appalachian mountaineers
      and, 113, 117, 118
    subculture, profile of, 56–67
    training (*see* Training courses for
      police)
    unionism, 212–214, 218, 220, 223
Police Benevolent Association (PBA),
    213, 214, 219
Police-community relationships. *See also*
    Community service programs
    in Britain, 348–353
    community relations councils in, 27
    community relations unit function in,
      26, 29
    conflict management program
      (Oakland), 281
    coordinator, job description, 345–347
    crisis intervention program
      (Dayton), 319–325
    family crisis intervention program
      (Oakland), 282–284
    landlord-tenant intervention program
      (Oakland), 284, 285

Michigan Institute on Community
    Relations and Administration of
    Justice, 260–268
National Institutes on Police and
    Community Relations, 257–260
North Philadelphia police-com-
    munity relations program,
    339–334
PACE project (San Francisco),
    312–318
para-military professionalism in, 26
patrolmen's attitude toward, 27
police function in, 25, 26
police-school liaison program (Flint,
    Michigan), 269-274
political power of police in, 28
POST training program (California),
    333–338
racial factors in, 31
ride-along programs, 308–311
Saint Louis police-community
    relations program, 293–299
San Francisco experiments in, 28–31
sensitivity training in, 275–280
social order in, 26
tension in, sources of, 151
traditional bureaucracy vs. human
    relations in, 23
violence prevention unit (Oakland),
    285, 286
Police-school liaison program. *See* Flint,
   Michigan, police-school liaison program
Police-youth relationships
    in black teen-age culture, 119–126
    in juvenile justice proceedings,
      153–184
POST (Peace Officer Standards and
   Training) program (California),
   333–338
    community profiles, 334–335
    course content, 334–336
    evaluation criteria, 337, 338
    objectives, 333
    police and social control, 335, 336
    results and recommendations, 338
    social change implications, 336
    subcultures, study of, 335
Prejudice
    based on individual experiences,
      80–82
    definition of, 85
    exercises to reveal, 83–85
    in perception, 82, 83
    sources of, 85

stereotypes rooted in, 86–89
techniques to curb, 90
types of, 86
Prosecutors, courts, and community
relations, 326–332
   black judges, 331
   community cooperation, 326, 328
   interagency cooperation, 330
   press relations, 331
   problem areas, 328, 329
   public concepts in criminal justice,
     326, 328
   role concepts, 326, 327
   trials videoed, 331
President's Commission on Law Enforcement and the Administration of
Justice, data from, 185
Probation
   juvenile, 167, 169, 171, 174, 181,
     182
   misdemeanant, 185–194
     insurance for volunteers in, 194
     limitations on, 187, 188
     origins of, 187, 190
     results of, 193
     Royal Oak, Michigan, program,
       189–194
     uses of, 185, 188
     varieties of programs in, 188,
      189
     volunteers in, 185, 190, 193,
      194

R

Recidivism, 167, 185, 188
Rehabilitation of offenders, 187–189.
   See also Attica prison riot, rehabilitation, ideal aims of
Ride-along programs
   arrests-transportation-booking,
     309, 310
   dispatching of calls, 309
   dress and appearance, 309
   ending the tour, 310
   females, 309
   host officer, 309
   identification, 309
   juveniles and minors, 309
   Kirkwood, Mo., program, 311
   Los Angeles County model program,
     308–310
   model stipulations, 308–310
   number allowed to ride, 310

   observer's report, 310
   officer's report, 310
   questions that arise, 310, 311
   selection of observers, 309
   who may volunteer, 308
Role, police, 51, 52, 56, 60, 212
   attitudes of victims of crime toward,
     19–21
   attributes, 35, 36
   community relations, 29
   conflict, 20, 21, 33, 34, 288, 289
   in criminal justice system, 335, 336
   law enforcement, 289
   police/community perceptions of,
     survey, 14–17
   social worker, 29
Royal Oak, Michigan, volunteers in
probation program, 189–194
Rumor
   aids to combat, 96
   circulation forms of, 93, 94
   definitions of, 92, 93
   fabricated, 94–96
   training exercise to detect, 97

S

Saint Louis police-community relations
program, 293–299
   awards, 298
   human relations training, 298, 299
   objectives, 294
   organization, 294
   projects, 296, 297
   youth programs, 297
San Francisco project PACE, 312–318
Sensitivity training
   as emotional process, 275, 276, 279
   as instrument for behavior change,
     278, 280
   misconceptions of, 275
   misuses of, 276
   negative aspects of, 276, 278
   police and, 279, 280
   police-community relations and,
     275, 280
   T-group (training group), 277–280
   as valid technique, 277
Sheppard v. Florida (1951), 198
Sheppard v. Maxwell (1966), 200
Southern Appalachian mountaineers,
109–118
   attitudes toward law enforcement,
     117

Southern Appalachian
mountaineers (*Cont.*)
    character of, 115, 116
    education of, 116, 117
    family patterns of, 115
    origins
        historic, 109, 112, 114
        regional, 114
    police and, 117, 118
Stroble v. California (1952), 199
Subcultures. *See also* Insular culture
  groups
    American, 335
    black teen-age, 119–126
    defined, 56
    police
        attitudes toward minorities, 64,
          65
        classes of people in, 58
        defined, 56
        diagram of, 59 (fig. 2–5)
        job attitudes, 57 (fig. 2–4), 60,
          63
        marginality, 60
        personality factors in, 59, 60
        public attitudes toward, 60
        related to roles, 56, 60
        shoptalk, 61
        social life attitudes, 65, 66
        status in, 60
        subgroups in, 58
Supreme Court decisions
    on desegregation and voting rights
      laws, 134
    on free press—fair trial issue,
      197–202

T

Tactical service officer, 291
Team policing, 291, 319, 320, 321
Training courses for police

crisis intervention, 323, 324
human relations, 3–9, 298, 299
Lohman, Joseph D., training texts,
    10–13
minority group relations, 10–13
PACE (Police and Community
    Enterprise), 313, 314
police-community relations, 10–13,
    298, 299
POST (Peace Officer Standards and
    Training), 333–338
sensitivity techniques, 275–280

U

Unionism, police, 212–214, 218, 220, 223
U.S. Commission on Civil Rights report
    on Mexican-Americans, 127–132

V

Victims of crime
    attitudes of
        in District of Columbia pilot
          study, 19
        in national survey, 20, 21
    complaints of, 39, 40
Violence prevention unit, 285, 286
Volunteers in Probation, Inc., 190, 193

W

Winston-Salem, North Carolina, com-
    munity services unit, 304–305

Y

Youth bureaus, 164, 166
Youth and police. *See* Police-youth
    relationships
Youth programs, 297